Top: **Pete Lavers and Dave Reid challenging Brighton keeper Peter Grummitt.**
Middle: **The Amateur Cup semi-final squad of 1973/74.**
Bottom: **Tanners come close to opening the scoring against AFC Wimbledon in 2005.**

SUBSCRIBERS

Martin Alsop	Mike Crouch	Brenda Mitchell
Michael Anderson	Gerald Darby	Tony Mitchell
Bob Belcher	Rob Davidson	Malcolm Munt
Clve Bennett	Steve Dennis	Christopher Peachey
Frank Bennett	Angela Doyle	Brian Pell
Tony Bennett	John Eaton	Goff Powell
Roy Beveridge	Ken Eaton	David Pope
Dave Blaszkowski	Tim Edwards	Gail Pope
Peter Bonney	Barbara Edwards	Alan Ramsey
Harry Bonney	Rod Ellis	Kevin Skudder
Denise Brazier	Ron Fruen	Michael Skudder
JWD Brealey	David Haines	Gordon Smith
Caroline Brennan	Mike Heather	Arthur Taylor
Peter Brown	Richard Hogsden	Colin Taylor
Mick Burberry	R Holmes	Fergus Trim
Mick Burt	Alan Jenkins	David Varney
Peter Chappell	Peter Lavers	Derek Wells
Keith Coburn	Matt Le Ross	Dick(Moler)Wilkinson
John Cooper	Richard Lilliman	A J Wilson
Audrey Crossley	Stuart McKay	David Zackheim

Graham
Mitchell
and
Dave
Johnston

©Graham Mitchell and Dave Johnston 2006

Printed and bound in Great Britain by NPL Printers Ltd - Unit 30, Bookham Industrial Park, Church Road, Bookham, Leatherhead, Surrey, KT23 3EU www.NPLprint.com

Cover design by Mark Stevens

THE

HISTORY

OF

LEATHERHEAD

FOOTBALL

CLUB

INCLUDING THE HISTORIES OF -	**LEATHERHEAD** 1886 - 1911 **LEATHERHEAD ROSE** 1907 - 1946 **LEATHERHEAD FOOTBALL ASSOCIATION** 1910 - 1916 **LEATHERHEAD UNITED** 1924 - 1946 **LEATHERHEAD** 1946 - 2006

Acknowledgements

We should like to express our thanks to the many people and organisations that have helped in various ways with the compilation of this book.

In particular to the; Surrey History Centre, Leatherhead and District Local History Society, Trinity Group of Newspapers, Leatherhead Advertiser, Surrey Advertiser, Leatherhead Museum, Dorking & District Museum, Isthmian League, Kingston Local History Centre, The Football Association, The Association of Football Statisticians, Sutton Library, Horsham Library, The British Newspaper Library and Frank Haslam's website at www.leatherheadweb.org.uk for much local historical information.

For the loan of and/or permission to use photographs in this book grateful thanks to - East Surrey and Sussex Newspapers, Surrey Advertiser, Leatherhead and District Local History Society, Eric Marsh, Leatherhead Football Club, www.katzpaw.co.uk/afc_wimbledon, The Argus Brighton, Bob Belcher, Goff Powell, Tim Edwards, Panther Studios (Farnborough Town) and John Hewlett. Additionally to Colin Ward for permission to use extracts from his best selling book 'Steaming In'. Despite our best endeavours we have been unable to trace a few of the photographers names or copyright holders of certain material used in the publication. We would welcome any information on this matter. Also to the assistance provided by various publications including the excellent 'The History of Non-League Football Grounds', the club histories of Bishop Stortford, Sutton United, Walton and Hersham and Woking and Mike Wilson's superb histories of the Athenian, Corinthian and Delphian Leagues, and of course Goff Powell's 'Up the Tanners'.

Thanks are due also to the numerous individuals who have contributed in some form or other to this project including; David Johnston (Senior), Chris Kelly, Billy Miller, Spencer Mitchell (Redhill FC) David, Debbie and Ross Mitchell, John North, Dorothy Lewis, Mark Stevens, Hilary Stokes, Mike Wilson, Matt Le Ross, Gerald Darby, Dick Wilkinson and Steve Dennis to name but a few.

Finally thanks to the players, officials and supporters of Leatherhead Football Club, without whom there would have been no story to tell.

(Next Page - Pete Lavers celebrates Chris Kelly's headed goal against Leicester City)

CONTENTS

KICK~OFF
FOREWORD - by BILLY MILLER

My first introduction to the book was on a sunny Saturday in May 2004. I was with the Middlesex Wanderers Football Club in Calais watching them play a representative match against Racing Club of Calais. There were several English supporters at the game and I was introduced to David Johnston. We chatted away and reminisced about the old days at Leatherhead FC in the 1970's and what great times to be remembered they were. David then told me that he and Graham Mitchell were compiling a book on the history of Leatherhead FC and asked if I would be interested in writing the foreword. I was obviously delighted and honoured to be associated with such an important part of Leatherhead FC's history, as will be recorded in the following pages.

My association with the club started, if memory serves me correctly, in 1957/58. I was asked to come down and play for the club by Roy Reader, the then first team goalkeeper. The officials of the club at this time were the manager Chris Luff, Tommy Rochester the coach, Ivor Gibbon the Chairman, Arthur Benn the Vice-Chairman, Leslie Ellis the Secretary, John Hewlett the Treasurer and Sidney Ranger the Committee PR man. We were competing in the Corinthian League, after having previously had several very successful seasons in the Surrey Senior League and then, briefly, the Metropolitan League.

In early 1961, Norman Douglas joined the club as manager from Dorking. He proceeded to do a fantastic job and I think this was the beginning of the advancement that the club needed to break into the top echelon of non-league football.

Time passed by and, sadly, Ivor Gibbon passed away. Arthur Benn took over as Chairman and the man who, in my opinion, became Mr. Leatherhead, Chris Luff, became Vice-Chairman. We progressed steadily under Norman and in 1963 gained promotion into the Athenian League. During the close season Norman was thinking of emigrating to Australia. Chris Luff, John Hewlett and Sidney Ranger, who had now taken over from Leslie Ellis as Secretary to the football club, resolved that they needed a new manager in place for the start of the 1965/66 season. They decided to interview me for the job. My abiding memory of this occasion was when Chris said, and I quote *"You will have every support from me and the committee but if you can't do the job I will have to sack you"*. Fair enough!

They were taking a great chance in appointing me as I had not played many first team games, not being the greatest of players. The previous year I had been coaching the first team under Norman and had passed my first FA coaching badge. I had also run the reserves for a couple of years. With all due respect to the other committee members who carried out sterling work in the background, it was Chairman Chris Luff, Secretary Sidney Ranger and Treasurer John Hewlett, who ran the administration side of the club and left me completely without interference to run the football side. This was the period when we were all in the right place at the right time; everyone was working as a team with the good of the club being the priority. Chris' main target for me as manager was to try to improve the team's performance year on year. Winning trophies would be nice, but to improve season upon season was the best way of achieving our ultimate aims. The team improved beyond all belief and achieved some fantastic results. At one stage we were regularly fielding seven amateur international players. The first pinnacle was reaching the 4th round of the FA Cup and playing with great credit at Leicester City's Filbert Street ground. The second, being both the proudest moment and on the other hand the saddest, was in reaching the FA Trophy final at Wembley. This was a wonderful achievement and gave me personally the greatest moment of my football life but sadly Chris Luff died just six weeks before the great day. Seeing the Tanners at Wembley would have fulfilled his greatest ambition. Chris, a non-drinker, always said to me *"Get us to Wembley and you can buy me a large brandy!"* It would have been my pleasure.

Unfortunately there has been a decline in the fortunes of the club since those heydays. Several reasons can be put forward as to why. Since the great days players have become fully professional. A small town club will always have problems raising the necessary cash to run a successful football team. Chris always referred to Leatherhead as a B & B town. There is a lot of truth in that statement. A high percentage of the population commute to London for their livelihood and we do not have enough chimney pots to give us a large enough guaranteed core support.

Tribute must be paid to those who have worked for the club and served on committees during these hard times. It is so easy when you are successful but when times get tough it can become a hard grind. I would like to mention my friend of many years, Gerald Darby, for his continuing dedication to the running of the club. At times this must have been a near impossible task. Still, it's great that there are always willing people to do this work. Good luck to Leatherhead Football Club for the future and it's great to see them on the up again.

▲Billy Miller - Leatherhead's longest serving manager by some distance. Billy clocked up nearly 900 games in charge of the Tanners between 1965 and 1980. Prior to becoming first team manager he spent 8 years at the Grove playing for both the reserve and first teams followed by a spell as reserve team manager before stepping into the Fetcham Grove hot seat at the tender age of 31.

FIRST HALF
CHAPTER ONE - GREEN SHOOTS

The town of Leatherhead lies at the geographical heart of Surrey, just eighteen miles from Central London. Although leather working and tanning were still thriving trades in the town as recently as 1905 the town's name is believed to derive from a ford (the old English words for a public ford being leode and ride) which crossed the River Mole in centuries past.

The Leatherhead (or Letherhead as it was still often referred to) of Victorian times was primarily a farming community, as it had been for many centuries. The majority of the population, numbering less than 4,000, lived and worked within the criss-cross of land formed by Bull Hill, Bridge Street, High Street and Church Street, or in the surrounding fields. Lacking mains drainage, sanitation in the town was rudimentary. Electricity was a luxury afforded only by the wealthy few and the horse and cart were still kings of the road. Despite improved communications (the railway arrived in 1859) with the outside world, travel to neighbouring towns was still a relatively rare and exciting adventure. Leatherhead remained essentially a self-centred sleepy little country town with its own tradesmen catering for most of its inhabitants needs.

The game of football in the late 1800's was also far removed from that of the modern era. The game was encouraged on the grounds that it was, "a pleasing and unobjectionable recreation". It was fully amateur, often with administration to match. Tape or string was used as a crossbar and goal nets had yet to be invented. There were no pitch markings other than the centre-line. Goals were often referred to as points, emphasising the close affiliation with rugby, as did many of the rules. Hacking was legal and goalkeepers, who could still handle the ball anywhere on the field, could be charged out of the way even if they did not have the ball in their possession. Indeed one of Leatherhead's early tactical ploys was for a colleague to fell the goalkeeper as a fellow forward was in the act of shooting!

Tactics were very different. The normal line up consisted of a goalkeeper, one back, two half-backs, three halves and five forwards with the forwards formation comprising a centre and a pair of wingers on either side. Football was also a game that crossed the usual class barriers with solicitors, clergymen, clerks and labourers competing side by side.

As the new century approached football was rapidly gaining in popularity. All over the country new clubs were springing up to take advantage of this upsurge in interest.

1886/7

It was against this backdrop (two years before the advent of the Football League) that twenty-year-old Albert Warren, whose parents' shop in Kingston Road overlooked the Recreation Ground, set about the task of forming the town's first football club. Encouraged by the turnout at several impromptu kick-abouts in the local park he decided to test the level of enthusiasm for the game within the town by calling a public meeting. He was delighted by the response.

A NEW FOOTBALL CLUB FOR LETHERHEAD

An account of that first meeting, on 27th November 1886, appeared in the West Surrey Times:
"A meeting was held on Wednesday last at the Rose Coffee Tavern for the purpose of forming a football club. The meeting was presided over by Mr. Albert Warren who, in an able speech, pointed out the benefits to be derived from this winter recreation. About twenty men gave their names in as members at the close and a committee was formed and officers elected. Entrance fee is 3d and

annual subscription 1 shilling".

After some debate the newly appointed committee christened their new enterprise Leatherhead Rose, the Rose stemming from the aforementioned establishment which was situated further along Kingston Road and run by one of the players, Tommy Hersey. The Tavern was to serve as the club's headquarters for most of the next decade. Kingston Road Recreation Ground was the obvious choice as home ground.

The rest of the first season appears to have involved recruiting players and raising funds to purchase balls and other items of necessary kit as no games seem to have been staged, although it has to be acknowledged that press coverage of these formative years was somewhat sketchy.

1887/88

The earliest recorded match took place in November 1887, the Rose losing 2-1 to Dorking YMFS with Songhurst the scorer of the solitary goal. This was followed by further defeats to St John's School and Cobham Hawks. The first victory did not arrive until January 1888, an 8-0 drubbing of printing works side, Caxtons with Chapman, Reverend Robert Gill and Campbell-Summer all chipping in with a brace of goals apiece. The only other success from the eight games contested in this first playing season came by a narrow 2-1 margin in a return fixture at Dorking YMFS.

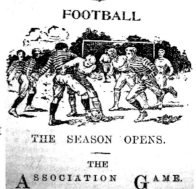

1888/89

A report in the Parish Magazine notes a 5-0 defeat at the hands of Cobham Hawks in the opening game of the season. Wins and goals remained few and far between, just two goals and two draws was the sum total in nine games against other club sides. The only two positive results came against scratch sides, although notable draws were achieved with Sutton Rovers and Saxons from Kingston.

Also on the field of play, referees replaced umpires as arbiters of the game. Previously the two club linesmen made the decisions with the referee only being called upon if the two officials could not agree. Power was now handed to the referee, presumably along with a whistle, and he was allowed onto the field of play for the first time to control the game as an independent official, although initially they were still only allowed to award free-kicks if a player actually appealed for one.

1889/90

This season saw the first signs of some improvement in playing performances. The Reverend Gill hit a hat-trick in a 4-1 defeat of Wallington and the double was completed over Danes Streatham.

Leatherhead at least now had a football team but they attracted little comment or interest from the citizens of the local community. At this time cricket was by far the most popular and important sport with the locals. The town supported no fewer than six cricket clubs of which three: Leatherhead (the Fetcham Grove square has staged cricket since at least the mid 1850s), Leatherhead Rovers and Red, White and Blues (based at Kingston Road), were well-established and successful teams. The football club in comparison struggled to gain a foothold. Outside of summertime, little interest was generated in the proceedings at Kingston Road, particularly as defeats continued to consistently outnumber victories, even though the majority of opponents were drawn from local schools and villages. Early adversaries included Ockley, Cobham Hawks, St John's School, Harcourt (Wallington), Saxons and Kingston Wanderers (the two forerunners of Kingstonian), Godalming YMFS, Shalford and Ditton.

Perhaps fortuitously, given the relative popularity of the two sports at the time, there was no overlapping of the cricket and football calendars. The football season did not get into full swing until late October, took a mid-winter break in December and January, and had normally ended by mid-March, well before the sound of leather on willow was heard. With a number of players participating in both, relations between the various cricket and football teams was cordial with matches at each others sport taking place between sides representing 'The Muddied Oafs' and 'The Flannelled Fools'.

1890/91

The Rose continued to toil away for little tangible reward, failing to register a single win in the first half of the season. Defeat in the club's first 'competitive' outing, 2-0 to Whitgift in the Herald Cup, was followed by a humiliating 10-1 reverse at the feet of St John's School, albeit by a team comprising both masters and pupils.

St John's had been the first team to play organised games of football in the town; although a rather wild and rumbustious form of football is reported to have been popular among local farm workers as early as the 17th century. Football had succeeded rugby as the main winter sport in 1885 and the school soon became one of the top teams in the area. The school was awarded senior status and entered the early Surrey Senior Cups. These games drew large crowds to see the players, wearing their customary coloured skull caps with tassels flying behind, take on the best teams in the county. Football remained the principal game at St John's until the First World War when rugby regained its former pre-eminence. The school was provided for sons of Church of England clergy and several former pupils and masters, along with other local clergymen, were to feature prominently both on and off the field for Leatherhead over the forthcoming years. Soccer was obviously considered good for the soul!

The arrival of the Hue-Williams brothers (Eric and Guy) from Charterhouse in late 1890 signalled a big change in the town club's fortunes. The Hue-Williams were part of a well-known local family. Their father, Frederick, was a keen sportsman who captained Leatherhead Cricket Club from 1870 until the early 1900s and later became chairman of the famous Swan Brewery in the town centre. A great local benefactor his generosity extended to making a point of employing players whenever he could. Another of his son's, Bertie, was to later join his brothers in representing the football club.

Galvanised by the presence of the Hue-Williams and the arrival of a number of other new faces in their wake, the team's improvement was both immediate and dramatic. Before Christmas one game was drawn and four lost with only three goals scored and eighteen conceded. The New Year, however, heralded a complete reversal of form. All five games played were won and sixteen goals scored without reply.

The encouragement drawn from the second half of the season was reflected in a new mood of optimism that was carried over into the following campaign.

1891/92

Rose again entered the prestigious Herald Cup, which attracted twenty one entries from across Surrey and South London. Carshalton, 2-0, and holders Balham, 5-1, were defeated in the early rounds, a hat-trick from Arthur Rutty and two by Hersey doing the damage in the latter game. Rose travelled to Hackbridge for the semi-final against Harcourt (Wallington), returning victorious by the only goal of the game, scored by Henry Moore. The local populace at last began to sit up and take notice of the achievements of the team and the prestige it attracted to the town. The prospect of winning such an important competition against much bigger and more established clubs ensured that there was standing room only on the trains carrying the supporters once more to Hackbridge, this time for the final. Due to the vagaries of the train timetable (no change there!) the match did not start until 4.00 pm by which time a record crowd had assembled to watch Leatherhead, wearing white, and opponents Battersea Albion, wearing colours, contest the final. Battersea were strongly fancied to win but the Rose players and supporters arrived full of confidence and expecting nothing other than victory.

The pitch was muddy and *"players had trouble keeping their perpendicular"*. Special football boots were still some years away, hence players often took to the field still shod in their ordinary working boots. Rose, adapting better to the tricky conditions, took the lead when, following a melee in front of goal, a Battersea back put the ball between his own sticks. However, the lead was short-lived as Albion equalised almost immediately. During the second half Rose gained the upper hand and two goals in quick succession on the hour mark, another own goal and a fine shot from Hersey, gave a final scoreline of 3-1.

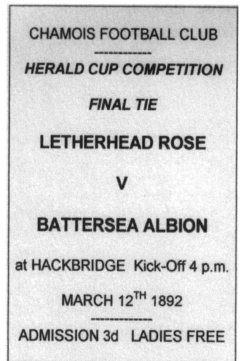

CHAMOIS FOOTBALL CLUB

HERALD CUP COMPETITION

FINAL TIE

LETHERHEAD ROSE

V

BATTERSEA ALBION

at HACKBRIDGE Kick-Off 4 p.m.

MARCH 12TH 1892

ADMISSION 3d   LADIES FREE

RAMPANT ROSE TOO HOT FOR THE ALBION

The Wallington and Carshalton Herald described events following the completion of the match, *"The teams and some sixty supporters adjourned to the Melbourne Hotel in Wallington where tea was provided and the cup and medals presented. A very jolly evening ensued with the Albion men atoning for their earlier defeat on the football field by beating Leatherhead hollow in the singing stakes"*.

Town pride and a desire to be the best team in the district burnt fiercely in local hearts and, despite the late hour, a large number of supporters gathered at the town's train station to see their heroes return. After much cheering and back slapping the players finally dispersed for the walk home, accompanied by groups of supporters who gladly carried their kit for them. The triumph provoked much celebration. With the town unaccustomed to such sporting success, the cup was proudly displayed in the window of Hewlins chemist shop in the town centre and its presence soon attracted large crowds of admirers, much to the shopkeepers delight no doubt.

The victory was not, however, met with universal approval. The local press received a number of letters from rival clubs complaining bitterly about the composition of the Rose team during the course of the tournament. As well as fielding players from St John's, the Reverend Beaumont (a master at St John's) was said to belong to the County, the brothers Rutty (sons of the headmaster of St John's) to Cambridge, Messrs Hue-Williams to Charterhouse and Ware to Epsom. A number of teams threatened to field players down from Oxford and Cambridge if the practice was not stopped and called for a tightening of the rules of eligibility. Only club members were eligible to play but players circumvented this by the simple expedient of becoming members or honorary members of more than one club allowing them to turn out for whoever required their services the most. Unless of course, they fell foul of the club's committee who would vet all prospective members and anybody deemed unsuitable would be rejected. There was some justification for the accusations of fielding other team's players as results outside of the Herald Cup were generally poor.

The success of the Herald Cup in attracting twice as many entries as the Surrey Senior and Junior

Cups combined, led to the Surrey Football Association trying to ban it on the spurious grounds that it constituted a form of advertising since the competition was run by the Herald group of newspapers. Ultimately a compromise was reached restricting the number of entrants to sixteen.

1892/93

Leatherhead's games, in common with most clubs at the time, were subject to last minute cancellation or delay, often almost at the whim or interest of the players. Fixtures were anything but 'fixed', shambolic was a more appropriate description. Spectators would turn up only to find a match had been called off. A variety of reasons were offered; a club could not raise a team, their opponents had failed to arrive or they had simply not received the telegram confirming the match details. Additionally travel to all games was either by foot, horse-drawn cart or by public transport hence advertised kick-off times tended to be 'flexible'.

As football became more popular with the masses so spectators became rather more partisan and less inclined to stay aloof from the action on the pitch. One game affected by both of these traits was the first match played in defence of the Herald Cup, a home tie with Sutton Rovers. On this occasion it was the referee who arrived thirty minutes late due to train delays and the game had to be curtailed with Leatherhead (Rose having been dropped from the title in the close season to identify the team more closely with the town as a whole) leading 4-1. Sutton protested to the cup committee on the grounds that at the appointed kick-off time Leatherhead had only eight players and had the advantage of a gale force wind in the first half to build up a 4-0 lead. In contrast and as a direct result of the delayed start Rovers only had the benefit of the wind behind them for twenty minutes before the game was halted due to the descending darkness. The committee upheld Sutton's appeal and ordered the tie to be replayed. If anything the replay was even more controversial. This time the game started promptly at three o'clock. Leatherhead had to kick-off with only nine players although the other two soon arrived, though somewhat out of breath. The early exchanges were marred by some heavy tackling which culminated in Charlie Edser receiving his marching orders. Despite this handicap two goals from Ernie Fuller secured a hard fought 2-1 win. The match was further tainted by some ugly crowd scenes. The events were reported in the following week's Wallington and Cheam Herald: *"The ground is not an enclosed one and the executives of the club are therefore unable to keep undesirable characters from lining the touch and goal lines. After the sending-off every decision by the referee was hissed and hooted by a section of the crowd and when the visitors and referee left the ground to return to the train station after the game they were followed by a disorderly mob who made themselves most objectionable"*.

Leatherhead became embroiled in further controversy in the second round, scheduled for the 17th of December. Unable to raise a team on that date, due to work commitments, a request was made for the match (against Wallington) to be rearranged. The cup committee granted the wish but ordered the game to be played at Hackbridge. On the appointed day Leatherhead failed to turn up and as a consequence the cup organisers summarily threw them out of the competition. Writing in the local press Albert Warren defended the team's action on the grounds that they felt harshly treated in being ordered to play the rearranged tie at a neutral venue. Not surprisingly it was more than a decade before the competition was entered again.

Leatherhead tasted league football for the first time with a brief sojourn into the West Surrey League. The league was divided into two divisions - Dorking and Guildford. Unfortunately, there were only three entrants in the former; Leatherhead, Dorking and the Guards Depot. The experiment of league football was not a success with three out of the four games being lost and the decision was taken not to renew membership of the league.

During the course of the defeat against the Guards Depot, Frank Haseman became the first

Leatherhead player to score a penalty. This followed the introduction of the penalty shot for certain infringements committed anywhere within twelve yards of the goal. Previously the only punishment for fouls perpetrated within the area was the award of a free-kick. The odds, however, still favoured the goalkeeper as he was able to stand anywhere within his six yard area and could charge out as soon as the kicker moved. It was not until another change in the law a decade later forcing goalkeepers to stay on their line that the chances of successfully converting a penalty were high enough to make unscrupulous troglodyte defenders have second thoughts before rudely interrupting fleet-footed forwards in full flight to prevent a likely goal. Skilled dribblers were much sought after but so equally were the cloggers who were favoured more for their brawn than their skill.

Players in the Victorian age were generally short, sturdy, muscular and stocky. Nicknames such as Hacker, Nailer, Chopper, Blaster, Bull, Tiny, Haystack, Cruncher and Masher were commonplace among the Leatherhead players and were not earned without good reason. Inevitably injuries were also commonplace with the Football Association, an organisation to which Leatherhead had become affiliated in October 1893, forced to issue a directive to the effect that, "*No player shall wear projecting nails, iron plates or gutta percha on the soles or heels of their boots*".

One of the sport's greatest early exponents, Lord Kinnaird, summed up the attitude of those early exponents of the game when upon being warned by his wife that his energetic style of play might lead to a broken leg, ebulliently replied, "*Perhaps, but it won't be mine*".

1893/94

Leatherhead pulled off something of a coup in being able to call upon the services of two full England internationals, A. M. (Arthur) and P. M. (Percy) Walters. Inevitably they were often referred to as 'Morning' and 'Afternoon' after their initials. The Walters were household names when Association Football was beginning to develop as a public entertainment and were as famous in their day as Jack and Bobby Charlton were some eighty years later. No England XI of the time was complete without them and they remain part of a select band of brothers to have played for England, joined only by the Charltons and Nevilles since 1900.

The brothers were a formidable pair of backs, characterised as, "*hard and rough in a gentlemanly way*". Arthur was described as "*short and square with shoulders like the west door of a cathedral*" (in other words the Victorian equivalent of a brick s***house). He was a fearless tackler within the bounds of the shoulder charge rule before the introduction of the Goalkeepers Protection Act provided custodians with some respite from his attentions. Between 1885 and 1890, whilst at University and later with Old Carthusians and the renowned Corinthians, the two were automatic choices for England, winning twenty two caps between them. They helped England to win their first Home International Championship, as well as a share of two others, and were generally considered to be the best backs of their generation. Percy captained his country on five occasions, the last in front of 30,000 fanatical Scotsmen at Hampden Park in 1890. The Walters' top class playing careers ended prematurely in tragic circumstances. Despite still being in their prime they reluctantly agreed to retire, at their father's request, after younger brother Hugh suffered a fatal injury when accidentally colliding with an opponent's knee during the course of a match for Oxford University.

The brothers resumed playing after a break of a year or so. As well as turning out for Leatherhead on an occasional basis, forming a close association with the club which was to last for many years, they also helped Old Carthusians to reach the 1894 and 1895 FA Amateur Cup finals.

Arthur, who lived in Kingston Road, was a solicitor by profession and an accomplished cricketer for Leatherhead. He also later became Chief Fire Officer of the town's Fire Brigade.

On the football field he soon displayed his enduring class when, playing in an unaccustomed forward role, he scored all four goals in a 4-3 win over Guildford.

The game of football seems to have been something of a family pastime in Leatherhead at this time. As well as the Walters, the Rutty brothers and up to three Hue-Williams appeared in the starting line-up at various stages during the year.

The fixtures for the season showed how much the club's stock had risen with several well established senior clubs having been added to the card. In all fifteen games were played, resulting in eight victories: Middle Mill 3-0 (Moore 2 and Poulter), Banstead 3-0 and 1-0 (Eric Hue-Williams), Dorking 1-0 (Rutty), Dorking Wanderers 4-0 (Rutty scored a hat-trick despite only playing for an hour as he had to leave to go to work), Guildford 4-3 (Walters 4), Preston House (Bookham) 3-1 (Reverend Jourdain 2 and Moore) and Chamois 3-0 (Poulter 2 and Moore). One game was drawn, 1-1 against Epsom and six lost: Epsom 0-3, Ewell 1-3 (Warren), Dorking 1-4 (Poulter), Guildford 0-5, Cobham Hawks 1-2 (Moore) and Middle Mill 0-2.

On occasions, problems were encountered in raising a full team for away games because of work commitments and the time and expense involved in travelling. Indeed against Middle Mill only seven players arrived and four unsuspecting travelling spectators were hastily press-ganged into playing to make up the numbers. A 2-0 reverse was a valiant effort in the circumstances.

Following the publication of letters in the local press urging the formation of a new club based nearer to the centre of the town it was felt necessary to call a meeting in an attempt to encourage the whole town to unite together to support the club. Correspondents had suggested that Kingston Road was too remote a venue and not readily accessible for the majority of players or spectators. In an effort to head-off any potential breakaway the meeting agreed that the club would: provide a ball for people to practice on the pitch at any time of the day, form a reserve side, reduce entrance fees to half-price for under-16's and seek an alternative site in a more central location.

1894/95

Leatherhead's growing stature within the county was underlined when Honorary Secretary Albert Warren, perhaps somewhat surprisingly given his past brushes with authority, gained election to the Surrey Football Association Council.

With a healthy bank balance to draw upon, the club was at last able to purchase an official strip. This first kit consisted of red and white halved shirts with red knickerbockers and red socks.

On the playing front an extremely harsh winter virtually wiped out football for the whole of January, February and March. The weather did relent long enough to allow a first appearance in the Surrey Junior Cup where Tooting Externes were overwhelmed 8-3 on a veritable swamp at Kingston Road before Balham Albion triumphed 3-1 at the same venue in the 2nd round.

In the few other games completed there were good victories over Epsom 4-0 and Kingston 6-0 and a well contested draw with the Idlers of Wanstead.

1895/96

Before the season began, the outlook did not appear very good, there were even suggestions that all fixtures would have to be cancelled due to "*a paucity of playing members*". As well as losing players through retirement, several of the squad had moved down the road to the newly formed Ashtead club. Fortunately a number of former members were persuaded to return enabling the programme to be fulfilled.

Fixtures continued to comprise almost entirely of friendly matches (although many were far from it). A first foray into Sussex was organised for Boxing Day. A goodly number of fans travelled down with the team to the uncharted wilds of darkest Horsham only to see one of many reverses. Supporters were left disillusioned by some dire performances, notable stinkers occurring at Ferry Works (0-11) and Dorking (0-8).

A rare bright spot was a decent run in the inaugural Surrey Junior Charity Shield. If the loyal supporters were harbouring any thoughts of silverware they were comprehensively crushed at the semi-final stage as they had to endure the sight of Herald League champions Sutton St. Barnabas administering an 8-1 thrashing to their heroes. In the previous round Reigate Institute had been beaten after a replay, a rare win in a very disappointing season.

Home games were by now being played at Thorncroft Park, in the grounds of Thorncroft Manor, a private school in the hands of Walter Lawrence who generously allowed the ground to be used free of charge. The adjacent Fetcham Grove cricket pavilion doubled up as changing room and clubhouse. The Park was considered to be a more accessible venue for both players and spectators alike and immediately proved popular helping to attract 30 new members, each paying the minimum club subscription of 2s 6d.

1896/97

By mid-1896 the club was flourishing with over 100 members. As well as the two Saturday sides a third team, which in due course entered the Redhill and District Wednesday League, was added to take advantage of the free afternoon afforded by early closing on Wednesdays. Many members worked as shopkeepers, assistants or bank clerks and were often expected to work to nine or ten o'clock on Saturdays and hence were only available for selection for the midweek games. Featuring alongside them in the midweek matches were many of the same players from the Saturday teams. Considering how rough and physical games were and that participation was largely at their own cost and expense, this was no mean feat. Injuries were frequent although the threat of an ice cold sponge usually did the trick, if not an injured player would be consigned to hobbling about on the wing for the remainder of the game. They obviously bred them tough in those days.

In the Surrey Junior Cup revenge was gained over Sutton St Barnabas with a 2-1 away win, Guy Hue-Williams netting both goals. Leatherhead, though, were indebted to young goalkeeper William Davis for a brilliant display between the sticks for ensuring victory. Davis was reported to be, "*marvellous, when age, size and weight were taken into consideration*". Bearing in mind that Victorian football was often brutal, that goalkeepers were targeted for special attention and were afforded little protection by the laws, it was not surprising that there were few volunteers for the position. As well as courage the unfortunate soul selected usually displayed one of the following attributes - considerable bulk (outwards, upwards or even better - both), nimble feet (to evade rampaging forwards who were intent on decapitating him) or be at least two sandwiches short of a full picnic. Any oddball in possession of all three was immediately snapped up. Davis seems to have been an exception to this rule. Barnes were toppled 4-0 before Kingston dashed thoughts of further progress in the 4th round.

Leatherhead enjoyed another good cup run to reach the final of the Surrey Charity Cup. Victories en route against Eversleigh (3-0) and, contrary to all expectations, over Herald League side Selhurst (3-1) in the semi-final set up a meeting with the Guards Depot (Caterham).
The final, at Reigate, was enlivened by the presence of an abundance of brightly painted top hats with the red and white colours of Leatherhead predominating. There was a sizeable crowd in attendance with "*a fair number of supporters from both sides with voices of the fog horn order*". Unfortunately Leatherhead failed to rise to the occasion losing 2-0. The defeat was blamed on the forwards being in a "*funk*" and the big weight advantage enjoyed by the Guards. Size did matter in those days! The team included three Hue-Williams brothers but only two survivors, William Hewlins and Guy Hue-Williams, from the 1892 Herald Cup triumph.
The full side read: *William Davis, William Hewlins, Bertie Hue-Williams (captain), William Killick, Bob Nash, Charles Wafforn, Eric Hue-Williams, Harry Shurville, Guy Hue-Williams, Edward Symonds and Harry Hook*

By now the fixture list had grown considerably with the season's record showing 17 wins and 6 draws from 37 games (including 14 for the Wednesday team) with 74 goals scored and 63 conceded. New names added to the list of opponents included Weybridge Rose, Ripley, Cranleigh, Kingston Hill and Dorking Early Closing.

Much of the credit for the team's improvement was down to the selection committee, which consisted of five senior players and officials. They took the brave decision to give several youngsters the chance to prove that they could stand up to the physical requirements of the game. In the process a side that contained a good blend of youth and experience took shape. In previous years reports had suggested that the presence of "*someone large, vicious and goal hungry*" would have made all the difference and 16-year-old newcomer Harry Shurville, who played with a fearsome vigour, certainly fitted the bill. According to contemporary descriptions, "*the centres were selected for weight, strength and charging powers as well as their talent as dribblers. The game being a bit strenuous and many goals got by hustling goalkeepers through their own goals all ends up*". The name of Shurville was to become synonymous with football in Leatherhead over the course of the next fifty or so years with four of Harry's older brother Alf's sons representing town clubs between the two World Wars. Harry along with three others of the younger element, William Davis (18), Bob Nash and Harry Hook (15), seized the opportunity presented to establish themselves in the first eleven and become the backbone of the team well into the 1900's.

The defence in particular improved markedly with Bertie Hue-Williams and William Blaker forming a solid combination at full-back and Bob Nash proving a tower of strength at centre-half. Winger Guy Hue-Williams continued to bamboozle opposing full-backs and fellow forwards alike, although he had a tendency to overdo the fancy footwork. The team's general lack of physique was usually compensated for by the extra speed and courage of youth.

1897/98

After eleven years at the helm Albert Warren stood down as Club Chairman in September of 1897, Bertie Hue-Williams assuming the role. A well-wisher paid off the club's debts enabling a new challenge to be sought. During the summer Leatherhead had been one of forty clubs invited to discuss the formation of a Surrey Senior League. In the event it was to be another twenty five years before it came to fruition but a County Junior League did result from the discussions with Leatherhead eagerly signing up for the new venture, which was due to commence the following season.

Ambition was not immediately translated into results with a poor season being experienced on the pitch. There were excellent wins over Guildford and Dorking but equally disappointing defeats to Banstead, Cobham and Cranleigh.

A brace of goals from Eric Hue-Williams was insufficient to prevent an early exit from the Junior Cup, 3-2, at the hands of Sutton Association (shortly to change their name to Sutton United).

The Management Committee struck on a novel way of ensuring the players did not over indulge over the Christmas period; they arranged two matches on Boxing Day! Clydesdale provided the opposition in the morning and Banstead the afternoon. These holiday games were always watched by large and jovial crowds with the result of the matches largely immaterial to the day's enjoyment. The Leatherhead players certainly seemed to be slightly less inebriated than the visitors, winning both games before retiring to the pub to dull the aches and pains.

1898/99

Leatherhead acquitted themselves well in the opening season of the Surrey Junior League finishing as divisional runners-up. Some impressive performances were turned in, most notably in defeating Cobham, Ripley, Woking Reserves and eventual champions Walton St Mary's.

In the Junior Cup Middle Mill were brushed aside 6-1 but, disappointingly, defeat ensued in the following round at Wallington.

The forward line was especially strong and included three players, 'Dasher' Davis (having dispensed with his goalkeeping duties) and the two Harrys, Shurville and Hook, who went on to net in excess of 375 goals between them over the course of the next ten years. Hook and Davis' goal-scoring prowess did not go unnoticed and was rewarded by selection for Surrey Juniors match against their Middlesex counterparts at Millwall. Another player to make an impact during the season was right-winger Edwin Utterton who tormented backs with his speed and close control. His father and Club President, Canon Utterton, was one of the most remarkable men in Victorian Leatherhead. A keen sportsman his association with the club went back to its formation when he was elected as the first President. The Canon was also responsible for the opening of the Rose Coffee Tavern in the early 1880's as a social centre. He actively encouraged people to become involved in the game and a number of his curates, including the Reverends Jourdain and Gill, were regulars in the Leatherhead team during the 1880s and 90s.

1899/1900

Following a successful 1898/99 "*prospects were of a very cheering character*" but results failed to live up to expectations.

DAVIS AND SHURVILLE HAVE A FIELD DAY AT THE ASYLUM

The season started well enough with a 16-0 tonking of Horton Asylum in a friendly with both Davis and Shurville scoring six times. Goals were more difficult to come by in the league programme and it was December before the first victory was recorded, 2-1 against Cobham. Local soldiers serving in South Africa were not forgotten with the proceeds from the game being donated to the Transvaal War Fund. After marching to the ground from the Letherhead Institute the Town Band proceeded to entertain the crowd before, during and after the game with a selection of music. The home sides win was greeted with a rousing rendition of '*See the conquering hero comes*'. In all £2 6s 1d was raised to help the war effort. Results remained mixed and a final finishing position of fourth out of six represented a major disappointment.

The loss of inspirational captain Guy Hue-Williams, due to a serious leg injury, for a large part of the season was undoubtedly a major factor. His absence affected the balance of the team resulting in much chopping and changing in an elusive effort to find the right combination. The half-back line was the exception, the Reverend Vernon's crunching tackling allied to the passing ability of Bob Nash and Brockworth making them a match for anyone. In attack the bullocking runs of Shurville were complimented by the rather more subtle skills of Utterton on the wing but the team lacked the strength in depth to cover for the inevitable injuries.

At the Annual General Meeting, Vice-President Walter Lawrence reminded everyone that, "*he let out his grounds for football and football spectators only. Anyone caught idling the afternoon away or playing the fool would be turfed out*". In a bid to deter these less desirable elements it was agreed to raise the entrance fee to 3d for all games. An extra half acre of land was also made available to the club. This allowed the fence surrounding the ground to be fixed instead of having to be moved backwards and forwards before and after every game in order to prevent spectators encroaching on to the adjoining farmland. The Treasurer announced total receipts of £22 11s 6d, £18 of which was raised by way of member's subscriptions, producing a healthy profit of £2.

CHAPTER TWO - PRIDE BEFORE A FALL

Edwardian Leatherhead was still little more than a village although the population had by now increased to over 5,000. The majority of people still worked locally with over 20% of the population employed as domestic servants in the many large houses that still flourished in the area.

The growing need for affordable new houses in the early 1900s fuelled by the town's proximity to and convenient rail links with London, coupled with the consequent increase in the value of real estate encouraged landowners to sell surplus acreage to the developers. Much of this expansion occurred to the north of the town centre around the Kingston Road area.

Football had enjoyed a phenomenal growth in popularity across the country but it had both its ardent worshippers and its strenuous detractors. The advocates believed that used as it should be, the training on the football field would make a man a better citizen or soldier whilst those opposed to the game said that football had been allowed to usurp the place which young men ought only to devote to the more serious business of life. However, football continued to provide rich entertainment for very little outlay and working men in their droves flocked to the matches.

Leatherhead had a football team but it had made little impression on the consciousness of the citizens either within or outside the local community. That was about to change. As the team's results began to improve so the local populace began to sit up and take note of the town team, a team of which they could now look on with pride not indifference.

1900/01

This was a season of undoubted progress although it did not start too auspiciously, Beddington, "*a very hot lot*", quickly putting paid to any ambitions of an extended run in the Surrey Junior Cup.

The following week's league clash with Weybridge was spoilt by a series of bad fouls climaxing in the dismissals of both Davis (for suggesting the referee did not know what he was doing - or words to that effect) and Shurville (for giving defenders a worms eye view of the grass once too often). Worse followed as Weybridge grabbed a late equaliser and then the ever combustible Shurville, noted for having a shorter fuse than Guy Fawkes, chinned two Weybridge players as they left the field. A letter was hastily dispatched to the visitors apologising for the "*regrettable incident*" and Shurville was immediately suspended for the rest of the season.

Despite Shurville's loss goal-scoring was not a problem. A new league record was set with a crushing 10-0 win over Hook. Two weeks later this was bettered when Thorpe St Marys were hit for twelve. 'Dasher' scoring five in the former and Hook five in the latter. Ironically it was a point dropped in a rare goalless draw sandwiched between these two high scoring wins that proved crucial. This, together with the point lost earlier due to ill-discipline, allowed Weybridge to pip Leatherhead to the divisional title. Nevertheless, it was still a good season with only four defeats suffered in twenty two games played.

Things did not look quite so rosy off the pitch though with a significant loss reported. A whip round at the Annual General Meeting raised over £3 to help clear the debts and put the club back, temporarily as it proved, on a sounder financial footing.

On a sadder note two respected club members left the fold. Walter Lawrence, who had been a good friend to the club for many years, moved from Thorncroft. In his stead an annual rent of £2 was negotiated with the landlords, Merton College, but it was evident that once a buyer was found for the manor, the club would have to find a new home.

Edwin Utterton, captain and Honorary Secretary, who was leaving the district to continue his religious studies, bade farewell at a smoking concert held at the Swan Hotel in April. Utterton, a brilliant dribbler and crosser of the ball, was one of Leatherhead's early stars. His skills would be sorely missed. The club's 61 members purchased a handsome inscribed four foot high revolving bookcase for his farewell present, indicating the esteem in which he was held by his peers. Speakers included his father and Club President Canon Utterton and the former international Arthur Walters. To round off an enjoyable evening the players and committee members provided their own comedy and musical cabaret (rather more refined than a curry and karaoke evening) to show that their talents were not confined solely to the football field.

1901/02

Notwithstanding the loss of Utterton, league form continued to improve with the first of three consecutive divisional titles coming to Thorncroft Park. Leatherhead dominated their division remaining undefeated, gaining twenty seven out of twenty eight points and keeping nine clean sheets along the way. The Junior League was divided into four geographical sections to reduce travelling with the overall title decided by play-offs between the four divisional winners.
In spite of controlling the semi-final for long periods Leatherhead succumbed 3-1 to the eventual champions Guards Depot, disappointing the big crowd of "*lusty lunged supporters*" (distant relatives of Moler perhaps?) that had travelled with the team to Sutton. After dominating the early exchanges, but failing to capitalise on the numerous chances created, McIntyre finally opened the scoring only for the Guards to grab a late equaliser and add two further goals in extra-time as the superior fitness of the soldiers told on a heavy pitch.

Despite the bruising nature of games a great camaraderie existed between the players. This was to be amply demonstrated, as were the potential hazards of football, in an early round of the Junior Cup. In attempting a tackle, Hennings, Surbiton Rangers centre-half, broke his leg in two places during his sides 6-0 defeat at Thorncroft. The game was held up for some considerable time whilst the local doctor was summoned. In the intervening period spectators helped to relieve Henning's suffering by offering regular swigs from their hip flasks. The doctor splinted his leg on the pitch before he was finally loaded on to a horse and cart for an uncomfortable and painful journey to the local hospital. An impromptu collection at the ground amongst players and spectators raised £3 (equivalent to about two weeks wages) for the unfortunate Hennings.

The hard men in Leatherhead's team still thought the wearing of shin-guards as somewhat effeminate and considered leg injuries to be an occupational hazard. However the 'Fancy Dans' out on the wings did take some precautions although this usually involved little more than the stuffing of a couple of sheets of folded newspaper down the socks. However, it would have needed the entire edition of the Sunday Times to provide any real protection against toe caps that felt as if they were made of pig iron.

It had been the best season yet. Twenty seven wins from thirty one starts and over a century of goals scored. It was unfortunate that the two worst displays were reserved for the two most important games, the defeat by the Guards and a Junior Cup exit at Old Tiffinians.

The sides strength undoubtedly lay in the forward quintet of Eric Hue-Williams and Harry Hook on the left side, Davis and Pauling on the right and Harry Shurville in the centre. Shurville in particular was in fine form returning from his suspension to terrorise opposition defences. His equally combative older brother, Alf, performed a similar function in defence. As a back, his main function was to dispatch objects over the sidelines, it did not seem to matter whether it was the ball, the winger or both! He was the type of back that nobody got past without suffering gravel rash.
It was a source of pride that success had been achieved in spite of only recruiting players from the immediate vicinity, unlike many other local teams who drew players from far and wide.

Success was also reflected in increased takings at the gate, up £3 to £10, putting the club's finances in a much healthier state.

1902/03

The loss of the Hue-Williams brothers, to concentrate on their business activities, allowed new stars to emerge in the form of the half-back pairing of returning captain Arthur Childs and E. M. Barnes. Throughout the season these two were exceptional in breaking up opposition attacks.

In the Junior Cup, Sutton United came out on top in the first confrontation between the two clubs, triumphing 1-0 in front of several hundred spectators at their Manor Road ground.

This proved to be a rare setback as Leatherhead's victorious march continued. Goals piled-up and the league season was completed without defeat. League whipping boys, Shalford, felt the full force of the team's potent attacking play, conceding nineteen goals in the two meetings. The two local derbies with Cobham were won handsomely 8-1 and 4-1 in front of large and appreciative crowds. A special train carrying over 200 partisans, harbouring high expectations of victory, travelled to Guildford for the semi-final clash with Farncombe. Once again they were to be hugely disappointed. Leatherhead had the tonic of being awarded a first minute penalty but things went rapidly downhill from then on. Hook missed from the resultant spot-kick and shortly thereafter Shurville was rendered hors de combat and reduced to the role of a passenger. Already missing the injured Davis the team, unsurprisingly, "lacked punch up front". Farncombe took full advantage to run out 2-0 winners and went on to beat Sutton United to take the overall title.

Surrey Junior League 1902/03

Team	Played	Won	Drawn	Lost	For	Against	Points
Leatherhead	**10**	**8**	**2**	**0**	**46**	**9**	**18**
Guildford Reserves	10	8	1	1	28	8	17
St Martha's	10	4	3	3	22	14	11
Jarbies	10	3	2	5	16	13	8
Cobham	10	2	2	6	14	26	6
Shalford	10	0	0	10	5	61	0

Despite falling at the penultimate hurdle terrific entertainment had been provided for the local football followers. Hook and Shurville were once more in prolific form contributing over 50 goals between them.

At times the football was the best yet seen. Early in the New Year supposedly superior neighbours Dorking were simply outclassed by a superb exhibition of quick passing and dribbling resulting in a final scoreline of 5-2 which did not do justice to Leatherhead's dominance.

1903/04

By this time club membership had reached an impressive figure of 130 enabling three powerful X1's to be fielded. The first team was strengthened by the return of a fit again Bob Nash (he had missed much of the previous season through illness) and the Blaker brothers, returning after a short spell at Dorking. On the debit side the services of Reverend Vernon were no longer available.

The Junior League moved Leatherhead into, what looked on paper at least, a tougher section centred on South London. This proved to be no hindrance as winning ways continued despite an early shock. The first reverse in a divisional fixture for over three years was suffered at home to

Wallington in October. The home team's position was not helped when Lionel Blaker was knocked senseless by his goalkeeping brother, Henry. In attempting to fist a cross clear Henry missed the ball completely and instead landed a haymaker, of which heavyweight champion 'Gentleman' Jim Corbett would have been proud, flush on the chin of his unfortunate sibling. Lionel continued after lengthy treatment but took the wise precaution of staying well out of his brother's reach for the remainder of the game.

The strong passions aroused by local rivalries were graphically illustrated when police had to be summoned to rescue the referee, besieged in his dressing room, from an angry mob of Sutton United supporters. They had been incensed by a string of decisions going against their team during the course of Leatherhead's 2-0 league win and were threatening to relocate the official's over-used whistle from his mouth to an altogether different part of his anatomy!

Back to events on the pitch and after the early hiccup the team went from strength to strength resoundingly defeating Ashtead 5-0 home and away and wrapping up the title in the penultimate game when gaining a revenge win over Wallington by 4-2.

Surrey Junior League 1903/04

Team	Played	Won	Drawn	Lost	For	Against	Points
Leatherhead	**10**	**8**	**1**	**1**	**28**	**4**	**17**
Guards Depot	10	6	2	2	35	11	14
Wallington	10	5	2	3	26	14	12
Sutton United	10	5	1	4	18	13	11
Croydon Reserves	10	2	1	7	11	32	5
Ashtead	10	0	1	9	7	51	1

It proved to be third time lucky as, despite falling a goal behind to Euneva at Dorking in a game watched by some 800 spectators, goals for Davis (from the penalty spot) and Hook ensured safe passage to the final for the first time. The supporters again turned out in large numbers for the final against Guildford at Ewell which, unfortunately, was to end in anti-climax. Once more Leatherhead under-performed when it really mattered, a late Hook effort was all they had to show for their endeavours as Guildford took full advantage of their below par efforts to secure the title by two goals to one. The team that took the field was: *Henry Blaker, Lionel Blaker, Harry Garland, Bob Stevenson, Bob Nash, Alf Shurville, Harry Hook, E. W. Taylor, 'Dasher' Davis, Harry Shurville and Tom Phipps*

Interest in the Junior Cup was ended at the 3rd round stage by local rivals Dorking, who went on to win the competition. Considerable ill-feeling had been generated in the run up to this game by a local correspondent writing under the byline of 'Chick' (no prizes for guessing where his allegiances lay) who circulated stories that the visitors intended to mete out severe punishment to Dorking's best players in order to nullify their superior skills. The prospect of a bloodbath drew a large and expectant crowd but in the event the game was actually played in a very good spirit, though Leatherhead probably regretted not resorting to rough house tactics as they were soundly beaten, 4-0.

To end another enjoyable campaign the famous touring side Middlesex Wanderers were welcomed to town although the hospitality did not extend as far as the pitch where the visitors were beaten by two goals to one.

Both sound defensively, with Nash shining at centre-half and Blaker keeping a succession of clean sheets, keen and resourceful in attack, where Shurville, Hook, Davis and Taylor all scored fifteen goals or more, the team again demonstrated itself ready to make the transition to a higher grade of football. In the last four seasons only 15 out of 100 games played had resulted in defeat.

1904/05

Leatherhead's success had not gone unnoticed and, along with Junior Cup winners Dorking, an invitation from the Mid-Surrey League to join their ranks was received and duly accepted.

Even before a ball had been kicked however, problems were encountered. The freehold of Thorncroft was acquired by Arthur Tritton JP who intended to use the property as a private residence and thus no football would be allowed to be played in the Manor's grounds. A short term solution was found in the shape of a new "*piece of turf*" off the 'old' Epsom Road. The entrance was near to the old turnpike road whilst the former turnpike lodge was utilised as the dressing rooms. Once again Leatherhead had cause to be grateful for the assistance of their friends in high places as the land was loaned to the club by local resident Walter Cunliffe (his family home was at Headley Court), the incumbent Governor of the Bank of England and soon to be a peer of the realm.

When the season kicked off hopes of a winning start at the new venue were scuppered by the Guards Depot who returned to barracks with both points after a 3-0 victory. Leatherhead continued to struggle in their new environs, winning just two of twelve league games and finishing only above neighbours Dorking. This was largely as a result of enjoying the better of the league meetings, drawing 1-1 at home and winning 5-3 at London Road with the prolific forward line of Hook (2), Shurville (2) and Davis sharing out the goals. Champions elect and Surrey Senior Cup finalists Redhill dished out a footballing lesson in the penultimate game romping to a 5-0 win. The season did at least finish on a high note. Over 1,000 spectators were entertained by both the musical offerings of the Town Band and an improved showing from the home players during the course of a 2-1 victory over Croydon.

Half-back Bob Stevenson and winger Tom Phipps were the pick of the team and earned selection to represent the Rest of the League in the season finale against champions Redhill.

The time and effort required to organise and run a football team was outlined by Arthur Walters who reported at the club's Annual General Meeting that during the course of the season a total of 365 postcards, 81 letters and 24 telegrams had been despatched to players and opponents notifying them of forthcoming fixtures. A decision taken at the same meeting was to have significant repercussions later on. The members agreed that players travelling expenses for away games should be met by the club. The extra burden placed on the finances was to eventually prove crippling.

1905/06

With the loss of the Epsom Road ground a new home had again to be found. The problem was solved when Merton College gave their permission for a field at the rear of Fetcham Grove Mansion, just a stones throw from the former ground at Thorncroft Manor, to be used. Considerable time, effort and money were expended to turn the field into a proper pitch fit to stage senior football. Unfortunately, the low lying field was prone to flooding and more often suited to growing rice or wallowing Hippos than for playing football. Attempts to play a more constructive game tended to get bogged down in the mud and the most effective ploy was often the big boot upfield followed by a mass cavalry charge. In wet weather games resembled mud polo played by twenty two grubby creatures all wearing the same indistinguishable strip in the same shade of grime and slime. With no proper changing facilities nearby the only running water available to wash off the mud was in the river. Not a pleasant prospect on a freezing winter's afternoon. The Old Rising Sun Pub (now Pangs Villa restaurant) at the foot of Hawks Hill served as the club's headquarters and no doubt many sorrows were drowned and successes celebrated there.

Elevation to the Mid-Surrey League had helped boost membership to a new high of over 150. It also brought with it senior status as a result of which the Surrey Senior Cup could be entered for the first time. Initial progress was made with a 2-0 defeat of Borough Polytechnic but ended by Croydon Wanderers, 5-0, in the next round.

There was some improvement in the league campaign with five out of eighteen games being won and a final placing of 8th attained. This would have been better but for a dreadful away record. The team fared worse on their travels than a short sighted learner driver who had forgotten his glasses. All nine games were lost and forty eight goals conceded. Goal-scoring remained a problem as did consistency. A record 16-1 thumping at league new boys Clapham was followed seven days later by a fine 1-0 win over the "*county towners*" from Guildford. Earlier a 4-2 win over Redhill followed a 5-0 defeat at the hands of the same opponents just two weeks previously. Wimbledon (in a taste of things to come) took maximum points in winning both league meetings 4-1, although the home game was interrupted by spectators angrily confronting the referee after he had awarded a dubious penalty to the Dons. Wimbledon went on to take the title and promptly left to join the West Surrey League.

On Wednesday March 7th 1906 Leyton became the first professional team to visit the town. In an early example of sponsorship Mr. George Brown, proprietor of the Swan Hotel, ensured the Southern League side's presence by guaranteeing their expenses, no doubt expecting to benefit from their patronage after the match to recoup his expenditure. Facing a team unbeaten in nearly a year, and more used to playing the likes of Tottenham Hotspurs, West Ham, Fulham and Southampton, a Leatherhead select side, bolstered by four players from the Guards Depot and two from Dorking, put up a brave fight in front of a large crowd before eventually succumbing 3-1.

1906/07

Old Tiffinians replaced Wimbledon but as a result of the expulsion of Redhill, for fielding a reserve side, only sixteen league games were played. Because of the small number of teams in many leagues, clubs would often field sides in more than one competition, in Redhill's case the South Eastern as well as the Mid-Surrey League. This practice led to the inevitable occasional fixture clash which, in this instance, led to Redhill's removal. Other teams in the South Eastern League at this time included the likes of Southend United and Clapton Orient.

It turned out to be another season of struggle. Six points was the final tally with maximum points gained just twice, against Old Tiffinians and Croydon Common, and single points twice in goalless draws with Balham and Wallington as Leatherhead finished 7th of the nine teams. Goals remained in short supply. The situation was not helped when centre-forward and erstwhile captain Harry Shurville departed for Dorking in mid-season. To rub salt in the wound he scored in both games as his new club did the double over his former colleagues on their way to claiming the league title.

Senior Cup success was again at a premium as the intriguingly nicknamed 'Lobsters' of Redhill put paid to hopes on a freezing afternoon with a 2-0 replay win in front of 250 hardy, frostbitten souls.

Folklore has it that Redhill's nickname arose because the colouring in the team's shirts was non-fast and when put in the wash the red and white stripes turned lobster pink in colour.

The summer of 1907 witnessed a major dispute between many amateur clubs and the Football Association over the rising tide of professionalism. The immediate cause of the trouble was a proposed amendment by the FA Council requiring a change to the rules of County Associations to admit both amateur and professional clubs to membership. Two associations, Surrey and Middlesex, held out against this change. They felt strongly that the introduction of professional clubs into formerly wholly amateur associations would be to the detriment of the amateur game. The dispute degenerated into a slanging match with the Football Association suggesting that class distinction and the old school tie were behind the amateur revolt, while the other side retorted that commercialism was the prime consideration of the FA whose only concern was with the professional game. Ultimately this dispute led to 40 clubs in Surrey, along with as many as 900 others up and down the country, joining the breakaway Amateur Football Defence Federation (later renamed the Amateur Football Association (AFA)). Some of the early giants of English football: Old Etonians, Old Carthusians, Corinthians and Cambridge and Oxford Universities were among those to break ranks. The split lasted until 1914 when, in a spirit of reconciliation, the AFA and the rebel clubs were welcomed back into the FA fold. The AFA still exists today in the guise of the Amateur Football Alliance. For the time being Leatherhead stayed loyal to the Football Association.

1907/08

The supporters started with low expectations and the players duly did their level best to live down to them. During the season victory was tasted on just three (out of twenty three) occasions.

The first excursion into the FA Amateur Cup proved to be short-lived. Norwood Association going through at **Leatherhead's** expense, winning at the third attempt after two drawn games. This was despite all three games being played at the Fetcham Grove enclosure since Norwood did not possess a suitable pitch of their own.

Early exits were also made from the Senior Cup, Woking from the West Surrey League handing out a 5-0 drubbing on a quagmire of a pitch, and the Surrey Charity Cup, Dorking winning 5-3.

The Mid-Surrey League was reduced to just five teams with the loss of Croydon, Croydon Common, Guildford and Old Tiffinians. Playing fewer games did nothing to reverse fortunes, however. Bottom place was occupied throughout a dismal campaign. The solitary victory came against ten men Balham, Watson on target three times in a 4-3 win that also contributed half of the goals for total for the season. This result at least gave some cause for celebration as it ended a three year drought since the last competitive win away from the Grove. To make matters worse Dorking, inspired by Shurville, won both derbies comfortably on their way to retaining the league championship trophy.

Two players, Harry Garland and Bob Mathieson did at least have the satisfaction of helping the Rest of the League defeat the new champions 6-3 in the traditional end of season fixture.
The reserves fared even worse, failing to win a game throughout the season.

Despite struggling on the field the club continued to enjoy the patronage of many local dignitaries, highlighting the continued social importance attached to the game of football. Due to his failing health Canon Utterton (by now Archdeacon of Surrey) stood down as President after twenty years, his drive and enthusiasm would be sorely missed. He was replaced by his successor as vicar of the Parish Church, Reverend Edward Nash.

Whilst Leatherhead continued to ply their trade at Fetcham Grove, on the other side of town moves were afoot to form a new club to rival the 'town' team. This was somewhat ironic in the light of the move away from the area a decade earlier because of its perceived remote location. The situation was now reversed with the local folk wanting a team to represent the fast expanding Leatherhead Common area.

Roy Watson was the prime mover and shaker behind the founding of the new club. In the belief that there was plenty of footballing talent in the area he issued a challenge to Headley FC stating that he could raise a team drawn from Leatherhead Common that would be more than good enough to beat them. Headley readily accepted the challenge. A relatively inexperienced side under the name of captain Phil Peters, who lived at Thistle Cottage in Kingston Road, travelled to Headley on 9th November and made good on the promise, returning victorious after a very close and exciting game.

Flushed with success the players decided to officially form a new club. To this end a meeting was held at All Saints School twelve days later. Reverend Taylor, curate of All Saints, was duly elected as the first President (and a player when duties permitted). The gathering voted in favour of resurrecting the name **Leatherhead Rose,** with the Rose Coffee Tavern being chosen as the club's headquarters. Home ground was at Kingston Road although it was now more commonly referred to as Leatherhead Common Recreation Ground. Club colours of green shirts (later changed to green and white) were selected. Another connection to the original Rose club was Albert Warren, one of its founders and now a well-known photographer, who filled the role of Honorary Secretary as well as occasional player for the new Rose.

Three weeks after the first fixture Rose and Headley met again, this time at Kingston Road, with the home team playing under the title of Leatherhead Rose for the first time. With Jack Port a tower of strength at the back Rose again came out on top, this time by the only goal of the game fired home by Harry Godwin. The full side read: *John Tarran (captain), Jack Port, Ivor Songhurst, Albert Legg, Percy Norwood, Bob Strickland, Alf Uncles, Albert Wafforn, George Reddick, Harry Godwin and Jesse Kemp*

The team continued to perform well throughout the rest of this first season, losing only three of the sixteen games contested. One of the better performances came in a 2-2 draw with a strong Leatherhead Postal side containing several of Leatherhead's Mid-Surrey League team in their ranks.

1908/09

The challenge offered by the emergence of a new team across town seemed to act as a spur to **Leatherhead**, the 1908/09 season proving to be their most successful in senior football.
The League increased to seven teams with Redhill, Norwood and Croydon renewing acquaintances whilst Balham bade farewell.

LEATHERHEAD FINALLY VANQUISH DORKING

After a poor start, five goals were conceded in each of the opening league games, attention turned to cup football and what turned into a two month long battle for local bragging rights with Dorking.

On the 17th October, Leatherhead returned from the short journey to Pixham Lane with a 2-2 draw in the Surrey Charity Shield. East Grinstead were summarily dispatched 2-0 in the Amateur Cup before the draw for the second round provided the Chicks with home advantage. This game resulted in a thrilling 3-3 draw. The replay drew the biggest attendance of the season of over 600 to the Grove. The majority went home disappointed though as the visitors grabbed the only goal of an error strewn game. The sides clashed again seven days later in the Charity Cup replay. Following complaints the previous week about the muddy condition of the approaches to the ground the committee had lain down duckboards to improve the situation. The majority of supporters accepted the mud, puddles and slippery ooze as an occupational hazard but the committee's efforts were particularly appreciated by the ladies in their fashionably long skirts. The Vicar kicked-off the proceedings and then sat back and watched, along with another sizeable crowd, as Leatherhead finally ended Dorking's dominance, coming out on top by four goals to two. The problem centre-forward position was filled by former Woking star Jack Kyle

ON DIT
* * *
That Leatherhead trounced Dorking in good style on Saturday
* * *
That they were a much superior team than the score of 4-2 represents
* * *
That the Leatherhead forwards were all mustard
* * *
Jack Kyle's centre forward play made an immense difference in the attack
* * *
That he was the cleverest forward on the field
* * *
That Capt Dyball found the old Woking man too slippery for him
* * *
That the Chicks always came off second best in their encounters
* * *
The Leatherhead defence played a sterling game
* * *
That the Chicks were easily held in check and never appeared dangerous
* * *
That their exit from the Charity Shield has not caused the Chicks to don sackcloth and ashes
* * *
Jack Kyle made all the difference and he provided the 'mustard to the beef'
* * *
That the gate on Saturday amounted to £9 10s
* * *
That Dorking's county players compared unfavourably with their counterparts
* * *
There were several weak spots in the Dorking defence
* * *
The Leatherhead club officials deserve the warmest praise for temporarily improving the approach to their ground

who responded with two goals, Davis and Watson the other scorers. Battle was recommenced on the 5th December, a hat-trick by Phipps helping to secure another win, this time 4-3 in the league. With honours just about even the teams took a welcome break from each other for a while.

Redhill and Metrogas soon ended interest in cup competitions for another season before the New Year saw the welcome return of Harry Shurville to lead the attack. He helped erase any lingering resentment over his shock departure two years previously by scoring the winning goal in three of Leatherhead's next four league games. He was unavailable for the other match as he was in Devon on county duty for Surrey. Unfortunately, he was still as volatile as ever and the red mist descended once more at the conclusion of the return league fixture with Dorking, at Easter, resulting in another suspension. Aware of his resemblance to a ticking time-bomb his former team-mates primed the touch paper but then failed to stand far enough back when he exploded. According to the match report the game would have been better, "*if less attention had been devoted to the man and more to the ball. Shurville was upset by some of the close attention he received and as the players were walking to the pavilion he struck his marker, Fuller, in the face and had to be restrained from having another go*".

Analysis of the season showed a big improvement on recent years, six wins and six losses resulting in a final finishing position of 4th.

Mid-Surrey League 1908/9

Team	Played	Won	Drawn	Lost	For	Against	Points
Guards Depot	12	8	4	0	30	10	20
Redhill	12	8	1	3	36	14	15*
Norwood	12	4	5	3	25	18	13
Leatherhead	**12**	**6**	**0**	**6**	**17**	**25**	**12**
Croydon	12	3	3	6	19	33	9
Dorking	12	3	2	7	25	28	8
Wallington	12	2	1	9	6	27	5

*Redhill had 2 points deducted for fielding an ineligible player

The team possessed strength in all departments, skipper Harry Garland was again masterly in defence and goals were more abundant. 'Dasher' Davis top scored with thirteen in all games, Harry Shurville contributed twelve (in only half a season) and Ed Watson nine. The ability to field a settled side was, undoubtedly, one of the main reasons behind the improvement, as was the return of Shurville to cure the lack of goals. The better results also brought about a welcome increase in attendances and hence revenue, although it was still considered necessary to disband the Wednesday team to reduce expenditure.

———————————

The **Rose** continued to gain experience through playing occasional ad hoc friendlies. These included a return match with Headley, won 4-0, and three games against Leatherhead Reserves that all ended in defeat, albeit narrowly. Fixtures, however, were still generally few and far between and so a solution was sought in order to enable the club to participate in extra and more meaningful matches.

1909/10

Leatherhead's best season was promptly followed by their worst. There were said to be only two things wrong with the team - the defence and the attack! The forwards carried all the attacking threat of a pirate with a rubber sword whilst the rearguard displayed all the defensive acumen of a sloth. If the squad's New Year's resolution was to lose every game then they succeeded admirably. Nash, Stevenson, Garland (although his performances were still good enough to earn him a County trial) and Jeeves were all now at the veteran stage and there were few youngsters around of sufficient quality to replace them. The long and distinguished careers of forwards Shurville, Hook and Davis were also drawing to a close. To make matters worse, Davis was missing for most of the campaign and Shurville from Christmas onwards. Goalkeeper H. Davies departed for Redhill, with another veteran, Blaker, returning to take his place. There was more vigour in the local old folk's home than was evident in this squad.

The first two months brought elimination from all cup competitions. Entry into the English (Football Association) Cup for the first, and only, time resulted in a 2-1 defeat in south-west London against Summerstown. Southern Suburban League Summerstown went on to reach the fourth qualifying round before bowing out to Wycombe Wanderers.

The FA Cup exit was followed by a shambolic 0-8 Charity Cup reverse on the Old Kent Road against South Eastern League side Metrogas where there was a collective dereliction of duty by the defence, prior to an extraordinary game in the Amateur Cup. Two goals from Shurville helped Leatherhead race into a 3-0 lead inside the first twenty minutes against old foes Guards Depot but the fans optimistic thoughts of an unlikely victory quickly turned to despair as Leatherhead were trailing 4-3 by the interval. Bob Mathieson headed an equaliser but some defending of the slapstick variety allowed the Guards to run in four more in the closing quarter of an hour to record an 8-4 triumph. As well as the Mid-Surrey League the Guardsmen also found time to participate in the Southern Suburban League alongside the likes of Sutton United, Dorking, Kingstonian and Tooting.

Clapham ended any hopes of lifting the Surrey Senior Cup for another year and things continued on a downhill path thereafter. Honorary Secretary R. V. Taylor announced his intention to resign and the services of several key players were lost during the latter part of the season which brought further heavy defeats at the hands of Croydon (8-1), Guards Depot (6-2) and Redhill (6-0) to leave Leatherhead propping up the table once again, having mustered just three points from eight games.

The trials and tribulations of a dreadful season were temporarily set aside for a special benefit game arranged to raise funds for Davis who had suffered a serious injury early in the season and been unable to work, enduring considerable hardship as a result.

As a consequence of the poor league form and with no protracted cup runs to retain interest, support had drifted away. Gate receipts plummeted from a record £44 to just £8. With travelling expenses amounting to £7 and postage nearly £4, even before taking into account ground and other sundry expenses, you did not need to be Albert Einstein to work out that the club were in financial difficulties. Despite members subscriptions helping to partly redress the balance the Treasurer confirmed that the finances were indeed in a parlous state with the balance sheet showing a deficit of £20 (somewhere in the region of £3,000 - 4,000 in today's money). Aided by good weather a hastily arranged summer fete raised the princely sum of £12 to help ease the financial crisis, at least for a while. Moving into senior football had placed an increasing burden on both the financial and playing resources of the club. The policy of only recruiting local players had backfired as the town was simply not large enough to produce sufficient players of senior level ability. With money extremely tight this policy was unlikely to be reversed in the near future. As a way of cutting costs and still remaining competitive the club's members were asked to consider a proposition to throw in their lot with the rival Amateur Football Association (AFA) and thereby revert to junior football.

At a stormy special meeting held in late April to debate the issue, the Walters brothers, among others, aired their points of view in support of the idea and the motion was duly carried. The decision may well have been partly influenced by the fact that Percy Walters was Vice-President of the AFA but the result was far from unanimous with more than a third of the members abstaining or voting against the resolution. Despite these misgivings a new constitution was drawn up for working under AFA rules and a fresh committee was appointed to negotiate for a new ground, preferably one at a cheaper rent.

If times were troubled down by the Mole at the 'town' club the opposite was true at Kingston Road. **Leatherhead Rose** officials, in particular Honorary Secretary Phil Peters, had played a major part in the formation of the Dorking and District League in May of 1909. The league was open to any club within a six mile radius of Dorking and attracted entries from Westcott, Dorking Reserves, Dorking St Pauls, Buckland, North Holmwood and Headley as well as Rose.

The season opener resulted in an 18-1 pummelling of Walton-on-the-Hill in a friendly but goals were much harder to come by in the league. This was largely as a result of Rose being unable to field their strongest side on a regular basis as only thirteen players were registered and eligible for league duty.

In all just twenty nine goals were scored in the twelve league games. With the attack misfiring badly it was superb defensive displays that won the day. Ten wins were ground out and only one defeat suffered, to nearest challengers Westcott. Games were invariably hard fought, close affairs: Buckland 2-1, Headley 3-2, Dorking Reserves 2-1 and 3-1, Dorking St Pauls 2-1, North Holmwood 3-1 and Westcott 1-1 were typical of the campaign as a whole. The title was secured in the final game with another narrow win, this time 2-0, over Buckland.

Dorking and District League 1909/10

Team	Played	Won	Drawn	Lost	For	Against	Points
Leatherhead Rose	**12**	**10**	**1**	**1**	**29**	**13**	**21**
Dorking St Paul's	12	7	2	3	39	17	16
Westcott	12	7	2	3	37	17	16
Dorking Reserves	12	5	2	5	29	24	12
Buckland	12	3	0	9	21	49	6
Headley	12	3	0	9	21	37	6
North Holmwood	12	2	1	9	12	27	5

To round off a memorable first season in league football, Rose took on the Rest of the League at Fetcham Grove. The match was heavily advertised with 50 bill posters and over 200 tickets printed to ensure there was a large gathering present. Cooke opened the scoring, the team's 100th in all games, and Taylor added a second late on. At the games conclusion the League trophy was presented to skipper Harry Godwin by J. H. C. Evelyn JP, who had donated it, to end a barren period of seventeen years since a Leatherhead team had last won some footballing silverware. The success was celebrated on the following Wednesday at a smoking concert held at the Royal Oak where a, *"capital programme of songs and recitations was rendered"* by the players and management committee.

PRESENTATION OF THE CUP.

At the conclusion of the match Mr. F. P. Ashdown, in asking Mr. J. H. C. Evelyn, J.P., to present the cup to the winners, said the League had been carried on very satisfactorily that year, and they hoped that next year more clubs would join, and that it would continue as prosperous as it had in the past. On behalf of the League, he would like to thank Mr. Evelyn for providing the beautiful cup he had for the winners, and he would also like to thank the Leatherhead F.C. for placing their ground at the disposal of the League for that match (cheers).

Mr. Evelyn having presented the cup and medals to Mr. A. Godwin (the captain of the Leatherhead Rose), and medals to the Dorking St. Paul's as runners-up in the League, said he would like to congratulate the Leatherhead Rose upon their success, which he understood had been thoroughly deserved (cheers). He was glad the League had made such an excellent start, and he hoped the success that had attended it would continue (cheers). He hoped that the cup he had had the pleasure to give the League would be an encouragement and an inducement to other teams to compete in the future (cheers). He very much ap-

they had been able to win the championship of the Dorking and District League (applause).

Mr. A. D. Childs proposed "Success to the Club," and said as an old footballer he was delighted that a football cup had been again brought to Leatherhead, and he heartily congratulated the Rose on having achieved that distinction (applause). He hoped the success they had achieved would be an encouragement to them, and that having won the cup they would make every effort to retain it (applause).

Mr. P. J. Peters (hon. secretary) said the club had had a most successful season, and although he had felt at times that his duties were rather arduous, he had been pleased to do what he could for the club, and it was a matter of considerable satisfaction to him that they had succeeded in winning the cup (applause). A capital programme of songs and recitations was rendered by Messrs. A. D. Childs, A. Bowden, P. Cropley, J. Harding, G. S. Clark, W. Budden, B. Bullen, Allen, and others, Mr. C. Smith presiding at the piano.

The health of the Chairman was drunk with musical honours, and Mr. Gregory having replied a successful evening was brought to a close with the singing of "God save the King."

CHAPTER THREE - PARTING OF THE WAYS

With outbreaks of hostilities both on and off the pitch as well as, rather more seriously, further afield in Europe, it was certainly an eventful decade in the life of the various clubs in the town.

The standard of living had improved significantly with main sewers lain and piped gas and electricity no longer luxuries afforded only by the affluent minority. Motor cars were by now a regular sight passing through the town centre.

The game of football had also taken on a more recognisable form. Crossbars, goal nets and kit were all now standard equipment and the rules and pitch markings more closely resembled those of today. From 1912 the use of hands by goalkeepers was restricted to the penalty area. Boots were purpose made but resembled clumsy armoured clodhoppers, reaching above the ankle and weighing a ton. One thing that hadn't changed was the ball. It was a miracle that anyone deliberately headed a rain soaked leather ball after the first collision between head and ball. A cannonball would have done little more damage to a skull and would not have left the imprint of the lace on the forehead!

1910/11

During the summer of 1910 those club members and supporters who were opposed to joining the ranks of the Amateur Football Association rallied support. In August some 30 disaffected past and present members gathered at the Prince of Wales pub to down a few pints and discuss local feeling that a town club should be affiliated to the Football Association. Following a strong show of support for the idea, the meeting agreed to investigate the possibility of forming a new club. With the objective of facilitating this, a second meeting was held a week later at which the new club, **Leatherhead Football Association**, was formally lodged with the Surrey Football Association representative present. He was more than happy to accept their registration given that he had been snubbed and treated most disgracefully by the committee of the 'old' club earlier in the day when he had made a last ditch effort to try and persuade them to remain members of the County Football Association.

The formation of the new club generated considerable enmity amongst loyal Leatherhead members. They were upset by the split as many disaffected members had not been present at the original meeting when they would have had the opportunity to put their points of view across. It was considered to be *"very bad form"* to go off and start a new club instead without at least consulting all concerned parties first.

Having been formed less than a month before the start of the new season it was too late to enter league football and the committee therefore decided to form a junior club with a view to entering senior football in 1911/12. Not wishing to make the same financial mistake as the existing club, the committee decreed that players would be expected to pay their own travelling expenses to away matches as well as forking out annual subscriptions of half a crown for the privilege of playing. Taking advantage of a now vacant Fetcham Grove, Leatherhead Football Association set up home there. With the town's playing resources split three ways it was always going to be an uphill battle to be competitive straight away.

Scattered among the many new faces that took to the field wearing the club colours of blue shirts with white sleeves, were a few more familiar ones. Harry Shurville, Tom Phipps, Chester and 'Dasher' Davis (appearing as a goalkeeper) all made appearances. Other players to join over the course of the next couple of months included the Tutt brothers and Fred Hatchwell as turmoil engulfed the by now ailing 'town' club.

Given the circumstances it was hardly surprising that an inauspicious start was made to the campaign. Heavy defeats were suffered at home to Dorking St Pauls (2-7) and to Leatherhead Rose (0-6) in the opening fixtures. Ashtead inflicted a crushing 6-0 beating in the Surrey Junior Charity Cup before results slowly began to improve, aided by an influx of new players. Effingham were beaten 6-0 and an under-strength Leatherhead Rose, 4-0 at the Grove.

Dorking Reserves were overcome in the Junior Cup before a meeting in the second round with local rivals Leatherhead Rose ended in a 5-2 defeat. Tragically nearly half of those players representing Rose in this match were to lose their lives in the Great War.

The inherent pitfalls of the formative months had at least been safely negotiated and with a stronger squad available the committee took the decision to sign up for league football for the following season.

With three clubs; Leatherhead FA, Leatherhead Rose and Leatherhead (AFA), now vying for their favour, the locals must have been mightily confused as to exactly who they should support.

The original club, **Leatherhead (AFA)**, fared the worst from the split, having the heart ripped out of the team. During the close season the majority of the 1st X1 either left or retired, although captain Garland, Nunns, Jeeves and Hatchwell initially remained loyal. Arthur Walters also stayed and continued in the role of President. The rest of the side contained a mixture of reserve and junior players who were thrown in at the deep end in order to fulfil the fixtures. The expectation that former public school boys would be attracted to a purely amateur side proved groundless.

Fetcham Grove was vacated as the use of Fortyfoot Recreation Ground had been offered at a lower rent. The Drill Hall in Poplar Road was utilised as changing rooms. The playing surface at Fortyfoot was considerably superior to that of the Grove enabling a more attractive style of passing football to be played. Unfortunately the only people to derive any benefit were the opposition. The only team to fail to win at Fortyfoot all season were - Leatherhead. Some valuable lessons were learnt, like how to pick the ball out of the net without hurting your back and how to be gracious in defeat.

One disastrous season was spent in the Surrey Amateur League during which time it was a continuous struggle to put a full side onto the park. Just two points from eighteen games were gleaned and no wins registered. Fielding a side largely unencumbered by any semblance of talent some heavy pastings were suffered along the way. Parthians won 9-0 and 6-0, Carshalton 6-0 and London County and Westminster Bank 6-0 before, mercifully, the season drew to a close.

Crowds were pitifully small (in fact they often couldn't really be classified as a crowd as there were usually more people on the No. 46 bus to Dorking than turned up at Fortyfoot) and they normally generated all the atmosphere of a dentist's waiting room. The majority of fans preferred to watch their football at the alternative venues of Fetcham Grove and Kingston Road, or simply stay away altogether and save their valuable time and money rather than witness another beating.

Not surprisingly it became increasingly difficult to make ends meet and eventually the remaining members accepted the inevitable and gave up the unequal struggle. The club folded, ending twenty five years of endeavour during which time it had helped to establish the name of Leatherhead on the local footballing map.

The **Rose** opened their defence of the Dorking and District League title with an emphatic 5-0 defeat of Buckland and with Smith, Taylor and former Leatherhead favourite Watson all finding the net with great regularity, goals came more freely than in the previous campaign. There was no shortage of excitement or eventful matches either. The short trip to Dorking St Pauls ended prematurely when, with Rose leading 3-2, large numbers of home supporters, angry at the impending outcome, invaded the pitch forcing the game to be abandoned. However, the League Committee ruled that the result should be allowed to stand. Three weeks later, on New Years Eve, Ashtead arrived at Kingston Road as the only other side sporting an unbeaten record. It remained that way. The match ended all square and set up the return two weeks later as potentially the championship decider. At Woodfield Lane, Ashtead made home advantage pay to record a 3-1 win that put them in pole position. Rose maintained the pressure with big wins over Headley and Westcott and when Ashtead slipped up on the run-in it allowed the gap to be closed. The teams finished level on twenty one points with identical records of ten wins and only one defeat from twelve games. Ashtead had a superior goal average but there was no provision in the rules for the title to be decided in this manner. Justice was done though as Ashtead comfortably won the championship play-off by four goals to nil in front of a healthy crowd numbering around 500.

Local rivals Leatherhead Football Association had been beaten in the Surrey Junior Cup but Epsom ended hopes of a prolonged run with a convincing 4-1 win in round three.

1911/12

Following the demise of Leatherhead (AFA), **Leatherhead Football Association** ambitiously tried to rest the initiative away from successful neighbours Leatherhead Rose by entering the Surrey Junior League and Cup, Profumo Cup, Junior Charity Cup and the Surrey Wednesday Junior Cup.

Alas it quickly became apparent that ambition had overcome a rational evaluation of the available playing strength and a string of defeats ensued. The heaviest was a 12-2 Boxing Day mauling at home to Paddington based Hawthorne that did nothing to soothe the player's hangovers. The games won column remained resolutely stuck on zero. The league's wooden spoon was won with some ease and early leave was taken from all cup competitions.

The defence was so porous it resembled a colander but the main problem was the forwards inability to locate the space between the uprights, with press reports wryly noting that, *"Leatherhead desperately need forwards well versed in goal geography"*.

Appearing in goal for **Rose** for the opening game was 'Dasher' Davis, whose career had now turned full circle. Fifteen years earlier, as a callow teenager, he had excelled in goal for Leatherhead before moving upfield to the forward line as he 'filled out'. Beset by leg injuries he reverted to his original position between the posts for the 1910/11 season. He spent one year with Leatherhead Football Association before completing the full set of local clubs by joining Rose.

Rose made a spirited effort to reclaim the league title. With the Taylor brothers and Reg Crocker cracking in the goals the team remained unbeaten well into the New Year. A series of postponements however, left a horrendous fixture backlog which ultimately proved too big an obstacle to surmount. The final nail in title aspirations was hammered home by arch-rivals Ashtead who inflicted a 3-1 defeat in April, a week after the sides had fought out a 2-2 draw at Kingston Road. Sadly the earlier game marked the last appearance of Davis. He sustained a badly broken leg, bravely diving at the feet of an onrushing forward, an injury that spelt the end of his career. To recognise his past services a benefit concert was held in his honour at which he, along with the rest of the squad, was presented with a silver medal for finishing as league runners-up. Chairman Henry White kindly agreed to liquidate the club's balance sheet deficit of 10s 11d to save the club from a similar fate to that of the Titanic, for which money was also collected during the evening for donation to the ship's disaster fund.

1912/13

Suitably chastened by the previous seasons debacle, **Leatherhead** (Football Association having been dropped from the title during the close season) took the option of regrouping in the rather more parochial and humble surroundings of the Dorking and District League.

The squad was bolstered by a number of new acquisitions. Former captain, Arthur Childs, returned to the fold (after a ten year absence) and Arthur and Fred Taylor arrived, having previously helped both Ashtead and Leatherhead Rose to win the Dorking League title. The balance of power shifted across town with them as Leatherhead were able to field their strongest team to date, despite losing popular captain Len Loxley, who had emigrated to Australia.

Once again Junior Cup hopes were swiftly laid to rest, by Epsom, but only after two close, hard fought games. The replay was the first match staged at the new home ground of Elmer Meadow.

Leatherhead got off to a winning start in the league and never looked back, enjoying the better of two fiercely contested local derbies. In the first Crocker scored a hat-trick for Rose but finished on the losing side as Harry Baker went one better for the home side. The return resulted in a rather more comfortable victory by 3-0. At Christmas Leatherhead sat on top of the table with six of seven games won, the only defeat occurring when an under-strength side travelled to Westcott. Brockham looked likely to put a spoke in title aspirations when they led 1-0 at half-time but the Taylor brothers had different ideas both scoring twice in the second half, as did Baker, to soothe the nerves. A point gleaned against nearest challengers Westcott brought the title closer before it was finally secured thanks to final opponents Walton-on-the-Hill scratching as they were unable to raise a side. The two points awarded were enough to claim the League Championship.
The League record read: Played 14 Won 12 Drawn 1 Lost 1 For 43 Against 14 Points 25
The handsome trophy was presented to team captain Fred Hatchwell by League Secretary H. W. Trimm following the final game of the season against the Rest of the League.

Key components in the side were a sound goalkeeper in Chandler, two capable backs in flamboyantly moustachioed Hatchwell (indeed most of the team sported facial furniture that made them look like refugees from a Gilbert and Sullivan Opera) and Fred Palmer, an experienced half-back line comprising of the Tutt brothers, Footman or Willie Shoosmith and plenty of firepower, supplied by the Taylor boys and Baker.

Despite the good results the committee were disappointed by the club's failure to muster greater support, but they expressed the hope that floating fans would be attracted now that Leatherhead had established themselves as the top team in town.

Suffering from the loss of several influential players, **Rose** failed to make an impact in the league and had to settle for a disappointing finish in the lower half of the table. This was all the more galling in view of the success across town. The loss of the Taylor brothers was an especially big blow, their keen eye for goal not being adequately replaced.

The away defeat at Brockham encapsulated the problems of a miserable season. Defensive mistakes gifted the home side a two goal lead, Rose then proceeded to miss a hatful of chances and Brockham held on to win 2-0. With the players already washed and changed the referee belatedly realised he had blown for time a full fifteen minutes early and had to summon the, none too eager, players back into the pouring rain. In the extra spell Rose contrived even more ways to miss clear cut chances, and when the final whistle went for the second time no further goals had been added.

1913/14

Leatherhead continued their recent nomadic existence, this time pitching tent at Fortyfoot Recreation Ground, which had recently been purchased by the local council.

Several older players, including the Tutt's (who had moved across town to Leatherhead Rose) left, but able replacements were drafted in to more than compensate for their loss. Despite the changes in personnel a flying start was made to the league campaign. The opening five games produced five wins and 27 goals. The run came to an end in late December in the local derby with second placed Leatherhead Rose. Honours finishing even after a 1-1 draw. This match was subsequently ordered to be replayed after an appeal to the Surrey County FA succeeded in overturning an earlier ruling by the Dorking League that Watson of Rose was eligible to play. A league rule stipulated that all players must reside within five miles of their team's home ground. Watson's parents lived in Kingston Road, just yards from the ground, but the County Association ruled that this was not his normal address and therefore he was ineligible. Strangely the ruling actually benefited Rose. Leatherhead could not raise a side for the rescheduled match and Rose collected both points. Three successive 1-1 draws followed before a depleted team were narrowly beaten at Headley to dash hopes of a repeat title. This proved to be an expensive defeat in more ways than one as the club also fell foul of the league's strict disciplinary code. A fine of one shilling was meted out for playing one man short (presumably numerically rather than vertically) another fine was incurred because not all players were wearing the club colours and a third fine was received for sending in the result card late.

In the County Junior Cup, a one-back formation was adopted for the visit of high-flying Westcott. After an even first half John Chilman opened the scoring from the spot but when a second penalty was awarded against the visitors they were so outraged that they refused to put anyone in goal. Amazingly, and much to his embarrassment, Chilman contrived to hit the upright from the spot-kick with the ball bouncing to safety. His blushes were saved when Fred Taylor slammed home the clincher ten minutes from time. There was to be no further progress though, as Leatherhead were comprehensively outplayed by neighbours Rose in the next round.

After a series of early exits **Rose** enjoyed an excellent run in the Surrey Junior Cup, finally coming to grief in the 5th round. Along the way neighbours Leatherhead were upset 5-1, in a very rough and exciting game, thanks to a hat-trick from Watson and two from his former strike partner from Leatherhead's Mid-Surrey League days, Tom Phipps. Dorking Reserves and the Guards Depot were also brushed aside, albeit the latter after a replay. A motor bus was chartered to take the players and supporters to the game at Godstone. The bus left the Common at 12.30 a.m. for the 2.30 p.m. kick-off. Perhaps the novelty of this form of transport or queasiness bought on by the bumpy state of the roads contributed to a below par performance that culminated in a 2-0 defeat.

Distracted by the cup run early league form was patchy with too many games drawn. Glimpses of the side's true potential surfaced from time to time. Brockham were on the receiving end of a 16-1 hiding and Headley were beaten at a canter 7-0. Visits to Dorking continued to be dogged by controversy. The game in February with Dorking Reserves had to be abandoned five minutes from time, with Dorking leading 3-2, after two players came to blows. The situation deteriorated rapidly as spectators waded into the fray. The referee sensibly abandoned proceedings before matters could get completely out of hand. In an exciting three way race for the title Rose's chances were dealt, what turned out to be, a fatal blow by Dorking. The replayed game, in April, resulted in the same scoreline as the abandoned match, 3-2, (the only league defeat suffered). The return a week later ended all square allowing Westcott to overhaul both teams to claim the championship. Rose and Dorking were locked together necessitating a play-off to determine the runners-up. This match also finished all square with the replay having to be held over to the following season.

The sound performances of half-back Fred Lowe earned him selection for the league team that took on Dorking at the season's conclusion. George Reddick, who was to win the Distinguished Conduct Medal in the forthcoming war, was also a valued member of the squad.

The hazards of travelling to away games were not to be underestimated as the Rose players found to their cost when involved in a near disaster returning home from the match at Westcott in March. Players and supporters were travelling in a horse drawn wagonnette driven by goalkeeper Joe Stevens when it was involved in a serious accident. A runaway carriage, whose brake had failed as it negotiated a steep hill, careered out of control and rammed into them at full speed. The occupants of the open sided carriage were thrown onto the road by the force of the impact, as were several of the passengers from the wagonnette. The casualties were attended to on the spot by some of the players before being transported to hospital for treatment to an assortment of head injuries and broken bones. Fortunately none of the injuries proved to be too serious.

1914/19

The outbreak of war quickly followed by conscription soon left teams short of players as countless young men joined the colours in response to Lord Kitchener's vigorous appeal. The Surrey Football Association suspended all competitions shortly thereafter and the vast majority of clubs closed up shop for the duration of the war.

There were, though, occasional friendlies staged. At Easter 1915 **Leatherhead**, in probably their last ever match, took on Claude Eliot FC from Hoxton in a game played at Barnett Wood Lane. The game, to help raise funds for the Cottage Hospital, ended in a 1-1 draw.
The following Easter a team representing Leatherhead Town took on one representing Leatherhead Common. The Town side ran out winners by the only goal of a keenly contested game played out in a distinctly unseasonable snowstorm.

With several of the senior administrators of the club having passed away in the intervening years the will and enthusiasm to revive the club at the end of hostilities was lacking and thus the Leatherhead club failed to resurface after the end of the Great War.

———

With many people's minds turning to Europe, football began to be almost an afterthought. Nevertheless, preparations for the new season went ahead. **Rose** lost the services of Len Songhurst and John Poulter who had joined the regular army and departed for the front line. Before the season opener, the replay against Dorking held over from the previous season, could take place war was declared. Rose were amongst the first club's to cancel all their fixtures and the game was never staged.

Upon the declaration of war a notice was posted at all local clubs stating that, "*The competitions and the clubs all realise that the Empire comes first and it is the business of footballers in common with everybody else to do their best to see that Kaiser Wilhelm is not going to referee everything and everybody*".

Clubs shut down for the duration of the war but Leatherhead All Saints (who appeared to be Leatherhead Rose in all but name) played a number of games including a fixture on Boxing Day 1916 against Leatherhead Wednesday. All Saints, nicknamed the 'Bing Boys', the origins of which have long since been lost in the mists of time, won 2-0 with the second goal scored by Collins from what was described as, "*an overhead drop shot*".

Sadly, many men who volunteered so eagerly to answer Kitchener's call to arms lost their lives in defence of their country. Among locals who did so were no fewer than five men associated with Rose. Four players: John Poulter, Harry Godwin, Fred Taylor and Bob Strickland plus committee man Albert Godwin all paid the ultimate sacrifice, with many others losing friends and family. On the 11th November 1918 the armistice was signed and the war was over. However, it was still some months before all units finally returned from the front and a semblance of normality was restored. Once the Great War was over the appetite to quickly reinstate the league and cup competitions was huge but it was to be fully ten months before organised football resumed.

1919/20

The Dorking and District League reformed in time for the start of the season with entries being received from nine clubs; Leatherhead Athletic (a newly formed club for ex-servicemen),Westcott, **Leatherhead Rose**, Dorking Reserves, Ashtead, Great Bookham, Effingham, Mickleham and North Holmwood.

Despite the casualties suffered during the war the Rose team was still a familiar one to their supporters. The half-backs of Small, Tutt and Fred Lowe remained intact and Phipps and Watson were still plying their trade in attack. In addition Len Chitty and Batchelor had turned out for Leatherhead Juniors pre-war and Arthur 'Lucky' Taylor for Leatherhead.

A potent forward line combined with a resolute defence made Rose formidable opponents. A goal laden start to the season was enjoyed; twenty seven goals in three games, including a crushing 14-1 win over Effingham. This form was carried through the rest of the season with the ultimate destiny of the league trophy never really in doubt. An enthralling all action pre-Christmas derby against Leatherhead Athletic had the crowd on tenterhooks until the final whistle. Play flowed from end to end and Rose showed great character to come from behind to eclipse Athletic by six goals to five. The only points dropped were in a New Year derby draw with Leatherhead Athletic and in a solitary defeat by nearest challengers Westcott in March. Handsome revenge was wreaked on Westcott three weeks later though with a 5-1 win in a stormy match that saw Taylor and an opponent sent-off for indulging in a bout of boxing. It was a win that sewed up the title.
Rose were comfortably the league's top scorers with Small and Watson particularly impressive.

Dorking and District League 1919/20

Team	Played	Won	Drawn	Lost	For	Against	Points
Leatherhead Rose	**16**	**14**	**1**	**1**	**82**	**24**	**29**
Westcott	16	12	1	3	55	17	25
Ashtead	16	11	1	4	65	15	23
Dorking Reserves	16	8	2	6	43	35	18
Leatherhead Athletic	16	7	3	6	50	41	15*
Mickleham	16	7	0	9	26	40	14
Great Bookham	16	6	1	9	49	44	13
North Holmwood	16	1	2	13	18	73	4
Effingham & Little Bookham	16	0	1	15	11	110	1

*Leatherhead Athletic had 2 points deducted for fielding an ineligible player

In the Junior Cup, progress was made to the fourth round where three absorbing encounters followed against top Redhill League side Horley. One hundred vociferous supporters accompanied the team to Horley to see a workmanlike performance earn a replay. The first replay again ended all square after Small had first scored and then missed from the penalty spot. There was more penalty drama in the second replay back at Horley. This time the referee awarded Rose no fewer than three spot-kicks. Small rattled home the first but the next two were saved and missed respectively whilst Horley managed to score three times without the assistance of penalties to progress to the next round.

▲Canon Utterton, Vicar of the Parish Church and the first President of Leatherhead Football Club, a role he fulfilled from 1886 to 1906

▲Kingston Road pictured in the early 1900's with the Recreation Ground on the right and the Rose Coffee Tavern directly opposite in, what still remains, a small parade of shops. The Recreation Ground was the first home of Leatherhead Football Club and also played host to Leatherhead Rose for most of their existence between 1907 and 1946. The ground is still in use today as a football pitch nearly 120 years after Leatherhead's first match was played their in November 1886.

▲The earliest known photograph of a Leatherhead team, taken at the Leatherhead Institute in 1896.

▲Leatherhead's highly successful team from the 1901/2 season line up for the camera. The team won 27 out of 31 games played and were Surrey Junior League Divisional champions.
Back Row: Charles Weller, Harry Hook, F. Watson, Bob Stevenson, Harry Shurville and H. Mann
Middle Row: Alf Shurville, Ernest Utterton, Guy Hue-Williams (captain), William 'Dasher' Davis and E. Brockwell *Front Row:* F. Barnes and J. McIntyre

▲Leatherhead Rose's Dorking and District League winning side of 1909/10 pictured with the trophy after the final match of the season against the Rest of the League at Fetcham Grove.
Back Row: Mark Rowland, John Poulter*, S. Hill, Jack Port, George Reddick, Bob Strickland*, J. Smith, Fred Lowe and William Holland *Front Row:* Edward Penfold, John Cooke, Harry Godwin*, Phil Peters, Henry Wild, Fred Taylor* and Albert Godwin*.
*Killed in the First World War.

▲Leatherhead (or is it the cast of a Gilbert and Sullivan opera?) - Surrey Junior League 1911/12
Standing: Referee Thorne, Footman, Tim Tutt, Fred Hatchwell, Edward Tinsley, Len Loxley, Walter Boswell, Willie Shoosmith, Benjamin Tutt and S. Kirkham
Kneeling: William Worsfold, Linesman's identity unknown

▲Phil Peters - one of the main driving forces behind the formation of Leatherhead Rose.

▲Henry White - a wealthy local stock and share broker noted for being a man of great kindness and genorosity. He was Chairman of Rose for 30 years.

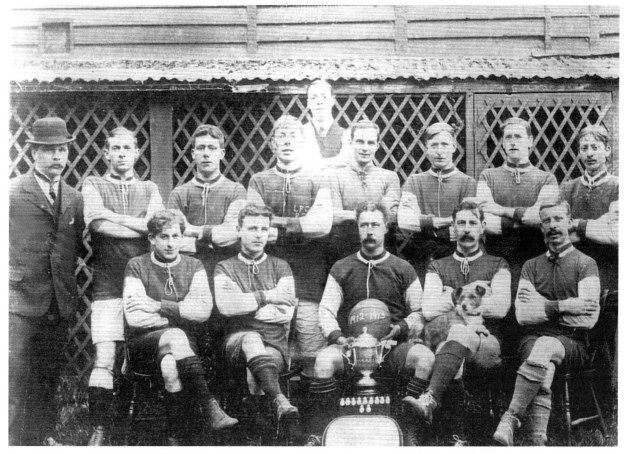

▲The Leatherhead team pictured at the end of the 1912/13 season outside the Old Rising Sun pub (now Pangs Villa restaurant) with the Dorking and District League trophy.
Back Row: Alf Shurville, Fred Palmer, Alfred Taylor, Benjamin Tutt, Arthur Searle (proprietor of the Rising Sun), Stan Loxley, Tim Tutt, Hutton and Arthur Taylor *Front Row:* W. Prutton, Footman, Fred Hatchwell, Harry Baker (with Billy the club mascot) and Fred Taylor

▲Leatherhead sent a large contingent of men to serve in the Armed Services during the First World War; among them were Privates Alfred, Fred and Arthur Taylor (*pictured above*) who had all turned out for Leatherhead and Leatherhead Rose in the years immediately prior to the war. Tragically Fred (May 1915) and Alfred (August 1917), along with three other brothers including Albert (who had also played for Leatherhead Rose pre-war), lost their lives during the conflict whilst a sixth member of the family lost a leg. Of the seven brothers who served their country only 'Lucky' Arthur remained physically unscathed and able to resume his playing career with Leatherhead Rose at the war's end.

▲The Leatherhead Rose, Dorking and District League championship winning squad of 1919/20.

CHAPTER FOUR - GREAT EXPECTATIONS

Although the Leatherhead club had failed to resurface after the war, a number of other local teams were formed, albeit in the cases of Leatherhead Athletic and Leatherhead Juniors they were to prove short-lived. However, it was not all doom and gloom as from the ashes of Leatherhead Juniors rose a new name, Leatherhead United.

Football club's finances were also affected by the recently introduced Government Entertainment Tax, which encompassed gate receipts, although some supporters would argue that there was often little of entertainment value on offer at the various football fields in Leatherhead!

With the break up of many of the large estates and the rapid expansion of suburban type council housing estates during the 1920s the character of the town changed from being partially a farming community with some light industries, to a commuter village. The countrywide industrial troubles, culminating in the 1926 General Strike and the world depression in 1929, had a profound effect on the town. Trading slumped forcing many shops to close, unemployment was rife leading to a fall in living standards which in turn caused considerable hardship. The town's football clubs were not immune from the fall out, as players found there were more pressing requirements for their time. The teams did their level best to keep the town's spirits up by winning a number of trophies and consolidating their position amongst the top junior clubs in the county.

Further afield the new home of English football, Wembley Stadium, was opened in 1923.

1920/21

In search of a fresh challenge, Leatherhead Rose transferred to the Kingston and District League (where they remained for the next 26 years) with the reserves moving up to the Dorking League. One development effected at Kingston Road was the introduction of a rope around the pitch perimeter to keep spectators at arms length from players and officials. The wingers, in particular, had previously faced an extra hazard. It was not uncommon for them to be upended in full flight by an outstretched foot 'accidentally' placed in their path by supporters of the opposing team. There had been a number of incidents at various venues; most notably in the game against Dorking the previous season with the visitors claiming that their goalkeeper had been impeded by spectators thereby preventing him from reaching a speculative long range shot that brought the first goal.

It took a while for the team to adjust to life in the new and undoubtedly stronger competition. Reigning champions Hampton Court Palace administered a 5-2 opening day beating. Rose held a four goal advantage after an hour in the next match against the Canaries from Hook but then conceded five in the last half-hour as the defence caved in. The league account was finally opened in November with a gritty 2-1 win over Oxshott. A game, according to the match report, in which not a single foul was committed! This victory failed to lead to a sustained upturn in fortunes and a final finish of ninth out of eleven tells its own story, although "*if the defence had been as virile as the vanguard*" the record would have been much better.

Travel to away games was now marginally quicker, if no less unpleasant, with many games involving a bumpy journey in the back of a motor lorry. This was not without its problems though. The vehicle transporting the team to Earlsfield for a friendly broke down (not an uncommon event) and on this occasion was unable to be repaired leaving the team stranded by the side of the road. When the team did manage to arrive the off field hospitality was greatly enjoyed, particularly at Depot East Surreys where the players and supporters were treated to a proper sit down tea in the Officers Mess at the conclusion of the match.

Dorking Reserves had accounted for Leatherhead Athletic in the Junior Cup but Rose, "*playing a very dashing and robust game*", destroyed the home side and restored local pride by avenging the defeat in emphatic style, 9-2, but participation in the competition was ended by a hefty defeat at Epsom Brotherhood in the following round.

The transfer of inside-left Archie Smith to Dorking (amid some acrimony as no official approach was made to the club only to the player) in mid-season weakened the forward line. The defence leaked too many goals although Eric Wild at right-half and George Budden, a goalkeeper of "*more than average ability*", turned in some fine displays but the intermediate line lacked cohesion. One player to make his mark was outside-right Eric Collins whose association firstly with Rose and later with the newly merged Leatherhead club was to span more than four decades.

Off the pitch Phil Peters resigned as Honorary Secretary after 14 years, his role being taken over by Fred Harwood.

A reunion match held in March 1921 saw the current team take on a Leatherhead Old Crocks side including Tom Phipps, Ed Watson, 'Dasher' Davis, Harry Shurville, Bob Nash, Bob Stevenson, Bob Mathieson and the Reverend Vernon. Despite an average age closing in on fifty the Old Crocks held the 'youngsters' to a 2-2 draw. The presence of the Town's Silver Band helped attract a healthy attendance enabling over £8 to be donated to the Cottage Hospital's building fund. The match was followed by tea and the presentation of commemorative medals at the Running Horse. During his speech, Club President Captain Gregory, suggested an amalgamation of all Leatherhead's teams to form a single club strong enough to match neighbours Dorking. Unfortunately his plea fell on deaf ears.

1921/22

Benefiting from the demise of Leatherhead Athletic (who had been unable to find a suitable permanent home ground), Rose recruited several new players including the free-scoring William Hibbett and his sidekick, Arthur Atkins.

Hibbett's goals featured heavily in a superb run in the Junior Cup, Rose battling their way through six rounds amid increasing excitement to reach the semi-finals for the first time where Farncombe barred the way to the final. Cup fever swept the town. Even London and South West Railways joined in the spirit, laying on a special train to take the fans to the game and offering cheap tickets on all other scheduled trains to Guildford. A crowd numbering close to 800, with Rose enjoying the bulk of the support, had assembled at the Guildford Sports Ground by kick-off. They watched an absorbing encounter in which Farncombe always just held the upper hand. A goal at the end of each half was enough to put them through to the final.
In an earlier round Rose had been involved in a titanic tussle with local rivals Great Bookham. In the first game at Kingston Road, Bookham looked dead and buried as they trailed 4-1 with ten minutes remaining. They managed to peg the score back to 4-4 to take the game into extra-time where they soon took the lead and seemed to be heading for victory until the game was abandoned as it had become too dark to continue. The replay was almost a replica of the original tie. Again it finished 4-4, Hibbett again scoring three times. Once more Bookham took the lead in the extra period only for the failing light to force a second abandonment. The third game was surprising, not only was it actually played to a conclusion but also because it turned out to be a no contest. Hibbett only on the mark twice this time as Bookham were overcome at last, 7-0.

In contrast to cup form, league performances were second rate. With eyes on the Junior Cup, league form suffered. Even so fifth out of eight still represented a slight improvement.
The team generally performed below standard but former Athletic men Alf Tidy and Reverend Brooks (the local Wesleyan Minister) excelled in goal and at half-back respectively. Bespectacled

Terence Potter also played well in defence and cultured centre-half or centre-forward John Bates was a revelation. Hibbett was the pick of the forwards scoring over half of the side's league goals. He was especially strong in the air and thrived on the corners and crosses from Eric Collins but he lacked sufficient support.

The wearing of glasses by players was fairly common and did not normally present a problem but during the course of a 6-2 Epsom Hospital Cup win over Ewell the following year Potter (Terence not Harry) broke his spectacles. To avoid him endangering his own goal as a result of his impaired vision his captain wisely moved him well out of harms way to the right wing where home supporters shouted instructions as to the whereabouts of the ball while visiting supporters tried to steer him towards the adjacent river!

Rose also participated in other local cup competitions most notably the Teck Charity Cup. The importance of this competition can be judged by the fact that an astonishing 6,000 spectators turned up at Kingstonian's Richmond Road ground for the final in April 1922 between Long Ditton Old Boys and Hampton Court Palace.

At the season's conclusion, Rose officials were invited to a meeting called by the Kingston League to discuss the formation of a new Premier Division to help raise standards on and off the pitch. The new division was duly created, unfortunately Rose's facilities and playing record were not deemed good enough to gain election.

1922/23

Rose kicked off in Division One having effectively been demoted now that the new Premier Division was in operation.

Hibbett started the season in spectacular fashion scoring twelve times in the opening seven league and cup games. His loss through injury in November for the remainder of the season was a major blow. Bates filled in whilst a replacement as the central pivot was sought. Although not a prolific scorer like Hibbett, Jock McKenzie proved a more than useful acquisition. He held the forward line together better and was more adept at bringing the other forwards into the game.

Performances remained solid rather than spectacular but 5-0 and 4-2 wins over Ham and Hampton Wick respectively showed that Rose were coming to terms with the competition.

John Bates again performed superbly in defence and half-backs Terry Potter, the Wild brothers (Eric and George) and Lindsell deserve mention as effective spoilers, compensating for the loss of Reverend Brooks who had left the parish for pastures new.

Highlight of the season was an appearance in the inaugural Leatherhead Hospital Shield final. This competition, along with many others, was instigated by the clubs who wished to play their part in helping raise funds for their local hospital, especially as it had been of great benefit to more than a few players who had met with misfortune on the field of play. Local rivals Leatherhead (*see page 46*) were knocked out in the semi-final in an exciting tie. Leatherhead held the initiative at half-time but Rose, kicking down the 'infamous' Fortyfoot slope, struck four times in the second half through Mckenzie (2), Bates and Jack Holland to progress.

The final, at Ashtead, drew an excellent crowd of 2,150. Epsom Town, Sutton and District League champions and Surrey Junior Cup finalists, took the Shield courtesy of a solitary, hotly disputed goal. Rose players and supporters alike convinced that the ball had not crossed the line before it was hacked clear. Nevertheless, the performance suggested that better times were not far away. Queen Marys Convalescent Home of Epsom were beaten for the third successive season in the Junior Cup but Leatherhead inflicted a surprise defeat in front of a large crowd at Kingston Road in the next round.

Still buoyed by a post-war boom in attendances and despite competing in a lower league gate receipts still reached a respectable £56, indicating average home crowds of around 200 - 300.

Elsewhere, the Surrey Senior League was finally formed with Dorking amongst the participants.

1923/24

In a bid to attract new members, the Rose reduced subscriptions to 4d. As part of the membership package the club made available a lorry on matchdays to transport supporters to away games.

Life in Division One continued to be more to the liking of Rose. The table was headed for much of the season until a poor run in March put paid to any chance of capturing the title. In a very close finish Rose occupied fifth place but just three points behind champions Teddington Central. Performance of the season was a 4-3 win at league leaders Teddington, Rose coming from behind three times before snatching a late winner.

The season began and ended with cup final appearances of contrasting fortunes.
In September, Epsom Town provided the opposition in the Epsom Hospital Cup final held over from 1922/23. Severely handicapped by an injury to Terry Potter, Rose battled on bravely with ten men for over an hour. A single goal defeat was no disgrace in the circumstances.

On Easter Monday, Ashtead played host to the final of the Leatherhead Hospital Shield. Some 2,000, almost universally cloth capped, spectators were treated to an enthralling humdinger of an encounter between Rose and newly crowned Sutton and District League champions, Banstead. Bates twice gave Rose, wearing an unfamiliar strip of red and white stripes, the lead in the first half only for Banstead to quickly equalise. Twice more in normal time and once in extra-time Rose took the initiative only for Banstead to claw their way back into the game each time. In order to try to reach a conclusion, a further ten minutes each way was played. With time running out and both sets of players exhausted, Eric Collins found sufficient reserves of energy to send over an inch perfect cross for Hibbett to head home to make the score 6-5 and finally break Banstead's stubborn resistance. Fittingly it was the team's captain Collins, whose fine wing play had created four goals, who was the man to be presented with the Shield amidst scenes of great jubilation.

LEATHERHEAD HOSPITAL SHIELD

(FINAL TIE).

LEATHERHEAD ROSE WINNERS AT SECOND ATTEMPT.

Leatherhead Rose were successful in securing the Leatherhead Hospital Shield on Easter Monday, after one of the most exciting, yet gruelling, matches that one could wish to see. Fifty minutes extra time was necessary before a decision was reached, and it can quite be understood that each side was played to a standstill. At no time during the match could the Rose get more than a goal lead, and thus it was that there was always "something in it," keeping the spectators on the tiptoe of excitement throughout.

The Rose took the field first in the unfamiliar colours of red and white stripes, when between 1,500 and 2,000 people had assembled. Banstead were also in neutral colours (white). Collins won the toss and elected to defend the slope during the first half. Leatherhead Rose opened the game with a determined attack on the Banstead goal, and during the first minute Creasey just missed with a fine drive. The Rose continued their attack and be-

The fans certainly got their money's worth from some eventful cup football during the season.
A 1-1 draw in the quarter-final of the Chambers Cup against Premier Division opponents Hampton sounds fairly straightforward but it was far from it. Hampton peppered the Rose goal with shots and forced twenty six corners and with the match official finding sufficient intent to award no fewer than four penalties, all for handball, created enough chances to win ten games. Four different players tried their luck from the spot but only one managed to aim sufficiently straight enough to force keeper George Holland into saving. Atkins, revelling in an attacking midfield role, scored a ripsnorter following a rare foray into Hampton territory. With Rose clinging on to their lead like an

alcoholic to his last drink a major upset was on the cards but with time running out, Hampton reaching for the kitchen sink and the Fat Lady readying her tonsils, a wicked deflection finally beat the outstanding Holland. Hampton converted their superiority into goals in the replay winning 4-0. Player of the season was undoubtedly centre-half John Bates whose outstanding performances gained him selection for the Surrey squad that met Buckinghamshire at Kingstonian's Richmond Road ground. One hundred and eighty players and members gathered at the Picture House to celebrate a successful season and, no doubt, to spend some of the club's Balance Sheet surplus of £14.

1924/25

As a result of restrictions placed on the use of the Recreation Ground, Leatherhead Rose were compelled to move to a new location. The local council decreed that the cricket club should have first use of the facilities and that ratepayers should not have to pay for a football team to use the Recreation Ground! Fortunately the use of a private ground just a couple of hundred yards further along Kingston Road was acquired, with the added luxury of adjoining dressing rooms.

Despite this upheaval Rose continued to flourish and a new youth team was set up to compete in the Surrey Youths Cup.

Three weeks prior to the kick-off, the team was rocked by the loss of cultured centre-half John Bates, who elected to move to Kingston to further his business career. The defensive problem was solved by the simple expedient of deploying an attacking formation designed to ensure that more goals were scored than conceded. By and large this tactic worked.

RIP-ROARING ROSE RUN RIOT

The first six cup and league games were won convincingly with thirty goals scored and only nine conceded. The revelation of the early weeks was young centre-forward Pickering. Sadly Pickering, a native of Birmingham, soon became homesick and returned home shortly after the turn of the year. His departure did not stem the flow of goals. Teddington Workmen were beaten 9-1 and 7-0, Surbiton Christchurch 6-4 and eventual runners-up Ham and Petersham 5-2, as Rose marched triumphantly to the title scoring 46 goals in gaining twenty one out of a possible twenty four points.

Kingston and District League Division One 1924/25

Team	Played	Won	Drawn	Lost	For	Against	Points
Leatherhead Rose	**12**	**10**	**1**	**1**	**46**	**14**	**22**
Ham & Petersham	12	9	0	3	54	17	18
Graham Spicer	12	7	1	4	40	25	15
Worcester Park	12	7	1	4	34	22	15
Surbiton Christchurch	12	5	1	6	26	25	11
Oxshott	12	2	0	10	18	44	4
Teddington Workmen	12	0	0	12	7	78	0

Bates' replacement George Stevens quickly matured into a fine stopper who sufficiently impressed Isthmian League Kingstonian for them to offer him a trial. He was ably supported by the Holland and Wild brothers as the defence coped much better than expected with Bates' loss.

Despite winning the William Hunt Cup as Division One champions promotion was denied by an early form of ground grading. The new ground was deemed not to be up to the standard required for entry to the Premier League, a disappointing footnote to an otherwise fine season.

The attacking policy was not without its risks. When the forward line didn't function properly the whole team struggled. Surbiton Old Boys inflicted heavy defeats at the quarter-final stages of both the Teck and Chambers Cups. Perennial party poopers Ashtead did likewise in the final of the Dorking Hospital Cup (having already knocked Rose out of both the Surrey Junior and Charity Cups). A crowd numbering around 1,000 and a whole host of local dignitaries were kept waiting for over an hour for the start of the Dorking Hospital Cup final because several Rose players were attending a funeral. It was hardly the ideal preparation for an important game and their sombre mood was certainly not improved by a 5-1 drubbing.

The grip on the Leatherhead Hospital Shield was ended by Ewell. This defeat came after a 3-1 win over Leatherhead United in an earlier round in the first meeting with their new cross-town rivals.

Leatherhead Juniors had been formed in 1920 and entered the Dorking and District League but made little impact in the following two seasons. Juniors was dropped from the title in 1922 as the club became the third in less than fifteen years to carry the town's name. Following a switch to the Sutton and District League, Leatherhead made a reasonable start to the 1923/24 league campaign but then their season fell apart. In November, Carshalton Wanderers were beaten 6-0, a result that put Leatherhead on top of the table, thereafter results went on the kind of downward spiral not normally seen outside of the Argentinian economy. Due to a catalogue of injuries and work commitments it became an increasing struggle to field a side. Matters finally came to a head in January when none of the scheduled fixtures were fulfilled. A crisis meeting of the members provoked a renewal of enthusiasm and agreement that the club should continue to fulfil its engagements in the league. Unfortunately, this enthusiasm proved short-lived and within a couple of weeks hope, along with most of the supporters and players, had drifted away. After failing to raise enough able bodied players to fulfil another fixture in early March the remaining members took the sad but inevitable decision to disband the club and the league accordingly expunged Leatherhead's playing record from the table.

Thanks to the determined efforts of two former Leatherhead officials, Messrs Fred Elliott and H. F. Harding a new club, **Leatherhead United**, rose from the ashes of the old Leatherhead club. A team was entered in the Dorking and District League, disregarding the fact that with only two months to go to the start of the new season, they had neither players or kit nor a ground to their name. Due to the unstinting endeavours of the two men a long list of locals were persuaded to become Vice-Presidents (newspaper tycoon Lord Beaverbrook, who lived at Cherkley Court, was among those enlisted) in return for a generous donation to the club's coffers. In addition the local Member of Parliament, Sir George Rowland Blades (later Lord Ebbisham) agreed to be President, although he maintained a foot in both camps as he was also a Vice-President of Rose. With sufficient funds now in place a new club kit of white shirts and black shorts was purchased and the use of Fortyfoot secured as home ground.

On the playing front, virtually the whole of the previous season's Leatherhead squad signed on including the Girdler brothers (Percy and Lou) plus Gale whose pace was a tremendous asset to the side. They were supplemented by the return of Fred Shurville from Dorking together with his teenage brother, Reg, and Dayman, both recruited from Leatherhead Rose. Reg, Albert, Fred and Ernie Shurville were all sons of Alf Shurville who had been a Leatherhead fovourite at the turn of the century, between them the brothers were to clock up over 50 seasons and some 1,500 games for United. The difference in attitude of the players under the new regime was immediately evident, undoubtedly aided by a successful start to the new campaign.

There were some notable performances. In friendlies, Merton Corinthians were powerless to stop a rampant United attack and were overrun 14-0, Lou Girdler scoring eight times. Little goodwill was shown to Leatherhead Wednesday in the Christmas Day fixture either. Creasey putting six of the eight goals scored past the hapless Wednesday custodian.

In the league United made the early running thanks to the goals of the Shurville and Girdler brothers. Nine of the first ten league games were won. Title rivals Westcott temporarily knocked United off the summit after scoring the only goal of a keenly contested game. Top spot was reclaimed seven days later following a 4-1 victory over Great Bookham and was not relinquished again until the final weekend when Capel won 4-1 at Fortyfoot to claim the top prize. Despite this disappointment runners-up spot was still regarded by all connected with the club as a notable achievement in the circumstances.

1925/26

With the benefit of hindsight it may well have been preferable not to have resurrected the former Leatherhead club in the guise of Leatherhead United as more of the local playing resources would have been available to bolster **Rose**. As it was the town's footballing strength was hopelessly fragmented and not only between Rose and United. Throughout the following two decades a succession of other clubs sprang up, although many soon withered and died. Among rivals to the two more senior teams were: Leatherhead Old Boys, Fetcham, Leatherhead Old Scholars and Leatherhead JEA, who all competed in various divisions of the Sutton and District League prior to the outbreak of the Second World War.

1925/6 witnessed the introduction of a new offside law. There now had to be only two opponents (not three) in front of the attacking player and he could no longer be offside in his own half of the field. The law was introduced to prevent the growth of sterile and boring football. Some teams had become so adept at the art of offside that up to 40 offside decisions in one game was not an uncommon occurrence (Arsenal's name springs to mind for some reason). In the long term the rule change ended the 2-3-5 formation which had prevailed for nearly forty years. The eventual result was a move to a 3-4-3 line-up. This change certainly had the desired effect and nets bulged as defenders struggled to cope with the new law, none more so than at Kingston Road (Rose had returned to the Recreation Ground once the problems with the council had been resolved) where over a century of goals were scored but also conceded. It was very much a season of two halves. Unbeaten in league or cup until January the good ship Rose, which up till that time had sported a watertight defence, inexplicably sprang a leak of Titanic proportions and hopes of any silverware sank without trace. It looked for a long time as though the league title would be successfully defended until a calamitous 10-1 defeat at the hands of Ham and Petersham in March was quickly followed by an 8-3 reverse at Shepperton. Any lingering chances were soon extinguished by a 2-1 loss to Esher.

Cup games did not lack goals or entertainment either. Leatherhead United, 9-1, and Ewell, 8-0, were crushed in the Junior Cup before the defensive fallibility resurfaced during the course of a 9-4 fifth round drubbing by Benhilton, with the defence in danger of being prosecuted under the Trade Descriptions Act. Ashtead won a Hospital Shield semi-final replay 7-2 whilst the heaviest defeat, 13-2, thanks to a performance that would have been an insult to headless chickens, was suffered at Premier League Surbiton Old Boys in the Teck Cup, as injuries and a huge fixture backlog took its toll.

For the third year running the influential Atkins topped the scoring charts with over 30 goals to his credit. He received excellent support from lively youngster Webb, the latest in a long line to be tried at filling the problem centre-forward berth.

_____

Meanwhile, **Leatherhead United** built on the foundations of success laid down in the first year.

United switched from the Dorking to the Sutton League and were placed in the First Division.

The new offside law was also welcomed. Defences had become so adept at springing the offside trap that when the United team arrived at Dorking station prior to a game and heard a guard's whistle, a wag chimed "*Blimey! Offside already*". The law change had the requisite effect though and goals aplenty were seen at Fortyfoot with the homesters accounting for the majority of them.

The league season commenced with a thrilling game (amply demonstrating the merits of the new rules) against Carshalton Hill, which was edged by the odd goal in nine. The attack continued to give opposing defences a torrid time, rattling in an average of four goals a game. The championship soon developed into a three horse race involving United, Brocks Pyros and Croydon Parish Church, with the outcome in doubt until the final game of the season. On 27th March, Croydon arrived at Fortyfoot knowing that a win, in what was their last game, would be enough to secure the title. However, they went home empty-handed as United enhanced their own chances with a well deserved 2-1 success. Two weeks later Brocks Pyros produced some early fireworks, putting paid to an unbeaten away record by recording a 3-2 victory. Even so the title could still be clinched with victory in the last game. Due to a string of cup commitments the final match was not staged until 8th May, fully six weeks after Croydon had finished their campaign. If there were any nerves they were not in evidence as the championship was won in style at Epsom Brotherhood, thanks to goals from Lou Girdler (2), Froese (2), Gale and Hoare to no reply.

Sutton and District League Division One 1925/26

Team	Played	Won	Drawn	Lost	For	Against	Points
Leatherhead United	**16**	**12**	**2**	**2**	**67**	**27**	**26**
Croydon Church	16	12	1	3	88	18	25
Brocks Pyros	16	12	1	3	71	26	25
Belmont	16	8	2	6	54	51	18
Lavender United	16	7	0	9	20	47	14
Epsom Brotherhood	16	5	0	11	29	48	10
Carshalton Hill	16	4	3	9	36	48	9*
Coles Athletic	16	3	2	11	21	79	8
Carshalton Rainbow	16	3	1	12	25	66	7

*Carshalton Hill 2 points deducted for fielding an ineligible player.

President Sir Rowland Blades took special delight in presenting the League Championship Shield to United; not only because it was to his own club but because he had also been the original donor of the Shield at the League's inception in 1921.

Despite a couple of heavy cup defeats, United did enjoy some success, reaching the final of the Epsom Hospital Cup before succumbing to Sutton Premier League side, Banstead.

The Wednesday section added to the collection of silverware with their first honour, winning the Rawson Cup by virtue of finishing runners-up to Crawley in the Redhill and District Wednesday League. All in all a terrific achievement for a club resurrected just two years previously.

The friendly rivalry that existed between the two senior Leatherhead teams was evident at the Annual General Meeting's, with both clubs inviting their rivals to attend. Rose's Secretary, Fred Harwood, took the opportunity afforded by his invitation to address the meeting to again express the hope that the clubs would amalgamate in the not too distant future to form a single club capable of returning to senior football.

1926/27

John Bates was welcomed back to the **Leatherhead Rose** fold and his presence ensured that the defence was harder to break down. Other than Bates the starting eleven was virtually unchanged. Atkins continued to rattle in the goals, becoming the first player to reach the century mark.

League form was patchy until the team put together an excellent unbeaten run which lasted from early February right through to the end of the season. This was sufficient to clinch second place behind Worcester Park. The reserves went one better by winning the Fourth Division title.

In cup football, Rose were engaged in a highly contentious run in the Junior Cup. After easily overcoming Ewell and Walton Heath the draw threw up a meeting with Leatherhead United at Fortyfoot. United won through, 3-1, but an appeal against the result was lodged on the grounds that one of United's players, Jones, had recently played as a professional and was therefore ineligible. The protest was upheld and United were thrown out of the competition. In the next round it was the supporters who got into trouble. The match at Epsom Athletic had to be frequently halted due to the antics of the travelling supporters during the course of a 3-3 draw. The club were left in no doubt by the County Football Association that any repeat in the replay would lead to serious consequences. Fortunately the rowdier element managed to control their feelings despite having to watch their favourites being dumped out of the cup.

The final of the Leatherhead Hospital Shield was made, only for Banstead to take home the spoils after a narrow 2-1 victory.

The Junior Cup dispute with United temporarily soured relations between the two clubs and preliminary merger discussions petered out as a result.

Having won promotion to the Premier Division of the Sutton League, **United** took the rather curious decision to return to the Dorking and District League. It did not turn out to be an inspired decision and a string of inconsistent performances ensured only a mid-table finish was achieved. The end of term report read - A strong rearguard but weak upfront, could do better.

There was little for the faithful fans to get excited about with the Junior Cup debacle mentioned above and poor league form although the final of the Epsom Hospital Cup was again reached. The Easter Monday final at Epsom Town was evenly balanced at one apiece at half-time, Reg Shurville tucking away the leveller after Epsom Athletic had taken an early lead. Injuries to Wild, Powell and Lawes during the second period, however, proved too big an obstacle to overcome. Despite a gallant rearguard effort United's depleted forces could just not withstand constant Epsom pressure and as the eight remaining fit men tired in the closing stages so Athletic made the game safe with three goals.

1927/28

Indifferent form in the first couple of months could be attributed to the first major overhaul of the **Rose** team for five or six years. Bates missed the majority of the campaign through illness and centre-forward Webb left for pastures new. George Stevens moved across town to United whilst Albert Potter was still recovering from a serious injury sustained at the tail-end of the previous season. This opened the door for several new faces of which right-half Dean and forward Taylor proved to be outstanding successes as performances steadily improved as the campaign wore on. Rose were again tough to beat at home but failed to accumulate sufficient points away from Kingston Road. Hopes of at least finishing second were entertained until defeat in two bruising, high scoring encounters in March and April with eventual champions Esher.

There was one solitary victory in eight cup matches, 15-0 over Epsom Brotherhood in the Junior Cup of which centre-forward trialist Lindsell scored seven. Indeed in spite of only finding the net in four games Lindsell still finished as second top scorer (behind Atkins) with fourteen to his credit.

There were also changes off the field with Arthur Griffin, later to become Chairman of Rose and subsequently of Leatherhead, taking up a position on the club's committee.

After a single season away **United** returned to the Premier Division of the Sutton and District League. As well as a new league the campaign also began on a new ground. Well-known wealthy local benefactor Herbert Reeves was rewarded with the club presidency after giving permission for United to use the pitch in the grounds of his property at Fetcham Grove House. Reeves thus commenced, what was to be, a lifelong association with the town's football clubs.

The signings of George Stevens, one of a rare breed to play for both United and Rose, and Fred Shurville, returning after one season in which he had helped Dorking to the Surrey Senior League title, augured well for the season ahead.

A rocky start soon put paid to title aspirations, although a strong recovery in the New Year resulted in a respectable fourth place finish. Derby confrontations with Great Bookham were always eagerly anticipated but had a tendency to boil over. The clash at Fetcham Grove degenerated into a brawl which led to Gale and two Bookham players receiving their marching orders. This was somewhat of a rarity. The following season a total of 900 players representing some 40 clubs played in nearly 300 games throughout the league's four divisions and only twelve were booked and just two sent-off during the entire season. That would probably be an average tally every weekend these days!

The youth side were successful in winning the inaugural District League and with a view to the future several of the squad were blooded in the first team with Friday, Pratt and Mills quickly establishing themselves as first choices. Another youngster to make his debut was Jack Bullen who, during the course of the next fourteen seasons, went on to become one of the club's best ever defenders, occupying every position in the back line with equal alacrity.

United emulated the previous two years performances by reaching the Epsom Hospital Cup Final, going into the match as strong favourites having beaten opponents Banstead 5-1 in a league encounter only three weeks earlier. As expected United dominated the game, but the forwards endured the sort of day in which they wouldn't have scored in a brothel and Banstead converted one of their few opportunities to snatch the cup.

1928/29

Even though finances were in a reasonably healthy state, **Rose's** committee took the decision to switch to the Sutton and District League in order to benefit from less travelling and the extra revenue generated by local derbies against Great Bookham and Leatherhead United. Fund raising at this time was no easy matter, particularly as the Football Association had issued a reminder to all clubs that sweepstakes and lotteries were illegal and "*calculated to bring the game into disrepute*".

The league season began in a flurry of goals, 8-2, 5-2 and 8-0, with Epsom Brotherhood being flattened 11-0 in the Junior Cup, Atkins scoring seven to take his tally to eighteen from the opening six games. The vertically challenged Taylor, usually the smallest and lightest player on the park, belied his stature to net the other four. A good Christmas, which included a 5-0 demolition of

United on Boxing Day, was followed by a disastrous six week spell in February and March which brought elimination from four cup competitions and damaging league defeats. Confidence was partially restored with a derby victory over Great Bookham and the first league defeat inflicted on runaway leaders Crown Road Old Boys for more than two seasons. A draw with United at Easter guaranteed runners-up spot and ensured some reward from a season that had promised so much early on.

Home form was again exceptional, unbeaten with sixty three goals scored in twelve fixtures. Rose possessed a forward line that was the equal of any in the league (Atkins topped twenty goals and finished as top scorer, both for the sixth year running) unfortunately, the same could not be said of a defence that shipped goals at an alarming rate.

United had their most successful season to date. A slick short-passing game allied to mobile forwards and good teamwork proving a highly effective combination. Although the defence was not as solid as in recent campaigns goals were in plentiful supply and, despite an occasional hiccup, a title challenge was maintained until April when fixture congestion finally took its toll. Just one point from the final three matches allowed Rose to snatch runners-up spot.

Sutton and District Premier League 1928/29

Team	Played	Won	Drawn	Lost	For	Against	Points
Crown Road Old Boys	16	14	1	1	47	25	29
Leatherhead Rose	**16**	**10**	**2**	**4**	**64**	**27**	**22**
Leatherhead United	**16**	**9**	**2**	**5**	**63**	**43**	**20**
Great Bookham	16	8	0	8	44	48	16
Banstead	16	4	5	7	29	35	13
Sutton Waterworks	16	6	1	9	47	57	13
Kelvin Works	16	6	1	9	43	67	13
Waddon Aircraft	16	6	0	10	43	52	12
Sutton Athletic	16	3	2	11	20	71	8

E. A. Gale, known to all as 'Wanna', returned to action after a long absence due to a serious arm injury sustained in a motorcycling accident. In a fortuitous move he was tried at centre-forward. 'Wanna' grabbed the opportunity with both hands netting twenty two times in cup games alone. His partnership with Charlie Froese, renowned for his powerful *"clinking"* long range shooting, produced in excess of sixty goals and was instrumental in the team reaching the final of three of the four Hospital Cup competitions entered.

A healthy turnout of 1,700 looked on as holders Ashtead retained the Leatherhead Hospital Shield but only after a tremendous tussle. Gale opened the scoring, Ashtead surged into a 3-1 lead, but United came close to forcing an equaliser in a rousing finale after Lawes had reduced the arrears in the eightieth minute.

DEADLY DUO SHOOT DOWN THE AIRMEN

The Cobham Hospital Cup also proved elusive, but there was better fortune to come with the Sutton Hospital Cup being won at the first time of asking. The deadly duo of Gale and Froese scored early on against Waddon Aircraft at Sutton United's Gander Green Lane ground and the Airmen rarely threatened thereafter, U's eventually running out 4-1 winners. This was United's first ever cup final victory following five previous unsuccessful attempts to break their duck.

1929/30

The vacancy at centre-forward, created by the retreat of ace marksman Atkins to a more defensive role, was filled with great aplomb by Welsh teenager Roddy Williams. After a slow start Williams made his first major impression when scoring all six goals in a league fixture against Hook. He repeated the feat one month later against doughty opponents Crown Road in the Junior Cup and ended the season with a club record 40 goals to his credit. As so often happened **Rose** could not hang onto their latest scoring sensation. Williams signed for Sutton United for whom he continued to find the net with great regularity. His eye for goal came to the attention of League scouts and he soon moved into the Football League where he enjoyed a long and successful career with Norwich City and a number of other clubs.

Despite Williams' goal-scoring prowess an indifferent league campaign was endured in which only third place was managed.

Cup football was a different matter entirely. In the Junior Cup, Epsom Athletic, Ashtead (after a replay), Ewell and Crown Road Old Boys were all overcome. The draw for the quarter-final brought Columbia to Kingston Road. On the day Rose had to play second fiddle to the visitor's superior play and could not stop their progress, which eventually ended with them lifting the cup.

Over Easter two finals were contested in the space of three days. On the Saturday, Roddy Williams was on target twice as Beare Green were comfortably beaten 5-2 in the Dorking Hospital Cup. The Easter Monday confrontation with bitter rivals Ashtead in the Leatherhead Hospital Shield was an altogether tougher proposition but the supporters were able to celebrate the winning of more silverware courtesy of goals from Len Holland and S. Williams (Roddy's brother) which secured a narrow 2-1 victory.

The line-up for both finals was: *Vic Hastings, Cyril Basson (captain), Terry Potter, E. Taylor, F. Parker, Len Holland, Arthur Atkins, S. Williams, Roddy Williams, T. Wafforn and Eric Collins*

In contrast **United** endured a very poor season failing to build on the progress made in 1928/29. Talented, good to watch, hard working, goal laden and hard to beat were just some of the words in no way associated with the team. The loss of influential skipper George Andrews, for the whole campaign, and Reg Shurville, for a large portion of it (both had signed for Sutton United), were major factors in the decline.

Just four of fourteen league games played were won and only the resignation of Bookham based works side Gillett Stephens in mid-season saved United from relegation. The team's apparent philosophy of treating goal prevention as a nasty chore to be tackled once the fun stuff up the other end was out of the way certainly didn't help the cause.

Cup football provided little cheer either with early exits being made from all competitions with the exception of the Leatherhead Hospital Shield. Even then it was neighbours Rose who had the last laugh defeating United 4-2 in a hotly contested semi-final.

There was some encouragement for the future though as the reserves won the Sutton and District Third Division title, finishing ahead of local rivals Fetcham and Leatherhead Old Boys. These promising youngsters would certainly be needed in the near future as several players, including 'Wanna' Gale, Froese, Lou Girdler and George Stevens, decided to call it a day at the season's end.

There was a small crumb of consolation as the continuing friendliness and hospitality of the club, on and off the field, was recognised by the award of the coveted League Sportsmanship Trophy.

CHAPTER FIVE - A MIXED BAG

Throughout the thirties the town was changing dramatically in appearance with many old buildings, including the famous Swan Hotel, torn down, regardless of their age, to be replaced by characterless blocks of shops and offices.

Recession was replaced by a new mood of optimism reflected in a building boom that gobbled up large tracts of Fetcham and provided much needed housing for the middle classes. For those able to afford them housing development continued apace, with a new three bedroom semi-detached house setting you back around £750. This compared to the average local skilled workers annual salary of around £150.

Growing affluence brought its own problems though as traffic congestion in the town was now a major problem with 850 cars an hour regularly passing through the High Street on a weekend. The feel-good factor was relatively fleeting though, the second half of the thirties was dominated by the increasingly gloomy news from abroad as war became inevitable.

On the footballing front, with Leatherhead United's star on the rise, Rose contemplated the question of how to halt their recent slide and regain their reputation as the town's number one club.

1930/31

Rose experienced an unproductive season. The loss of the Williams brothers affected morale although Roddy's replacement, George Armstrong, strove manfully to fill the void.

Despite an unbeaten eight match run late in the year, performances failed to match the high standard of the previous campaign. The New Year heralded a drastic downturn in results with heavy defeats suffered in the League, Charity and County cups. Just two wins in the final seven league games ensured a finishing position no higher than third.

There was still hope of some consolation in the shape of the Dorking Hospital Cup. In the final Rose were pitted against arch-enemies Ashtead. Rose could hardly have asked for a better start, left-back Basson converting a first minute penalty. The lead lasted well into the second half until the incident that changed the course of the game - Ratcliffe being badly injured bravely diving at an onrushing forwards feet in a vain attempt to prevent an equaliser. The stand-in keeper, Alf Holland, then had the misfortune to concede two soft goals in the remaining minutes to enable Ashtead to make off with the victor's laurels. The loss was all the more galling as the winners paraded several former Rose favourites, including Goodway and Frewin (who both scored), in their ranks.

United started the season deceptively well with a run of six straight league victories. Reg Shurville again led the way, scoring all the goals in an impressive 7-0 home success over Ewell.However, United fared little better than Rose (or the turkey) come Christmas time. Form and confidence gradually ebbed away as the winter months progressed. Mitcham Green scored five times in the final twenty five minutes on a mudbath of a pitch, not suited to United's more cultured short passing game, to win 6-2. An even more damaging defeat was inflicted by prospective champions Sutton Water. Even so thoughts of finishing as runners-up were still harboured until a final day defeat by Cheam allowed Banstead to claim second place.

Results of cup matches made grim reading and it was obvious that fresh blood was required to rejuvenate the squad. With neighbours Dorking adding to the misery by lifting the Surrey Senior League championship there was little to lift the spirits of either set of Leatherhead club's supporters.

In an effort to combat the previous season's failings **Rose** recruited heavily. The forward line was rebuilt with Linn, Hough and Dobson drafted in. The team's strength though, lay in the half-back line, with Wafforn and Collins developing a fine understanding, and in a solid defence where left-back Basson, centre-half Taylor and, another newcomer, Jim Strudwick, particularly impressed.

Early season league form was reasonable rather than spectacular but the turning point came with a tremendous 4-0 victory over leaders Hampton. Heartened by this performance the team went from strength to strength and were soon vying for top spot with the Metropolitan Water Board. The Watermen were the only team to have put a blot on the copybook but that 3-1 defeat was reversed in style in late January and was followed by a six game unbeaten run. Recovering from a 2-0 half-time deficit to win 4-2 in the game at Esher proved crucial in maintaining a one point advantage over the chasing pack. Rose finally celebrated a first league title since 1925 on the final day of April with the gaining of two points at Hampton, Hough, Linn and Dobson on target in the 3-1 win.

Kingston and District League Division One 1931/32

Team	Played	Won	Drawn	Lost	For	Against	Points
Leatherhead Rose	**18**	**13**	**3**	**2**	**61**	**32**	**29**
Metropolitan Water	18	13	1	4	93	31	27
Surbiton Christchurch	18	9	5	4	64	58	23
Graham Spicer	18	8	5	5	44	30	21
Esher	18	10	1	7	45	53	21
Hampton Reserves	18	8	2	8	52	44	18
Kingston Polytechnic	18	6	5	7	43	57	17
Malden Labour	18	6	4	8	40	43	16
Hook	18	2	1	15	31	46	5
Surbiton Electric	18	1	1	16	15	77	3

It was just as well that Rose succeeded in winning the league crown because cup form was truly atrocious.

At the end of the campaign record goal-scorer Atkins decided to hang up his boots. He had scored over 190 times in some 300 appearances during the course of his eleven year stint with the club.

United relied mainly on the existing squad supplemented by the return of Dayman, after a long spell at Ashtead, and keeper Dave Wareham, fit again following a lengthy lay off through injury.

The side's strength lay in a powerful forward line. There was a positive goal glut in the early weeks. Dorking Technical were made to pay for the impertinence of taking the lead in the opener being routed twice - 12-2 and 11-1. Dorking Reserves and Holmbury conceded seven and Capel eight, all in the Dorking League to which United had once more reverted. Consecutive defeats at Effingham and Ashtead prompted a positional reshuffle in which centre-half George Andrews moved to centre-forward in a rearranged front line. Having recently played at a higher level with Sutton United he found little difficulty in bypassing opposition defences. Andrews found the back of the net eighteen times in January alone and finished with a half century, the last forty one coming in only sixteen matches. His tally included six both home and away against hapless Headley, his haul at Fetcham Grove containing no fewer than five headers (despite him not being the biggest of men).
The title hinged on the encounter with Dorking St Pauls in mid-April. Unfortunately, the forwards chose this occasion to have a rare off day allowing the Saints solitary goal to claim the points and

ultimately the championship. United were by far the league's highest scorers, 113 (in 22 matches), and goals came equally freely in the various cups.

The fourth round of the Junior Cup was reached for the first time before bowing out to Ashtead but it was in the Hospital Cups that United really made a mark.
In the final of the Dorking version Surrey Junior Cup finalists and old adversaries Ashtead provided the opposition. The game was closely contested until United struck four times in a golden spell midway through the second half, Reg Shurville (2), Dayman and Thomas the scorers.

OLD BOYS SENT PACKING BY RAMPANT UNITED

The Cobham Hospital Cup was soon added to the trophy cabinet. Kingston League side Ditton Old Boys could not contain U's rampant forward line; Reg Shurville, George Andrews and Dayman on the scoresheet this time. The final was followed by tea and a concert at the village hall to which both players and spectators were welcome. Following the formal presentation of the cup and medals an evening's jolly entertainment was provided by the Cobham Amateur Players.
The same eleven represented United in both finals, namely: *Dave Wareham, W. Molloy, Fred Shurville, F. Pratt, Jack Bullen, William Atkin (captain), Herbert Creasey, George Andrews, W. Dayman, Reg Shurville and J. Thomas*

The chance to make it a unique hat-trick was initially denied because the Leatherhead Hospital Shield final had to be held over to the following season, no suitable date being available for the tie in such a crowded calendar.

Nevertheless, it was still the most successful season to date. The success was built on the back of fine team play but especially on the prolific forward quintet of Shurville, Dayman, Thomas, Creasey and Andrews who scored nearly 150 goals between them.

1932/33

In order to take up their place in the Premier Division of the Kingston League, **Rose** vacated Kingston Road and moved to a new private ground located at Mr. Holly's farm in Barnett Wood Lane. Through the generosity of President Henry White, funds were made available for a pavilion. This was erected during the summer months thanks to the unstinting efforts of the members and boasted: two dressing rooms, a bathroom with copper tank for hot water, a canteen from which tea could be dispensed and a store room. As well as a welcoming cup of tea the pavilion also at last provided some shelter from the elements for the long-suffering home supporters.

When the league campaign got under way the faithful supporters were poorly rewarded for forking out the increased admission charge of 4d. Rose found the new company, generally considered to be the strongest junior league in the county, considerably tougher. In those days status was more a matter of choice than a reflection of actual playing ability. After a succession of heavy defeats Rose seemed destined to be relegated straight back to Division One. However, the team gradually adapted to the higher level and successive victories in April over Shepperton and Cobham were just sufficient to lift Rose off the foot of the table and thereby avert the threat of demotion.

In what was the poorest season for five years no solace was to be found in cup competitions either, early departures again being made from the various tournaments.

The season marked a definite shift in the balance of power in the town. Leatherhead Rose had been top dog for the best part of a decade but now **United** assumed that mantle. Despite appeals in the local press for more support Rose still commanded the loyalty of the majority of the town's fans. Improved transport links to many professional and semi-professional clubs had also eaten into both teams traditional support.

After what many believed to have been a retrograde step in joining the Dorking League the committee changed tack completely and endeavoured to entice more followers through the gates by playing a higher grade of football. As the first step towards this goal a successful application was made to join the Surrey Junior League.

League form was very up and down, although there was rarely a shortage of goals. Kenley were beaten 10-5 and 10-0, Hadleigh Surbiton 6-1 and Southern Foundries 5-0. On the other hand thumpings were received at the hands of Croydon Gas (9-5) and Cane Hill (8-1). On the whole though a fifth place finish, out of eight, was not an unsatisfactory outcome.

It was in the cup competitions that United again really excelled. The team opened by claiming the Leatherhead Hospital Shield for 1931/32, in somewhat controversial circumstances, to complete a unique hat-trick of victories in local hospital competitions. Opponents Ashtead raced into a 3-0 interval lead before goals from Reg and Fred Shurville and George Andrews levelled things up in the second period. To the bemusement of everybody else the Ashtead players then refused to play extra-time and walked off. With no other option available the Shield was duly presented to United captain Atkin. Subsequently, following an appeal from Ashtead, the organising committee amended their decision decreeing the match to be a draw and ordering the Shield to be shared between the two clubs. The Shield was retained outright on Easter Monday when horns were locked once more with Ashtead. It was the fifth cup meeting between the two sides in six months with the score standing at two victories apiece. A large crowd was in attendance for the showdown. Those expecting another close fought game were disappointed though as United took an early grip on the game and were never seriously troubled, cantering to a 3-0 success.

Old Dorkinians were seen off, 3-2, as the Dorking Hospital Cup was also retained but the heavy toll inflicted by a third cup final in eight days proved too great an obstacle to overcome to retain the Cobham Hospital Cup. As fatigue set in during the second half Cobham simply overran United, scoring seven without reply.

Defensively the captain William Atkin was again in imperious form. He was joined at centre-half by Andrews whose aerial power was considered to be a greater asset utilised in defence. In his absence Neville and Booth led the front line to good effect. Reg Shurville netted his 100th goal for the club - the first and indeed only player to reach that milestone. The only unfortunate aspect of the season was the sacking of popular keeper Dave Wareham for disciplinary reasons. Wareham, a character prone to the odd Vesuvian eruption, was shown the exit door after he exploded during the course of a Junior Cup defeat at Ashtead. Upset by a late challenge he proceeded to launch a single-handed attack on the entire opposition forward line before being dragged away and sent for an early bath. Unfortunately the club committee took a dim view of his actions and suggested he sought a new club since he would not be allowed to darken Leatherhead's door again.

The decision to switch leagues was vindicated with the announcement at the club's AGM that gate receipts had more than doubled from the previous season.

1933/34

Wholesale changes were made to the squad but it failed to have the desired effect. **Rose** could just not compete with teams who were allowed, under league rules, to field as many as six players who had played football at a senior level.

The entire season was spent sloshing around in the depths of the relegation zone. The sole league victory was actually a walkover when Shepperton failed to appear. Only two further points were gleaned from the other seventeen fixtures and relegation was inevitable from an early stage. There were few bright spots but the form of Arthur Waite and centre-half Jim Strudwick in the backs and Dai Pritchard in midfield gave some desperately needed cause for optimism for the future, especially as stalwarts Potter and Collins decided to call it a day at the season's end.

Cup football provided some relief for the die-hards who had forked out for the newly introduced season tickets. The semi-finals of both the Cobham and Leatherhead Hospital tournaments were reached but further progress was denied by Ditton and Leatherhead United respectively.
In the Dorking Hospital Cup, Rose marched through four rounds to reach the final where neighbours United stood between them and the cup. However, due to United's success in various competitions, the final had to be held over to the following season.

UNITED ON THE UP AND UP

Whilst Rose were enduring a miserable season, by contrast **United** enjoyed a record breaking campaign. Having taken one season to find their feet the team took the Surrey Junior League by storm. After three comfortable wins the style was really turned on as Mitcham Works were crushed 13-0. In an exciting tussle nearest challengers Acc and Tab were edged out 2-1. Goals flowed freely once more in the return fixture with Mitcham, the final verdict proving to be a club record winning margin of 21-0, Roebuck setting another club record by netting eight times. The return match at the jauntily named Accounting and Tabulating (Acc and Tab for short) proved decisive. The civil servants led 2-0 early in the second period but the United players showed admirable fighting qualities to restore parity by the end. With the winning post in site nerves were set jangling in late April by a first defeat. The victors Radcliffe, along with Acc & Tab, could still snatch the title if they won their games in hand. United did themselves no favours by losing their final match but the chasing duo also stuttered in the closing weeks and United were crowned as champions by dint of a vastly superior goal average.

Surrey Junior League 1933/34

Team	Played	Won	Drawn	Lost	For	Against	Points
Leatherhead United	**14**	**10**	**2**	**2**	**74**	**20**	**22**
Radcliffe	14	9	4	1	44	20	22
Accounting & Tabulating	14	8	3	3	60	20	19
Warlingham	14	7	4	3	34	21	18
Kenley Elmwood	14	4	4	6	31	46	12
Sutton Water Company	14	5	0	9	23	41	10
Croydon Gas Company	14	2	4	8	30	40	8
Mitcham Works	14	0	1	13	13	112	1

No fewer than twenty one cup ties were contested. Leatherhead Rose could be counted among the victims of a good run in the Junior Cup that eventually ended in a replay defeat at Ashtead.

The semi-final of the Surrey Junior Charity Cup was reached for the first time before Redhill League side Horley inflicted the season's only heavy defeat (1-6).

There were goals galore as the Dorking Hospital Cup final was made for the third year in a row,

although the final was held over to the following season due to fixture congestion, and the Leatherhead version was retained again after a third consecutive meeting with Ashtead.
Two cup victories over Rose confirmed United's new found ascendancy.

With no outstanding individuals, success was based on superb all round team play. The defence was well marshalled by Jack Bullen (who displayed *fine headwork*) together with Molloy. With Joe Roebuck, who was only signed shortly before Christmas, contributing an impressive total of 33 goals, Reg Shurville close behind on 30 and Thompson (signed from Dorking By-Pass), Booth and even 'Wanna' Gale (returning to the district) contributing double figures there was plenty of firepower available.

The next step towards the club's stated long-term goal of senior football was taken. Membership of the Surrey Intermediate League was sought and accepted.

1934/35

Rose made a blistering start to life back in the First Division of the Kingston League. The opening seven games were all won, however, a disastrous beginning to the New Year put paid to title aspirations. A late revival, which included a 16-0 trouncing of Hook, came too late to achieve anything higher than a third place finish.

Once again more cup games (seventeen) than league games (sixteen) were played. Victories were recorded in the early rounds of all five competitions entered but ultimately defeat ensued in the later rounds, apart from in the Leatherhead Hospital Shield. Rose lifted the Shield for the third time thanks to goals from Dai Pritchard and Steadman in a hard fought victory over Effingham.
The side that took the field was: *E. Taylor, Charlie Budd, Bill North, Alf Goodhew, Jim Strudwick, Cyril Basson, A. Thorpe, Dai Pritchard, Arthur Waite, T. Carter and Mark Killian*

In the Surrey Junior Cup the tie with Wallington had to be replayed after the original game was abandoned in bizarre circumstances fifteen minutes from time, with the scores tied at two apiece. The reason was that the club's entire stock of balls (three) had been put out of action. Incredibly two had burst and the third had then been dispatched into a nearby garden by an over exuberant defender. After several altercations between players and the grumpy homeowner in question, stretching back over a number of years, the council had stepped in and decreed that any ball landing in the neighbour's garden became his property and could not be retrieved. The home players, knowing of the ruling, were therefore rather more circumspect when clearing the ball but opposing defenders could not always be relied upon to be so subtle. Fortunately, only one ball was required for the replay, although Wallington did not get to play with it very much as they were on the wrong end of a 10-0 hiding.

This result was one of the few high spots as the gaps left by the loss of several older faces had not been adequately plugged. Burly youngster Bill North was the exception, impressing alongside Arthur Waite in a reconstructed defensive unit, nevertheless, the signs were not overly encouraging for a quick return to the top flight.

Fielding virtually an unchanged squad **United** made a slow start to life in intermediate football. Netherne Mental Hospital, one of four hospital sides in the division, overpowered United 6-2 in the opening game. Three further defeats followed before Oxshott were beaten 3-1 at Fetcham Grove to earn a welcome two points. This proved to be a false dawn and points remained hard to come by. Cane Hill Mental Hospital administered another footballing lesson handing out a 9-2 caning, a defeat that left United rooted to the foot of the division. The team gradually got to grips with the higher standard of intermediate football and form picked up considerably from February onwards. Defeat was tasted only once in the last nine games as United charged up the table to finish in a highly creditable seventh position. During the course of the run-in excellent wins were registered over Guards Depot (5-1), Trojans (5-1 and 4-0), Colliers Wood (3-0) and Caterham Old Boys (4-0). Roebuck and Shurville were again the principal goal-getters but lacked the support they had enjoyed at junior level. Despite this the fine end of season form provided the supporters with hope of better things to come.

The season had commenced with United claiming the Dorking Hospital Cup for 1933/34 with a comfortable 3-1 win over neighbours Rose in the first cup final meeting between the town's two premier clubs. For once it was Jack Bullen's brother, Len, who grabbed the headlines with two goals in an outstanding display. The trophy was retained at Easter, the fourth time in succession, with victory over Brockham.

United were prevented from adding to this tally by the decision taken at the club's AGM to disband the reserve side thus making the club ineligible to participate in any of the Hospital Cup competitions, only clubs represented in junior football were permitted to enter.

Off the field progress towards senior status was also being pursued with some vigour. This aim was greatly aided by the assistance of club member Mr. Dickinson who generously donated a pavilion for use as changing rooms and refreshment bar.

1935/36

Rose now found that they were overshadowed by United both on and off the pitch. The traditional support was also ebbing away, lured by the prospect of a better quality of football at Fetcham Grove. Events on the field of play did nothing to reverse this trend.

Once again Rose flattered to deceive early on. A decisive 8-0 walloping of Hook was backed up by seven further wins in the next nine outings. The initial promise soon evaporated though and just three points were gleaned from the remaining eight fixtures. This left Rose languishing in fourth place, nine points adrift of champions Hackbridge.

Cup football offered up no joy either, the green and whites bidding farewell at an early stage in all six competitions entered.

Arthur Waite and Bill North again formed a solid barrier in central defence but the team lacked a cutting edge to convert some excellent approach play. An injection of new blood was desperately needed to put the club back on an upward path.

_____

Disappointingly **United** were unable to carry forward the form from the end of the previous campaign into an expanded division which now boasted fifteen teams.

Points were not picked up on a regular enough basis, mainly due to alarming inconsistency. A 6-0 defeat by Cane Hill was swiftly followed by the tonic of a 7-1 win over Dorking Reserves. The good work was undone by a toothless performance in a heavy reverse at Netherne Mental Hospital. This was soon put to one side as Trojans were turned over on their own patch and high-flying Sutton Waterworks were beaten thanks to a superb all round team performance. Any benefit derived was again thrown away as the team returned from lowly Oxted with nothing more than dirty laundry to show for an inept performance. The frustration continued until the side finally found some consistency late in the day, losing only once in the final seven games. Again the rally came too late to haul United above mid-table.

In the County Intermediate Cup the Guards Depot were engaged in a ding-dong tussle at the Grove. The lead changed hands repeatedly in the first ninety minutes. Andrews seemed to have secured safe passage into the third round with his third goal of the game to make the score 5-4 deep into extra-time. Astoundingly the referee, despite vehement protests from the home players and amid suggestions that darkness could not possibly have impaired his vision any further, chose to abandon the match due to the failing light with barely ninety seconds remaining. The replay was equally action packed. United built up a four goal advantage in the opening hour only for the soldiers to remorselessly chip away at the advantage and finally draw level in the very last minute. Neither side could break the deadlock in the added period. The Guards took full advantage of their reprieves to win at the third attempt and progress to the next round and thereby end any hopes United had of winning a trophy.

The team were hampered by a lack of goals, just 70 in the 35 league and cup matches. The return of George Andrews from Dorking, after a three year absence, only partly alleviated the problem, especially as he missed most of the second part of the campaign through injury. Indeed injuries and unavailability of key players contributed greatly to the poor form shown away from home.

It was the first time in fourteen years that both Leatherhead club's - United and Rose, had ended the season without a trophy to their names.

1936/37

In more ways than one this turned out to be the worst season in **Rose's** history. New President, Charles Leach, a shipping entrepreneur, could hardly have picked a worse time to replace long time incumbent Henry White.

League form was mediocre, the team just unable to string a winning run of any significance together with the mid-table berth representing the club's lowest ever finishing position. The shortcomings of the squad were such that Eric Collins came out of retirement to cover for injuries and unavailability.

Cup form was little better but the season was overshadowed by events during a rugged County Junior Cup clash at Barnett Wood Lane with Epsom Old Boys. A simmering undercurrent of aggression had been evident throughout the game. This finally exploded when, with the Old Boys 4-2 ahead late in the second half, a bad foul led to a brawl between several players. This quickly escalated to the point where home supporters joined in the fracas. The referee, fearing for his and the opposition players safety, immediately abandoned the game. He and the Old Boys players were subjected to further attacks and abuse as they beat a hasty retreat from the ground. The Surrey Football Association, unsurprisingly, took a dim view of these "*disgraceful happenings*" and had no hesitation in expelling Rose from the competition. In addition they ordered the ground to be closed for a period of two months, forcing home games to be played at Ashtead and Cobham. Furthermore, the club were fined and warned as to the future behaviour of players and spectators, backed up with a warning as to the dire consequences of any further transgressions.

Prior to the season's start **United's** supporters' harboured confident expectations of a good showing. Thanks to the generosity of President Herbert Reeves the Fetcham Grove dressing rooms had been upgraded. The finances were on a firmer footing, aided by the introduction of a season ticket (cost of five shillings) which was made available to all honorary (non-playing) members and provided admission to all home league games. In a bid for greater fitness training was stepped up to twice a week - Tuesdays and Thursdays.

All this optimism proved to be badly misplaced. After a reasonable start United came a cropper at Caterham. The defence was conspicuous by its absence as the Hospital side chalked up ten. There was the promise of a revival with successive home wins over Achillard Sports, Trojans and Sutton Water Company but injuries to key players exposed the old flaw of lack of depth in the squad, and inexperienced teenagers had to be thrown into the fray. The outcome was nine defeats in ten outings, including a number where the defence again went AWOL. The words all going and pear shaped were never far away. Away from the Grove, United were pathetic losing all nine games and conceding forty eight goals into the bargain. The side plummeted down the table and come the end of the season were relegated.

One of the few bright spots in an otherwise disastrous season was the emergence of three youngsters; 19-year-old centre-forward Rueben Leverington, right-winger Doug Street and powerfully built right half-back Ernie Harvey. They possessed three things the majority of the squad lacked, namely youth, pace and hair. Leverington, who possessed a terrific shot with his left foot, scored twice on his debut and finished as second top scorer and, like the other two, proved to be a great servant to Leatherhead football in the years to come.

1937/38

Having plumbed the depths the **Rose** bounced back in style. The revamped team clicked straight away and were in with a shout of honours until the final weekend of the season.

The season was a personal triumph for new centre-forward Bill North. The sixteen stone North forsook his defensive duties and used his attributes to great effect to hit 35 goals, including all eight against Metropolitan Water Board and eight more in a resounding 13-0 Junior Cup victory over neighbours Ashtead. His two month absence during the run-in proved costly. Avorians from Cobham were the only serious rivals for the league crown. It was Avorians who inflicted the first defeat in late January. This proved to be a minor blip with six successive wins following to set up the return at Barnett Wood Lane as the title decider. Up to that point the defence had been practically impregnable at the Lane notching up ten clean sheets in thirteen matches. Avorians, playing some sparkling football, breached the defence four times in an hour. In a thrilling finish Rose reduced the arrears to 3-4 but could not force, what would have been, a vital equaliser and had to be content with second spot as a result.

As well as Ashtead, Caterham and Mitcham were ousted from the County Cup before Thornville, who had earlier evicted United, put an end to the run.

The final of the Dorking Hospital Cup was reached for the first time since 1934 but Effingham proved too strong in a disappointing final.

Right-half George Rand and centre-half Arthur Waite's contribution to the fine defensive record was recognised by their inclusion in the League Representative side. Keeper Peddar, signed from Leatherhead JEA, and evergreen left-back Basson also shone in the league's meanest rearguard. Another player to appear was Bunny Oram, who was to feature behind the scenes at Leatherhead for many years and whose son, Keith, was to manage Leatherhead FC during the 1980's.

United's fortunes were now on the wane. Despite finishing as runners-up back in the Premier Division of the Sutton and District League the team never looked capable of winning the title and ended well adrift of champions Mill Green Rovers. Rovers completed a league double in the fixture at Fetcham Grove in March to seal the title with a month still remaining. United at least had the satisfaction of enjoying the better of two well attended and hard fought derbies with Leatherhead JEA. The first match at Kingston Road was an exciting affair that ended all square at two apiece whilst the meeting in the final game of the season at the Grove saw United walk away with both points after a fine 4-1 win.

Early leave was taken from the Hospital Cups and a feeble performance, which highlighted the failings of a decidedly mediocre season, led to a 6-2 drubbing at the hands of Thornville in the County Cup.

Cross-town rivalries were temporarily set aside for a specially arranged fixture at the Grove in aid of the Leatherhead Cottage Hospital rebuilding fund, a combined Rose and United eleven taking on a JEA/Fetcham Old Boys selection. The presence of the Town Silver Band helped to draw a large crowd to see the Rose/United X1 come out on top by 6-2. Unfortunately, the two clubs had no immediate plans to make this a more permanent merger.

1938/39

Building on the foundations lain in the previous campaign **Rose** secured the Division One title for the third time. The success was built on the back of a tremendous team spirit and a never say die attitude that led to some thrilling fightbacks. North was again the main spearhead, netting 36 times. He benefited from the support he received from Ernie Shurville and Armstrong, who both topped the twenty goal mark, whilst Alec Peters, Jimmy Harrison and R. Gravett all reached double figures. With the defence as hard to break down as before Rose were extremely tough to beat.

GOALS GALORE AS ROSE MARCH TO LEAGUE TITLE

The tone for the season was set when works side British Thermostar (who subsequently withdrew from the league) were blown away by a club record margin of 20-0, Shurville and Cliff Dean contributing thirteen goals between them. A battling 6-5 success over Surrey County Staff was the precursor to a January double over nearest challengers Malden which opened up a comfortable cushion over the chasing pack. Points dropped in two nervy, drawn games allowed Malden to close the gap but decisive wins over Molesey Athletic and Littleton Sports ensured there was to be no slip up.

Kingston and District League Division One 1938/39

Team	Played	Won	Drawn	Lost	For	Against	Points
Leatherhead Rose	**14**	**11**	**2**	**1**	**57**	**23**	**24**
Malden	14	11	1	2	41	20	23
Littleton Sports	14	8	2	4	34	20	18
Kingston Rovers	14	7	3	4	43	38	17
Molesey Athletic	14	7	0	7	39	31	14
Graham Spicer	14	3	1	10	19	38	7
Surrey County Staff	14	2	1	11	23	54	5

In the County Cup neighbours Leatherhead United and Fetcham Old Boys had their colours lowered prior to a stunning 10-4 defeat of Rollasson Sports. Eventual winners Mill Green Rovers could count themselves fortunate to edge past Rose 3-2 in the round of the last sixteen.

The last competitive meetings with Leatherhead United produced the best and most exciting derbies witnessed for many seasons. Rose led 2-0 in a County Charity Cup 2nd round clash only to be pegged back. The replay was again close but the green and whites prevailed 2-0. The run continued with an excellent victory over previously unbeaten Thornville and an easier passage against Pagomacs. Dreams of a first County final appearance were disappointingly dashed at the semi-final stage by Thelma and Beddington.

Once more the finals of both the local Hospital competitions were contested. Six hundred paying customers saw defences dominate in the Leatherhead final leading to a rare nil-all draw. Effingham came out on top in the replay and completed the double by winning the Dorking version as well.

Such was the late season fixture congestion caused by good progress in so many trophies that the team were forced to play two important games on one Saturday in March. It says much for the team spirit that Old Dorkinians were defeated 4-0 in the semi-final of the Leatherhead Hospital Shield in the morning before the squad travelled to Kingston for a vital league encounter with Kingston Labour. The players managed to push their tired limbs through another ninety minutes and secure a 3-0 win to boot to stay on course for the title.

Thanks to the success on a number of fronts, no fewer than twenty one cup ties were contested, the club's finances received a timely boost with gate receipts more than double those of the previous season.

United signalled their intentions early on with an 11-0 hammering of Chessington Labour, future Leatherhead favourite Jackie Collins making a goal-scoring debut, and a superb 6-2 demolition of reigning champions Mill Green. Despite a narrow defeat at Mill Green in the reverse fixture title prospects still looked bright thanks to a string of fine performances. Unbeaten league leaders Epsom Athletic came to Fetcham Grove in February intent on kicking United out of the race. Their overly robust approach upset the homesters and didn't exactly endear them to the referee either. He responded by awarding four penalties. Teenager Rueben Leverington converted two but also had a spot of bother and missed the other two enabling Epsom to escape with an undeserved point.
The return fixture in April was equally explosive. A decidedly physical opening period culminated with Leverington and an Epsom defender having their handbags confiscated and receiving their marching orders following a bout of fisticuffs. The remaining United players kept their heads and turned in a brilliant display to emerge 4-0 victors over their previously undefeated hosts. Chances of league glory were dealt a fatal blow though when, forced to field a weakened side for a midweek match, United came a cropper against lowly Sutton Wanderers. The pressure was kept up by completing the league programme with two comprehensive wins which left Mill Green needing to win their last game to deny United and retain their title, which they duly did.
Fetcham Grove remained a fortress with just a solitary league defeat now suffered in the last two seasons of league football.

Cup results were as successful as an ice cream salesman in the Antarctic on an especially cold day.

There were some encouraging individual performances. The form of sound tackling veteran right-back Fred Shurville, evergreen Jack Bullen, Molloy (returning after a three year absence) and young captain Bonnett, whose jovial disposition made him a popular skipper as well as a being a consistent keeper, proved a formidable obstacle for opposing attacks to surmount. Up front Doug Street set a club record by netting 32 league goals and Leverington also again impressed with his consistently solid performances.

Total income for the season reached £105 5s 4d of which only £14 7s 3d was generated by gate receipts, the remainder coming principally from members' subscriptions and donations.

After urgings by the Supporters Committee the possibility of joining the Surrey Senior League was investigated, but war clouds were gathering and the idea was shelved as more important considerations came to the fore.

1939/40

By 1939 many players were being called up into the armed forces. Within days of football resuming, Hitler marched into Poland and war was declared. All sports were initially banned by order of the Government. This restriction was soon lifted with competitive sport actively encouraged as a way of keeping up the spirits of the population.

The majority of league competitions though shut down for the duration of the hostilities. The Kingston League was one of the few to continue. With such a dearth of men and the imposition of travel restrictions the rulings concerning eligibility were ignored with teams often sharing players or fielding 'guests' to make up the numbers. The distinction between amateur and professional was also dispensed with. Clubs with large numbers of soldiers stationed nearby reaped the benefit. It is rumoured that two full Scottish internationals, based locally with their army units, appeared for **Rose** during this period.

In the prevailing conditions Rose acquitted themselves well on their return to the Premier Division, winning four and drawing two of the twelve matches played in a truncated programme. Highlights were a 5-5 draw with Worcester Park (a game in which recent recruit Cecil Weller scored the first of many hat-tricks for his new club) and an 11-3 annihilation of Avorians. Something of a masterstroke had been pulled off in persuading Weller, who had been dogged by injuries, to drop down from senior football in order to take up the post of player-coach at his home town club.

Most cup competitions were cancelled but the Leatherhead Hospital Shield was competed for. Ashtead were squeezed out in a semi-final replay to set up a first meeting with Fetcham Old Boys. Urged on by a large crowd both teams played fast attacking football. The Old Boys led 2-0 at the break but in a pulsating second period Rose clawed back the deficit, took the lead, fell behind again and drew level once more at 4-4 before the final whistle sounded. The fightback proved to be in vain as the Old Boys scored three without reply in the extra period to claim the Shield for the first and only time.

Those serving abroad were never far from the thoughts of those at home and the proceeds from the Boxing Day fixture with Leatherhead Wednesday were used to send cigarettes to the troops.

The Sutton League temporarily suspended operations but after discussions with club representatives decided to continue, albeit reorganised into four area leagues to ease transport problems. **United** were thus faced with a host of local derbies. Emphatic wins were enjoyed over Epsom Spartans -11-4, Goblin Sports - 7-3 and Leatherhead Old Scholars - 6-1 but these were interspersed with some narrow defeats to leave United becalmed in mid-table. The league programme was not completed due to the large number of postponements caused by clubs being unable to raise a side.

Defeat came at the semi-final stage of both the Sutton and Leatherhead Hospital tournaments. In a generally disappointing season the performances of Doug Street again stood out. His call up in February was the prime cause of a late season slump.

CHAPTER SIX - WAR AND PEACE

For the first time war arrived on Leatherhead's doorstep. During 1940 the town took a pummelling from German bombs. Nearly 600 high explosive bombs and 4,000 incendiaries landed in the vicinity, claiming eight lives (including former player and Old Contemptible Fred Hatchwell who was killed by a stray bomb in the Reigate Road) and injuring scores of others. The majority of players were involved in the war effort in some way, those who had yet to be called up for the Armed Services participating nearer to home in part-time civil defence work such as the Home Guard or ARP. Residents grew used to hardship and personal tragedy and went about their daily business as best they could.

Following the outbreak of hostilities football provided a focal point for the release of tension and a temporary escape from the privations and horror of the war, not to mention a useful boost to morale when the local team was successful.

1940/41

Football carried on but could not help but be affected by the prevailing circumstances, especially as the town lay under the German bombers flight path to London and matches were often punctuated by the wail of air raid sirens. As rationing began to bite everybody was encouraged to "*dig for victory*". To this end the Surrey War Agricultural Office claimed the ground at Barnett Wood Lane for use as allotments. **Rose**, therefore, had little option but to return to their old stamping ground at Kingston Road where the amenities remained rudimentary, the bathing facilities amounting to the culvert that ran alongside the pitch, not very enticing on an icy winter's afternoon.

On the field the forwards benefited hugely from Cecil Weller's coaching, plundering close to 200 goals between them. Weller himself led the way topping fifty, despite injuries restricting him to fewer than twenty appearances.

The Kingston League reorganised into four divisions based on areas rather than playing strength and this led to several mismatches. Big wins became commonplace rather than the exception.
On average Rose managed a goal for every six minutes played throughout the season.
With the Battle of Britain raging overhead the football season commenced in a welter of goals. Imperial Sports were hammered 7-1 and 14-0, Claygate pulverised 16-0 and 8-1, Hackbridge and Powered Mountings both thumped 6-1. Unfortunately, none of these sides managed to see out the campaign and their records were accordingly expunged, much to the chagrin of Rose. Hersham Boys Club did at least last the course but probably wished they hadn't, being on the wrong end of 19-1 and 11-0 thrashings. With the squad decimated by call ups a makeshift team suffered a series of narrow reverses in the closing stages of the season condemning Rose to third place, a long way adrift of Molesey United and Kingston Belmont. The challenge was not helped when on one occasion the team played shorthanded because two, unnamed, players had been arrested and carted off to jail for breaking wartime curfew restrictions.

With the closure of the Sutton and District League, **United** opted for a full programme of friendlies. Matches were organised in the main against Company or Regimental representative sides drawn from the various branches of the Armed Services. The Royal Canadian Army was just one of the overseas units introduced to the game whose understanding of the rules left something to be desired. Other matches were arranged with any local side that had sufficient men to form a team.

Matches tended to be only sporadically covered by the restricted press. What is known is that the last ever meeting between United and Rose went the way of the former by a 3-2 margin.

The fact that players played for the love of the game and nothing else was amply illustrated by the number of men who used large chunks of their priceless leave (forsaking rather more obvious pleasures) to kick a leather ball around a patch of grass for ninety minutes. On one such occasion Doug Street dashed home from his unit in time to net five times against the Welsh Guards. As well as the finishing power of Street the Guards simply had no answer to the trickery of diminutive left-winger Stan Stone. Stone tormented defences throughout the season laying on chances galore for his attacking colleagues. His efforts played no small part in helping the team to compile an excellent record of twenty four wins and just two losses in the twenty eight games played.

1941/42

There was some doubt over whether or not **Rose** would continue until a successful appeal for new players enticed a mixture of schoolboys and veterans along to Kingston Road, but these new recruits were often no more than bystanders witnessing the exploits of Cecil Weller at first hand.

The team continued in the Kingston League, revamped again into just two sections, but the season was all about one man - centre-forward and captain Cecil Weller. Short of bricking up the goal, mining the penalty area and arming defenders with baseball bats no one came up with a really workable plan to stop him from scoring at will.

WELLER THE DESTROYER AS ROSE HUMBLE THE MEDICS

Cecil started slowly, scoring only a treble in a close tussle with Hersham Claremont before really hitting his stride. The visiting Royal Corp of Signals defence communicated with all the confidence of a short-sighted man peering at semaphore signals as Cecil, almost single-handedly, tore them to shreds. He collected a league and club record twelve goals before Ken Skilton chipped in with a thirteenth. Seven days later he scored a mere ten (out of eighteen) as the unfortunate Eagle Components side were dismantled. There then followed a positive drought as he managed only fifteen in the next six games. He rediscovered his shooting boots in the New Year helping himself to a double hat-trick as Hersham Old Boys were crushed 10-1. Poor Sutton and Cheam Rescue were desperately in need of help themselves in a Sutton Hospital Cup tie.Cecil again provided a masterclass in the art of finishing; reaching double figures for the third time and with his team-mates adding a further eight the final tally was 18-0. Weller managed just six in the return fixture with Eagle Components and a paltry four in the next two games. An injury suffered in a 5-0 win over Parnells Athletic in early March sidelined him for six crucial weeks. Prior to his injury Rose were unbeaten in eighteen matches but in his absence the team contrived to lose three times and were pipped by works side Vickers to the league crown.
Cecil returned in time for the Sutton Hospital Cup Final at Sutton United's Gander Green Lane ground. Whilst his solitary effort forced extra-time it was not enough to prevent Croydon Leaguers Phillips Sports taking the cup, courtesy of a last gasp winner.
Barring his injury Cecil would surely have achieved the remarkable feat, at any level of the game, of reaching a century of goals in a season. As it was he netted a club record 70 league and cup goals in just 17 matches and 87 in 21 games in all games (another record).
His goals per game were as follows - 2,3,5,3,12,10,3,2,4,2,2,2,6,4,10,6,1,3,1,5 and1.

Off the park things were looking brighter. The club's insistence on playing the game in the right manner was recognised by their peer's award of the League's Sportsman Trophy for the best sporting spirit and hospitality.
In addition the financial position was healthier than ever allowing donations to be made to the Wings for Victory and Aid for Russia campaigns.

The Football Association requested that clubs should give as many matches as possible to Service teams in the cause of morale. **United** were happy to oblige and played friendlies against X1's representing the likes of the Royal Artillery, Royal Engineers, Royal Tank Corp, Royal Army Ordnance and the Royal Air Force. Many of these Service sides fielded former professionals and leading amateurs and, if nothing else, could always be relied upon to be very fit.

However, it was becoming an increasing struggle for United to field a full side. By now no fewer than sixteen members of the club were serving in some branch of the Armed Services. After a narrow 1-0 defeat by the Royal Ambulance Corps on the 10th January the committee took the decision to mothball the playing side and wait for the end of hostilities before reforming.

1942/43

Leatherhead Rose were now the only local side still playing regularly. The Kingston League continued but Section 'A' was reduced by further withdrawals to only six participants.

With Cecil Weller again in prime form in front of goal Rose dominated proceedings, dropping only one point. Whilst the scoring wasn't quite on the same scale as 1941/42 there were still some thumping wins. Hawkers Athletic were swamped 10-2 and 6-1, Molesey 6-0 and Hersham Claremont 8-2, but it was a gutsy 3-1 win over Walton Reserves that banished any lingering doubts as to the destination of the league title.

Kingston and District League Section 'A' 1942/43

Team	Played	Won	Drawn	Lost	Points
Leatherhead Rose	**10**	**9**	**1**	**0**	**19**
Walton Reserves	10	7	2	1	16
Hersham Claremont	10	6	1	3	13
Hawkers Athletic	10	4	0	6	8
Molesey United	10	2	0	8	4
Hersham Boys	10	0	0	10	0

The Leatherhead Hospital Shield was recaptured after a gap of eight years. Rose were involved in a stirring semi-final encounter with Chessington Athletic. In a thrilling end to end match the lead changed hands regularly. After ninety minutes the scores were level at four apiece. Another thirty minutes of great entertainment ensued before Rose could finally be declared the winners by 7-6.

ROSE UPSET THE ARMY BOYS TO TAKE SHIELD

The final, at Epsom Town's West Street ground, was no less exciting. The Royal Army Medical Corp (RAMC), with three professionals in their ranks, represented formidable opponents. In another see-saw tussle Rose, wearing their favoured green and white quartered shirts, gained a deserved reward for attacking enterprise, edging home by the odd goal in nine. A treble, almost inevitably, from Weller and one apiece from Cordier and Stone doing the trick.

The joy was tempered by the knowledge that popular player and club member Dennis Girdler had recently lost his life on operations overseas. His loss placed the victory in its proper perspective.

1943/44

Bolstered by the addition of former United stars Doug Street, Fred Shurville, Freddie Graffham, Chester and Cordier the new campaign again opened brightly. Hawkers were dispatched 10-1 and the Military Convalescence Depot were left in need of some rest and recuperation themselves after being humbled 14-0. In the return fixture a much strengthened and refreshed Depot side inflicted the first home league defeat since 1941 by an 8-4 margin. The decisive moments proved to be the two clashes with Byfleet. Both were close, exciting contests that ended in favour of Byfleet who went onto lift the league title with Rose losing out on the runners-up spot on goal average.

League football took a back seat to the team's cup exploits, however. The best run for over twenty years in the reconstituted Surrey Junior Cup was greatly enjoyed by all. Marzick were crushed 9-0, Salford Wanderers 6-2 and Ramblers 6-0 to set up a quarter-final meeting with Sutton United Reserves. A faultless team performance earned a 4-1 win and only Monotype Sports of Redhill stood between Rose and a first County final appearance. In a rousing match, holders Monotype clinched a final place with a last minute winner after an under-strength Rose had shown tremendous resilience to draw level four times. The outcome was particularly disappointing for Charlie 'Battler' Stone who had demonstrated his dedication and commitment by disembarking from his ship on the South Coast early that morning and hot footing it across country via train, bus, taxi and finally foot to join up with his team-mates just prior to the kick-off.

The Leatherhead Hospital Shield was retained thanks to a fine 2-1 victory over RAMC Banstead. The final was a fast and exciting affair played before a large crowd at Pixham Lane, Dorking. Hampshire produced a fine display in goal and Bill North impressed at centre-half but it was that man Weller who struck the winner ten minutes from time after the RAMC keeper had failed to hold a fierce shot from Harris.

The largest crowd of the season assembled at Kingston Road in April to witness a cracking match in the Sutton Hospital Cup, against Tooting and Mitcham's second string. Another late goal saw Rose home in a seven goal thriller. The RAMC halted further progress at the semi-final stage, thereby gaining vengeance for their Shield defeat.

At the seasons end long-serving Fred Shurville finally hung up his boots after over 500 appearances, the majority for United, whilst another veteran, Jim Strudwick, featured in all 33 games in his 20th season with the club. Cecil Weller's season was again blighted by injury but he did record his 200th goal for the club whilst Bill North reached the century mark.

Finances were now in their healthiest ever state, the cup runs helped the club to generate a surplus of over £20 and sport a very healthy bank balance of £145 (equivalent to around £5,000 today).

1944/45

Although the tide of the war was running firmly in favour of the allies the citizens of Leatherhead and district could not relax. During the course of the year sixteen V1 rockets, flying bombs or doodlebugs fell on the area causing casualties and considerable damage to property. Against this backdrop soccer was of secondary importance but served to keep up spirits through a bitterly cold winter that was dogged by fuel shortages.

By now Leatherhead were having to field a mixture of players on leave from their units, older men, semi-juveniles or men excused military service on health grounds or because their normal work was of national importance.

The team, sporting many new faces, were outplayed by Olivers Garage on the opening day. There then followed a fantastic run which garnered twenty four points from the next fourteen league games and propelled Rose into the final of the Leatherhead Hospital Shield and the penultimate round once more of the Junior Cup. This spell included a superb 4-1 win over eventual champions

Hersham Claremont and knocking-out holders and previous season's nemesis Monotype 1-0 in the third round of the Junior Cup.

The Easter Monday clash with Vickers of Weybridge to decide the destiny of the Shield drew a good crowd of 1,000, generating gate receipts of £32 to be donated to local charitable causes. Vickers fielded their Surrey Senior League team but Rose matched them for ninety minutes before finally succumbing to a late winner in the extra period.

South West Middlesex League team North Sheen provided the opposition for a place in the County Junior Cup final. Walton's ground was the venue. Again a lacklustre display was turned in on an important occasion. Despite failing to live up to their normal high standards Rose still led 2-1 early in the second period but the game was tipped firmly in favour of the Middlesex side when Rose keeper Greenaway cracked three ribs in an abortive attempt to save the equaliser. He gamely continued but was unable to prevent Sheen from grabbing a winner in the remaining twenty minutes.

Stalwart left-back Cyril Basson finally hung up his boots after nineteen seasons and over 400 games for the club. At the other end of the age spectrum the newly reformed youth team enjoyed instant success, winning the Epsom and District Youth League at the first attempt.

On a wider scale there was plenty to celebrate elsewhere. The German's surrender was greeted with all the euphoria of a victorious peace.

1945/46

The two sections of the league were amalgamated to form two new divisions with Rose competing in the top flight. With a record of won twelve, drawn three and no defeats the title was very much in sight. Only three further points were required from the final three outings. A shock defeat by Kingston Belmont preceded a comfortable win over Leyland Motors that set up an intriguing final day clash with title rivals Hersham Claremont. Needing just a draw the Rose strikers proceeded to spurn a hatful of chances and almost inevitably Hersham scored late on from a penalty to take the points and the league crown to boot on goal average.
The side that turned out, in what proved to be Leatherhead Rose's final game, was:
A. Greenway, G. Weatherall, Cyril Basson, Jimmy Harrison, Cecil North, A. Kerrage, Arthur Waite, Tommy Temlett, Cecil Weller, Tommy Nunn and Freddie Graffham.

Lady Luck also deserted the team in the Junior Cup. Once more comfortable progress was made to the semi-final stage. Hopes of a first final appearance were literally blown away though. With the backing of a gale force wind Farnham Town had built up a six goal lead by the interval. After the teams changed ends the fickle wind decided to follow suit and there was no way back for Rose. This defeat provided the prelude to a downturn in form that ended the Rose's hold on the Leatherhead Hospital Shield and any attempts to reclaim the other local cup competitions.

Just six defeats in thirty three matches represented another good season but ultimately with no tangible reward at the end of it. Charlie Stone took over Weller's mantle enjoying a fruitful season with over 40 goals to his credit but the defence shipped too many goals at crucial times. Many of the players had the ability to play at a higher level and indeed ten of the Rose squad went on to appear in, and help win, the Surrey Senior League title for the newly merged Leatherhead FC.

The end of the war and gradual return to normality also signalled a new beginning for football in the town as the merger of the town's clubs, that had first been mooted some twenty five years earlier, finally came to fruition.

▲Leatherhead Rose - Leatherhead Hospital Shield winners 1923/24.
The magnificient Shield is currently on display at Leatherhead Museum.

▲The Leatherhead Rose side (containing three sets of brothers; the Wilds, Potters and Hollands) pictured prior to the Dorking Hospital Cup Final defeat against Ashtead at Dorking FC in April 1925.

▲Eric Collins
Eric spent eighteen years with Rose as a player before spending a similar length of time as a committee member, firstly at Rose and then, after the merger with United in 1946, with the newly formed Leatherhead club.

▲Leatherhead United's team from their first season in1924/25

▲Leatherhead Rose - Leatherhead Hospital Shield and Dorking Hospital Cup winners 1929/30

THANK YOU!

──

The Management Committee beg to express their grateful thanks to:—

Our President—C. H. McComas, Esq., M.D., Donor of Cup and Medals.

The Vice-Presidents for their continued interest and financial support.

The Dorking Football Club for permitting the use of their ground, free of cost, on March 7th and to-day, also for their help with ground arrangements, in addition to handing over the profits from the tea.

The Leatherhead United Football Club for permitting the use of their ground on March 21st, free of cost, and in giving us every assistance.

The Dorking and District Hospital Management Committee for kindly presenting Ball used in to-day's game.

Mrs. R. H. Wilson, Holmwood, and Mr. S. Fuller, South Street, for providing Footballs for the Semi-Finals.

The Dorking Town Band for rendering selections to-day, also for handing over the proceeds of their collection to our funds.

The Ladies and others who are helping to-day.

The Dorking Advertiser for their many free insertions.

The Proprietors of the Pavilion Theatre for their generosity in providing Free Seats in connection with the sealed number programmes, and for exhibiting slide free of cost throughout the week.

The Referee and Linesmen for giving their services in this and other matches.

The Clubs who take part in the Competition and all other willing workers who, in some way or other, helped forward The Dorking Hospital Cup Competition.

MANY thanks are due to the various clubs that have taken part in this season's Hospital Charity Cup Competition which is brought to a conclusion by to-day's Final.

This is the eighth occasion of the issue of this programme, and an appeal is made again to spectators for their continued support of a charity which is deserving of the utmost help.

To date £655 has been raised by Junior Clubs, including last year's amount of £70. At the moment the funds are slightly less than at the corresponding stage in 1930, but with your help to-day, it is hoped that the seventy mark will be reached again.

Little need be said of to-day's teams. Leatherhead Rose (holders) and Ashtead have met in a previous final, and a splendid game should result, played in the usual fine spirit which has marked all previous finals, so that the tradition created may be worthily maintained.

If the number of your programme is announced at half time you will be entitled to one of the Free Seats kindly presented by the Management of the Pavilion Theatre.

Ball Tickets, 1d. each, entitle the owner of the winning number to the Football used in to-day's match.

Tea can be obtained on the ground.

The teams will line up as follows:

ASHTEAD
(RED & WHITE).

Right.   Left.

F. COOKE

A. COOK   W. DODMAN

L. JACKSON   J. BIRCH   A. E. GOLDSMITH

C. WELLER   R. DAWSON   W. H. GOODWAY   H. NEVILL

J. HOLLAND

Referee: Linesmen:
Mr. E. DENYER   Mr. S. DENYER
(Dorking)   Mr. J. MAY

G. ARMSTRONG

A. HOLLAND   L. GRAVETT   T. WOFFORN   E. COLLINS

R. RICE   E. TAYLOR   J. STRUDWICK

C. BASSON   J. COULSON

F. RATCLIFFE
Left.   Right.

LEATHERHEAD ROSE
(RED & GREEN).

▲The programme produced for the Dorking Hospital Cup Final played in May 1931 at Dorking's Pippbrook Mill Ground. Ashtead ran out winners by 3 goals to 1.

▲Roddy Williams

Leatherhead Rose 1929 - 1931. After leaving Rose, Roddy enjoyed a highly successful career in the Football League with Norwich City, Reading, Exeter City, West Ham United and Clapton Orient, scoring 71 League goals in 118 appearances before the Second World War intervened.

▲Leatherhead United's squad of 1931/32 that achieved a unique treble by winning the Dorking, Cobham and Leatherhead Hospital Cup competitions.
Back Row (standing): Edward Trunkfield, F. Pratt, Jack Bullen, Dave Wareham, William Atkin, Stan Haynes, Walter Murton and F. Creasey
Middle Row (seated): Reg Buckley, Herbert Creasey, W. Dayman, George Andrews, Reg Shurville, J. Thomas and Len Bullen
Kneeling: A. H. Miles (Honorary Secretary) and F. Bullen
Sitting: W. Molloy and Fred Shurville

▲The Leatherhead Rose side that finished as Dorking Hospital Cup runners-up in1933/34
Back Row: Arthur Griffin (Chairman), Cyril Basson, Arthur Waite, K. Maine, Jim Strudwick, G. Florence and unknown committee member *Front Row:* Mark Killian, D.Thorpe, Dai Pritchard, F. Parker, Cocker and Fred Reddick

▲The Leatherhead Rose team that enjoyed a highly successful campaign in 1938/39, finishing as Kingston and District League Division One champions as well as runners-up in both the Leatherhead Hospital Shield and the Dorking Hospital Cup.
Standing: Cyril Basson, Bunny Oram, Syd Peddar, C. Stedman, Arthur Waite and D. Bartholomew
Kneeling: George Armstrong, Ernie Shurville, Bill North, Alec Peters and C. Berry

▲The triumphant Leatherhead Rose side pictured at Dorking FC after defeating RAMC Banstead 2-1 in the 1944 Leatherhead Hospital Shield Final.

▲Cecil Weller
Between 1936 and 1950, Cecil scored a combined total of 327 goals in just 266 appearances (despite the last 65 being as a full-back) for Leatherhead Rose and Leatherhead.

Matches to remember

12th March 1892   Herald Cup Final
Leatherhed Rose 3 v Battersea Albion 1

A record establishment gathered to watch this game. It was a good gate for the district and proved that the winter game was getting a good hold among sport loving residents of suburban Surrey. Albion set the ball in motion and for the first few minutes penned Rose inside their half of the field and continually swarmed around in front of goal, though without scoring. The pressure was eventually relieved and transferred to the Albion end. Following a scrimmage in front of goal, an Albion back contrived to put the ball between his own sticks and the first goal was scored amidst the loud cheers of the large body of supporters who had travelled from Leatherhead to witness the contest. The Rose joy was short-lived. From the re-start Albion rushed the leather up the field and almost before one could say Jack Robinson the score had been made equal, the right-wing sending in a shot just beyond the reach of the custodian, Watson. Despite strenuous efforts by both sides no further score was made in the first half.

During the second moiety the game was much more one-sided. Though the Albion made a gallant fight, it was plain they were outmatched. Rose lasting out better were soon busy round the Battersea goal, and after about an hour, were rewarded by two goals, one put through his own net by an Albion man and the second scored by Hersey. With two points against them Albion rallied but though they got within shooting distance now and again they were never really dangerous. When the whistle blew for the termination of the game Rose left the field as winners of the cup by three goals to one, with their delighted followers swarming around, cheering and back-slapping their heroes.

No one, least of all the losers, grudged Leatherhead their victory. It was gained by hard work and the display of a considerable amount of skill. Childs and Ware were particularly strong in defence. Both saved splendidly and kicked with a certainty which made their assistance most valuable. The passing runs of right forwards Beaumont and Hewlins were extremely pretty, though the want of a good centre-forward was most noticeable.

Until the present year Rose has been of little moment at all in the football world, but since the Messrs. Hue-Williams became members it has forged ahead and now promises to make some of its near neighbours - Dorking and Guildford - look to their laurels.

Team: *William Watson, William Ware, Arthur Childs, Arthur Dexter, Guy Hue-Williams, Albert Warren, Charles Poulter, Henry Moore, Reverend Harry Beaumont, William Hewlins and Tommy Hersey*

6th March 1897   Surrey Charity Shield Semi-Final
Leatherhead 3 v Selhurst 1

Contrary to the expectations of many, Leatherhead succeeded in winning this engagement with Selhurst. The result could hardly have been any other than it was, the homesters being on their best form and combining capitally.

However, at the start matters were not at all pleasant. The visitors immediately began to press and in a very few minutes registered a goal, which was headed through by Johnson. This reverse had the effect of putting Leatherhead on their mettle. They at once made a dash for goal and, with Guy Hue-Williams doing the needful, made matters level.

For some time afterwards play was of a very even character until just before half-time when Hue-Williams scored again. In the second half Selhurst strained every nerve to equalise but the home defence were impregnable. Just on time Shurville shot another goal from a difficult angle to complete the scoring and secure a memorable triumph.

Team: *'Dasher' Davis, Bertie Hue-Williams, William Blaker, James Wafforn, Bob Nash, William Killick, Fred Caiger, Sid Neate, Guy Hue-Williams, Harry Shurville and Eric Hue-Williams*

26th March 1904   Surrey Junior League Semi-Final
Euneva 1 v Leatherhead 2
A large crowd at Dorking's excellent ground had the excitement of watching a thoroughly hard fought game between two strong teams. A remarkable pace was kept up from start to finish although this began to tell on the players towards the end. There was no score in the first half though Leatherhead had a little better of the game. Both goals were once or twice in danger but both custodians were absolutely safe with Blaker making a fine double save to deny Arget.

Euneva attacked strongly in the second period and were the first to score. In a moment of indecision the Leatherhead defence were defeated and Ayris shot swiftly high into the corner of the net giving Blaker no chance of saving. In response Leatherhead pressed forward and were soon awarded a penalty. Davis, who had been fouled, equalised with a low shot. Leatherhead now attacked repeatedly and it came as no surprise when Taylor, taking the ball beautifully up the wing, gave to Hook who, from a difficult position, sent in a beautiful cross-shot which put his team safe on the winning side and into the final for the first time.

Team: *Henry Blaker, Lionel Blaker, Harry Garland, Alf Shurville, Bob Nash, Bob Stevenson, Harry Hook, E. W. Taylor, 'Dasher' Davis, Harry Shurville and Tom Phipps*

28th November 1908   Surrey Charity Shield 1st Round
Leatherhead 4 v Dorking 2
Dorking were soundly beaten to break a long and monotonous series of defeats inflicted by the Chicks in the previous few seasons. The game initially swung from end to end with both sides missing chances until Fuller opened the scoring for Dorking. Within a few minutes Leatherhead equalised, Davis getting in a swift shot along the ground. From a hot attack Fuller again gave his side the lead. This was countered when Watson got in a beautiful centre which ex-Woking forward Kyle transferred into the net. Following a poor clearance Watson fastened onto the ball and sent in a lightning shot which gave the goalie no chance.

On the re-start Leatherhead continued to hold the upper hand and the Dorking goal had several narrow escapes before Kyle took a good pass from Davis and, rushing through the defence, scored easily for the homesters to complete the scoring. This was a very fine performance, all the Leatherhead men played up to their best form. The defence was superb in holding Dorking's forward line which included three County men and Leatherhead's forwards were all mustard. The game attracted a large attendance producing a gate of £9 10s.

Team: *H. Davies, Harry Garland (captain), Rev. W. Seddon-Cooper, Dick Evans, Bob Nash, Fred Hatchwell, Bob Mathieson, Herbert Jeeves, Jack Kyle, 'Dasher' Davis and Ed Watson*

5th November 1910   Surrey Junior Cup 2nd Round
Leatherhead Rose 5 v Leatherhead FA 2
There was a large crowd at the Recreation Ground to witness this first competitive encounter between the two local rivals. From the kick-off Rose took up the attack and eventually the pressure told when Poulter centred for Watson to score. Despite strenuous efforts by both sides no further goals were registered in the first period.

The second half produced some exciting play. Rose extended their lead when Poulter put in a fine centre which enabled Smith to beat the goalie. Port muffed a long punt forward with the result that Boswell secured and scored. Just afterwards the scores were tied. Walter Tutt rushed the ball up the field and passed to Boswell who scored at long range. After these reverses Rose pulled themselves together and after a series of corners Poulter fired home. Then Crocker gave Watson a beautiful forward pass which enabled that player to score the fourth. Rose monopolised play to the finish and Taylor scored a splendid goal after good work by Lowe to complete the scoring.

Teams: Rose - *Jack Port, Henry Wild, Bob Strickland, Reg Crocker, George Reddick, Fred Lowe, Harry Godwin, P. Smith, Ed Watson, Fred Taylor and John Poulter*
Football Association - *'Dasher' Davis, C. Tearo, Hawes, Rupert Bennett, John Chilman, W. Steere, Walter Tutt, Bob Tutt, Walter Boswell, Len Loxley and Fred Agate*

4th November 1922   Surrey Junior Cup 2nd Round
Leatherhead Rose 2 v Leatherhead 5
It had been a long time since Leatherhead football enthusiasts had been provided with the excitement of a local derby. The match at Kingston Road was not found wanting in keen and thrilling football. The game was one of the cleanest and fastest seen for many years.

Leatherhead made a very successful debut in the competition and thoroughly deserved the win. Girdler (2) and Creasey put Leatherhead three nil up before goals from Bates and Collins put Rose back in the game. Further efforts late on from Percy and Lou Girdler put the result beyond doubt. Leatherhead had a well-balanced side with the forwards combining cleverly and always remembering where their opponent's goal was. Percy Girdler led the line in sparkling fashion, scoring a hat-trick, and was undeniably the best forward on the park but honours of the game must go to centre-half Reid whose constructive work laid the foundation to their success. He was also prominent in breaking up many attacks and showed little respect for the opposing forwards. Rose's failure was due to a weak goalkeeper and a lack of cohesion among the inside forwards.

Teams: Rose - *Joe Stevens, Terry Potter, Rob Hersey, J. Filchett, Len Chitty, W. Lindsell, George Small, Eric Collins, John Bates, William Hibbett and Ed Watson*

Leatherhead - *George Budden, Wilf Girdler, George Wild, E. Lawes, G. Reid, S. Richardson, C. West, Lou Girdler, Percy Girdler, Fred Shurville and Herbert Creasey*

26th April 1924   Leatherhead Hospital Shield Final
Leatherhead Rose 6 v Banstead 5
Rose were successful in securing the Shield on Easter Monday at Ashtead in one of the most exciting yet gruelling matches that one could wish to see. Fifty minutes extra-time was necessary before a decision was reached by which time both sides had played themselves to a standstill. The 2,000 spectators were kept on tiptoes of excitement throughout.

Collins won the toss and elected to defend the slope. Rose attacked from the start and within five minutes Dayman was unfairly brought down in the box. Bates scored from the rebound after Webb saved the penalty. Almost immediately Banstead won a penalty for handball and Bond banged the ball into the net. Bates brought down the house by scoring a great goal with a terrific free-kick from fully thirty five yards, bringing cheers from all around the ground. Again Banstead replied quickly, via Flack. Creasey restored the lead, meeting Collins fine centre to head a brilliant goal. Banstead forced several corners and eventually equalised through Wright. Another accurate Collins cross was turned home by Atkins, however, as time ran out Flack headed another equaliser to send the game into extra-time.

In the first extra period a Banstead defender had the misfortune to put through his own goal but back they came to draw level yet again, through Wright, before time expired.

With no provision for a replay it was necessary to continue playing until a conclusion was reached. Therefore a further ten minutes each way was played. Another model centre from Collins was converted by Hibbett and this time there was no way back for leg weary Banstead. Fittingly the Shield was handed to man of the match Collins amid ringing cheers.

 Team: *George 'Dutch' Holland, P. Songhurst, Eric Wild, John Bates, A. Wickett, Eric Collins, George Small, W. Dayman, William Hibbett, Arthur Atkins and Herbert Creasey*

20th April 1932   Dorking Hospital Cup Final
Leatherhead United 4 v Ashtead 0
On a wretched evening at Dorking, United surprised Ashtead and thoroughly deserved their victory. United faced the wind and slope in the first half and defended strongly. United keeper Wareham was in outstanding form being tested by several long range shots and in particular made one incredible point blank save from the Ashtead centre-forward. United were quick on the ball and the anticipation of Bullen frequently thwarted Ashtead's attacks. Despite dominating Ashtead were unable to make a breakthrough.

On resuming United, with the elements in their favour, combined cleverly and pressed consistently, until a hard shot from Dayman found the back of the net. The game continued to be contested in a fine spirit and on fairly even terms, although United just had the edge. On seventy minutes Thomas scored a fine goal with a wonderful cross shot. Ashtead fought back but the United backs were giving nothing away. Towards the end United gained complete mastery and Reg Shurville twice beat Cook to complete the scoring and bring an end to a game worthy of two fine, sporting teams.

Team: *Dave Wareham, W. Molloy, Fred Shurville, F. Pratt, Jack Bullen, William Atkin (captain), Herbert Creasey, W. Dayman, George Andrews, Reg Shurville and J. Thomas*

27th January 1934   Surrey Junior League
Mitcham Works 1 v Leatherhead United 21
United recorded their record victory over a poor Works side. The unfortunate home side were never in the picture and it seemed incredible that eleven players, who tried in vain throughout, could form such a weak combination. United started scoring after ten minutes and then scored with such monotonous regularity that the game seemed little other than the players walking back to the centre to re-start. By half-time United had the ball in the net ten times without reply and after the change-over added another ten before Mitcham got a consolation goal. Roebuck then completed the scoring. The players who contributed to this avalanche of goals were; Roebuck - 8, Thompson - 4, Booth - 3, Stevenson - 3, Reg Shurville - 2 and Bullen.

Team: *C. Townsend, Fred Shurville, W. Dodman, F. Pratt, Jack Bullen, R. Dunn, H. Booth, Reg Shurville, Joe Roebuck, A. Thompson and J. Stevenson*

20th January 1939   Surrey Charity Cup 2nd Round
Leatherhead Rose 2 v Leatherhead United 2
One of the best derbies for many years was played out at Barnett Wood Lane. Peddar made several good saves early on but Rose settled down and after twenty minutes Bonnett unluckily slipped when dealing with a shot from Gravett and the ball rebounded for North to score.

The second half opened with Rose attacking and from a Thorp corner Harrison headed home to double the lead. On the hour mark United got back in the game with a rather fortunate goal. Street's shot being deflected into the net by Kirkham. Rose had the chance to sew the match up when they were awarded a penalty for hands but Peters shot wide from the spot. United made the most of their reprieve when, with ten minutes remaining, Collins nipped into equalise.

Extra-time was started but after the first period the referee was forced to abandon the game as darkness descended.

Teams: Rose - *Syd Peddar, R. Kirkham, Cyril Basson, Jimmy Harrison, Arthur Waite, R. Gravett, A. Thorp, Alec Peters, Bill North, Ernie Shurville and L. Gravett*
United - *A. Bonnett, W. Molloy, Rueben Leverington, G. Ham, Jack Bullen, Alf Cook, Jackie Collins, Fred Shurville, Doug Street, G. Padgham and J. Cliff*

25th October 1941   Kingston & District League
Leatherhead Rose 13 v Royal Corp of Signals 1
The game was not as one-sided as the score suggests but simply the Rose had Weller and the Army side did not. Weller set a record that will take a lot of beating, scoring twelve goals. To score twelve goals in a match is no small feat and Weller established a league, as well as a club record. He was simply unstoppable and had the happy knack of continually being in the right place to despatch his team-mates passes and crosses. Try as they might the Army men just could not shackle him.

The visitors made the mistake of giving Weller too much rope and, with the rest of the team playing up to him, he gave the goalkeeper no chance with his scoring shots and headers. Leading by five goals at half-time the Rose carried their score to thirteen by the end. Skilton scoring the final goal with a good shot from the wing but the day belonged to the exceptional Weller.

Team: *S. Rhodes, J. Fuller, Cyril Basson, Jim Strudwick, D. R. G. Seymour, G Weatherall, L. Harvey, John North, Cecil Weller, F. Attwood and Ken Skilton*

10th April 1944   Leatherhead Hospital Shield Final
Leatherhead Rose 2 v RAMC Banstead 1

Played at Pixham Lane, Dorking before a large crowd this was a fast and exciting game which resulted in Rose retaining the Shield. In the first half the Royal Army Medical Corps were the more dangerous, without being able to record a goal thanks to the brilliant work of Hampshire in the Rose goal and Bill North keeping a tight hold on the lively Wadsworth, the RAMC centre-forward. Rose came closest to scoring on the break but the first half ended goalless.

On resuming, the Rose forwards combined well and had more of the play. After twenty minutes Harris opened the score. He fastened on to a capital pass by Weller to cut in and score with a fine drive from a narrow angle. RAMC soon replied, a centre from the left being headed in by the ever dangerous Wadsworth. Play was very exciting, each side attacking in turn. With a little over ten minutes remaining Rose scored what proved to be the decisive goal. Harris raced away on the left wing, his shot could only be pushed out by the Banstead goalkeeper, Parramore, allowing Weller to collect and promptly drive the ball into the net. RAMC strove hard for an equaliser but the Rose defence held firm.

Team: *R. Hampshire, Jim Strudwick, Cyril Basson, Charlie Stone, Bill North, Dick Chester, A. Cordier, N. Salter, Cecil Weller, S. Felgate and B. Harris*

Early Stars

Arthur Atkins

1921 - 1932 (Inside-Forward) Leatherhead Rose: Appearances - 305 Goals - 190

Arthur joined Rose in1921 after spending two seasons with Leatherhead Athletic. He was renowned for his nifty footwork which often left defenders non-plussed and on the seat of their pants. Although initially playing in midfield he quickly made a name for himself with his eye for goal. His goal-scoring prowess was soon recognised with a move into the forward line where he scored more than twenty goals and was leading scorer for six successive seasons from 1923/4. In total he amassed around 190 goals. Arthur made a successful transition to defence in his last couple of seasons before retiring in 1932.

Cyril Basson

1926 - 1945 (Left-Back) Leatherhead Rose: Appearances - 450 Goals - 22

Cyril was a tall, elegant and accomplished full-back who was Rose's longest serving player. In total he clocked up around 450 appearances during a nineteen year career, winning more than twenty medals during this period. His popularity and leadership qualities saw him serve as club captain for more than a decade. He was also the side's regular penalty taker and his calmness under pressure ensured that he rarely failed from the spot.

Eric Collins

1920 - 1937 (Outside-Right) Leatherhead Rose: Appearances - 320 Goals - 56

Eric's association with football in Leatherhead, firstly as a player then as a committee member, spanned more than four decades. He made his first appearance in 1920 and established himself as a regular in Rose's starting line-up the following season. He tormented opposing full-backs with his fine wing play and created numerous scoring opportunities for his colleagues with his accurate crosses and corner kicks, as well as chipping in with his fair share of goals.

Collins retired from first team action in 1935 but put his boots back on to help out during an injury crisis in the 1936/37 season.

He held the post of Honorary Secretary from July 1933 until the merger of Leatherhead Rose with Leatherhead United in 1946 at which time he was elected Secretary of Leatherhead, a post he held well into the 1950's.

William 'Dasher' Davis

1896 - 1920 (Goalkeeper / Forward) Leatherhead: Appearances - 250 Goals - 127 Leatherhead Rose: Appearances - 25 Goals - 0 Leatherhead FA: Appearances - 10 Goals - 0

A labourer by trade Davis made his debut as an 18-year-old goalkeeper. He was soon converted to the right-wing where he earned the nickname 'Dasher' for his fleet of foot. As well as supplying the other forwards with numerous chances he scored more than his fair share of goals.

At various stages of his career 'Dasher' turned out for all four local teams, he represented Leatherhead from 1896 to1910, Leatherhead Football Association (1910-11), Leatherhead Rose (1911-20) and Leatherhead Wednesday.

His outstanding performances earned him representative honours with Surrey Juniors.

Injuries and advancing years eventually rendered his sobriquet somewhat less than apt and he was forced to return to goalkeeping duties after suffering a serious leg injury that forced him to miss most of the 1909/10 season. He was often too brave for his own good and his comeback was continually dogged by further injuries until a broken leg sustained in 1912, while playing in goal for Rose, effectively ended his career although he did make a few appearances for Rose after the end of the First World War.

Reginald (Guy) Hue-Williams

1890 - 1902 (Half-Back) Leatherhead: Appearances - 165 Goals - 35

The Hue-Williams family were instrumental in turning around the fortunes of the club in the early years. Guy's father, Frederick, a well-known local businessman, was a key figure off the field in organising the club and putting the club's finances in order whilst on the field no fewer than three Hue-Williams brothers (Guy, Eric and Bertie) were involved.

Guy joined the club along with his brother Eric from Charterhouse School, one of the early powerhouses of English football, at the tail-end of 1890. Their impact was immediate and for the first time in the club's short history victories outnumbered defeats.

In his second season Guy's inspirational defensive performances helped Rose lift their first ever trophy with victory in the Herald Cup. Guy continued to excel at half-back before converting to centre-forward in 1896. He showed his versatility by expertly leading the line and was top scorer in both that and the following season. With the emergence of youngsters Harry Shurville and 'Dasher' Davis, Guy was able to return to his more preferred defensive duties. He was appointed club captain and proceeded to lead by example with a string of top class performances. Unfortunately he missed most of the 1899/1900 season with a serious leg injury although he did recover sufficiently to win the football kicking competition at the town's famous Easter Games with a prodigious toe-punt of two hundred and eleven feet.

He resigned as club captain in 1900 because his availability was increasingly affected by his role as Lieutenant and main Recruiting Officer for the local volunteer force. Later, during the First World War he led a battalion of the East Surrey Regiment into action in France.

Guy regularly turned out for the town cricket team, another club in which a number of Hue-Williams family members were also heavily involved.

Bob Nash

1894 - 1911 (Centre-half) Leatherhead: Appearances - 325 Goals - 9

Leatherhead's appearance record holder, Bob stood out as an outstanding centre-half in the junior game and but for injury would surely have played at a higher level. Cool under pressure he was an excellent tackler and fine passer of the ball.

He established himself in the side as a teenager at the same time as Davis and Shurville. Nash was one of the few Leatherhead players to readily adapt to the higher demands of senior football.

He stayed loyal to the club during the turbulent times and continued to turn out for them to the bitter end. After retiring from playing he continued to be involved in local football and after the end of the First World War served in the capacity of Chairman and President of another local club, Leatherhead Juniors.

Bill North

1934 - 1946 (Centre-half / Centre-forward) Leatherhead Rose: Appearances - 280 Goals - 122

Bill was a larger than life character in more ways than one. At six foot plus and weighing in at over sixteen stone he dwarfed most of his playing colleagues and opponents alike.

He made his debut as a centre-half in 1934 and performed admirably in that role over the next three seasons. He was given a trial at centre-forward and made an immediate impact twice scoring eight times in a game in his first five matches. Bill topped 35 goals in each of his two seasons leading the line before the arrival of Cecil Weller saw him return to his former position as a stopper. Unsurprisingly he was very difficult to knock off the ball as well as being strong in the air.

He finished third in Rose's all-time scoring list, behind Atkins and Weller, with over 120 goals to his credit. North, described as an Oxo cube of a man, was one of three footballing brothers. His younger brothers, John and Cecil, both played for Rose during the war years and also for the new Leatherhead club in their Surrey Senior League days. In John's case this was despite having to overcome the handicap of losing an eye in the war. Their sister was married to another well known Rose player, George Armstrong.

Fred Shurville

1920 - 1944 (Right-back) Leatherhead United: Appearances - 410 Goals - 52
Leatherhead Rose: Appearances - 30 Goals - 2

Another member of the Shurville clan (son of Alf), Fred was originally an outside-left but was converted into a quick kicking, sound tackling right-back. Renowned as a dead-ball specialist he was United's regular penalty taker and scorer of a spectacular free-kick against Ashtead in 1925 that was reputed to have been taken from inside his own half.

Fred made his debut for Leatherhead Juniors in 1921, after spending one season with Leatherhead Athletic, before joining United following Juniors demise in 1924. His consistently solid performances won him Sutton League representative honours on several occasions.

Apart from brief spells with Mickleham and Dorking (whom he helped to win the Surrey Senior League title in 1923/4) he remained a regular in United's line-up until their mothballing in 1942 at which time he moved across town to play for Rose for a couple of seasons before finally calling it a day at the age of forty one in 1944.

Harry Shurville

1896 - 1911 (Centre-forward) Leatherhead: Appearances - 200 Goals - 125
Leatherhead FA: Appearances - 6 Goals - 2

Harry made his debut as a sixteen-year-old and was soon among the goals. A bricklayer by trade he was *"a big bull of a man, a fearsome sight as he bulldozes his way through opposing defences"* who, to say the least, had a somewhat chequered disciplinary record, twice receiving his marching orders for striking opponents. Despite these misdemeanours he, along with 'Dasher' Davis and Harry Hook, was responsible for providing the bulk of the team's goals for more than a decade.

He was suspended for most of the 1900/01 season but soon bounced back to help Leatherhead become one of the top junior teams in the county. Harry announced his retirement in 1905 due to persistent injuries but was soon persuaded to reverse his decision and was duly appointed club captain. He spent eighteen months with Dorking helping them to the Mid-Surrey League title before being warmly welcomed back to Fetcham Grove in 1908.

Harry gained representative honours for Surrey in the prestigious County Championship tournament. He hung up his boots following the acrimonious split in the club but continued to serve on the committee of Leatherhead Football Association and indeed made one or two appearances as a player to help out when the team was short of numbers.

Reg Shurville

1921 - 1942 (Centre-forward) Leatherhead United: Appearances - 420 Goals - 198

United's record goal-scorer, Reg was another one of the members of the Shurville family dynasty that was involved with football in Leatherhead for more than sixty years. He made his debut in 1921 as a seventeen-year-old with Leatherhead Juniors and was soon scoring freely.

Reg had a brief spell with Dorking in 1923/4 before joining United in their first season. He signed for Sutton United in 1929 but returned for the following campaign where he continued to find the back of the net with great regularity. Reg's goals were crucial to United's success in the Thirties. He carried on playing until United's demise in 1942 and then served on Leatherhead's committee during their successful period in the Surrey Senior League.

Reg was also a stalwart of Leatherhead Cricket Club for whom he notched up an incredible fifty playing seasons before finally retiring in 1972.

Cecil Weller
1939 - 1950 (Centre-forward) Leatherhead Rose: Appearances - 155 Goals - 260
Leatherhead: Appearances - 111 Goals - 67

Cecil's first senior club was Wimbledon for whom he appeared at outside-right in the 1935 Amateur Cup final defeat against Bishop Auckland at Dulwich Hamlet's ground.

He subsequently enjoyed spells with Sutton United and Woking in the Isthmian League and then Epsom Town, where he was out of the game for some time through injury. When fit again he was persuaded to take over as player-coach and captain at Leatherhead Rose in 1939.

He soon made his presence felt, reaching a half century of goals in his first full season and then breaking every club and league record in the course of scoring 87 times the following year, including twelve in one game (another record). He continued in a similar vein and soon broke the all-time scoring record, finishing with over 250 goals to his credit in just over 150 matches.

A local man, he ran a tobacconists shop in the town, he was among those responsible for the formation of Leatherhead Football Club where his 48 league and cup goals were instrumental in helping secure the club's first Surrey Senior League title.

He carried on breaking goal-scoring records including hitting six of eight against Farnham in a Surrey Senior League Charity Cup match in January 1948, before, despite being well into his forties, filling the left-back spot with great success for much of the 1948/49 season. A very versatile player he appeared in every position, including goalkeeper, before hanging up his boots in December 1950 to concentrate on his new role as club coach.

A good club member and all round sportsman (he was a prolific run maker for Ashtead Cricket Club) who played for the love and enjoyment of the game.

Roddy Williams
1929 - 1931 (Centre-forward) Leatherhead Rose: Appearances - 35 Goals - 48

Noted as a hard working and tireless centre-forward the Welsh teenager only played one full season for Rose but made a tremendous impact, scoring 40 goals including two double hat-tricks. His exploits did not go unnoticed and he signed for Isthmian League Sutton United for whom he continued to find the net regularly. Roddy quickly came to the attention of League scouts and was snapped up by Crystal Palace. He spent a short time in the reserves before a change of manager precipitated his move from Selhurst Park to join Norwich City in the summer of 1933. He scored on his League debut and helped the Canaries to win promotion to the Second Division. After failing to establish a regular first team berth at Carrow Road he moved to Exeter City for whom he netted (what still remains) a club record 37 goals in just 48 games in his only season with the Grecians before leaving briefly for Reading in exchange for a sizeable fee. First Division West Ham United then splashed out £4,000 for his services towards the tail-end of the 1937/38 campaign. He was an instant hit with the Upton Park faithful, netting five times in his first nine appearances for his new club. However, with a wealth of forward talent available to the Hammers management Roddy was unable to hold down a regular first team place and he soon moved on again, this time to Clapton Orient where he soon made his mark. In his first season with the O's he finished as the club's leading marksman. In all Roddy totalled 71 League goals in just 118 appearances for his various clubs before the intervention of the war brought a premature end to his first class career.

Selected seasons in full

Leatherhead - 1903 / 04 (Surrey Junior League)

Date	Opponents	H/A	Competition	Result	W/D/L
19/09	Ewell Reserves	H	Friendly	9-0	W
26/09	Cobham	A	Friendly	4-0	W
03/10	Guards Depot	A	League	4-0	W
10/10	Wallington	H	League	0-1	L
17/10	Ashtead	H	Friendly	2-2	D
24/10	St Martha's	A	Friendly	3-1	W
31/10	Croydon II	A	League	4-0	W
07/11	Reigate Priory	A	SJC 2	3-1	W
14/11	Ashtead	H	League	5-0	W
21/11	Old Externes	A	Friendly	3-0	W
28/11	Dorking	A	SJC 3	0-4	L
12/12	Sutton United	H	League	3-0	W
26/12	Carleton	H	Friendly	5-0	W
09/01	Eversleigh	H	Friendly	4-1	W
16/01	Ashtead	A	League	5-0	W
06/02	Wallington	A	League	4-2	W
13/02	Sutton United	A	League	2-0	W
20/02	Guards Depot	H	League	1-1	D
27/02	Guildford 'A'	H	Friendly	4-0	W
05/03	Cobham	H	Friendly	2-1	W
12/03	St John's School	A	Friendly	3-1	W
19/03	Croydon II	H	League	w/o	W
26/03	Euneva	N	SJL s/f	2-1	W
02/04	Lorn	H	Friendly	0-1	L
09/04	Middlesex Wanderers	H	Friendly	2-1	W
16/04	Guildford 'A'	N	SJL Final	1-2	L

Season's record: Played - 26 Won - 20 Drawn - 2 Lost - 4 Goal For - 75 Goals Against - 19

Leatherhead - 1908 / 09 (Mid-Surrey League)

Date	Opponents	H/A	Competition	Result	W/D/L
05/09	Wimbledon	H	Friendly	2-1	W
12/09	Sutton Court	H	Friendly	1-1	D
19/09	Norwood Assocation	A	League	0-5	L
26/09	Guards Depot	H	League	1-5	L
03/10	St John's School	A	Friendly	1-0	W
10/10	Clapham Rangers	H	Friendly	3-0	W
17/10	Dorking	A	SCS 1	2-2	D
24/10	East Grinstead	H	AC 1	2-1	W
07/11	Dorking	A	AC 2	3-3	D
14/11	Dorking	H	AC 2r	0-1	L
21/11	Dorking	H	SCS 1r	4-2	W
28/11	Beddington Corner	A	Friendly	1-0	W
05/12	Dorking	H	League	4-3	W

Date	Opponents	H/A	Competition	Result	W/D/L
12/12	Redhill	A	SCS 2	0-2	L
26/12	3rd Grenadier Guards	H	Friendly	2-3	L
09/01	Richmond Town	H	Friendly	4-0	W
16/01	Woodford Town	H	Friendly	1-1	D
23/01	Metrogas	H	SSC 1	3-3*	D
30/01	Metrogas	A	SSC 1r	1-3	L
06/02	*Croydon*	*A*	*League*	*1-0*	*W*
13/02	Wallington	H	Friendly	1-0	W
20/02	3rd Grenadier Guards	H	Friendly	6-2	W
13/03	*Norwood Association*	*H*	*League*	*1-2*	*L*
20/03	*Wallington*	*A*	*League*	*2-1*	*W*
27/03	*Redhill*	*H*	*League*	*2-1*	*W*
03/04	*Dorking*	*A*	*League*	*0-1*	*L*
10/04	*Guards Depot*	*A*	*League*	*0-3*	*L*
12/04	Fulham Albion	H	Friendly	4-1	W
17/04	*Croydon*	*H*	*League*	*3-0*	*W*
24/04	*Redhill*	*A*	*League*	*2-4*	*L*

Season's record: Played - 30 Won -15 Drawn - 5 Lost -10 Goals For - 57 Goals Against - 51

Leatherhead United - <u>1933 / 34</u> (Surrey Junior League)

Date	Opponents	H/A	Competition	Result	W/D/L
02/09	Dorking By-Pass	H	Friendly	2-0	W
0909	Leatherhead JEA	H	LHS 1	6-0	W
16/09	*Kenley Elmwood*	*A*	*League*	*4-1*	*W*
23/09	*Warlingham*	*H*	*League*	*5-2*	*W*
30/09	Selhurst	A	CCC 1	2-1	W
07/10	*Radcliffe*	*H*	*League*	*1-1*	*D*
14/10	Epsom Athletic	A	SJC 2	7-1	W
21/10	Reigate Heath	H	DHC 1	9-0	W
28/10	*Croydon Gas Co*	*A*	*League*	*4-1*	*W*
04/11	Croydon Ramblers	H	CCC 2	5-0	W
11/11	Leatherhead Rose	H	SJC 3	5-2	W
18/11	Sutton Gas Company	H	SCC 1	5-1	W
25/11	*Mitcham Works*	*H*	*League*	*13-0*	*W*
02/12	Ashtead	A	SJC 4	3-3	D
09/12	Ashtead	H	SJC 4r	1-2	L
23/12	*Sutton Water Co*	*H*	*League*	*1-0*	*W*
30/12	*Sutton Water Co*	*A*	*League*	*5-2*	*W*
06/01	*Acc and Tab*	*A*	*League*	*2-1*	*W*
20/01	Ashtead	H	SCC 2	2-1	W
27/01	*Mitcham Works*	*A*	*League*	*21-1*	*W*
03/02	Ashtead	H	SCC 2r	6-3	W
10/02	Croydon Gas Co	H	SCC 3	7-1	W
24/02	Leatherhead Rose	H	LHS s/f	4-0	W
03/03	Radcliffe	H	SCC 4	2-2	D
10/03	Radcliffe	A	SCC 4r	3-1	W
17/03	Horley	H	SCC s/f	0-6	L
24/03	Warlingham	A	CCC 3	2-5	L

Date	Opponents	H/A	Competition	Result	W/D/L
31/03	*Kenley Elmwood*	*H*	*League*	*6-0*	*W*
02/04	Ashtead	N	LHS Final	4-1	W
07/04	Dorking St Pauls	A	DHC 2	5-5	D
14/04	*Acc and Tab*	*H*	*League*	*2-2*	*D*
21/04	*Croydon Gas Company*	*H*	*League*	*7-0*	*W*
23/04	Dorking St Pauls	H	DHC 2r	3-0	W
28/04	*Radcliffe*	*A*	*League*	*3-6*	*L*
02/05	Charlwood	N	DHC s/f	3-1	W
05/05	*Warlingham*	*A*	*League*	*0-3*	*L*

Season's record: Played - 35 Won - 25 Drawn - 5 Lost - 5 Goals For - 160 Goals Against - 56

Leatherhead Rose - <u>1943 / 44</u> (Kingston and District League Section 'A')

Date	Opponents	H/A	Competition	Result	W/D/L
11/09	Siemens Navy Club	H	Friendly	7-1	W
18/09	Epsom Town II	A	Friendly	1-3	L
25/09	*Hawkers Athletic*	*H*	*League*	*10-1*	*W*
02/10	*Military Conv. Depot*	*A*	*League*	*14-0*	*W*
09/10	*Tolworth Athletic*	*A*	*League*	*2-1*	*W*
16/10	Surrey Police	H	Friendly	7-3	W
30/10	*Military Conv. Depot*	*H*	*League*	*4-8*	*L*
06/11	*Berrylands*	*A*	*League*	*6-2*	*W*
13/11	*Byfleet*	*H*	*League*	*2-3*	*L*
20/11	TMA (Epsom)	A	Friendly	4-0	W
27/11	*Tolworth Athletic*	*H*	*League*	*5-1*	*W*
04/12	Stoneleigh Wardens	A	Friendly	4-2	W
11/12	Marzick	H	SJC 1	9-0	W
18/12	TMA (Epsom)	A	LHS 2	6-2	W
01/01	Benham Sports	H	SHC 1	4-0	W
08/01	*Byfleet*	*A*	*League*	*1-2*	*L*
15/01	Salford Wanderers	A	SJC 2	6-0	W
22/01	Goblin Sports	H	Friendly	3-2	W
29/01	*Hersham Claremont*	*A*	*League*	*2-1*	*W*
12/02	*Berrylands*	*H*	*League*	*1-0*	*W*
19/02	RASC	H	Friendly	3-0	W
26/02	Pioneer Corps	N	LHS s/f	7-0	W
04/03	Stoneleigh Wardens	A	Friendly	0-3	L
11/03	Tooting & Mitcham	H	SHC 2	4-3	W
18/03	Ramblers	H	SJC 3	6-0	W
01/04	Military Conv. Depot	H	Friendly	2-0	W
10/04	RAMC Banstead	N	LHS Final	2-1	W
15/04	Sutton Utd Reserves	H	SJC 4	4-1	W
22/04	RAMC Banstead	H	SHC s/f	0-5	L
29/04	Monotype	N	SJC s/f	4-5	L
05/05	*Hersham Claremont*	*H*	*League*	*4-2*	*W*
12/05	*Walton Reserves*	*H/A*	*League*	*9-2*	*W*

Season's record: Played - 33 Won - 26 Drawn - 0 Lost - 7 Goals For - 143 Goals Against - 54

Cup Final Appearances 1886 - 1946

Leatherhead

Season	Opponents	Competition	Result	W/D/L	Attendance
1891/92	Battersea Albion	HC	3-1	W	
1896/97	Guards Depot	SCC	0-2	L	
1903/04	Guildford 'A'	SJL	1-2	L	500

Leatherhead Rose

Season	Opponents	Competition	Result	W/D/L	Attendance
1922/23	Epsom Town	EHC	0-1	L	
1922/23	Epsom Town	LHS	0-1	L	2,150
1923/24	Banstead	LHS	6-5*	W	2,000
1924/25	Ashtead	DHC	1-5	L	1,000
1926/27	Banstead	LHS	1-2	L	
1929/30	Ashtead	LHS	2-1	W	
1929/30	Beare Green	DHC	5-2	W	350
1930/31	Ashtead	DHC	1-3	L	
1933/34	Leatherhead Utd	DHC	1-3	L	500
1934/35	Effingham	LHS	2-0	W	
1937/38	Effingham	DHC	1-3	L	
1938/39	Effingham	DHC	0-2+	L	
1938/39	Effingham	LHS	1-2	L	
1939/40	Fetcham Old Boys	LHS	4-7*	L	
1941/42	Phillips Sports	SHC	1-2*	L	
1942/43	RAMC Banstead	LHS	5-4	W	
1943/44	RAMC Banstead	LHS	2-1	W	
1944/45	Vickers Armstrong	LHS	2-3*	L	1,000

Leatherhead United

Season	Opponents	Competition	Result	W/D/L	Attendance
1925/26	Banstead	EHC	2-5	L	
1926/27	Epsom Athletic	EHC	1-4	L	
1927/28	Banstead	EHC	0-1	L	
1928/29	Ashtead	LHS	2-3	L	1,700
1928/29	Surbiton Christchurch	CHC	1-3	L	
1928/29	Waddon Aircraft	SHC	4-1	W	
1931/32	Ashtead	DHC	4-0	W	
1931/32	Ditton Old Boys	CHC	3-1	W	
1931/32	Ashtead	LHS	3-3#	D	
1932/33	Cobham	CHC	0-7	L	
1932/33	Old Dorkinians	DHC	3-2	W	
1932/33	Ashtead	LHS	3-0	W	
1933/34	Ashtead	LHS	4-1	W	1,100
1933/34	Leatherhead Rose	DHC	3-1	W	500
1934/35	Brockham	DHC	3-1	W	

Major Cup Results

Leatherhead

Season	Opponents	H/A	Competition	Result	W/D/L
1905/06	Borough Polytechnic	A	SSC	2-0	W
1905/06	Croydon Wanderers	H	SSC	1-5	L
1906/07	College Park	H	SSC	4-3	W
1906/07	Redhill	H	SSC	0-0	D
1906/07	Redhill	A	SSC	0-2	L
1907/08	Woking	H	SSC	0-5	L
1907/08	Norwood Assocation	H	AC	2-2	D
1907/08	Norwood Assocation	H	AC	1-1*	D
1907/08	Norwood Assocation	H	AC	0-2	L
1908/09	Metrogas	H	SSC	3-3*	D
1908/09	Metrogas	A	SSC	1-3	L
1908/09	East Grinstead	H	AC	2-1	W
1908/09	Dorking	A	AC	3-3	D
1908/09	Dorking	H	AC	0-1	L
1909/10	Clapham	H	SSC	0-2	L
1909/10	Guards Depot	H	AC	4-8	L
1909/10	Summerstown	H	FAC	1-2	L

KEY		KEY	
AC	Football Association Amateur Cup	+	After 0 - 0 draw
CCC	Croydon Charity Cup	SCC	Surrey Charity Cup
CHC	Cobham Hospital Cup	SCS	Surrey Charity Shield
DHC	Dorking Hospital Cup	SHC	Sutton Hospital Cup
EHC	Epsom Hospital Cup	SJC	Surrey Junior Cup
FAC	Football Association Challenge Cup	SJL	Surrey Junior League
HC	Herald Cup	SSC	Surrey Senior Cup
LHS	Leatherhead Hospital Shield	w/o	Walkover
r	Replay	*	After extra-time
s/f	Semi-final	#	Cup shared

Complete League and Cup Playing Records
1886 - 1946

Team	League Seasons	Played	Won	Drawn	Lost	For	Against	% wins
Leatherhead	1892 - 1911	170	72	19	79	314	361	42
Leatherhead FA	1910 - 1916	45	22	9	14	120	82	49
Leatherhead Rose	1909 - 1946	503	293	63	147	1698	1002	58
Leatherhead United	1924 - 1940	272	158	27	97	905	583	58

Team	Cup Seasons	Played	Won	Drawn	Lost	For	Against	% wins
Leatherhead	1890 - 1910	54	21	7	26	105	118	39
Leatherhead FA	1910 - 1916	11	2	2	7	13	25	18
Leatherhead Rose	1909 - 1946	300	150	32	118	870	681	50
Leatherhead United	1924 - 1940	153	83	15	55	453	355	54

HONOURS BOARD - 1886 - 1946

Leatherhead (1886 - 1911)

Herald Cup: *Winners (as Leatherhead Rose) - 1891/92*
Surrey Junior Charity Shield: *Finalists - 1896/97*
Surrey Junior League: *Overall Runners-Up - 1903/04 Divisional Winners - 1901/02, 1902/03 and 1903/04 Divisional Runners-Up - 1898/99 and 1900/01*
Representative Honours: Surrey County - Harry Shurville **Surrey Juniors -** William Davis and Harry Hook **Mid-Surrey League** - Harry Garland, Bob Mathieson, Tom Phipps and Bob Stevenson

Leatherhead Rose (1907 - 1946)

Dorking and District League: *Champions - 1909/10 and 1919/20 Runners-Up - 1910/11, 1911/12 and 1913/14*
Dorking and District League Division Two (Reserves)**:** *Runners-Up - 1931/32*
Dorking Hospital Cup: *Winners - 1929/30 Finalists - 1924/25, 1930/31, 1933/34, 1937/38 and 1938/39*
Epsom Hospital Cup: *Finalists - 1922/23*
Kingston and District League Division One: *Champions - 1924/25, 1931/32 and 1938/39 Runners-Up - 1926/27, 1937/38 and 1945/46*
Kingston and District League Section A: *Champions - 1942/43 Runners-Up - 1941/42*
Kingston and District League Division Four (Reserves)**:** *Champions - 1925/26, 1926/27 and 1942/43 Runners-Up - 1933/34*
Kingston and District League Sportsmanship Trophy: *Winners - 1931/32 and 1941/42*
Leatherhead Hospital Shield: *Winners - 1923/24, 1929/30, 1934/35, 1942/43 and 1943/44 Finalists - 1922/23, 1926/27, 1938/39, 1939/40 and 1944/45*
London Railway Cup (Reserves)**:** *Finalists - 1925/26*
Surrey Junior Cup: *Semi-finalists - 1921/22, 1943/44, 1944/45 and 1945/46*
Sutton and District League Premier Division: *Runners-Up - 1928/29*
Sutton Hospital Cup: *Finalists - 1941/42*

Leatherhead Football Association (1910 - 1916)

Dorking and District League: *Champions - 1912/13*

Leatherhead United (1924 - 1946)

Cobham Hospital Cup: *Winners - 1931/32 Finalists - 1928/29 and 1932/33*
Dorking and District League: *Runners-Up - 1924/25 and 1931/32*
Dorking Hospital Cup: *Winners - 1931/32, 1932/3, 1933/34 and 1934/35*
Epsom Hospital Cup: *Finalists - 1925/26, 1926/27 and 1927/28*
Leatherhead Hospital Shield: *Winners - 1931/32, 1932/33 and 1933/34 Finalists - 1928/29*
Redhill and District Wednesday League: *Runners-Up - 1925/26*
Surrey Junior League: *Divisional Champions - 1933/34*
Sutton and District League Premier Division: *Runners-Up - 1937/38 and 1938/39*
Sutton and District League Division One: *Champions - 1925/26*
Sutton and District League Division Three (Reserves)**:** *Champions - 1929/30*
Sutton Hospital Cup: *Winners - 1928/29*

UNITED COMPLETE CLEAN SWEEP

CLUB RECORDS - 1886 - 1946

Leatherhead

Goal-scoring: In one game	6 - **Harry Shurville** and **Dasher Davis** v Horton Asylum (1899/1900), **Harry Hook** v Norwood Rovers (1902/03)
In a League season	15 - **Harry Shurville**, Surrey Junior League (1902/03)
In a season: All games	25 - **Harry Hook** (1902/03)
Career	127 - **William 'Dasher' Davis** (1897 - 1909)
Most Appearances:	320 + - **Bob Nash** (1896 - 1911)
Biggest Victory: Home	16 - 0 v Horton Asylum (1899/1900)
Away	9 - 1 v Shalford (1902/03)
Heaviest Defeat: Home	1 - 10 v St Johns School (1890/91)
Away	1 - 16 v Clapham (1905/06)

Leatherhead Football Association

Goal-scoring: In one game	6 - **Harry Baker** v Epsom Reserves (1910/11)
Most Appearances:	100 + - **Harry Baker** (1911 - 1914)
Biggest Victory: Home	13 - 0 v North Holmwood (1913/14)
Away	10 - 2 v Epsom (1910/11)
Heaviest Defeat: Home	2 - 12 v Hawthorne (1911/12)
Away	0 - 9 v Tarrants (1911/12)

Leatherhead Rose

Goal-scoring: In one game	12 - **Cecil Weller** v Royal Corps of Signals (1941/42)
In a League season	59 - **Cecil Weller**, Kingston and District League Section 'A' (1941/42)
In a season: All games	87 - **Cecil Weller** (1941/42)
Career	260 - **Cecil Weller** (1939 - 1946)
Most Appearances:	450 + - **Cyril Basson** (1926 - 1946)
Biggest Victory: Home	19 - 1 v Hersham Boys Club (1940/41)
Away	20 - 0 v British Thermostar (1938/39)
Heaviest Defeat: Home	1 - 10 v Army X1 (1942/43)
Away	2 - 13 v Surbiton Old Boys (1925/26)

Leatherhead United

Goal-scoring: In one game	8 - **Joe Roebuck** v Mitcham Works (1933/34)
In a League season	32 - **George Andrews**, Dorking and District League (1931/32) and **Doug Street**, Sutton and District League Premier (1938/39)
In a season: All games	50 - **George Andrews** (1931/32)
Career	198 - **Reg Shurville** (1925 - 1942)
Most Appearances:	420 + - **Reg Shurville** (1925 - 1942)
Biggest Victory: Home	14 - 0 v Merton Corinthians (1924/25)
Away	21 - 1 v Mitcham Works (1933/34)
Heaviest Defeat: Home	1 - 7 v Epsom Athletic (1929/30)
Away	2 - 11 v Ashtead (1925/26)

CHAPTER EIGHT - THE GREEN, GREEN GRASS OF HOME

Not everything connected with the club takes place on the pitch, indeed if it were not for the dedicated supporters and officials who have worked tirelessly, giving their time and energy (not to mention hard earned money), behind the scenes the club would have been unable to survive. The following account of the development of Fetcham Grove is a tribute to their endeavours.

Fetcham Grove was described in the 1978 edition of Rothmans News as follows:
"On leaving the town centre one descends the steepish hill, crosses the bridge spanning the River Mole, and is soon inside the delightful Fetcham Grove ground. Here, in a tree-lined setting, is the very quintessence of the pastoral sward, enhanced by the rusticity of the village green".
Whilst the writer may have imbibed rather too lengthily in the clubhouse the Grove certainly still retains a rural feel to it, especially when the mist rolls in off the Mole on a cold winter's night.

1905 - 1920

The Fetcham Grove 'enclosure' has been staging football matches since 1905 when Leatherhead were granted the use of a field by the owners, Merton College, Oxford. This makes it one of the oldest grounds in the county to still be staging senior football.

Fetcham Grove takes its name from the mansion in whose grounds the pitch originally lay. Parts of the mansion remained in use for many years until finally being demolished in 1998.
The first game played on the ground was a reserve match against Holmethorpe on the 16th September 1905. The first senior game was a friendly against Guildford (Pinks) a week later. Lewis had the honour of scoring Leatherhead's first goal at the Grove in a 2-1 defeat. Other early visitors included Woking, the professionals of Southern League, Leyton and the famous touring side Middlesex Wanderers.

Tenancy of the Grove was acquired by Leatherhead Football Association in 1910 following the demise of the original town club. The new club only stayed for a couple of seasons with the Grove subsequently playing host to a number of local junior teams including; Leatherhead Creamery, Leatherhead Police, Leatherhead Athletic and Leatherhead Bus Garage Depot, as well as a flock of grazing sheep during the First World War. The Garage side competed, with considerable success, in the wonderfully titled East Surrey Traction Company Inter-Garage League.

Unfortunately, with its proximity to the river, the low lying field was prone to flooding and often more suited to growing rice than playing football. It was so boggy that if you stood still for too long you sank. The consistent theme throughout early match reports was the state of the pitch. Many games at the Fetcham Grove 'mudflats' were postponed due to a waterlogged pitch and many more went ahead even though the pitch was variously described as: a quagmire, muddy, saturated, sodden, soaked or heavy. At times conditions were so bad lifeguards not ballboys were needed.

1920 - 1945

Wealthy local benefactor Herbert Reeves, who had purchased the Grove from Merton College in 1918, offered its use to Leatherhead United for the 1927/28 season. The offer was gratefully accepted and United continued to play there until the outbreak of World War Two.

In 1934 the first facilities arrived thanks to the generosity of Mr. Dickinson. He donated a pavilion for use as changing rooms and a refreshment bar. Two years later Herbert Reeves, by now United's Club President, provided further funds to enable the dressing rooms to be upgraded.

Despite this the ground remained no more than a roped off pitch in a field, bounded by tall trees like sentinels behind the far goal, with entrance money paid into collection boxes handed around the ground during the match. This remained the case until the merger of United and Rose in 1946. In these inter-war years the Grove staged many local cup finals with the Leatherhead Hospital Shield regularly attracting crowds of over 1,000.

During the Second World War the Grove experienced several near misses, the closest coming in the summer of 1944 when a doodlebug fell in the nearby grounds of Thorncroft Manor, spraying the pitch with debris and damaging the adjacent cricket pavilion.

1945 - 1960

Herbert Reeves gave his permission for the newly merged Leatherhead club to use the ground, however, much work was required to bring it up to a playable standard as the ground, along with Thorncroft Manor and many of the surrounding villages, had been occupied by the Canadian Army during the war. Through the unstinting efforts of enthusiastic volunteers the dressing rooms were refurbished and enlarged, plunge-baths installed, the pitch cleared and levelled and a cinder track lain around the playing surface, all in a matter of weeks in time for the start of the 1946/47 season.

In 1946 Reeves donated the Grove and surrounding land to the District Council on the condition that the land was restricted in perpetuity to be used only as playing fields.
The ground has also staged some rather more unusual events. In the years immediately following the war an open air boxing tournament and a grand cycle polo match were but two examples of events organised by the supporters club to raise funds for ground improvements.

It was during the summer of 1948 that the club made a big stride forward with the building of a new 200 seat stand incorporating, club room, dressing rooms, referee's room, committee room and canteen. Thanks to the sterling efforts of the committee and supporters the project was completed in just ten weeks at a cost of £600. The Supporters Club donated £60, committee members loaned £400 interest free, and the balance was funded via a well supported half-crown appeal. The opening ceremony was performed in August by the Chairman of Leatherhead Council, Mrs. E. Levett. More than sixty years later the stand still remains as the centre-piece of the ground. The club now possessed the best facilities in the County League.

A new ground attendance record of 2,597 was set in October 1948 for the visit of Sutton United in the FA Cup, surpassing the previous record of 2,000 against Carshalton Athletic for an Amateur Cup tie eleven months earlier. During 1949 the Guildford Road end was banked with the assistance of a bulldozer in anticipation of a bumper crowd for the visit of Hayes for another Amateur Cup tie. The intention was to concrete the banking to form a terrace but it was to be nearly fifty years before this finally came to fruition.

As the fifties arrived so further improvements were made as the club progressed to a higher standard. These included a social club for the use of members and players, rounded steel goal posts to replace the old wooden ones and the playing area being enclosed by metal tubing.
New training lights allowed a number of local sides, Ashtead, Bookham and Leatherhead Rovers, to make use of the facilities for midweek training and take advantage of the first licensed bar.
Over the next three seasons the stands were extended to increase the covered terracing which then boasted 500 seats and cover for 2,000. The work was paid for out of supporters club funds and from the proceeds of a successful Ground Improvement Fund appeal that raised over £200.

On 6th June 1953, Elizabeth II's Coronation Day, the Grove played host to a parade followed by five hours of entertainment provided by a variety of local organisations.

Herbert Reeves passed away in the mid-fifties and in his will he bequeathed most of his buildings and land to the local council. In his stead the council continued to charge a peppercorn rate for the use of the Grove until adopting a more commercial attitude in the 1980's.

In the summer of 1958 the rough land behind the main stand was cleared and made into a sizeable car park. Slowly but surely over the next twenty years the ground changed cosmetically, although never losing its rustic appeal.

1960 - 1975

Work on installing floodlights, at a cost of £6,000, began in October 1963 with the work being undertaken by local firm Buchanen and Curwen. Watched by a large crowd, numbering over 3,000, the lights were officially switched on for the first time by Club President Stuart Surridge in November of that year for the visit of a strong Fulham side that included England Internationals Johnny Haynes, Bobby Robson, Alan Mullery and George Cohen in their ranks. So flush was the club at this time, thanks to a highly successful weekly Tote, that the bill for the lights was settled a year early. Erection of the lights elevated Leatherhead into the top flight of amateur clubs in the county. At this time the only other Athenian League club to possess lights were Erith and Belvedere.

During the following summer £2,500 was expended on a new drainage system and on ploughing and levelling the pitch. Installation of the drains helped alleviate some of the problems with the pitch which had been described as, *"like playing on cold porridge"*, and led to Tanners being dubbed the 'Mud Masters' as they stormed to successive promotions. Despite this few games were cancelled, indeed only a solitary first team fixture was postponed between 1946 and 1962 due to the state of the pitch (although it has to be said that they were not too fussy about the playing surface, games went ahead so long as the players could cope without the aid of skis or flippers!).

Many T.V. stars appeared at the Grove in the 1960s and 70s in charity matches which drew large crowds. A reported crowd of 9,000 crammed in to watch a match between two teams of celebrities in 1964 although, if the figure is anywhere near correct, it is hard to imagine how more than half of those present could have actually seen anything.

A fence was erected around the ground in 1965 to fully enclose it and the council even discussed the possibility of erecting a bridge over the Mole opposite the ground to improve access from the town. The Grove may have changed beyond all recognition if ambitious plans had been approved around this time. The council granted a new four year lease but proposed that the Grove should be turned into a multi-sport site with a running track around the pitch and a swimming pool and bowls green built on adjoining land. Fortunately these plans were shelved in favour of a new Leisure Centre.

The visit of Hendon in February 1967 for an Amateur Cup quarter-final tie drew a new official record gathering of in excess of 4,000, with cars lining the roads all the way into Fetcham.

New pay-boxes and the Ivor Gibbon Memorial Gates (named in honour of the former chairman) were next on the agenda, with a public address system added whilst the wooden seats in the stand were covered with canvas - supposedly for added comfort!
To the delight of all the long suffering car and coach drivers the council finally laid a decent entrance road into the ground thus eliminating the huge potholes that had previously existed.
A deluxe club shop - or at least a converted shed (later replaced by a caravan) selling programmes, rosettes, scarves, lapel badges, car stickers, pens and mugs did a roaring trade on matchdays.

In 1968 Tanners took on the might of BBC United with the proceeds going towards the Leatherhead

Theatre Club's building fund for the Thorndike Theatre. One or two familiar names appeared in the BBC line up; singer Craig (Kung Fu Fighting) Douglas, actor Norman Rossington and ex-boxer Terry Mancini. The "*gorgeous*" Virginia Stride kicked-off the proceedings. Other events to be staged at the Grove included five-a-side and darts competitions, club fetes, Snoopy's Disco Club, Sunday Totes, programme fairs, Surrey Senior and local league cup finals.

In June of 1968, Club Secretary John Hewlett had outlined a highly ambitious three stage ground redevelopment scheme to cost £50,000 (equivalent to a mammoth £500,000 at current values) over a ten year period to include a new grandstand, clubhouse and terracing of both ends of the ground. However, these plans were dealt a major setback when the town suffered its worst ever flooding in September 1968. Four and half inches of rain fell in just six hours and the River Mole swelled to half a mile in width. The floodwater rose until it nearly covered the goal posts and stands. The Entrance Hut was last spotted merrily sailing off downstream towards Cobham. Beer barrels and terrace sleepers were also washed away and the clubroom was wrecked. Once again club stalwarts came to the rescue. Within a week the ground was transformed from slime covered shambles to spotless and freshly repainted in time to stage an FA Cup tie with Molesey. A Flood Appeal Fund was set up to recoup some of the loss. One of the fund raising ideas was a Marathon Challenge between Leatherhead and Woking supporters. The challenge was to walk from Fetcham Grove to Kingfield and back, a distance estimated at 36 miles, in less than ten hours. For the record Woking's ramblers triumphed by eleven to six. Due to the delays the projected cost of the plans had increased significantly and as a result a number of items were dropped from the original building agenda. Despite the revised plans it still required a substantial outlay of £30,000 to enable the new clubhouse, incorporating canteen, kitchen, dressing rooms, bar and boardroom, to be erected and the old clubroom refurbished to provide some of the best amenities in non-league football. The new clubhouse was built with a flat roof as the intention was to add a second story when finances permitted. Unfortunately, they have yet to do so. A perimeter fence was also erected which at last segregated the club from the adjoining waste land (now one of the Leisure Centre car parks) and solved the problem of people gaining free access. The new facilities were officially opened in August 1973 with a cocktail reception for League and Council officers and were to be the last major improvements for some years.

Additional banking was built and the pitch surround filled with wooden picket type fencing prior to the 1974 FA Cup match with Colchester which drew a slightly disappointing crowd of 3,500.

1975 - 1990

Rather fewer people saw one of the earliest performances of up and coming young band The Jam at Tanners 1975 New Year bash. Staying on a musical theme, two years later over 5,000 people turned out to see a Top Ten XI (including Gary Glitter) take on the stars of Capital Radio.

A new official attendance record of 5,500 turned up on a cold Tuesday night in mid-December 1976 to witness Tanners fall to their bogey side, Wimbledon, in another FA Cup tie.

In the same year the club was given full control of the pitch for the next 60 years by the landlords, Mole Valley District Council, who had previously been responsible for its maintenance and had done much to improve the standard of the playing surface.Advertising boards appeared around the pitch perimeter for the first time in the autumn of 1977.

In February 1980 a tournament was held to open the new all weather floodlit five-a-side court. Windsor and Eton overcame the hosts, Brighton and Fulham to emerge victorious.
As details of financial difficulties emerged in the 1980's the ground began to look rather dilapidated and the club came under the threat of closure. Already in arrears with rent and rate payments the

council, in accordance with the terms of the full and repairing lease, demanded repairs to a list of identified defects at a cost of some £30,000. Tanners' officials put themselves in debt by taking out personal loans to prevent the retraction of the lease and save the football club from closure. Even so extra funds had to be found in order to comply with more stringent ground grading requirements. A concrete walkway was laid, a new players tunnel constructed, directors seats installed in the stand, new trainers dugouts erected, a new roof put on the stand, the lower bar renovated and the upper bar redecorated (at a cost of £2,000) and reopened as 'The Swans Lounge Bar', all in anticipation of promotion in 1984 which was ultimately denied by the Football Association's unfortunate deduction of points. The walkway was welcome but anybody venturing into the wilds of the far side of the ground was still well advised to come equipped with umbrella, wellies and sou'wester.

Problems with the pitch led to a spate of postponements and a visit from officials of the Isthmian League. The pitch had sunk in the middle and looked as though the Household Cavalry exercised on it daily. Remedial work was carried out to satisfy the league and allow matches to be played. Crystal Palace played some of their Football Combination games at the Grove following Charlton's move to Selhurst Park but their supporters complained that it was too far to travel and the experiment was soon shelved.

The football club also played host to the Round Table's annual fireworks displays in the 1980s and 90s which regularly attracted in excess of 2,500 spectators. Rather fewer saw the cast of Starlight Express display their abilities on the football field although they were obliged to wear boots rather than roller skates. On a different level the likes of England Internationals Bobby Moore, John Hollins and Bobby Charlton have graced the Fetcham Grove grass in various exhibition and friendly matches. Charlton also ran a coaching course for the youth team but word of his presence soon got out and in the event any youngster who turned up with his boots joined in. By the end of the session over 100 lads covered the pitch and Bobby spent a long time happily signing autographs. In more recent times Tottenham Legends took on a local Charity side before 500 spectators. Former England star Martin Chivers was just one of the well-known names in the Spurs line-up.

1987 saw the award of an 'A' grade from the Isthmian League Ground Grading committee following extra paving and fencing work. The Grove escaped lightly from the Great Storm in October of that year. Two trees fell on the perimeter fencing and some panels were blown down together with the telephone lines to the clubhouse but no major damage was reported.

The floodlights were upgraded at the start of the 1988/89 season to meet new standards for FA Competitions (having already been made 75% brighter in 1979 it must have been pretty murky before then!).

1990 - 2006

In the 1990s extra finance was generated by leasing the old clubhouse to a company for use as a disco/nightclub, with the company paying the £10,000 refurbishment costs. The club reopened as the 'Tanners Shack' and the 'Whispers' nightclub. This proved to be a short-lived venture though as the club closed within six months due to a lack of patronage.

In the close season of 1993 the clubhouse was redecorated, a seated American diner style replacing the old tea bar. The car park was re-surfaced with shingle, however, floods in October caused £6,000 worth of damage to carpets, furniture and the electrics in the recently refurbished bottom clubhouse. Further misfortune followed when arsonists destroyed the Tanners Bar in early 1994 causing its closure for some four months and yet more bad luck struck in the shape of floods in December of that year that damaged the nightclub and boiler room.

When an enthusiastic new board took over the following year the ground began to get a much needed facelift. The Guildford Road end was finally terraced, the perimeter fence was renewed, a Press Box erected at the rear of the stand, further terracing lain behind the Leisure Centre end goal and additional seating installed in what used to be 'The Shack'. The clubroom and snack bar were refurbished and reopened as 'Marchants'. This work ensured the ground obtained the 'B' grading required by the Isthmian League to preserve the club's status as a full member.

The long-running dispute with the council over rent arrears and their seemingly unhelpful attitude towards the club threatened to see the Tanners evicted but in the end common sense prevailed and the settling of eighteen months outstanding rent eased relations between the two parties.

As the Grove is a greenfield site development is a thorny issue but planning permission was granted for a roof over the terracing although, due to a clerical error (having the map the wrong way up!), permission was nearly sought to cover the wrong end. Fortunately this mistake was discovered in the nick of time. The roof was duly erected in 1998 and the structure (partly funded by Barbara Edwards) named the Bernie Edwards Stand in honour of the man who did so much to keep the club afloat during the dark days of the 1980s. New breezeblock retaining walls were also built, partly funded by a sponsor-a-brick campaign.

With the threat of closure again in the air in 2000, summer working parties made up of supporters, players and committee members carried out pitch maintenance and various redecorating jobs. Despite the financial climate the resources were cobbled together to re-roof the new clubhouse and, thanks to sponsors Milners, the premises were adorned with new carpets.

Facilities were further improved when a new boardroom was built in the 'old' clubhouse but the twin problems of flooding and burglaries have continued to blight the club and create financial headaches. The wettest winter for 200 years resulted in the old clubroom being flooded three times in as many months between November 2000 and January 2001. With insurance cover hard to come by the receipt of a couple of thousand pounds from the FA's Flood Fund helped to put right the worst of the damage. The clubhouse is currently home to Pitstop to whom royalty paid a visit in 2000. The Duke of Gloucester met charity workers and club officials to see at first hand the work done by this charity.

Relations with the local and county council's improved considerably, leading to the erection of road signs directing visitors to the ground from around the town. The signing of a new twenty five year lease with Mole Valley District Council in April 2002 ensured continued membership of the Isthmian League.

Thanks to the tremendous efforts of the ground staff and volunteers the ugly mud heap of a pitch has been transformed in recent years into a beautiful green carpet and one of the best playing surfaces around which has deservedly won many plaudits from visiting fans and players. Since stricter criteria have been introduced ground capacity has been cut from 7,500 to around 3,000. This has yet to be seriously tested with the largest crowd in recent years being the 1,814, swelled by Wimbledon's visiting hordes, to watch the 2005 promotion clash.

Fetcham Grove celebrated 100 years of staging football matches with the visit of Hampton and Richmond Borough for an FA Cup tie in September 2005. The Tanners marked the occasion with an excellent 2-1 win over their high-flying Isthmian Premier League opponents.

To coincide with the club's 60th anniversary an exciting £50,000 Diamond Project was announced in February 2006 that will see three sides of the ground developed. Due to the dictates of the Health and Safety Executive the grass banking will be replaced with stepped terracing; although some grass will be retained to maintain the ground's rural character. These changes will hopefully enable senior football to continue at the Grove well into the 21st or even the 22nd century.

▲The main stand at Fetcham Grove, pictured shortly after its completion in August 1948.

▲The same main stand sporting a new roof (as well as covered terracing that was added to either side in the early 1950s) pictured some fifty seven years later as Tanners host Farnborough Town in an FA Cup Third Qualifying round tie in October 2005.

Contrasting views of Fetcham Grove; snowbound in 2004▲, flooded in 1998◤and 2000▼during two of the, all too frequent, floods, and under floodlights on a frosty December night in 2005▼.

SECOND HALF
CHAPTER NINE - UP AND RUNNING

The early post war years were a golden era for English football generally and Leatherhead in particular. After the austerity and rigours of the war years and despite food, clothing and other goods continuing to be rationed well into the 1950's, the general populace was determined to go out and enjoy itself again. With the lifting of restrictions, all forms of leisure activity quickly became extremely popular. Football, still very much a community based sport, enjoyed a particular surge in interest and record attendances were seen at all levels of the game. Workers finished at noon on Saturday and would go straight to the match, with perhaps a small diversion to the pub first.

Locally, another housing boom followed the end of the Second World War and a new traffic scheme, the first of many, attempted to ease congestion in the High Street.

In the aftermath of the war the thoughts of the clubs' committee members turned to the future of football in the town.

1946/47

Having lost the use of the Barnett Wood Lane ground the officers of Leatherhead Rose considered the possibility of joining forces with Leatherhead United, who had been in 'mothballs' for five years. The plan was to form a team that would bring senior football back to the town after a gap of over thirty five years. To this end exploratory talks were held in April 1946 to which representatives of Rose, United and Fetcham Old Boys were invited, although the latter declined to attend. The meeting ended with general agreement on the idea. On 6th May, Rose's members and their United counterparts formally agreed to merge. At a further, this time public, meeting on the 27th May, the decision was ratified and Leatherhead Football Club was officially formed. The financial resources of Rose and United (a total of £200) were pooled together and put at the disposal of the new club. Herbert Reeves was elected as the first President with Arthur Griffin (Chairman), Edward Griffin (Honorary Treasurer) and Eric Collins (Honorary Secretary) - all former officials of Rose; Alan Peters (Vice-Chairman) and Reg Shurville (Honorary Assistant Secretary) - formerly of United, completing the list of newly elected officers. One man delighted to see the return of senior football to the town was Albert Warren, founder of the original club way back in 1886 and still going strong in his late seventies. A further meeting was held at the Plough Inn, in July, at which a supporters club was formed, the membership fee set at one shilling.

United's old ground at Fetcham Grove was to be used, thanks to the generosity of owner Herbert Reeves, although a great deal of work was required to bring it up to a playable standard.

Despite the constitution of the revived Surrey Senior League having been announced some six weeks earlier, at the eleventh hour Leatherhead were accepted as new members. Three other teams were to be fielded; the reserves in the Surrey Intermediate League, an 'A' team in the Sutton and District League and a youth side in the Epsom and Ewell Youth League. The club were fortunate in securing the services of both a coach/manager – ex-Preston, Huddersfield and Brentford professional Bob Gilboy and a trainer - Jack Copping, at short notice. Final trials to select the squads were held just two weeks prior to the start of the season.

With little time to prepare it was perhaps not surprising that it took a while for the team to gel and they did not exactly set the league alight in the early stages. The opening fixture was at Stompond Lane against Walton and Hersham Reserves on September 7th 1946. Walton started a man short, with Leatherhead quickly taking advantage when Charlie Stone had the honour of scoring the new club's first goal after just two minutes, turning in a cross from winger Tommy Temlett. Stone soon added a second but Walton, by now at full strength, pulled one back shortly before half-time. An own goal restored the two goal advantage, but Walton again reduced the arrears and then grabbed an equaliser only three minutes from the end. The local press were far from complimentary about the game stating that, *"the standard of football was not high and both sides will need to improve"*. The Leatherhead line-up on that historic day was: *Syd Peddar, Cyril North, Rueben Leverington, Bryn Evans, Ernie Harvey, S. Russell, Jackie Collins, Tommy Rochester, Charlie Stone, Ernie Trout and Tommy Temlett.*

WALTON & HERSHAM FOOTBALL CLUB.
CORINTHIAN LEAGUE.
WALTON & HERSHAM
Red

Right   Left
STONE 1
MC DAVITT 2 — FARROW 3
ROOKE 4 — TOWNSEND 5 — LICKFOLD 6
ALMOND 7 — AITKIN 8 — C. STENNING 9 — OSBORNE 10 — EVANS 11

Referee: C. F. HARLEY
Linesmen: F. M. ROBINSON, A. N. OTHER

TEMLETT 12 — TROUT 13 — STONE 14 — ROCHESTER 15 — COLLINS 16
RUSSELL 17 — EVANS 18 — HARVEY 19
LEVERINGTON 20 — C. NORTH 21
TEDDAR 22
LEATHERHEAD
Green & White
Left — TEAMS SUBJECT TO ALTERATION — Right

MAKE
L. SILK
YOUR GOAL!
2a, BRIDGE STREET. — WALTON-ON-THAMES.
FOR FIRST CLASS CLEANING and "HAND" PRESSING.
We specialise in "TURNING" Overcoats and Costumes.
Alterations carried out under Personal Supervision.

WALTON & HERSHAM FOOTBALL CLUB.
SATURDAY, 7th SEPTEMBER 1946.
WALTON & HERSHAM WILL PLAY LEATHERHEAD AT 3.30
NOTES.

We extend a most hearty welcome to our visitors this afternoon. Leatherhead F.C. is the product of an amalgamation of the Leatherhead Rose and Leatherhead United Clubs. The former had a wonderful record in Kingston Senior League circles before and during the war, but the latter, in pre-war days competed in the Surrey Intermediate League, ceased to function when war broke out. The new Club should prove a powerful combination, and we look forward to a ding-dong game.

Our game last week with Epsom was an interesting match, resulting in a draw. There seems to be general feeling that the forward line of our Surrey Senior League Team has not yet found its feet for co-ordinated attack, but it is perhaps a little too early to judge.

Our Corinthian Team played a magnificent game against Windsor & Eton, winning by 7 goals to 3 in a spirited contest which augurs well for the future. Goals were scored by Peach (2); Hoyle (2); and Hayes (3) who, after an excellent display, obtained his third goal in the last few moments of the game.

We take this opportunity of repeating our remarks regarding the Supporters' Club, for interest and support means much to any Club, and our own Supporters' Club aims to increase its membership very considerably; and the membership fee is still 1/-, (one of the very few things in life today that has not increased in price!) Why not join NOW? And we make this special addition, an appeal for timber for repairs and improvements to the Tea Kiosk. If any member of the Supporters' Club (or any one else, for that matter) can help by offering timber of any kind for this

The Act with a "KICK" in it that ensures a "WINNING" success at all
Concerts, Cabarets and Private Functions.
BERNARD AYRES, I.B.V.
PREMIER
VENTRILOQUIST
Enquiries to: BM/SHOW, LONDON, W.C.1 or 18, North Road, Surbiton.

There was no immediate improvement as the first home game produced a 1-1 draw with Camberley, this followed by a 3-1 defeat at Cobham. With no league fixture for the last week in September, a friendly was arranged against Banstead Hospital. Jack Coppin had succeeded Bob Gilboy as manager and had much to do with the excellent team spirit that quickly developed as an outstanding feature of the season. The game resulted in an 11-0 win and, with confidence restored, proved the catalyst for a remarkable goal spree. Forty nine goals were scored in winning the next six league games. Leyland Motors suffered most, being thrashed 9-0 at Kingston, with both Ernie Trout and Tommy Rochester netting three and faring even worse at Fetcham Grove as they were hammered 13-1, with four from Cecil Weller. This scoreline still stands as Leatherhead's biggest ever victory. Ample revenge was taken on neighbours Cobham to the tune of 12-0, Chertsey were beaten 7-1, in a game which saw the club's first official programme issued, priced at 2d. Devas Institute and Guildford (Pinks) escaped lightly with 4-1 defeats. It was usually a case of Leatherhead's small nippy forwards proving too much for the lumbering defenders pitted against them.

In November the search for a nickname had begun as some supporters thought 'Come on Leatherhead' was a bit long-winded. Tanning had been a major industry in the town from at least the 17th century. The present day Minchin Close had been the site of a tannery mill (owned by the Chitty Family) that prospered at Leatherhead Bridge until its demise in the 1870s. Tanning was also something Leatherhead were doing regularly to the opposition. 'Tanners' seemed an appropriate choice and was duly adopted as the club's nickname. It was also apt that the record victory against Leyland Motors was achieved on the same day that the appeal was launched.

With clothing still rationed the supporters club requested donations of clothing coupons to help purchase a new playing strip for Christmas. There was no sponsorship around in those days! Most of the older supporters remember the green and white quartered shirts but Leatherhead first turned out in green and white stripes, the change not coming until early 1948.

In the New Year the Surrey Senior Cup was entered with a visit to Corinthian League leaders Walton and Hersham. The tie attracted one of the largest crowds of the season including a significant contingent of travelling supporters. Unfortunately, Leatherhead's interest in the competition was ended by a 3-0 scoreline, but they were far from disgraced against their illustrious neighbours, including the great Jack Neale, England International and captain of the Great Britain team that competed in the 1948 Olympics under the guidance of Matt Busby.

Meanwhile, back in the league, a 4-0 victory over Devas took Leatherhead to the top of the table and they were determined to stay there. Walton Reserves arrived with only seven players and on a frozen snow covered pitch the game was reduced to thirty five minutes each way. This still left enough time for the Tanners to skate to a 10-0 win. Lagonda Sports conceded 17 in two games as Leatherhead topped 100 goals for the season. The match at Lagonda was a pantomime (Oh yes it was!). The pitch was covered with three inches of soft slushy snow. Large white sprays appeared every time the ball was kicked and it stopped dead wherever it landed. The players were exhausted after an hour and could barely manage a trot thereafter. Further high scoring wins against Brookwood and Vickers and a vital 3-1 victory over Camberley followed.

Cup commitments and a 2-1 Easter Monday defeat by Dorking in front of a near 2,000 crowd meant that Leatherhead had to wait until 19th April for a 6-1 win at Chertsey to clinch the title.

Surrey Senior League Final Table (Top 3)

Team	Played	Won	Drawn	Lost	For	Against	Points
Leatherhead	**24**	**17**	**3**	**4**	**127**	**29**	**37**
Camberley	24	16	3	5	72	47	35
Vickers	24	14	3	8	77	53	30

The League Charity Cup Final brought a 2-1 success over Dorking, before 3,000 spectators at Epsom, although the opposition scored all three goals. Chicks' centre-forward Allcock netted at the right end and the unfortunate Dorking defender, Andersen, twice beat his own goalkeeper. The Leatherhead Hospital Shield was added to the trophy cabinet after a 3-2 victory over Walton and Hersham.

Not to be outdone the 'A' team won the junior section of the Hospital Cup, dishing out an 8-3 hiding to Fetcham Old Boys, and then added the Ronson Cup for good measure.

It had been an incredible first season. The committee's aim to provide a team worthy of representing the town had succeeded beyond their wildest dreams. In all 157 goals were scored in just 33 league and cup games. In a bitter winter Weller did his utmost to keep opposing goalkeepers warm and ended as top scorer with 47 strikes to his credit. Undoubtedly one of the main reasons for the success was being able to field a settled side. Harvey, Trout, Temlett, Evans, Collins, Parker, Leverington, Weller, Goodall, Nunn, Chester and Weatherall were the mainstays. Leverington, Nunn and Rochester all gained further recognition for their efforts, being chosen to represent the Surrey Senior League during the season.

Because few people had cars, the Supporters Club laid on transport to away matches in the form of special buses from the bus garage or via Luff's Luxury Coaches.

At the Annual General Meeting, Arthur Griffin advised that a nominal rent had been agreed with the council and continued use of the ground was assured for another season.

1947/48

With Bill Parker retiring, Temlett moving to Sutton and Weller unavailable due to cricket commitments, several new players were given the chance to prove their worth in the early games. The first three league matches were won comfortably enough with Walton and Chertsey each being hit for five.

Leatherhead's name appeared in the FA Cup for the first time in 40 years, but it could hardly have been a tougher assignment, a trip to Kingfield to meet Isthmian League Woking. Despite a 2-0 reversal they acquitted themselves well but Fred Stenning, described as a forward of *"thinning hair and wicked grin"*, failed to impress on his debut. According to the local press *"he failed to hold the forward line together*". What hair Fred did have was centre-parted and slicked down with enough oil to lubricate 'The Flying Scotsman'. He might well have played at a higher level but had missed trials with Spurs in order to volunteer for service with the Royal Artillery in 1939. It did not take him long to find his shooting range at Leatherhead, with his first goal coming against Lagonda Sports on the Saturday following the Woking game.

Local rivals Dorking and London League side Post Office Telecoms were defeated in the FA Amateur Cup before a record crowd of 2,000 saw Leatherhead progress to the 4th qualifying round. A narrow 1-0 win over Corinthian Leaguers Carshalton Athletic was achieved, courtesy of a Stenning goal to follow his hat-trick against Telecoms. A protest was lodged with the Football Association, alleging that Temlett, who had returned to the side that day, was ineligible to play. The FA ruled that he was eligible on the grounds that he had played for Leatherhead in a friendly in September, prior to signing professional forms for Millwall for whom he had already played as an amateur in a reserve game. A week after defeating Carshalton, 400 supporters made the journey to Erith and Belvedere to watch Leatherhead take on the Corinthian League leaders. An injury-weakened side fought back from 2-0 down, to take the game into extra-time. Erith scored again and despite a sustained onslaught, which included hitting the bar in the final minute, the Tanners just could not force an equaliser.

The disappointment of exiting the Amateur Cup was evident in the next match. A lacklustre display culminated in a surprise defeat at home to Vickers in the County Cup. This was Leatherhead's first home defeat in a competitive game. The match was marked by crowd disorder and some bizarre refereeing decisions. Two Fred Stenning goals were disallowed; one having been given initially and the visitor's third goal in a 4-3 win arose from a drop-ball, after the referee reversed his original decision to award a free-kick for a foul on Leatherhead keeper Jay. A match report stated that, "*a certain element in the crowd adopted a menacing attitude towards the referee and he had to be escorted from the field protected by players and officials*".

Leatherhead quickly recovered their composure and walloped Metropolitan Police 7-2 before Camberley inflicted a 2-1 defeat. This proved to be a minor hiccup, as nine of the next ten games were won. A remarkable match against league leaders Farnham in the Charity Cup saw Farnham take a 2-0 lead before a staggering burst of scoring by the Tanners. Weller hit six and Stenning two with a further goal at the other end in-between, final score 8-3. Farnham exacted full revenge though handing out a 6-0 hiding in the league. After three successive defeats, Weller was rested and Fred Stenning temporarily switched to centre-half, with his brother Charlie, who had played for Halifax Town during the war, coming in at right-half. Title nerves were dispelled as the old sparkle returned with four wins on the trot. Goodall scored a hat-trick against Guildford at Woodbridge Road and Fred Stenning got three in the Easter derby with Dorking. Leatherhead now required just one point from the last four games to retain the title. Having failed at McLaren (formerly Lagonda) Sports, both points were picked up in the return game with Guildford. A record crowd turned out at Cobham to see the newly crowned champions thrash their neighbours 7-3.

Surrey Senior League Final Table (Top 3)

Team	Played	Won	Drawn	Lost	For	Against	Points
Leatherhead	**26**	**20**	**1**	**5**	**88**	**41**	**41**
Carshalton Athletic	26	14	5	7	60	42	33
Chertsey Town	26	12	7	7	73	57	31

Amazingly, despite this success, it was considered necessary to call a public meeting due to criticism from some supporters of tactics and the style of play. Trainer A. W. Smith made a long speech explaining team selection and the tactics used. In the event those who were most eloquent in criticism on a Saturday were quite taciturn for the meeting on a Monday and only general questions were asked.

Dorking prevented further silverware from reaching the Grove by securing a 3-2 extra-time win in the Leatherhead Hospital Shield. However, both the reserve and youth teams won their respective leagues.

At the end of May, the club's annual dinner was held at the New Bull Hotel. The presentation of cups and trophies was followed by a musical programme, to which anyone could contribute. W. L. Lamden presided and chief guest at the dinner was Mrs. Levett, the Chairman of Leatherhead Urban Council.

1948/49

Leatherhead Football Club embarked on a new campaign boosted by having a smart new stand and associated facilities in place at Fetcham Grove. The previous season's squad remained largely intact. Fred Chitty moved to Epsom, where he played for many years and had a spell as manager in the 1960s. Goalkeeper Eric Bristow arrived from Woking and Ernie Hawksworth, with his Brylcream permanent centre-parting, came in from Byfleet. Hawksworth had played reserve and 'A' team football with Sheffield United, Huddersfield and Barnsley pre-1939 and for Colchester during the War.

Tanners started brightly, beating the Rest of the League 2-1 in the traditional curtain raiser for the defending champions, and then defeated Carshalton Athletic in the Sutton Hospital Cup semi-final, held over from 1947/48. This game featured one of the finest goals ever seen on the ground. Nunn took a free-kick twenty yards out and sent in a long swerving centre. The next thing anyone saw was Fred Stenning hurtling through the air from nowhere to meet the ball with his head and send it crashing into the back of the net, almost before a defender had moved.

The first part of the season was dominated by cup football with good runs being enjoyed in both the FA and Amateur Cup competitions. The extra preliminary round of the FA Cup, against Vickers, was safely negotiated although at the cost of a broken nose for Hawksworth.
It was a struggle to overcome Cobham in the next round, before a record crowd of 2,547 flocked to see the visit of Athenian League Sutton United. Leatherhead had been contemplating moving to a higher class league (Corinthian or London), but the magnitude of that step was brought home to them. Honey and Case scored early goals for the visitors, who contained Leatherhead's much vaunted attack with some comfort thereafter. This game may also go down in the annals of history as the first time a spectator caught a rabbit on the field of play whilst the match was in progress. The lucky spectator received good value for his 9d admission - a game of football and his dinner.

In the Amateur Cup Tanners hit top form, rattling in seven goals in disposing of RASC Farnborough, both Stenning and Rochester grabbing hat-tricks, much to the delight of Tommy Rochester who had returned to the club in the role as player-coach following the resignation of A. W. Smith in early September. Local derby victories over Epsom Town and Dorking brought top Athenian side Redhill to the Grove for the next round. With sixty seconds of extra-time to go and a large crowd on their feet ready to acclaim a notable Tanners victory, Cornish rapped in the goal that earned Redhill a replay. Even then Leatherhead should have won but Weller missed a penalty, Bryn Evans having already failed from the spot earlier in the game. With Leverington unfit and Evans a passenger for most of the game, Tanners went down 3-0 in the replay.

In the league the goals were flying in, particularly from Fred Stenning. Hugh Tudor stepped up from the reserves and quickly became a firm favourite with the fans. Camberley were one of the teams on the receiving end of the Tanners' strike-force. Having conceded seven goals on the field one of their players had his misery compounded on returning to the dressing rooms to find that his false teeth had been stolen. Both the first team and reserves reached Christmas undefeated in the league. The 1st eleven were lying 4th, four points behind leaders Carshalton but with no less than seven games in hand.

The Surrey Senior Cup tie with Isthmian League Wimbledon looked to be heading for a replay but two defensive errors in extra-time settled the issue in the Dons favour. The culprits shall remain anonymous; nevertheless, it had been an impressive performance against far more senior opponents. The only cloud on the horizon was the resignation of Bryn Evans who had been centre-half and captain since the club's formation. He was unhappy at losing his place to Charlie Stenning.

Goals and points continued to pile-up in the league. The crucial top of the table clash with Carshalton lived up to it's billing with both teams playing fast clever football. Leatherhead won with two goals in the first half-hour, almost inevitably both scored by Stenning. Tanners replaced Carshalton at the top of the table and had virtually assured retaining the title. After 18 straight wins the invincible tag was finally removed as Camberley deservedly inflicted a 3-1 defeat. Their long passing and constant hustling knocked Leatherhead's close passing game out of gear. This and a heavy beating at Chertsey were only minor blemishes, as the season was finished in style with a six game unbeaten streak. The title was wrapped up on Easter Monday with victory over Dorking.

Surrey Senior League Final Table (Top 3)

Team	Played	Won	Drawn	Lost	For	Against	Points
Leatherhead	**26**	**23**	**1**	**2**	**96**	**30**	**47**
Carshalton Athletic	26	17	3	6	78	45	37
Dorking	26	15	3	8	80	50	33

Stenning had a tremendous season, notching up 61 of the 131 total goals scored. In one golden spell he netted 25 in 10 matches. This was even more remarkable considering that he allegedly, on occasions, turned up for games slightly the worse for wear, and it was not uncommon for a nip of brandy to replace the more conventional cup of tea at half-time. He was ably supported by Tudor and Hawksworth in the scoring department, with winger Trout continuing to be the main supplier. Defensively, Nunn and Leverington again formed a solid bedrock, supplemented by Charlie Stenning, diminutive goalkeeper Bristow and Weller (now nearing 40), who enjoyed a new lease of life after changing position to fill the problem left-back berth. John North played a number of games, despite having lost an eye during the War. Stenning, Trout and Evans all won league representative honours.

The reserves also enjoyed considerable success, retaining their league title with some ease and reaching the League Cup final. As the club grew in size, a 3rd XI had been re-formed, competing in the Kingston and District League. The club was also in a healthy state financially. Success had brought with it an increase in revenue. The accounts revealed a surplus of £325 on the year, this despite payments of thirty shillings or more, per match, in 'boot money'. In these days the unsanctioned paying of, reputedly amateur, players was common practice.

The Supporters Club continued to be active. A sum of £60 was donated towards the Football Club's building fund, new team shirts were provided from supporters' clothing coupons and an open-air boxing tournament was held at the ground.

1949/50

An application was submitted to the Corinthian League, but this proved unsuccessful and

Leatherhead remained a big fish in a little pond.

Bill Whittaker, a former Amateur international and half-back for Blackpool and Brentford, was engaged as first team coach. His appointment led to Rochester departing for Surbiton Town. Collins also left, for Epsom. Several new faces appeared in the opening league fixture at Camberley but it was an old one, Stenning, who once again grabbed the headlines with three of the goals in a 4-2 win.

Fetcham Grove had become something of a fortress and it therefore came as a shock when Athenian League Hounslow Town dumped the Tanners out of the FA Cup, 6-2.

There was also to be no repeat of the long unbeaten league run of the previous season, Guildford (Pinks) upsetting the Greens in the third game. Pinks were a totally different side to Guildford City, although they in fact played in the Southern League before City, albeit for just one season - 1895/96. The absence of Trout, through injury, and Tudor, on RAF duties, disrupted Leatherhead's free-flowing attacking football for a while. A surprising and unsuccessful experiment was to move Fred Stenning into the half-back line. Once restored to the centre-forward position he celebrated in style by scoring all six, a treble in each half, against McLaren Sports, to emphatically answer those critics who had suggested that he was past his best. Cobham held a 2-0 lead at Fetcham Grove, but a flurry of six goals in twenty five minutes of the second half saw the Tanners victorious, Doug Caswell contributing three.

Meanwhile, another decent run was being put together in the Amateur Cup. Wins were chalked up over Chertsey, Guildford, Banstead and Farnham, with a last gasp decider from Stenning against the latter. Leatherhead then had three weeks to prepare for the visit of mighty Hayes and what turned out to be an extraordinary serial of events, long remembered by all who witnessed them. To help accommodate the anticipated record crowd, a bulldozer was used to build a bank at the Guildford Road end. Lavatory accommodation for both men and women had also been erected. On the big day the gates were opened two hours before the 2.30 kick-off, to cope with the expected influx. Thirty coaches and two special trains packed with the Middlesex club's followers were anticipated, but this failed to materialise and the eventual crowd 'only' numbered around 2,500. Hayes fielded five internationals but Leatherhead, no respecters of reputations, tore into the visitors and were rewarded with an early goal from Stenning. Unfortunately, mist and fog rolled in off the river forcing the game to be abandoned before half-time. When the game was replayed Tanners again looked to be heading for victory, leading 2-1 with less than five minutes to go, when the referee incredibly abandoned the match due to bad light. Not surprisingly he had to be escorted off the pitch by police officers to prevent the angry home supporters from lynching him. Wishing to avoid the risk of the match official being hung drawn and quartered, the FA wisely appointed a new referee for what proved to be the final act of a dramatic trilogy. In his matchday notes the programme editor referred to how unlucky Leatherhead had been in the previous weeks but how sorry he was to see the club's supporters demonstrate against the referee and the Hayes players. He used his jottings to appeal to the fans to stop booing the visiting club and FA officials and finally pleaded with the person on the terraces who had a whistle to stop blowing it whenever a Leatherhead forward had a shot at goal (was this the first appearance of the phantom whistler of Fetcham Grove?). In front of another large crowd and a host of Fleet Street's finest, expecting the sensational defeat of the Athenian Leaguers, Leatherhead failed to rise to the occasion at the third time of asking. After two dry runs Hayes finally perfected their tactics, successfully starving Leatherhead's wingers of the ball and ran out comfortable 3-1 winners. It was certainly third time lucky for Hayes but on this occasion the home fans swallowed their bitter pill with remarkable stoicism.

In the Surrey Senior Cup Woking triumphed 3-2, before over 2,000 people, but in a storming finish Leatherhead almost turned the tables.

League form improved and confidence returned after a patchy spell. There was a setback when Ernie Hawksworth was indefinitely suspended (along with 138 players from other teams) in relation to an FA commission investigating the thorny subject of illegal payments. The ban was, however, lifted after two months. Popular winger Temlett returned following a spell as a professional. Leatherhead completed the double over championship rivals Farnham and gained an important point at league newcomers Banstead, who were also in the title hunt. A fourteen game unbeaten run came to an end at Easter, at home to Dorking. This was the Tanners' first ever home league defeat, coming nearly four years after the club's formation. The return meeting with Banstead on April 24th was now set up as a crunch game. It was played in strange weather conditions, a mix of blizzards, which left a thick carpet of snow, and bright sunshine. Temlett nipped in to score what proved the decisive goal although Tanners were indebted to Bristow for several fine saves to preserve the lead and swing the title race in their favour. Leatherhead were then involved in their first ever goalless draw, against Surbiton, but Dorking did them a big favour by beating Banstead, in the Merland Rise club's final game. This left the teams level on points but Leatherhead still had a game in hand. The luckless Guildford (Pinks) were no match for a rampant Tanners as both Stenning and Trout netted four times, to clinch the title in style and become the first club to win four consecutive Surrey Senior League championships.

Surrey Senior League Final Table (Top 3)

Team	Played	Won	Drawn	Lost	For	Against	Points
Leatherhead	**26**	**19**	**5**	**2**	**85**	**35**	**43**
Banstead	26	18	5	3	95	35	41
Farnham	26	16	5	5	74	53	37

In the semi-final of the League Challenge Cup, a sparkling performance saw Farnham hammered 5-0 before 1,000 spectators at the Grove. To crown another brilliant campaign Banstead were beaten 5-2 in the final and the League Charity Cup was secured a week later in a one-sided final against Hawker Athletic, Stenning helping himself to five more goals.

Several new players made their mark during the season including Doug Caswell, Ernie Francis and young half-back Tommy Wheeler, who looked destined to have a bright future ahead of him. Fred Stenning was again in stunning form, scoring with monotonous regularity. A six, a five, 4 fours and 8 further hat-tricks contributed to a final tally of 71 in 41 games, an all-time record for one season, unlikely to be broken. The level of support was encouraging and gate money for the season totalled £1,056.

Leatherhead's home league record in four years membership of the Surrey Senior League was quite extraordinary: Played 52 Won 47 Drawn 4 Lost 1 Goals for 231 Goals against 52.

A social club for use by players and members had been formed. One loyal follower, Mrs. Jean Jones, knitted tops for the club's stockings. Former Leatherhead Rose player George Holland was now serving as Assistant Secretary, otherwise the club's officers remained unchanged from those elected at the inaugural meeting in 1946.

An application to join the Corinthian League was rejected but a new era was ushered in when an invitation to join the Metropolitan League was accepted. Following Leatherhead's departure, Banstead went on to win the Surrey Senior League for the next four seasons.

ORIGIN AND PROGRESS OF

Members of Metropolitan League

LEATHERHEAD F.C.

WINNERS Surrey Senior League

SEASONS
1946-47
1947-48
1948-49
1949-50

OFFICIAL HANDBOOK   Price 1/-

CHAPTER TEN - DELPHIAN DAYS

People's way of life was transformed by the advent of television and by the greater mobility afforded by the increase in car ownership and air travel. Crowds at sporting events began to decline as people made the most of their newly found freedom or simply stayed at home to watch the latest offerings on the goggle box.

Two great ambassadors of Leatherhead football, Albert Warren and Herbert Reeves, passed away during the course of the 1950s, a decade in which Leatherhead had to come to terms with the fact that their all conquering days were over.

1950/51

A new decade opened with a fresh challenge in store in the Metropolitan League. The change meant new opponents to face, more travelling and extra games. With a number of professional sides, the class of football was much faster and more skilful than the Surrey Senior League had been. However, some of the ground facilities were basic to say the least, often involving long walks from the changing rooms to the pitch.

Tanners were given a baptism of fire in their new surroundings. The first two games brought the previous season's top two clubs to the Grove. A solitary goal from who else but Fred Stenning, was enough to see off Dagenham; but any illusions about repeating recent triumphs were soon shattered by reigning champions St Neots. Their extra class shone through and they ruthlessly exposed defensive shortcomings in a 4-1 win. The lessons seemed to have been learnt and victories ensued over Luton Town 'A' and Callender Athletic. Inside-right Hall, and goalkeeper Graham Lindsay came into the side but Fred Stenning suffered a blood clot in his leg and was out for six weeks.

Only limited progress was made in cup competitions. Walton and Hersham advanced to the next stage of the FA Cup at Tanners' expense after a hard fought 3-1 win.

In the Amateur Cup Hawker Athletic were beaten but Leatherhead were then the victims of an upset. Surrey Senior Leaguers Devas Institute had lost all nine of their previous encounters with Tanners. However, it was the home supporters who were left Devas-tated, after seeing the Greens concede two late goals to go down 5-4.

Mixed results continued for the rest of the season. Due to the indifferent form Leatherhead's supporters, who had become accustomed to uninterrupted success, soon began to voice dissatisfaction with the team's play. The discontent was such that the Supporters Club were lobbied for their views on boycotting matches until performances improved. How fickle people can be!

A 3-2 win in a thrilling end to end game against league leaders Headington United (soon to become Oxford United) silenced the detractors for a while. Against a poor Chipperfield side, destined to resign from the league shortly after, Leatherhead ran riot. Doug Caswell replaced Stenning at centre-forward and scored five times in a final winning margin of 11-0. This proved to be a false dawn, however. Performances remained fitful, not helped by a terrible sequence of nine successive league and cup defeats on their travels. The mutterings of discontent grew. Bill Whittaker jumped before he was pushed, resigning after 18 months in the Fetcham Grove hot seat. Veteran Cecil Weller was appointed player-coach but immediately hung up his boots to concentrate on the coaching side. Two weeks later the club was rocked by the resignations of Fred and Charlie Stenning, captain Ernie Francis and Ken Soane. Fred and Charlie followed their former manager to Malden Town.

It was probably not the best time to face Tooting and Mitcham at Sandy Lane in the Surrey Senior

Cup. So it proved, Tooting were always on top, winning comfortably by three goals to nil.

Within a month of his departure Charlie Stenning wrote to the club, apologising for his actions and asking if he could return. The committee initially rejected his plea, but were persuaded by Weller that the club needed his services and he duly returned in mid-February to bolster a shaky defence. Another well-known face to return to the Grove was Tommy Wheeler. Wheeler had earlier moved to Luton Town and had played a prominent part in helping the Hatters to a 4-2 win over the Greens. The loss of many influential players affected team morale and as a consequence results suffered. The remainder of the season was used to experiment with various permutations and to blood some promising youngsters. Tanners had to settle for a mid-table league finish.

At one game, Caswell was receiving abuse from an individual in the crowd. After enduring it for some time, he eventually walked into the crowd and chinned the offender before calmly returning to the pitch and continuing with the match as though nothing had happened. There was another incident involving spectators when it was alleged that a referee went for an involuntary swim in the Mole, the ground then being open down the side adjacent to the river. The Surrey FA fined the club two guineas and ordered that strong warning notices be displayed prominently at the ground for a period of one month.

There was at least a small measure of cheer for the supporters as some silverware did end up at the Grove. Leatherhead were the inaugural winners of the Epsom Challenge Cup, defeating Epsom 2-1 on aggregate. Then in May, Leatherhead, along with seven other local sides, competed in a six-a-side tournament as part of the Festival of Britain celebrations. The Leatherhead team of: *Doug Caswell, R. Norman, Ernie Francis, Alec Dawkins, Ernie Trout and Freddie Graffham* defeated Ronson Sports 2-0 in the final to win the competition and were presented with medals provided by the Urban District Council. One report described the proceedings as "*a lively afternoon's entertainment without any heights of football skill*".

In March, Leatherhead had been among fourteen clubs represented at a meeting to discuss the formation of a new league. It was felt that because of the closed shop policy operated by the Athenian, Corinthian and Isthmian Leagues, together with the fact that the Metropolitan League contained a mix of amateur and semi-professional clubs, that a top class amateur only league should be formed. The result was that Leatherhead became one of the founder members of the Delphian Football League, motto - 'To the peak of amateur football'.

1951/52

The new Delphian League consisted of fourteen teams, Leatherhead and Dagenham from the Metropolitan league, nine clubs from the Spartan League and three from the London League. There were several new names on the Tanners' team sheet for the opening day, including Len Barnes and Don Smith who, along with Graham Lindsay, were destined to be ever presents for the season. Tommy Nunn and Jackie Collins returned for second spells at the Grove.

It was a tough beginning in the new surroundings as Dagenham romped to a 7-2 win. Tanners recovered well to win the next three fixtures, including an away victory over eventual league champions Brentwood and Warley, prior to meeting Cobham in the Amateur Cup. Cobham, inspired by two goals from Fred Stenning, who had rejoined his first club at the start of the season, led 3-1 early in the second half and had also missed a penalty. Leatherhead rallied however, to win 4-3 thanks to two strikes by Watson in the last five minutes. In the following round Haywards Heath were beaten by the same 4-3 scoreline, Caswell netting a hat-trick. Cranleigh based Skyways and then Banstead provided stubborn opposition, Tanners requiring replays in each case, in order to progress to a meeting with Sutton United. The U's proved too good, racing into a 4-0 lead by half-time and despite two goals from Trout in the second period, United were comfortable winners in front of a 2,500 strong crowd.

Sutton also ended participation in the County Cup, scoring five times at Gander Green Lane, after saving themselves with a last minute equaliser at the Grove.

An eight season absence from the FA Cup commenced this year. The Football Association had brought in new criteria for entry. Attendances, gate receipts and ground facilities were taken into account and Leatherhead were one of the teams to suffer.

Tanners saved their best performance of the campaign for the return match with unbeaten league leaders, Dagenham, gaining revenge for the opening day defeat courtesy of a solitary Ernie Trout goal. League form remained inconsistent however, and led to the appointment of Bill Berry as manager. A late flourish, that produced sixteen points from the last nine games, pushed Leatherhead up to a highly respectable 4th position and featured wins over several of the top sides. Aylesbury (3-1) and Woodford Town (1-0) were among the victims during this purple patch.

An unaccustomed lack of firepower, just 51 goals in 26 league games, remained a constant problem. Don Smith and Ernie Trout were joint top scorers with 17 each. Fred Stenning returned briefly to Fetcham Grove, playing his final games for the club, finishing with an overall total of 185 goals in only 139 appearances.

The reserves reached the final of the Surrey Intermediate Charity Cup where they fought out an exciting three-all draw with Farncombe. In the days before penalty shoot-outs, it was agreed that the teams should share the trophy.

Fund raising events included a Mile of Pennies Fund and a well attended Football Forum that boasted such distinguished names as Dennis Compton and Charlie Buchan as members of the panel of experts. Admission to Fetcham Grove to watch the boys in green and white quartered shirts now cost the princely sum of one shilling (5p) and programmes could be obtained for 2d (less than 1p). Arthur Griffin, formerly Chairman, became Club President with Robert Bishop taking over the Chair. George Holland, previously Secretary, took on the Treasurer's role.

1952/53

Charlie and Fred Stenning were no longer mainstays of the Leatherhead side and Laurie Holland, a former Tooting and Mitcham left-winger, was appointed coach.

The season started well enough with five wins and a draw in the first seven league games. A five match sequence without a victory followed, but this was ended by an astonishing win at high-flying Dagenham. The Daggers were 3-0 in front with only fifteen minutes left to play before an amazing Leatherhead comeback, goals from Collins (2), Drury and Smith sealing a 4-3 success. However, Dagenham went on to win the championship by an eight point margin while the Tanners slipped down the league, eventually to finish in a comfortable mid-table position of ninth. There were too many defensive errors overall while up front it was the lowest scoring season to date.

Attendances fell considerably, leading to financial problems for the first, but not the last, time. Overall, gate receipts were less than £600. Stability was restored by generous assistance from the Supporters Club and through a fund raising friendly with a Fulham side including the legendary 'Tosh' Chamberlain.

Dave Bennetton and Pete Rogers were among the new players appearing for Leatherhead this season, but in January a walkout by three players (Lindsay, Hall and Don Smith) prompted Chairman Robert Bishop to announce that "*the spirit of the Club was not the same*". Ronnie Reed, a 17-year-old left-half, had been showing outstanding form, but in early 1953 was called up for National Service.

Haywards Heath and Newhaven were defeated in the FA Amateur Cup, Leatherhead were then 2-0 ahead inside eight minutes against a third Sussex side, East Grinstead, but seemingly eased off and ended up losing 2-3.

It was not all doom and gloom at the Grove. The Tanners did win the inaugural Wells Cup competition, beating Dorking 4-2 on aggregate over two legs. The cup was donated by Mr. A. F. Wells a Vice-President of Leatherhead Football Club, and owner of a local builders merchants that was later acquired by Hall and Co. Celebrations were limited slightly because the Allotments and Recreation Committee of the council had turned down the club's application for a liquor licence, a decision described by Robert Bishop as "*grandmotherly*". Despite this lack of alcohol, after each game both teams and match officials used to have a full sit down meal together in the clubroom.

Peter Rogers and Ken Tester were both selected for the League's representative team, while Jack Bastable was also serving as an amateur on Crystal Palace's books.

Leatherhead applied to join the Corinthian League for the following season but the application was unsuccessful.

1953/54

There was no sign of the dreadful season to come when Leatherhead, with Tommy Rochester now installed as coach, won their opening game 5-2 against Woodford Town. In fact just three more league games and one cup tie produced victories throughout the rest of the campaign. At Bishops Stortford, the players were upset by a referee who awarded three penalties to the home side while ignoring a blatant fist off the line by a Stortford defender. An FA enquiry followed the game at Brentwood; where young left-back George Allen was sent-off and subjected to shingle thrown by home supporters as he left the field. There was one sequence of nine consecutive defeats and Tanners' heaviest loss so far was suffered when thrashed 0-9 at Yiewsley. Generally the team lacked co-ordination and the will to win. They played "*along the ground football*" but the finishing was atrocious. The rare good performances usually came when least expected. After the nine consecutive losses, the previously undefeated league leaders, Rainham, were overcome 3-2 at the Grove, surprising even the staunchest Leatherhead supporter. A week after the thrashing at Yiewsley, Bishops Stortford's long unbeaten run was ended by the Tanners. Going into the final match, every away game had been lost. Leatherhead then proceeded to hold Rainham to a draw at Deri Park. The results against Rainham played an important part in the destination of the title as the Essex club finished one point behind the champions, Aylesbury. Leatherhead meanwhile, finished seven points adrift at the foot of the table. Reserves and youngsters such as 16-year-old goalkeeper Cliff Landsell were tried out. Vic Honey, Dennis Ford and Bill Goddard all arrived from Epsom Town.

Doug Caswell was one of the few players who remained with the club through these difficult times. Ernie Trout retired, having made 255 appearances and scored 127 goals and Dave Benetton went to Football League side Leyton Orient, as an amateur. The O's came down to Fetcham Grove for an end of season friendly that Leatherhead won 2-1.

Many of the players also turned out for Leatherhead Cricket Club in the summer months, although whether they had more success on the cricket pitch is not known.

The supporters did their best to give encouragement to the team. Hand rattles or bells could be borrowed from the Supporters Club hut for use during matches. The ground had a bar for the first time, housed in a new building adjacent to the stand. It is surely just coincidence that this arrived at the time of Leatherhead's worst season to date!

1954/55

George Hollings took over as team manager with former Leatherhead Rose player Jim Strudwick taking charge of the reserves. Hollings was able to pick the team rather than it being selected by committee. This was a bold step at the time and led to some improvement in performances and a better team spirit.

Tufnell Park, Edmonton, (now Haringey Borough), newcomers to the Delphian League, were Tanners' first opponents of the season. Leatherhead lost 2-1 and could only gain one point from their first seven games. Victory over Hornchurch led to some better form, including a 3-1 success against Rainham, a 1-1 draw at Aylesbury and the first away successes for nearly two years at Stevenage and Brentwood. However, a run of six straight defeats at the end produced a low finishing position, albeit an improvement on the previous year.

Once again there was little progress in cup competitions although an injury time 25-yarder from Doug Caswell earned a draw with Corinthian League Eastbourne in the Amateur Cup, before the replay was lost 0-2 in front of 3,100 spectators.

Fulham sent a side, including nine players with first-team experience, for a prestigious friendly, the Football League side winning 5-1.

On the playing staff there were numerous comings and goings. Caswell, Eric Bristow and John Hoy remained. Bert Willox and George Mannings, the only player to figure in the first and last games of the season, came into the side. Roy Springett was among the new recruits. Roy was a cousin of the England International goalkeeper Ron and played outfield as well as in goal. Tommy Wright, an ex-Epsom striker, Wally Pointer, Vic Reynolds and Bert Westland were some of the others appearing for the first time.

The club now had a new President, Percy Greenwood, Chairman Ivor Gibbon (replacing Ron Bishop after five years) and Secretary Leslie Ellis, while John Hewlett was also involved on the committee. The gate revenue, at just £408, had more than halved in two seasons.

1955/56

Delphian League form was sufficient to earn mid-table respectability with Roy Springett, Tommy Wright and Jackie Hughesdon contributing many of the goals. Ken Allbutt (ex-Sutton and Carshalton), Peter Martin, Lew Loader and Sid Gillett also made their mark.

En route to the away game at Tufnell Park, the coach broke down and the players had to hitchhike to the ground, arriving in various cars, vans and taxis. The match kicked-off half-an-hour late and in the circumstances Leatherhead did well to win. The champions, Dagenham, were beaten 2-0 at Fetcham Grove and but for a poor sequence towards the end of the campaign, the final league position would have been better.

It was in the Surrey Senior Cup that the Tanners made their mark this year. Having negotiated three qualifying rounds, Leatherhead won 2-1 at Dorking (watched by a crowd in excess of 2,000) to reach the second round proper for the first time. The cup holders Wimbledon, then in the Isthmian

League, were drawn to play at Fetcham Grove, where a magnificent 3-1 victory was achieved, the only time that Leatherhead defeated the Dons in a cup tie. Allbutt (2) and Bob Taylor scored the all important goals. In the semi-final the Tanners again fought hard, only losing 0-1 to Tooting and Mitcham United, in front of a 3,665 strong crowd.

Taylor left Leatherhead towards the end of the season and later signed for Gillingham, making 31 Football League appearances and scoring 5 goals. He then played two games for Millwall before returning to the part-time game in 1960.

Fulham made another visit to Leatherhead to commemorate the extension of the stands and the illustrious visitors were defeated this time, 2-1. Even with the added comfort for supporters attendances declined further, the programme editor of the time bemoaning the fact that 'only' 700 turned up to see the 3-0 win over lowly Woodford Town, on the Saturday before Christmas. By way of contrast, over 2,000 were at Victoria Road when Dagenham beat Leatherhead 3-1.

For the second time Leatherhead applied to join the Corinthian League, again unsuccessfully.

1956/57

W. Stuart Surridge, who captained Surrey County Cricket Club during their record run of seven consecutive County Championships, became Club President following the annual general meeting, and famous singer Alma Cogan, who lived in the Fetcham area, was now a Vice-President. Ron Gunner was appointed coach under George Hollings' management early in the season. Gunner was an experienced coach who, while at Sutton United, had gained a fearsome reputation for putting players through their paces during training. It was also about this time that the club's playing strip changed, the green and white quartered shirts being replaced by deckchair green and white stripes. The Tanners side included Wally Pointer, Bill Godfrey, Doug Caswell (in his final season at Fetcham Grove) and Joe McLaughlin who played for Portsmouth as an amateur on Saturdays and for Leatherhead in midweek. McLaughlin was a very talented player - with his left foot. A single cross with his right would warrant a mention in any match report. There were also several army players, such as Tommy Johnson and Matt Dunsmore. Johnson was a fearless tackling Scot with an FA Amateur Cup winners medal from his time at Crook Town, while Dunsmore went on to play for West Bromwich Albion. Jackie Hughesdon was called up for the National Emergency, but was released after two weeks with the Parachute Regiment. He claimed that they could not find a rank high enough for him.

The season was again not particularly notable from a playing point of view, but improvement did follow five consecutive defeats at the start. The final league match was marred by some strange refereeing decisions and resulted in a 9-3 defeat at Bishop's Stortford. The Surrey Advertiser diplomatically claimed, possibly a little tongue in cheek, that the referee may have been unsighted for four of Stortford's goals, three being yards offside and another punched into the net.

The final qualifying round of the Amateur Cup was reached, but Redhill gained a comfortable 5-1 victory at this stage. In a previous round, Johnson, Dunsmore and Hartley, all missed the tie at Croydon Amateurs, having been involved in a military train accident. Leatherhead still won the tie 1-0 and hit the woodwork no less than seven times!

The Tanners had their initial meeting with foreign opposition, Dutch club Hengelo being defeated 5-2 at Fetcham Grove. The game was treated as a major occasion and played under international rules with a substitute allowed for each side. National anthems preceded the match and about 100 Dutch supporters were in the crowd. In other games, where substitutes were not yet permitted, the team were often reduced to nine or ten men through injury and needless to say, this frequently affected the outcome.

The 2nd XI managed to gain some silverware, beating Berkhamsted Town 2-1 in the final of the Delphian League (Reserve Section) Challenge Cup.

Associate Membership of the Football Association was granted to Leatherhead Football Club and ground improvements continued. The club purchased its own welding gear and when the pitch needed rolling a tractor was borrowed from Nash's of Ashtead to pull the heavy roller. Leatherhead Rovers, who had been adopted as Leatherhead's "A" team, and several other local sides used Fetcham Grove for training. The pitch was often ankle deep in mud giving rise to cries like "*stop teasing the ball and give it a good whack*" during matches.

Membership of the club, entitling admission to the clubhouse and an unreserved seat for all league matches, now cost the sum of one guinea (£1.05). A profit of £87 was made, with the Supporters Club contributing nearly three times as much as gate receipts. There was a suggestion that those unable to attend matches send a shilling to the club instead. Entry to the FA Cup was still denied, due to an FA requirement that competing clubs have an average attendance of 500, Leatherhead's average being 400 at the time. Mole Valley rivals Dorking were attracting double that figure in the Corinthian League.

1957/58

A marked improvement in form took place, particularly in the goal-scoring department. The signing of Surrey County striker Gordon Cairns from Carshalton in October 1957 was a critical factor. Cairns finished the campaign as top scorer with 37 goals, including six in the 7-0 home win against Berkhamsted, which equalled Fred Stenning's six in a game record achieved in 1949. Billy Clack also contributed well to the goal tally, unless his wife was watching when he found it difficult to score! Tommy Johnson, Ken Allbutt, Mick Simmonds (who also represented Surrey in the left-back position) and Joe McLaughlin were other stalwarts as Leatherhead finished sixth in the Delphian League. Doug Caswell had now retired and Jackie Hughesdon moved to Dorking, where Johnson was to join him a year later.

There were some convincing victories achieved including Aylesbury (7-2) and Berkhamsted (7-0) in consecutive home games during November. The team scored four or more goals on a dozen occasions and there was a remarkable comeback at Woodford Town, from 0-4 down to win 5-4. On February 8th 1958, a minute's silence was observed before the game with Ware and black armbands worn, as a mark of respect to the victims of the Munich air disaster. For the away match with the same opponents the Tanners were forced to play with ten men, due to a car breakdown at Kew.

Cup success was again sparse but Epsom were defeated over two legs in the Wells Cup. The reserves retained the Delphian League (Reserve Section) Challenge Cup, beating Tufnell Park (Edmonton) 2-1 in the final. A new full-back named Billy Miller took part in this triumph. Tommy Millard and Reg Carter scored the goals.

A club crest and badge, with a swan as its central theme, had been introduced, as had a new playing strip of all green jerseys with white collars. Entry charges were one shilling for adults and sixpence for under-14's with OAP's admitted free. Fetcham Grove now provided enhanced facilities for supporters. It may have been more comfortable but safety was not guaranteed. Leatherhead official, Lt Commander Sid Ranger was knocked out and had to receive medical attention, having been struck on the head by a powerful clearance from a Hornchurch defender.

Leatherhead's latest application to the Corinthian League was successful and after seven seasons in the Delphian League it was time to move on. Relations with fellow Delphian clubs had been very friendly, so much so that several Woodford Town officials were Vice-Presidents of Leatherhead and vice (president)-versa.

1958/59

Chris Luff was appointed joint-manager for the commencement of Leatherhead's first campaign in the Corinthian League. Sandy Tait, who had been trainer, retired and was replaced by Fred Lipscomb. John Hewlett was appointed Treasurer. The team was strengthened by the arrival of goalkeeper Roy Reader (possibly the first custodian to wear a baseball cap), right-winger Ken Fitch and inside-left Sid Law.

The opening league match, at home to Erith and Belvedere, finished as a 2-2 draw, with four consecutive victories following - 2-1 at Edgware, 3-2 at Slough Town, 4-2 at home to Worthing and 6-2 at Epsom and Ewell. The return meeting with Edgware produced the first defeat. League form continued to be fairly good and a five match unbeaten run at the end, including a thrilling 6-5 success at Uxbridge, led to a very respectable fifth place in the final table. An injury crisis in November drew Doug Caswell out of retirement for two further games. His final tally of 210 appearances had only been exceeded by Ernie Trout (255) at this time.

	Maidenhead	Leatherhead
Goals	3	3
Shots	11	10
Corners	7	7
Throw-ins	36	20
Free kicks	5	7
Offside	2	4
Goal kicks	12	14

The report in the local paper of the game at Maidenhead in April carried a very concise statistical analysis of the game

Yet again there was little joy in the major cups, heavy defeats occurring in the Amateur Cup (1-5 at Carshalton), Surrey Senior Cup (0-7 at holder's Dulwich Hamlet) and Corinthian League Memorial Shield (0-6 at Horsham).
The East Surrey Charities Cup was won when Banstead Athletic were defeated 3-1 in the final at Redhill. Billy Miller made his first team debut in this match, after which the cup was presented by Surrey cricketer Mickey Stewart.

Jimmy Forrester, Johnny Lewis, new captain Johnny Jones, an inside-forward signed from Basingstoke, and Kilby Edwards, a Welsh striker signed from Welwyn, had now made their mark in the side. Ken Allbutt and Roy Reader were ever present for the Tanners in first team matches and Kilby Edwards was top scorer with 16 goals, achieved in just 13 games. Edwards, only 20-years-old, also signed on as an amateur for Chelsea, on condition that Leatherhead had first call on his services! Chris Luff was now sole first team manager (following the tragic death of George Hollings at age forty six) with Jim Strudwick as his assistant. Hollings had been renowned as a true sportsman, displaying unfailing integrity and conscientiousness.

The best home attendance of the season was 600 for the Wells Cup match with Kingstonian. OAP's could get free season tickets on production of their pension book and the club now had a flag that was proudly flown over the ground. The playing surface at Fetcham Grove was very highly regarded at the time, although in January 1959 Leatherhead suffered their first postponement of a home match due to adverse weather since the club's formation.

A 2-1 success away to defending champions Dagenham got Leatherhead's season off to a perfect start. The next four games yielded seven points but a narrow 2-1 defeat at eventual champions Uxbridge followed. League form dipped and at the turn of the year Tanners were mid-table. A good spell from the end of January saw Uxbridge defeated 1-0 in the return match. However, further deterioration took place, eight of the last nine matches were lost and a final placing of twelfth resulted. For the game with Edgware, Kilby Edwards and Brian Williams were missing. As teachers they were on duty with their pupils for a schoolboy international at Wembley Stadium.

The Football Association Cup was entered for the first time in nine years but Sutton United trounced the Greens 6-0. However, the Amateur Cup produced Leatherhead's best run to date. It was an inauspicious start as a hatful of chances, including a penalty, were missed in the draw against Ulysses, a side newly formed from ex-London University students. Ulysses and then Chertsey were beaten in replays before Surbiton Town and Addlestone each received 8-0 thrashings. A large crowd saw the Tanners through the final qualifying hurdle for the first time. Despite having to start the game with only nine men because Williams and Edwards were delayed by traffic jams in London, Sheppey were defeated 2-0 to set up a first round proper tie with Athenian Leaguers, Redhill. Leatherhead played some fine football in a magnificent game to achieve a 1-1 draw at the Memorial Ground but narrowly lost the home replay 0-1. Another momentous clash with Redhill took place in the first round of the Surrey Senior Cup. On this occasion a goal in the dying seconds gave the Reds a 5-4 victory.

Tommy Rochester had returned to Leatherhead as coach, while Arthur Benn linked up with Chris Luff as joint team manager. Leatherhead's second eleven, with Billy Miller and Ted Richards filling the full-back positions, won the Surrey Intermediate Charity Cup. Horley were defeated 5-3 in the final, Kilby Edwards scoring four goals. Edwards had begun the season with Isthmian League St Albans City but soon returned to Fetcham Grove, struck a dozen times in his first six games back and again finished up as top scorer for the first team, with 34 goals. Jimmy Forrester actually requested to be demoted to the reserves at one point so that he could play in his favoured right-half position. Debut making players included Arnold Bates, the new captain, signed from Redhill, Dave Mollatt, Ray Dowse, one of several players signed from Kent outfit Herne Bay, and the wonderfully named Johnny Blizzard whose first appearance was unfortunately in a downpour of rain rather than a snow storm. Ken Allbutt, a player noted for his gentlemanly conduct, had left the club to take up a coaching job and Roy Reader departed for Dorking towards the end of the season, to be replaced by Army regular Dave Burchall in goal. Johnny Phipps, Neil Goodman and Brian Pell were also at Meadowbank at this time where Norman Douglas was coach.

The biggest attendance at Fetcham Grove was 1,100 for the Corinthian Memorial Shield clash with Dorking. Leatherhead's support was quite vociferous but not always 'for' the team and a programme article complained of barracking from "*the terrace Internationals*". The membership fee was now one guinea and the cost of a season ticket had risen to one shilling and sixpence. The winners of the lucky programme draw received two tickets for the Crescent Cinema, to see films such as '*Some like It Hot*' starring Marilyn Monroe, Jack Lemmon and Tony Curtis or '*Genevieve*' with Dinah Sheridan and Kenneth More.

▲Surrey Senior League champions 1948/49
Standing: Mr Lush (Trainer), Cecil Weller, Tommy Rochester, Eric Bristow, Charlie Stenning, Tommy Nunn, Ruben Leverington, Mark Rowland (Assistant Trainer)
Seated: Jackie Collins, Hugh Tudor, Fred Stenning, Ernie Trout (captain) and Ernie Hawksworth

▲The Leatherhead committee with the three trophies won by the team in the 1949/50 season: Surrey Senior League, Surrey Senior League Cup and Surrey Senior League Charity Cup. *Standing:* G. Strudwick, L. Beasley, F. Lipscombe, R. Tulett, J. Strudwick, R. Chester, A. Strudwick, G. Holland (Asst Hon. Secretary) and V. Harvey *Seated:* W. Merton (Team Secretary), E. A. Griffin (Hon. Treasurer), A. P. Griffin (Chairman), E. A. Collins (Honorary Secretary), E. Shurville (Press) and W. Jelley (Canteen Manager)

▲Leatherhead take on Dorking in the Corinthian Memorial Shield in March 1960. Dave Mollatt dives in amongst the flying feet but this acrobatic effort just failed to find the target.
Leatherhead dominated the match but missed a host of opportunities and had to rely on a solitary strike later in the game from Mollatt to settle the issue in their favour. This derby game was watched by a season's best attendance of 1,100.

▲Johnny Phipps and Johnny Haynes lead out their Leatherhead and Fulham sides prior to the match to officially open the new floodlights at Fetcham Grove in November 1963.

▲Corinthian League champions 1962/63
Standing: Neil Goodman, John Lewis, George Ives, Jock Wood, Brian Pell and Reg Oakes
Seated: Dave Mollatt, Terry Dobbs, John Phipps, with the Corinthian League championship trophy, Norman Douglas (manager), Ken Harris and Kevin Brittin

▲Neil Goodman scores for Tanners in a 6-2 win over Epsom and Ewell in March 1964.

▲Brian Pell, Jock Wood and Johnny Lewis push through triumphant crowds celebrating Tanners promotion to the Athenian League Premier Division in late March 1964 after defeating Worthing 3-0.
◤Mr. Leatherhead, Chris Luff who did so much to further the cause of Leatherhead FC.

▲Neil Goodman wheels away after completing the scoring in a 4-0 hammering of Edgware Town.

▲Tanners fans invade the pitch at the end of a memorable 3-2 win over Kingstonian in the FA Cup of 1963/4. ▼Jack O'Malley and his defence under pressure against Guildford City in a home FA Cup tie in 1964. The Southern League professionals scraped through by 2-1 thanks to two goals in the final ten minutes of the match in front of a crowd in excess of 2,000.

▲Larry Pritchard *(far left)* scores with a tremendous shot from the edge of the penalty area to put Leatherhead two ahead inside twenty minutes against Sutton United in the 1965 Surrey Senior Cup final at Richmond Road, Kingstonian, but Sutton hit back to win 3-2.

▲Leatherhead skipper Alan Brazier exchanges pennants with the Marlebach captain prior to the final of the John Grun International tournament final in Luxembourg in May 1966.

◀Clearing the Fetcham Grove pitch of snow before the Amateur Cup tie with Pinehurst.

▶Billy Miller, Norman Douglas, Kevin Brittin and partners relaxing at an end of season fancy dress party.

▲Part of the then record crowd of over 4,000 that flocked to a muddy Fetcham Grove to watch the FA Amateur Cup quarter-final against Isthmian League giants Hendon in February 1967.

▲Hendon's John Swannell brilliantly saves
Ian Meekin's penalty in the Amateur Cup.
Hendon went on to win the tie 3-0.

▲Alan Brazier finally lifts the Surrey Senior
Cup for the first and, to date, only time after
Tanners defeat Redhill 3-1 in May 1969.

▲The Tanners team and supporters celebrating the senior cup triumph.
Back Row: Bobby Taylor, Barry Webb, Micky Cuthbert, Kevin Brittin, Ian Meekin
(partly hidden), Brian Caterer, Billy Miller and Tony Slade. *Front Row:* Nobby
Skinner, Barrie Davies, Alan Brazier, Keith Mills, Bobby Adam and Johnny Phipps

CHAPTER ELEVEN - PROGRESS, PROGRESS....
THAT'S LEATHERHEAD

"If you can remember the 1960s, you weren't there". Leatherhead Football Club were most certainly there. Refusing to be distracted by the beat boom, flower power or sexual revolution, they advanced to become a highly respected amateur side. Mini's were very much in vogue, both the car and the short skirt becoming icons of the swinging sixties, however, there was nothing mini about the revival in fortunes of Leatherhead FC. The Tanners began to make a name for themselves as cup fighters of renown, enjoying several impressive runs in national cup competitions.

Football began to suffer a drop in popularity, there was a marked increase in foul play, and fewer goals were scored as defences got tighter and defenders more cynical.

The town's artistic status was also enhanced, with the opening of the Thorndike Theatre and on the wider scale, there was the little matter of England hosting and winning the World Cup.

1960/61

There was a large contingent of Welshmen on the Leatherhead playing staff for this season. Kilby Edwards, now captain, was joined by Johnny Lewis, Dai Lloyd, amateur international Gordon Griffiths and youth international Marsden Hubbard. Johnny Phipps and Dave Wall, both later to play important roles on the backroom staff, also appeared in the first team. Edwards and Ray Dowse were the only members of the squad to retain a first team place for most of the season, as 55 different players were used. Three appearances were made by a young Dario Gradi, later to enjoy an illustrious career with Sutton, Wimbledon etc. and, at the time of writing, the longest serving manager in the Football League, with Crewe Alexandra. Gradi, a local schoolteacher, continued to recommend players to Leatherhead for a number of years after his departure.

An abundance of goals flowed in Tanners' matches. One twelve match sequence between mid-September and mid-December produced 88 goals as follows:- 4-3, 2-6, 3-4, 3-5, 3-4, 1-3, 5-2, 6-2, 2-5, 6-2, 6-3 and 4-4. At Christmas, Leatherhead had both the highest goals for and against tallies in the league. One of the best victories was the 5-2 success against defending champions Uxbridge, Tommy Millard netting a hat-trick. Unfortunately, over the season as a whole, far more goals were conceded than scored. Thrashings at Edgware (1-8), Eastbourne (0-7) and Worthing (0-6) contributing to a goals against tally of 93 (only the bottom club, Slough, conceded more) and a lowly final league placing of thirteenth out of the sixteen competing teams.

There was no cheer provided by any of the various cup competitions either. Kilby Edwards led the side by example however, and in a poor season for the club generally, can take great personal credit in finishing top scorer for the third year running with 38 goals.

In February 1961 Chris Luff stepped down after two years as unpaid team manager, due to pressure of work and shortly afterwards former Chelsea, Exeter City and Peterborough United player Norman Douglas moved from Dorking to Fetcham Grove as manager/coach. Douglas had been very successful at Meadowbank and under his guidance Leatherhead's playing reputation was to make great strides forward. However, it was not until his sixth game at the helm that a Tanners victory was achieved. The building of a decent side was going to need a little time.

Bingo evenings had replaced whist drives as one of the main events for supporters, aimed at both social enjoyment and fund raising. Bunny Oram and Geoff Otway were among those supervising these evenings. On a sadder note Jim Strudwick, one of the club's founders, a former centre-half with Leatherhead Rose and reserve team manager for twelve years, had passed away.

1961/62

Captain and top scorer for the last three years Kilby Edwards (88 goals in 83 appearances overall), left for Tooting and Mitcham in the 1961 close season but Norman Douglas began to put together a good settled side. Former Aldershot and Army goalkeeper Arthur Hammond, Reg Oakes and Kenny Harris (both Amateur Cup finalists with Kingstonian), Jimmy Finlayson (ex-Guildford City), Robbie Foster, Ron Philpott, Neil Goodman and Brian Pell joined established players such as Lewis, Phipps, Hickey and Mollatt. Douglas insisted on all players training at Fetcham Grove at least once a week. Although still amateur the outlook was becoming more professional.
Having scored 13 goals in 13 games, striker Phil West transferred to Hayes. Newcomer Pell, signed from Banstead Athletic, was a master tactician and playmaker whose hobbies included golf and sleeping! His colleagues reckoned that he could fall asleep on a clothesline if he had to.

League results were decidedly mixed but the defence was much tighter and many of the defeats were by the odd goal. Following an eight match winless run the programme editor bemoaned "*a lack of finishing thrust*". A 5-1 success against Horsham followed. Other highlights included a 5-1 drubbing of local rivals Dorking on the Saturday before Christmas, a 2-1 conquest of Epsom and Ewell, thanks to two goals in the last three minutes, and a 6-0 victory over high-riding Edgware in the penultimate game of the season. All this gave some notice of the promising things to come and the final league position of 10th was an improvement of three places on the previous year.

Cup progress was once again limited but the Tanners greatly inconvenienced Isthmian League Kingstonian in the FA Cup, only losing 2-4 after extra-time in a replay. This was the first match Leatherhead had played under floodlights. The Tanners had led 2-1 almost until full-time despite keeper Arthur Hammond being nearly immobile with a leg injury.

In December 1961 Arthur Griffin, who had played such a large part in the club's foundation in addition to serving as Chairman and President, sadly died at the age of 85. Griffin, along with his son (who was Tanners' Treasurer for many years), had owned a cobbler's shop in Kingston Road. At the annual meeting Ivor Gibbon warned that unless there was an improvement in attendances and greater financial support, senior football would cease.

The season ended with a four-day tour of Belgium. A party of twenty players and officials paid £10 each for the trip, which required a flight by Dakota from Southend to Ostend. Two games were scheduled, but only one played, against amateur side SK Vorwaerts, Leatherhead winning 5-1. Facilities were a bit basic. Only half the pitch had been cut, it had not been rolled for months and there were no showers, just eleven bowls of cold water to wash in. Nevertheless, the trip was hugely enjoyed by all and it was proposed that further tours take place.

1962/63

The 1962/63 season was marked by the coldest winter since the 1740s. It was so severe that some leagues were unable to finish their fixtures. Fortunately this did not happen in the Corinthian League as Leatherhead, in their best season to date by far, won the championship with a team that was described as "*fast moving, fighting for every ball and willing to shoot from any angle or distance*".

A 5-0 victory at Slough Town and a 5-1 success at home to Dagenham gave notice of the Tanners' intentions in the first two matches. At the turn of the year only Letchworth Town and Uxbridge had defeated the Greens with two further matches drawn. Champions for the previous two years, Maidenhead, were routed 7-1. The big freeze caused a five week lay-off but this did not affect Tanners' form. A thirteen match unbeaten run, including ten straight victories, took Leatherhead to the top of the table. Letchworth, including ex-Tanner Kilby Edwards, came to Fetcham Grove as league leaders, but were well beaten, 5-2.

The demanding end of season schedule, often playing three games a week, brought mixed results but in the final reckoning Leatherhead were Corinthian League champions, seven points in front of Erith and Belvedere, equalling the league points record set by Maidenhead a year earlier (49 out of a maximum 60). The fixture pile-up meant that the planned tour of Belgium had to be cancelled.

Corinthian League Final Table (Top 3)

Team	Played	Won	Drawn	Lost	For	Against	Points
Leatherhead	**30**	**22**	**5**	**3**	**88**	**36**	**49**
Erith & Belvedere	30	18	6	6	61	32	42
Wokingham Town	30	18	5	7	53	41	41

The Tanners went straight out of the FA Cup losing 1-4 at home to Wimbledon in front of a 1,500 crowd. The Dons included five England Internationals. Centre-forward Eddie Reynolds did most damage and later in the season he scored all four goals with his head when Wimbledon won the FA Amateur Cup at Wembley. In the Corinthian League Memorial Shield, almost the entire reserve side was fielded for a second round replay with Edgware, not played until the end of April. The match was only lost to a solitary extra-time goal. Success was more forthcoming in the other cup competitions however.

Hermes, Epsom Town, Molesey, Malden Town and finally Athenian League Carshalton Athletic were beaten in the qualifying rounds of the Amateur Cup. For the first round tie with Wiltshire club Pinehurst, A.L. Wells and Son loaned two tippers and a six-ton loader to enable an army of volunteers to clear 300 lorry loads of snow from the pitch and replace it with twenty tons of sand, before the match could take place. Their efforts were worthwhile as Leatherhead, with two goals from Goodman and one from Pell, won 3-0 to make the second round for the first time. A bitterly cold wind kept the crowd down to 500 and Leatherhead had to pay for thirteen first-class rail tickets for their opponents, as well as splitting the gate receipts. The spectators who did turn up in the sub-zero temperature may have regretted their decision as the game commenced in a strong cross-wind that blew the sand into every crevice and finished in a snowstorm of "*extreme velocity*". In round two the run ended with a 4-1 defeat inflicted by Athenian's Hitchin Town, watched by 1,424.

The Tanners also equalled their furthest progress in the Surrey Senior Cup. Isthmian League Corinthian Casuals were defeated 3-1 in the second round in what was the Casuals first match at Dulwich's Champion Hill ground following twelve years at The Oval. The very strong Sutton United side that reached the Amateur Cup Final that year barred the way in the semi-final and in front of a best of season 1,913 spectators at Fetcham Grove, Leatherhead lined-up to applaud the visitors onto the pitch, then crashed 0-4 in the match.

Newcomers in green and white this season included Kevin Brittin and Gordon 'Jock' Wood, both signed from Addlestone. Brittin was Leatherhead's answer to George Best, at least with regard to the number of young ladies that followed him around; Wood was an ever present throughout the campaign. Irishman, jazz lover, insurance clerk and goalkeeper, Jack O'Malley arrived from Sutton, for whom he had made a winning debut in the London Senior Cup Final, ex-Dulwich, Sutton and Kingstonian player Terry Dobbs also joined the ranks. Dobbs and Brittin provided "*rhythm and goal eagerness to a previously stuttering attack*". Lewis, Phipps, Oakes, Harris, Hickey, Pell and Goodman were the other mainstays in a fine side. The top four scorers contributed 100 goals between them: Brittin 34, Goodman 27, Pell 22 and Hickey 17. The same eleven or twelve players were used almost exclusively, a lack of injuries certainly assisting the cause. Indeed the same starting eleven played 19 consecutive games between early November and late April. When Ken Harris dislocated his knee against Wokingham, it was simply popped back in and Harris played on as normal.

Ground improvements continued apace and a Development Fund was set up to enable the installation of floodlights, as more and more top amateur clubs were lighting up. A new tote competition helped to raise much of the required money. Bingo sessions, raffles and blanket collections also took place. There was a fairly steep rise in admission prices, although most of the complaints were from OAP's who were still being admitted free of charge. John Hewlett stated that the club reserved the right to withdraw the free pass from any pensioner making a nuisance of them self.

The playing surface at the time was in excellent condition. During the 'big freeze', Fulham, Crystal Palace and Reading all used Fetcham Grove for training and practice matches after Leatherhead became the first club in the country to clear their pitch of snow. The ground was repeatedly harrowed with sand mixed in to prevent it from re-freezing. A fair amount of national press coverage was received, although The Times referred to a *"Leatherwood FC"* [sic]. The club also experimented (successfully) with the waterproofing of footballs, which led to them keeping their shape and not getting so heavy.

At the end of the season, Dagenham and Maidenhead United were elected to the Premier Division of the Athenian League, although Leatherhead had performed convincing double victories over both sides. However, the Corinthian, Delphian and Athenian Leagues now merged and the Tanners, along with most fellow Corinthian sides, became members of the new First Division of the Athenian League.

And finally (in the style of the last item on News at Ten), a pet rabbit was discovered in the social club. No-one claimed him, so he was adopted by a committee member and given the name 'Tanner'.

1963/64

Leatherhead were fortunate that they were able to retain most of their championship winning side for the new campaign in the Athenian League. Left-back Ken Bird and winger Colin Spriggs were the only significant newcomers. Several of the old guard had earned nicknames, such as 'Old Bandy Legs' Neil Goodman because of his Popeye stance that made him look as though he had lost his horse and 'Wild Bill' Hickey, who returned from a close season tour of Canada with crew-cut and suntan (a bit more imaginative than Giggsy, Keano etc.). During the winter months indoor training sessions were held at RAF Headley Court.

K'S BEATEN BY TEN HEROIC TANNERS

Things started splendidly with three league wins and a 4-0 thrashing of the Rest of the League in the annual Championship Challenge match. During the opening game at Slough, it was reported that *"Leatherhead chased the ball like terriers, as though it contained fivers from the Great Train Robbery"*. An even more impressive 3-2 success against a Rod Haider inspired Kingstonian side continued the run and provided a first FA Cup victory for fifteen years. This was achieved despite being reduced to ten men for an hour, outfielder Brittin having to go in goal when keeper O'Malley went off with a broken nose. Leatherhead hung on after being 3-0 up, Neil Goodman's hat-trick giving him a goal tally of twelve in the first four games of the season. At the end of the match Goodman left the field ashen faced with exhaustion, socks round his ankles, mud stained and shirt outside his shorts and had to fight his way through cheering, back-slapping crowds to reach the changing rooms. An excellent crowd of 3,074 attended the 2nd qualifying round tie at Guildford City. The Southern Leaguers proved too strong, however, winning 5-1.

Redhill were beaten 2-0 in the Amateur Cup before 1,400 spectators at the Grove. The traditional shout of 'Redhill' was probably not required in this match. This shout originated in 1927 during the FA Amateur Cup semi-final at Highbury when the Reds took on a very strong Northern Nomads side. Redhill lost their goalkeeper through injury in the opening minutes and the remaining ten men were in danger of being overwhelmed by their bigger and more physical opponents. In a bid to head off a heavy defeat by wasting as much time as possible the Reds players resorted to booting the ball as far out of the ground as they could at every opportunity. The crowd soon cottoned on to this practice and shouted 'Redhill' every time this happened. Unfortunately, despite their antics, Redhill still lost 7-1.

Leatherhead stopped overnight for the first time, prior to the first round tie at Harwich and Parkeston, but a closely fought match was lost 2-4, the Tanners failing to make the most of their chances.

Walton and Hersham eliminated the men in green from the Surrey Senior Cup, albeit only after extra-time in a replay.

League form continued to be good, although not as spectacular as the previous season. For the game at Eastbourne in November, the players wore black armbands in memory of United States President Kennedy, following his assassination. A run of victories from the end of February pushed Leatherhead to the top of the table with only five games, all against their nearest challengers, to come. Erith and Belvedere were defeated home and away, 250 Tanners supporters travelling down for the game in Kent. Edgware were overcome 4-3 and, in front of 1,400 spectators, Worthing went down 3-0. A 3-5 defeat at the hands (and feet) of Worthing in the return match did not matter, the Greens were champions again by just one point from Worthing and Edgware, with Erith fourth. The victorious team made the short journey along the coast from Worthing to Brighton to paint the town green in celebration.

Athenian League Division One Final Table (Top 3)

Team	Played	Won	Drawn	Lost	For	Against	Points
Leatherhead	**26**	**18**	**3**	**5**	**86**	**45**	**39**
Worthing	26	18	2	6	76	40	38
Edgware Town	26	17	4	5	72	40	38

Neil Goodman ended the season as top scorer with 46 goals in only 37 matches. Kevin Brittin with 25 and Brian Pell with 22 also contributed significantly to the goals tally. Brittin was beginning to earn a reputation for spectacular overhead volleys, long before Mark Hughes came on the scene. Ken Harris and, for the second season running, Jock Wood, were ever present in the Tanners line-up, while Wood, Johnny Lewis and Brittin were all selected to represent the Surrey County FA during the season. Norman Douglas, employing a 4-2-4 formation, was proving to be a highly successful manager, although he did have to chain-smoke his way through matches.

Leatherhead's reserve side, now managed jointly by Billy Miller and Tom Dixon, reached the final of the Neale Trophy, a league cup competition for Athenian League reserve section members.

Fetcham Grove's first floodlights, consisting of eight 60 foot high towers providing 96,000 watts, were switched on in November 1963. The opening ceremony was filmed by the BBC and shown on 'Town and Around'. Club President Stuart Surridge flicked the switch and presented the team with a new red-numbered playing strip to mark the occasion. The inauguration match was against a Fulham side including George Cohen, Alan Mullery, Bobby Robson and Johnny Haynes. Haynes, who had recently become the first £100-a-week player,

scored the final goal in a 3-1 victory for the Cottagers, in front of an attendance of around 3,000. The first competitive game under the Fetcham Grove lights took place in December, against Dorking.

In March 1964 Leatherhead were honoured by being granted full membership of the Football Association. Gate receipts for the season nearly doubled again to £1,354. Sales of season tickets, priced at 32s 6d, had also increased markedly.

The Tanners were no slouches on the cricket pitch either. They won the Leatherhead Sports Association's 18-over a side competition, defeating Ashtead Cricket Club by six wickets in the final, Ken Harris contributing 32 not out.

One sad point to note was the death of Ivor Gibbon who had been Chairman for ten years and had served on the committee since the club's inception. Arthur Benn became the new Chairman.

1964/65

Having won the Division One championship, Leatherhead were duly promoted and now took their place in the Premier Division of the Athenian League. The close season had been busy with work carried out on drainage, levelling and general improvement of the pitch which led the referee of the seasons opening game to comment that the playing surface was now, "*the best for miles around*". There was no summer break for the players who continued to train throughout and benefited from a series of coaching courses run by future England manager Bobby Robson.

The Tanners kicked-off with a largely unchanged side captained by John 'Pepper' Phipps for the third consecutive season. The opening game resulted in a 3-2 loss at home to Leyton. Barnet were held in the second match, and then Southall were defeated 5-2, these three games attracting a total of 2,250 spectators. League results continued to be inconsistent as the side adjusted to the higher level. Highlights included the double against both Carshalton and Dagenham and a 2-1 success at Hayes whose side included Dave Bassett and Willie Smith as the Greens finished just below halfway in the final table.

'Shamateurism', or the payment of 'boot money' to supposedly amateur players, was rife and the Football Association attempted to stamp it out. There had been calls to either abolish amateurism altogether or revamp football in order to drastically sort out the way clubs were run, many blatantly paying 'boot money' to entice those who would rather earn tax free than turn professional and pay their dues. A new rigidly controlled expenses form and statutory declaration was enforced by the FA. Walton & Hersham Chairman, John Leech, threatened to, "*blow the lid off*" and name names. Amid the ensuing arguments several players walked out of Stompond Lane. Larry Pritchard, Peter Keary and Ray Francis all came to Leatherhead. In protest Walton held up Pritchard's registration for nearly a month. A few weeks later the Tanners played Walton away. In an unpleasant atmosphere a bad-tempered match took place, finishing 2-2. Leatherhead signed the FA declaration that no payment of any sort, other than expenses, would be made to players. They also reported a couple of unnamed clubs to the FA for offering illegal payments as an inducement to sign.

There were two stirring FA Cup ties at Fetcham Grove. Kingstonian were beaten 1-0 in front of a 2,325 crowd in a 2nd qualifying round replay before a narrow 2-1 loss to Guildford City at the next stage watched by another 2,000 plus gate. Leatherhead had taken the lead with twenty minutes to go but two late goals sealed victory for the Southern League professionals.

Isthmian League Woking were among the sides defeated as Leatherhead reached the Surrey Senior Cup Final for the first time. Here their opponents were Sutton United, the match played at Kingstonian in front of a disappointing 2,000 crowd. Larry Pritchard scored twice to give the Tanners a 2-0 advantage inside seventeen minutes and the supporters in green chanted "*easy*", but Sutton with Dario Gradi, Ted Powell and Keith Blunt among their ranks recovered in the second half to win 3-2 with goals from Trevor Bladon (2) and Blunt. Pritchard soon moved to Sutton gaining 50 England Amateur international caps in a long and distinguished career with the Gander Green Lane club.

There was also an appearance in the Surrey Invitation Cup Final. Woking were again defeated in a semi-final replay, Cards legend Charlie Mortimer scoring his final goal for the club, but the final was lost 2-1 to Guildford City.

Fetcham Grove was honoured to stage the Athenian Premier versus Athenian Divisions One and Two representative game in which Kevin Brittin, Jack O'Malley and Gordon Wood appeared for the Premier Division XI. Wood also became the first Leatherhead player to win a full Surrey County FA cap while Billy Miller and John Phipps completed the course and examination leading to FA coach status.

Neil Goodman, Brian Pell and Kevin Brittin were again at the head of the goal-scorers list. In what was now a very experienced Tanners side, nine players had passed 100 games for the club overall by the end of the season. Goodman (108 goals in 133 games) and Johnny Lewis who failed to score in 152 games, made their final appearances for the club. Apart from the Walton trio, new players appearing during the season included Les Gilson, a centre-half signed from Tooting and Mitcham, Barry Webb, an 18-year-old half-back or inside-forward signed from Bexley United, ex-Sutton United veteran Ted Shepherd and Brian Gibbs from Hayes.

1965/66

A change of management took place at the start of the 1965/66 season. Norman Douglas announced his impending departure to Australia and in order to avoid mid-season disruption, Billy Miller, a 31-year-old telephone engineer, who had been running the reserves and serving as Douglas's right-hand man, was appointed first team manager. Johnny Phipps, having retired from playing (although he did return for two further first team games), became assistant coach and reserve team manager. Miller's appointment was a popular decision amongst the players, despite his noted lack of leniency in training matters. By his own admission, Miller had not been a great player, but he was a great thinker about the game. He subscribed to Danny Blanchflower's philosophy, "*It's a great fallacy that the game is first, and about winning last. It's nothing of the kind. The game is about glory. It's about doing things in style, with a flourish, about going out and beating the other lot, not waiting for them to die of boredom.*". He was a good motivator; although once expletives had been deleted there was little that could be reproduced in print. Under Miller the progress started by Douglas was to be taken on to a new level.

Prominent players such as Jack O'Malley, Ken Harris, Ray Francis, Colin Spriggs, Kevin Brittin and Brian Pell remained and were bolstered by some important new signings. Bobby Adam, who had played centre-back for Sutton in the Amateur Cup Final, full-back Alan Brazier from Croydon Amateurs, winger Micky Goodall from Sutton and striker Keith Mills from Hendon all came into the side, Brazier becoming team captain. Goodall was only 5 feet 4 inches high but was a small bundle of explosive energy who could often out-jump six foot tall defenders. Mills had scored a hat-trick for Hendon against the England Amateur side.

There was an average start to the league campaign, but from the end of September, commencing with a 2-0 win over Finchley, the Tanners embarked on a fine run, only losing once in fourteen games up to March. That solitary defeat came at the hands of eventual champions Leyton. Form dipped again towards the end, as goal-scoring became a problem. Many Tanners games this season, totally dominated territorially on the balance of play, were lost by the odd goal, missed chances proving costly. A very creditable 4th place was achieved nonetheless.

Having defeated Chertsey, Guildford City provided the opposition for the third year running in the FA Cup. Leatherhead were just three minutes away from victory at Fetcham Grove but Guildford scrambled a 2-2 draw and went on to win the replay

In the Amateur Cup the Greens made their mark, starting rather than finishing at Wembley (Wembley FC that is). Wembley, Oxford City and Maidenhead United were removed as the 3rd round proper was reached for the first time. Lowly Hayes were the opponents at this stage and with a certain Peter Lavers leading their front line, their performance belied their league position. Captain Brazier, who was now playing at half-back, scored the two goals which earned a rematch at Hayes in which the Tanners triumphed 1-0, Brian Pell the scorer. Cup fever hit Leatherhead for the first time. 'Leatherhead for the Cup' was daubed on an Ashtead residence and national publicity received, one paper describing Leatherhead FC as, "*A little village side from the country*".
The quarter-final draw paired Leatherhead with Isthmian League Wealdstone. On the Middlesex club's Lower Mead ground 5,000 spectators witnessed a valiant fight by the Tanners which ultimately ended in a 1-2 defeat. The deciding goal was scored just four minutes from time, when a replay was the least that Leatherhead deserved. Stones went on to win the cup, conquering Hendon 3-1 in the final.

The Surrey Senior Cup saw an embarrassing 3-0 home loss to Athenian Division Two outfit Croydon Amateurs but over Whitsun 1966, Leatherhead took part in a four team international tournament at Mondorf-les-Bains in Luxembourg. Barnet had been previous English winners of the competition, named after Luxembourg's World Champion weightlifter, John Grun. A fete and dog show were among fund raising events organised to help pay for the trip. Home club Red Boys Differdange, including several players who had represented their country in the qualifying competition for the 1966 World Cup, and Stade Olympique Marlebach from France were each beaten 2-1 as the Tanners won the competition.

The Premier Midweek Floodlight League was also introduced this season. Leatherhead, along with many other Athenian clubs and Southern League sides such as Guildford, Crawley Town and Hillingdon Borough, became founder members, but with limited success initially. The first victory was not achieved until the seventh game, at Hounslow in February. The final game provided the Tanners with a splendid 3-2 victory at Guildford, in a match played as a four-pointer. The competition guaranteed regular midweek matches, which broke up the tedium of training and helped finances. For the spectators evening football in autumn and winter was something of a novelty with matches at the like of Slough, Wimbledon and Guildford attracting attendances in excess of one thousand in the early years of the competition.

Keary, Pell and Goodall were chosen to represent the Surrey FA, Pell was also selected for an FA Amateur XI and Alan Brazier appeared for the Civil Service side during the year.

The club, not for the first time, received a letter of congratulation from the FA, "*for the high standard of sportsmanship shown by Leatherhead Football Club on the field of play*".
In March, Kevin Brittin had sprung a major surprise by announcing that he had lost interest in playing and no longer wanted to be considered for selection. He left for Addlestone at the end of the season, generally though the club continued to inspire great loyalty amongst its players, fringe players such as Chris Harlow and George Ives spending many seasons in the reserves whilst making only an occasional first team appearance.

Off the pitch developments continued and plans were announced for the building of a new clubroom to include dressing rooms and boardroom, a scheme scheduled to cost in the region of £12,000. As usual a small band of supporters worked hard with paint brushes and carried out other odd-jobs in the close season, a practice continued to this day and vital to the continued running of the club.

1966/67

England's World Cup win brought about a resurgence of interest in the professional game. Amateur football was still racked by the continuing 'boot money' controversy, however. Many supposedly amateur players in the Isthmian and Athenian Leagues were said to be earning more money than the 'honest' professionals in the Southern League.

Substitutes were used for the first time in the 66/67 season, although only one per side at this stage and they were only supposed to be used in the event of injury. Ken Bird sat on the bench for the Tanners' opening game at Finchley. Ray Pert became the first playing substitute for Leatherhead during a Floodlight League match at Maidenhead.

Billy Miller was able to keep a largely settled side although a 4-3-3 formation was reverted to due to a lack of wingers. Alf Ramsey's wingless wonders had something to answer for. John Hilliard and Ian Meekin, both signed from Sutton, were the only significant first team arrivals, the red-headed Meekin arriving in November, to fill the problem centre-forward position. Brazier, O'Malley, Gibbs, Adam, Keary, Pell, Mills, Goodall and Francis remained as the core of the team. Most of the squad gained some form of representative honour at League, County or FA level. The team also had a new playing kit of emerald green shirts and shorts.

Leatherhead began their league campaign with a five match unbeaten run, this sequence ending with a 4-0 hammering by eventual champions Leyton. At home the Tanners were almost unbeatable, 10 clean sheets and a solitary defeat, with only Harwich taking maximum points from Fetcham Grove. If away form had been better the club would have improved upon, rather than equalled, their best league placing of fourth. Missed penalties also proved expensive, various takers failed to find the back of the net on six separate occasions.

Younger supporters were warned not to play their own games on the grass banking during matches, as it was disturbing to spectators. In some previous seasons the action on the grass bank might have provided more entertainment than that on the pitch, but this was not likely at this time.

Impressive performances took place in all three cup competitions. The new system of zoning FA Cup draws enabled Leatherhead to meet a more wide ranging spread of opponents. Isthmian clubs Barking and Clapton, as well as Maidenhead United, were dismissed as the final qualifying round was reached for the first time. At this stage Athenian Division One side Chesham United 'giant-killed' the Tanners, 2-1. Three days later Chesham were defeated in the Floodlight League. Bobby Adam was sent-off for the third time in less than a year, as some scores were settled from the cup meeting.

The Amateur Cup produced away victories at Bishop's Stortford, then top of the Athenian Premier, Northern League Tow Law Town and Isthmian's Clapton. The Tow Law match had taken Leatherhead into uncharted territory, and to one of the highest grounds in the country. The team left Kings Cross at 6 p.m. on the Friday and stayed overnight in Darlington. Two trainloads of Tanners supporters and one intrepid person on a scooter (motorised presumably) travelled the following day. In the game itself, Tow Law missed a penalty shortly before Pell scored the only goal for Leatherhead and thereafter Tanners "*defensive curtain*" held firm. The players return train journey was delayed by some fifteen minutes because one of the players was busy celebrating the team's success with a young lady on some handy mail sacks and was not prepared to board until he had completed his conquest. The Durham based side later came to Fetcham Grove on the eve of the Amateur Cup final for a friendly, with the Tanners again victorious, this time 2-0. Johnny Phipps was sent on spying missions to watch forthcoming opponents and Billy Miller was always confident of victory, whoever the opposition. The quarter-final round again proved to be the stumbling block, but it took probably the best amateur side at the time to remove Leatherhead from the competition. Hendon had reached the last two Amateur Cup finals, winning the trophy in 1965, and their side contained five Amateur internationals. Fetcham Grove saw its then record attendance of 4,100. The town was abuzz, with cars parked all the way down to Fetcham village. One supporter marched round the ground banging a large drum and chanting *"Tanners…Tanners"*. He was soon joined by an army of small lads, waving their scarves. Hendon goalkeeper John Swannell was pelted with lumps of mud, but this experience did not put him off his game (or prevent him signing for Leatherhead some years later). As Hendon played in green, the Tanners had to wear a change strip of amber and black. After half an hour of action a Meekin penalty was brilliantly saved by Swannell. In the ensuing scramble some fans ran onto the pitch believing the Tanners had scored but Hendon cleared the ball and swiftly broke away to score the opening goal. A second shortly after the interval negated Miller's half-time team talk and Hendon went on to claim a 3-0 success.

Three Isthmian clubs were beaten as Leatherhead progressed to their second Surrey Senior Cup final. Dulwich Hamlet, who had twice thrashed the Tanners in previous meetings, Woking and Sutton, then top of the Isthmian League, all fell to the Greens. Eight times previous winners of the Surrey Cup, Kingstonian, were the opposition in the final played at Tooting and Mitcham's Sandy Lane ground. K's, including England Amateur international Rod Haider, were 'gifted' a two goal lead through defensive errors, but Leatherhead stormed back in the second half, with a superb strike from Ian Meekin. He was being forced away from goal when, appropriately for a Tanner, he turned on a sixpence and unleashed a thunderbolt shot that the keeper hardly saw until it was in the net. Goodall hit the post and there were several other near misses. Many of the crowd thought Pell had scored, but it was in the side netting, just the wrong side of the post and K's clung on to win 2-1

Leatherhead finished last of the twelve clubs competing in the Premier Midweek Floodlight League but did record a notable 6-2 thrashing of Guildford City in this competition.

At the end of the season, Arthur Benn resigned as Chairman due to work commitments and was replaced by Chris Luff who had already carried out tremendous work in furthering the interests of Leatherhead Football Club.

Several new faces appeared in the side towards the end of the season. Dave (Nobby) Skinner, a 20-year-old striker came from Leatherhead Casuals and soon became known for his defence splitting runs and spectacular goals, gradually inheriting the centre-forward role from Brian Pell. Skinner had previously spent six months at West Ham United, only to be rejected by Ron Greenwood who declined to fork out the £500 sum decreed for an amateur under FA rules. Goalkeeper Micky Cuthbert stepped up from the reserves and Bobby Taylor arrived from Sutton United. Taylor had received a call-up for the England Amateur side, until it was discovered that he had in fact been born in Northern Ireland! A planned tour to Germany had to be cancelled due to problems with the travel agents.

1967/68

Leatherhead Football Club had 'come of age', reaching their 21st anniversary in 1967 and a special dinner was held at Tyrells Wood Golf Club to celebrate the occasion. There were further changes on the Board, Sidney Ranger replacing Leslie Ellis as Secretary and F. C. Dean taking over from John Hewlett as Treasurer. The Leatherhead team were being described as big, skilful, determined and quick moving. Manager Miller had attended the same summer coaching course as Jack Charlton and Bobby Robson while Ken Cuthbert, father of goalkeeper Micky, was the new trainer.

On the playing front the season got off to a tremendous start with eight wins and a draw in the first nine matches, taking the Tanners to the top of the league. Unfortunately, the bubble burst with defeat by lowly Maidenhead. With another shock loss to Southall, a poor 90 minutes on the pitch was followed by a 90 minute grilling in the dressing room by Miller. They were made to suffer again in training on the following Tuesday. With injuries not helping, league results suffered and early exits were made from the major knockout competitions. By March 1968 rumours were circulating of Miller's impending dismissal. The Management Committee reacted quickly and blaming, *"certain busy-bodies with a self-advertised lack of intelligence"* for the rumours, had no hesitation in unanimously reappointing Miller as manager for the following season. Results did improve towards the end of the campaign, including a 9-0 thrashing of Hemel Hempstead in which Ian Meekin scored five goals, and a respectable final league standing of 5th was achieved. There was another fiery clash with Walton and Hersham. Keith Mills punched the Swan's Ted Crow, among numerous off-the-ball incidents, prompting the referee to call all the players to the centre-circle and give out a stern warning to *"cool it"*.

The Tanners did appear in the Surrey Senior Shield final, but lost 2-3 to Woking. Sammy Malcolmson, playing only his third game for the Cards, scored a hat-trick and went on to represent New Zealand in World Cup qualifiers.

Ken Bird, Colin Spriggs and Micky Goodall had left the club, Goodall to play for a Hampshire League side nearer to his home. O'Malley and Cuthbert shared goalkeeping duties, with prominent outfield roles played by Gibbs, Adam, Brazier, Keary, Meekin, Mills, Webb, Taylor, Skinner and Pell. Jimmy Cooley from Chesham, Phil 'The Tank' Dade from Tooting and Mitcham and Dave Juneman from Wimbledon, who topped the appearances chart, all came into the side. Juneman was said to be the double of Peter Osgood in terms of looks and gait. The use of substitutes was growing and it was beginning to appear that a number of 'tactical injuries' were being incurred. A series of 'meet the players' evenings was held throughout the season in an effort to get supporters to identify more closely with the club and perhaps to try and reduce the barracking of players from some sections of the crowd. There was also a brief tour of Jersey at Whitsun. Due to a misunderstanding, the only football played was on the beach. Peter Keary earned the nickname 'Potato' for his consumption levels of the famous Jersey vegetable, while Ray Francis and Dave Wall provided the in-house comedy.

Strenuous efforts were made to raise extra revenue for the club to meet the cost of the ambitious ground development plans. Bunny Oram, former player Tommy Temlett and Harry 'Taff' Jones and his wife Jean were among the helpers. A Junior Tanners Association was also set up to encourage youngsters to assist with the running of the club. Leatherhead still found time to help other bodies and a fundraising match against a celebrity BBC United XI was held in aid of the Thorndike Theatre Project. Many of the BBC players were in a 'soap' of the time called 'United', which was not quite as successful as 'Eastenders'. The Crescent Cinema had recently been demolished to make way for the new theatre that was to be opened by Princess Margaret in 1969.

1968/69

The various Surrey County FA competitions provided most progress on the field of play. In the two FA knockout tournaments Leatherhead came up against very strong opposition at an early stage. Molesey were defeated in the 1st qualifying round of the FA Cup, but at the next stage the Tanners were drawn away to Walton and Hersham, then top of the Athenian Premier with a 100% league record. A near 2,000 crowd watched the match which Walton eventually won 4-1. The Greens had held the home side to 1-1 at half-time but faded after the break. Even so, two goals in the last five minutes were required to give the final score a comprehensive look.

In the Amateur Cup mighty Isthmian League champions and leaders Enfield, whose side contained seven Amateur internationals, were the opposition in the 1st round. A battling performance by the Tanners, with Caterer and Adam superb in defence secured a deserved 0-0 draw at Southbury Road.

Unfortunately, on the day of the replay Nobby Skinner was involved in a different type of match and strenuous efforts to bring the time of his wedding forward were to no avail! Despite the absence of Skinner's dynamite boots, Leatherhead again held Enfield, this time 1-1 after extra-time. Micky Cuthbert had a fine game in goal, Ian Meekin scored, and in the last minute a Barry Webb shot brought a miraculous save from Wolstenholme in the Enfield goal. A third meeting of the two sides took place at Dulwich, in icy conditions which nullified ball skills, and on this occasion Enfield edged home 1-0 through a Tony Harding header.

A series of narrow victories earned Leatherhead a place in the Surrey Senior Cup final for the third time in five years. Dorking (in a replay), Walton and Hersham (sweet revenge) and Tooting and Mitcham were all pipped by the same 1-0 scoreline. Gander Green Lane, Sutton staged the final with Redhill and this time the Tanners were victorious with a fine team performance. Skinner was set up by Webb and Mills for the first, after quarter of an hour. A back header by Webb and a fine shot by Mills put Leatherhead 3-0 up with a late consolation effort from the Reds leaving a 3-1 scoreline. The attendance was just below 1,200, not helped by the fact that the Home Internationals were being shown live by the BBC at the same time.

Redhill were also defeated in the Surrey Senior Shield final, this time by 1-0, Webb the scorer from the penalty spot. Barry Webb was a constant hard worker and deadly from 12 yards, greatly improving Leatherhead's spot-kick success rate. Micky Cuthbert also played despite having received three cracked ribs in the Senior Cup final. With further honours gained by the reserves in the Surrey Intermediate Cup (2-0 v Chessington and Hook in the final) history was created. It was the only time that one club had won all of the Surrey Senior and Intermediate Challenge Cups in one season. A civic reception was held and the Surrey FA presented the club with a special commemorative plaque to acknowledge the achievement. For good measure, Leatherhead also reached the final of the East Surrey Charities Cup, which had to be held over to the following season, and Leatherhead Casuals won the Surrey Junior Cup.

For a change league form was indifferent at the start of the season but improved later. There was a bad tempered game at Hornchurch during which Bob Taylor became the first Tanner to be sent-off for three years, along with two Urchins. Future Chelsea legend Micky Droy was part of a strong Slough side that completed the double over Leatherhead. However, from mid-November until the end of the campaign, the only league defeat was by a narrow 2-1 margin at Walton in another unpleasant game, which highlighted the running feud between the sides. The match, watched by over 2,000 spectators, threatened to boil over and there were numerous late tackles. A report stated that the match, "*would not have been out of place in Buenos Aires*". The Stompond Lane side suffered only two losses all season on their way to the championship. The Tanners, utilising swift counter attacks allied to a solid defence, finished fourth for the third time in four years and with their highest points tally so far.

Alan Brazier, Bobby Taylor, Bobby Adam, Phil Dade, Keith Mills, Ian Meekin, Nobby Skinner, Barry Webb and Micky Cuthbert were all significant first team members during the year but there were several changes on the playing staff. No fewer than three players - Peter Keary, Brian Pell and John Hilliard - were forced to give up the game through injury, although Pell (having set a record at the time of 281 first team appearances, scoring 111 goals), returned to play a few reserve team games the following season. Jack O'Malley (260 games for the club) and Brian Gibbs retired, O'Malley becoming the first player to be elected to the club's Management Committee. Dave Juneman moved to Southall and later set up some sort of record by converting 42 consecutive penalties for Tooting and Mitcham between 1974 and 1977. Kevin Brittin returned from Addlestone and the squad was further strengthened, particularly in the half-back department, with some major new arrivals. Barrie Davies, a Welsh midfield dynamo from Hendon, British Army player Alan Goucher, accomplished former Chesham and Hayes centre-back Brian Caterer and winger Tony Slade from Wealdstone all made their mark. Caterer made his debut for Brentford and a day later played for Leatherhead in a Floodlight League match at Redhill. Slade had been in the Tooting and Mitcham side that took Nottingham Forest to a replay in the FA Cup 4th round of 1958/59. Ian McGuire, a highly regarded young goalkeeper from Tooting, also came to the Grove. The first team kept 27 clean sheets during the season with a game plan based on strong defence and swift counter-attack. These methods were not always appreciated by the fans. John Hewlett once again called for more support and attacked the apathy of many local townsfolk.

The ground development plans continued apace. Planning permission was obtained, architects instructed, artists impressions drawn of the new clubhouse and by April 1969 the Bills of Quantity had arrived. A charity match against the International Club was played to help raise funds for the new buildings. Johnny Haynes, John Byrne, Bobby Robson, Jimmy Hill, Dave Sexton and Billy Wright were among the stars appearing. Hill was the star of the show, not yet offering match analysis, but keeping the crowd entertained with flashy shots, passes and flicks as well as witty asides to the crowd and much arm waving. The club's ambitious plans received a setback in September 1968 when Fetcham Grove suffered its worst ever flooding. Incessant rain caused the River Mole to burst its banks. Water poured through the town engulfing 200 houses and the football club, being right beside the river, inevitably suffered. Hundreds of pounds worth of damage was caused. Everything was covered in thick cloying mud and slime but, in true fighting spirit, many volunteers helped with mopping-up operations. One lady, who had turned up at the club for the Friday night bingo session, gave the situation a quick appraisal and promptly removed hat and coat and commenced scrubbing walls. Remarkably, only one first team match had to be postponed.

1969/70

A Charlton Athletic reserve side came to Fetcham Grove for a pre-season friendly. Former Ipswich Town and England forward Ray Crawford scored for Charlton but Leatherhead triumphed 3-1. A few years later Crawford was one of the heroes, scoring twice, as Colchester defeated Leeds in the FA Cup.

After an inconsistent start, the highlight of which was scoring three goals in the last ten minutes to win 4-2 at Redhill, league form settled down nicely. In a fifteen match run from the end of September, Hayes were the only side to lower the Tanners' colours and a top of the table spot was achieved. As the championship race hotted up, Leatherhead had to endure a six-week spell without an Athenian League game. This lay-off may well have contributed to the crucial defeats in the two ensuing matches, 2-0 at home to Slough and 2-1 away to Bishop's Stortford. The Tanners slipped to a finishing position of fifth, albeit with their highest points tally yet.

Once again the men in green were unfortunate enough to draw very tough opposition in the early rounds of the major cup competitions. Walton and Hersham won 1-0 at Fetcham Grove in the FA Cup. An anticipated crowd of 1,500 turned out to be 2,400 and Walton suffered some frightening intimidation, fuelled no doubt by past grievances.

Sutton United barred the way in both FA Amateur and Surrey Senior competitions. It was a much weakened Leatherhead side that went to Gander Green Lane for the Amateur Cup first round tie. In addition to injuries, Adam, Mills and Davies were all suspended, having been sent-off in previous matches. Aggressive performances could prove costly. This despite the fact that you had to practically decapitate an opponent before the referee would even consider putting your name in his little black book. Davies had tigerish qualities, but was often more in trouble for arguing with referees. In front of 1,700 spectators the normally reliable Barry Webb did not have a good game. He missed a second minute penalty and then gifted Sutton the first of their two unopposed goals. The Tanners returned to Sutton in the Surrey Senior Cup, just a week after the U's had taken on the mighty Leeds United in the 4th round of the FA Cup. Leatherhead lost again, this time 3-0, with the last goal scored by John Faulkner. Faulkner signed for Leeds shortly after and later enjoyed a successful spell at Luton Town.

Leatherhead did have their most successful season in the Premier Midweek Floodlight League. Unbeaten in their fourteen section games, they qualified for a three way play-off for the championship. Wycombe Wanderers were held 2-2 on the Loakes Park slope, the Tanners coming from 0-2 down to draw, amid ugly scenes, as a section of the Wycombe supporters, incensed by some heavy tackling and poor refereeing, jostled and pushed the Leatherhead players and match officials as they left the pitch. Walton and Hersham were defeated 2-1 at Fetcham Grove in the next match, but a 3-1 home defeat by Wycombe cost the title. At this game about 100, mainly skinheaded, youths invaded the pitch intent on revenge for the events at Wycombe. John Hewlett made a loudspeaker plea for calm while stewards and police intervened to prevent a major disturbance. Walton failed to play the return match with Leatherhead and at a meeting of the league's committee, Wycombe were awarded the championship with Leatherhead runners-up.

A brief tour of Jersey at the end of May brought convincing victories over Georgetown, 4-0 and First Tower United, 8-1.

Kevin Brittin (94 goals in 187 appearances), Ray Francis (163 appearances) and Tony Slade had either retired or left the club, with Ian Meekin departing mid-season. Meekin, who was very accomplished in bringing the ball under control from any angle (or had a good first touch in modern terms), played 124 games for Tanners, scoring 47 goals. New arrivals in the first team squad included Micky Howard and Tony McGuiness, a defender from Wealdstone. The rest of the side remained fairly constant with Adam, Davies, Cuthbert, Taylor, Caterer, Goucher, Mills, Skinner, Brazier, Dade and Webb all featuring prominently. Skinner and Webb topped the scorers chart. Webb was reported at the time as being, "*deceptively slow*" - is this a compliment?

The reserve side, managed by Dave Wall, had a highly successful campaign, winning the Athenian League Premier Division (Reserve Section) championship. Peter Keary assisted Wall with running the team and Brian Pell even played a few games to help out during an injury crisis.

Leatherhead's links with Surrey County Cricket Club were strengthened. Stuart Surridge had been President for some years and now former Surrey and England batsman Ken Barrington joined the Management Committee at Fetcham Grove.

Social and fund raising activities were thriving. The Freddie Lunn Duo provided music for a Christmas dance, the club shop was doing a roaring trade in Terylene ties at 18 shillings each and the Junior Tanners Association had over 50 members. There was also an Away Travel Club, a 200 club, a darts team and the ever popular bingo sessions. The ground development proposals however, were only progressing very slowly and had to be trimmed down due to rising costs.

Overall, another fairly good season and Leatherhead Football Club's name was beginning to spread. Charles Buchan's Football Monthly ran a whole page article on the club headed 'Progress, Progress… that's Leatherhead'. This piece was written by Norman Acland, the celebrated sports writer, aged eighty at the time and also the father of actor Joss.

CHAPTER TWELVE - THE GLORY YEARS

The 1970s heralded an era of short shorts, long hair and, for Leatherhead, long cup runs. It was to be the greatest period in the club's history and put the town well and truly on the football map. The introduction of decimalisation saw an end to the faithful tanner coin but in its stead a new Tanner became equally famous.

It was an age of mass mobility. Increasing car ownership meant that people could easily travel further to watch top flight League football. The post-war feeling of community had largely gone and decreasing numbers identified with their local town team. The combined population of Leatherhead and Fetcham had now reached 17,500.

Criminal acts were committed against society in the form of hooliganism and fashion sense. New musical forces emerged from progressive rock to disco and on to punk and new wave. A little known punk classic of the time was 'Nothing to do in a town like Leatherhead'. That song's creators, The Head, had presumably not been to Fetcham Grove on a Saturday afternoon.

1970/71

During the season the Leatherhead side underwent a number of changes in playing personnel. Bobby Taylor (Tooting and Mitcham), Brian Caterer (Hayes), Alan Goucher (Oxford City), Tony McGuiness and Mike Howard departed. Howard was harshly described as, "*brilliant with his head but useless with his feet and no great loss to the team*". Goucher went on to take part in the longest running FA Cup tie on record. Oxford City and Alvechurch took six games to force a result in their 71/72 4th qualifying round encounter and Goucher scored Oxford's equaliser in the second replay at Birmingham City's St. Andrews ground. Cuthbert, Strong, Brazier, Davies, Mills, Skinner and Webb remained as the backbone of the team and there were some important new arrivals. Former Slough and Southall players Freddie Slade and highly rated striker Peter Lavers came to the Grove. Dave Reid, the son of the former Portsmouth and Scotland international Dougie Reid, was signed from Andover. He had also appeared in the youth teams at Portsmouth and Southampton, helping introduce Mick Channon to football. After three games up front, a tactical switch saw 'Reidy' moved to centre-half where he was to remain for over 500 games, gaining renown for his power in the air and rocket like free-kicks. Adrian Hill, later to manage Leatherhead and serve Epsom and Ewell as both player and manager had a few months with the Tanners before returning to his former club, Redhill. Derek Gamblin, the England Amateur international right-back, came from Sutton United but despite playing for his country and for the Great Britain Olympic side, failed to hold down a regular place at Leatherhead and departed before the season was over.

Only Grays lowered Leatherhead's colours in the first eight league matches as the Tanners challenged Dagenham at the top of the table, although officials were concerned about flagging gates. A run of three straight defeats followed including home reverses against Walton and Hersham and Dagenham.

It was, however, as cup fighters that the Fetcham Grove outfit were becoming renowned. Lavers scored his first hat-trick for the club as Barking were dispatched 3-1 in the 1st qualifying round of the FA Cup. Another Isthmian club, Tooting and Mitcham United, were seen off 2-1 at Sandy Lane and fellow Athenian's Grays comprehensively beaten 3-0 at the Grove. Mighty Southern Leaguers Wimbledon were the opponents in the final qualifying round. In front of a 1,350 crowd, Keith Mills put the ball past Dickie Guy to give Leatherhead the lead. Mills' boisterous style of play was ideally suited to the rough and tumble of cup football. Leatherhead outplayed Wimbledon for long periods and with time running out it was beginning to look as though a place in the competition proper was to be achieved. Eddie Bailham had other ideas however, and two goals by him in the last twenty minutes saw the Dons progress at the Tanners expense.

League form meanwhile, continued to be patchy. For the home match with Hayes, supporters shovelled snow from the touchlines and used pickaxes to chip away ice from the centre circle to get the game on. They then wished they had not bothered, as the team slumped to their fourth consecutive loss without scoring a goal. This put paid to any realistic hopes of Athenian League glory and was not the best preparation for the Amateur Cup campaign.

What was to be a marathon run began at Eastern Counties club Stowmarket Town with a 2-2 draw. The slope was so bad that it was described as, *"like playing on the side of Box Hill"*. Gamblin gave a goal away when his back pass failed to negotiate the incline and a home forward nipped in to score. The replay at the Grove again finished 2-2 and it took a rare pair of goals from Barrie Davies and one from Mills to end the Suffolk club's stubborn resistance, by 3-2, in a third match played at Enfield. There was growing support for Davies (known as 'Mighty Atom' or 'Mr Perpetual Motion' in the press and as 'Mickey Mouse' to his team-mates) to be honoured by Wales at Amateur international level. The next three rounds produced very tough matches, all going to replays before Tanners' battling spirit (and not a little luck) won the day. Mills scored the only goal over two games with Dulwich and Nobby Skinner got the extra-time winner against Boreham Wood after a mazy George Best like run. Skinner was probably still 'fired up' after a fiery exchange of words with Billy Miller at the start of the extra period. Over 2,600 spectators watched the quarter-final at Hayes, another Skinner goal ensuring a 1-1 draw. 1,500 attended the Fetcham Grove replay, striker Ronnie Fruen, who had only recently signed from Hayes, netting the only score against his former club. Great scenes of jubilation followed the match, with supporters dancing on the pitch and singing in the clubroom.

Nevertheless, the lack of support from the town prompted one follower to pen a poem:

> 'Now all you folk in Leatherhead, take heed of what I say
> You've got a really smashing football team
> They've reached the semi-final and you really should be proud
> The way they play is really quite a dream
>
> You seem so darned half-hearted, you never cheer them on
> They need encouraging, the same as we
> I know they'll play their hearts out, if you just give them a chance
> It doesn't cost you much, a cheer is free'

It's unlikely that the Poet Laureate at the time was concerned about losing his job.

One step from Wembley in the Amateur Cup, but the Tanners faced a 230-mile trek to Bolton's old Burnden Park ground for the semi-final with powerful Cheshire club Skelmersdale United. Seven coach loads and many more under their own steam followed Leatherhead. The Northerners, who had thumped Wycombe 3-0 away in the quarter-final, were too strong on the day and in front of 7,085 spectators, goals by Dickin on 70 minutes and Windsor, a minute from time, shattered the Leatherhead dream. Skelmersdale went on to defeat Dagenham 4-1 in the final before turning semi-professional and joining the Northern Premier League. Miller was disappointed but proud of his team and fine hospitality was shown to the Leatherhead followers in the Bolton Wanderers Supporters Club after the game.

A very good Walton and Hersham side, marshalled by Dave Bassett and destined for the Isthmian League, ended the Tanners' interest in two other competitions. The Stompond Lane side triumphed by 3-1 in a semi-final replay of the Surrey Senior Cup marred by crowd trouble. A Leatherhead supporter was hospitalised after being slashed and a Tanners coach was 'bricked'. In the Premier Midweek Floodlight League Walton were victorious by 1-0, also at the semi-final stage, after

Leatherhead had won their section for the second year running.

The progress made in the various cup competitions left the Tanners with a fixture pile-up and for the last couple of months three or four games a week had to be played. Not surprisingly league form remained inconsistent and the final position of sixth was quite reasonable considering. Players making their first team debuts during this crowded end of season run-in included teenagers Derek Casey, who was also appearing in the reserve and youth teams for Fulham, Derek Wells and John Cooper, a 19-year-old utility player who had been with Fulham reserves and the youth teams of West Ham and Brentford. A mark of the toughness of Leatherhead's training regime is borne testament to by Cooper who, despite being used to full-time training, was physically sick after his first Leatherhead training session at Headley Court.

Representative honours were commonplace among the Leatherhead players. In addition to Derek Gamblin being in the Great Britain amateur side, Nobby Skinner was in the England squad, Reid, Hill, Skinner, Brazier and Adam appeared for FA XI's and Brazier, Reid, Davies and Strong performed for the Athenian League team. In just eight years of Athenian membership no fewer than 20 Tanners had appeared for the League's representative sides. Bobby Mapleson, then a 17-year-old in the reserves, represented Surrey Youth. Overall it was a highly successful season despite the lack of medals and trophies. Top scorers for the campaign were Keith Mills with 27 goals and Pete Lavers with 21.

Off the pitch, the hard working committee pressed on with their ambitious ground development plans despite apathy from some quarters. Fencing and painting work was carried out in the close season and a Supporters Club shop, run by Dave Deluce and Bob Belcher, had been set up just inside the main gates at the ground.

1971/72

Paul Proctor, a midfielder from Addlestone, was the main newcomer to the Leatherhead ranks, although youngsters Barry Friend and in goal, Chris Jolly, began to appear as the season wore on. Bobby Adam (288 appearances) and Keith Mills (266 appearances, 91 goals) left for Horsham early in the season, Jimmy Strong going to Sutton United. Ron Fruen was constantly barracked by a section of supporters, who were told to, "*leave off him*" by Miller.

J. R. Garrett became the new Club Treasurer with most of the other places on the Board remaining unchanged. Among other 'behind the scenes' personnel were Dennis Brennan, Sidney Ranger and Jean Jones heading the Social Committee and Mick Bellerby with the Tanners Supporters Club.

Pre-season friendlies included a weekend trip to the Midlands to play Alvechurch and Moor Green and once the competitive matches began the Tanners had a good settled side. Only one of the first fourteen league and cup games was lost, this run including excellent league results at home to Slough (1-0) and away to Dagenham (1-1) and FA Cup progress at the expense of Erith and Belvedere. Leatherhead had needed a last minute equaliser from Pete Lavers to earn a replay with Erith but at the next hurdle the Tanners went down 2-3 at Bexley United, despite two more goals from the prolific Lavers.

Athenian League form remained consistently good. Slough were held 1-1 away in a top of the table encounter, three goals in the last twenty five minutes rescued a point at Tilbury and there was only one defeat in ten matches prior to the start of the Amateur Cup campaign.
Dagenham were drawn to play at Fetcham Grove in the opening round and in a cracking match, played out in front of a 1,500 crowd, the Tanners celebrated the announcement that they had been elected to the Isthmian League for the following season with a 2-1 victory. The referee said that the

game was one of the most exciting he had ever officiated at and would have graced the final itself. It took a Webb penalty five minutes from time to settle it. Seventeen other clubs, including Dagenham, had challenged for a place in the Isthmian League. Leatherhead's election was a tribute to the lobbying and hard work of Chairman Chris Luff in particular.180 Leatherhead supporters travelled by coach alone for the next Amateur Cup tie at Oxford City. The result was a comprehensive 3-0 success, and another Isthmian club, Leytonstone, were defeated after a replay in round three as the Greens continued to suggest that they were most deserving of a place in the higher league.

Renowned cup fighters from the north-east, Blyth Spartans, who had only narrowly lost to Reading in the FA Cup, opposed the Tanners in the quarter-final. 4,000 spectators attended the match in Northumberland, a fine shot by Lavers providing the second half equaliser to Blyth's scrambled first half effort. The Fetcham Grove replay was a niggly, scrappy affair. Six players were booked and Leatherhead, sorely missing Skinner and the suspended Lavers, went down 1-0, Nixon scoring the only goal. The gate of 2,500 included about 1,000 Blyth supporters and drew comment from several quarters. Describing the 'low crowds', the programme editor believed that Leatherhead may have previously been an ostrich preserve, with it's inhabitants burying their heads in the sand, oblivious to the town's Amateur Cup runs. Some complained about 'the exorbitant admission charge' of 20 or 30 pence for cup ties, compared to 15 pence for league games. Decimalisation had only just taken place.

Football hooliganism was rife at the time. Even Leatherhead were affected, particularly at big cup ties when many supporters who would normally watch a Football League team would attend. Police were called to deal with fighting before and after the Blyth game. Colin Ward, in more recent times Commercial Manager at Leatherhead, wrote in his best selling book 'Steaming In' about his life with the hooligans and recalled his early teenage days following the Tanners. At the Blyth game the Geordies placed a flag and two scarves in the shape of a cross in the centre circle. Ward and three mates decided to run onto the pitch and grab the scarves:

> 'I was immediately struck by how muddy the pitch was. I could hardly keep my feet. We ran out to the centre to the cheers of the Shed ringing in our ears. I snapped the flag in half, and we stamped on the scarves then held them aloft like Indians holding up scalps. All four of us were laughing aloud! What a giggle! We showed the Geordies. I didn't even hear the growling and swearing coming from the Blyth fans' section, but the next thing I knew there were four gorillas coming across the pitch at us. I don't think a discussion of football was on their minds. Trevor was already heading back to the Shed, and it was every man for himself.
> 'Grab the scarves,' shouted Trevor.
> Keith and I snatched them up and we headed off towards the goal. I suddenly realised that these Geordie loonies wanted Keith and me. I tried to speed up but the faster I tried to run, the slower I seemed to be going. I turned around and one of them seemed to have gained twenty yards in ten paces. I dropped the scarf I was holding and so did Keith, and we headed away towards the sanctuary of the Shed. They reached the scarves, picked them up, gave a 'V' sign and turned away. We were feted like returning war heroes.'

'The Shed' or 'Shack', located next to the player's tunnel, was the preferred area for the Tanners' hard core supporters. When 'I was born under a Leatherhead shack' was sung to the 'tune' of 'Wand'rin' Star', by the massed green and white ranks, Lee Marvin might have wished he had stuck to acting.

Sutton United removed the Tanners from the Surrey Senior Cup at the first round stage although Leatherhead dominated the game at Fetcham Grove and the U's had trailed 1-0 until the very last minute, before forcing a replay, which they won 3-1.

The cup defeats affected league performances to some extent and several losses put the championship out of reach. Nevertheless, Leatherhead bowed out from the Athenian League with their highest final placing of 3rd, behind Slough and Dagenham.

The Athenian League's reserve section had been wound up and the Tanners 2nd XI (managed by Dave Wall and Peter Keary) became founder members of a new reserve team competition, the Suburban League. They had a fine season winning 23, drawing 4 and losing 3 of their 30 league games to become inaugural champions by one point from Sutton and then defeated Metropolitan Police 3-1 in a replay of the League Cup final, to clinch the double. Among this reserve side were Norman Cairns and Jimmy Rochester, both sons of former club stalwarts, the veteran Kevin Brittin and a very young Jimmy Richardson.

Barrie Davies at last got his amateur international call-up for Wales, making his debut against England, and Dave Reid was in the England squad against Scotland. In addition to these two, Nobby Skinner, Derek Wells and Alan Brazier all appeared for FA XI's.

1972/73

Chris Kelly, the former Sutton, Tooting and Epsom striker, arrived at Fetcham Grove and promptly scored a hat-trick in a pre-season friendly at Epsom and Ewell. With Micky Cuthbert approaching retirement and Chris Jolly going off to University, goalkeepers Peter Smith and Dave Roffey were signed, Smith becoming the regular custodian.

The Tanners made an inauspicious Isthmian League debut losing 1-0 at home to Walthamstow Avenue, picked up their first point in a 2-2 draw at Tooting, despite having Pete Lavers sent-off and claimed their first victory in the third match, 2-0 at Enfield, Derek Casey scoring both goals. A run of four straight defeats came soon after. Billy Miller was baffled by his side's inconsistency and the struggle to score goals, but Leatherhead began to put their game together and were soon racing up the table. Only four further league games out of thirty three played were lost. A home and away double was achieved against Wycombe Wanderers during this sequence. There were over 2,000 patrons at Loakes Park to see Kelly sent-off and Nobby Skinner score an injury time winner. At Fetcham Grove, Barry Friend got the only goal in a match dominated by Wycombe, and Dave Reid was booked after squaring up to team-mate Barrie Davies, something of a mismatch apart from anything else. There was a general clampdown on foul play that led to a marked increase in the number of bookings and dismissals. Tanners had 2 sent-off and 16 booked during the course of the season. When Hendon came to the Grove in March their 1-0 success clinched the championship with the Leatherhead forwards unable to find a way past John Swannell and a rock solid defence. The Tanners finished in third place, a position that, at the time of writing, has not been bettered.

With a 42 match league programme to complete, as opposed to 30 games in the Athenian, Leatherhead withdrew from the Premier Midweek Floodlight League. Possibly through concentrating on their new league status, the Tanners found little joy in cup competition. A semi-final place in the Surrey Senior Cup was attained, but Kingstonian were 3-2 victors at this stage.

Various successes were achieved in the international arena however. An Easter tour of the Channel Islands yielded victories over the 'national' sides of both Jersey and Guernsey. A 6-2 win in Jersey won Leatherhead the Sir Cyril Black Visitors' Trophy and a 1-0 triumph over Guernsey saw Tanners take the Victory Cup. Guernsey had defeated Wycombe Wanderers the previous year. Peter Smith missed the tour in order to represent the Middlesex Wanderers in Japan and Korea.
Dutch club Zandaam visited Leatherhead at the end of the season. In the 1920s they had been one of the top amateur sides in Holland and winners of both the national League and Cup. They had more than 1,000 players on their books and ran 40 sides, the strongest of which appeared at Fetcham Grove, but the Tanners defeated them 4-1. Further international honours followed when

Barry Friend played and scored for England against Scotland in March. He then went on tour with the national amateur side in July. Many Tanners supporters were annoyed that Friend was not a regular in the Leatherhead team, yet good enough to represent his country. Davies received his Welsh cap from Tanners Chairman Chris Luff, prior to the game with Corinthian Casuals. The famous Casuals had Surrey and England cricketers Mickey Stewart as manager and Graham Roope in goal, at this time.

Manager Billy Miller and coach Johnny Phipps were certainly building a fine side, although there were a couple of hiccups. Barrie Davies quit to join Wycombe, but returned within two months, after telling Wanderers' boss Brian Lee "*to stuff it*" when he was relegated to the sub's bench. Back at Leatherhead, Davies ran foul of management again and was axed for a while due to a breach of club discipline. Nobby Skinner was set to resign, after being dropped, but then changed his mind and stayed. Alan Brazier still captained the side while Wells, Reid, Webb, Cooper, Casey and Lavers were all performing consistently. Covent Garden porter Pete 'The Meat' Lavers was top scorer with 23 goals, Kelly and Webb also reaching double figures.

A new monthly magazine, 'The Tanner', appeared in September 1972 and was possibly one of the earliest non-league fanzines, in Surrey at least.

Dave Wall's reserve side had another fairly good season and were runners-up in the Suburban League Cup final. The Tanners Supporters Club was running a side in the Leatherhead and District Sunday League.

John Hewlett's long involvement at Fetcham Grove was strengthened when he became Vice-Chairman of the Football Club as well as Chairman of the Social Club. In 1972 he had also been elected Chairman of the Surrey County Football Association. Other officials with long periods of service for Leatherhead included Assistant Honorary Secretary Jack O'Malley and committee men Leslie Ellis and Peter Keary.

1973/1974

There were few changes in the playing staff for the 1973/74 season. Alan Brazier's first team appearances became more limited after a troublesome knee injury, but he did complete the FA coaching course. Dave Reid took over as captain. Peter Lavers and the, "*moody but magnificent*" Barrie Davies transferred to Slough, although both were later to return to Leatherhead, Lavers within a few months. John Cooper switched from midfield to a back four position and in October, Barry Friend was taken on by Fulham, where he was to make three first team appearances. The only major new signing was Peter McGillicuddy, a midfielder/winger from Wycombe Wanderers and prior to that with St Albans City and Ilford. Regular midweek training was taken by RAF physical education instructors at Headley Court. The players certainly had to work hard and Chris Kelly for one was not too keen on the training side.

The new clubhouse and changing room complex was completed and the old 'lower bar' refurbished ready for the start of the Tanners second season in the Isthmian fold. The league took on a pioneering role with Rothmans becoming sponsors, the introduction of the 'three points for a win' system and the use of goal difference as opposed to goal average. There were also cash awards for wins by a three goal margin and a sportsmanship pool, all designed to reward successful and sporting play, while reducing the emphasis on defence.

Clapton, Woking and St Albans were all defeated as Leatherhead made a fine start but the next three games, tough fixtures against Wycombe, Hendon and Hayes were all lost. More consistency was gained as Lavers returned, including a run of five convincing victories; 5-0 versus Sutton, 4-2 at Ilford, 6-0 at Bromley, 4-0 at Woking and 5-1 at home to Barking.

In the FA Cup, Erith and Belvedere and Ilford were defeated before Leytonstone dismissed the Tanners following two hard fought games. The London Senior Sup was entered for the first time but Leatherhead were unfortunate to draw Amateur Cup holders Walton & Hersham away in the first round and went down 1-0.

January 1974 saw the Tanners commence a fine run in the FA Amateur Cup. Amateur football was to be abolished by the FA from the end of the 73/74 season, mainly in order to stop the illicit payment problems. Stories had abounded of players unable to get their boots on because they were so stuffed with fivers. Amateur Cup entrants would either join clubs that were already semi-professional in the FA Trophy, which had started in 1970, or enter the new FA Vase competition. Leatherhead started their last ever Amateur Cup campaign in style, taming Enfield 4-0, then travelled to Mid-Cheshire League champions Middlewich Athletic. A large crowd, anticipating an upset, were stunned as Leatherhead made light of a strong wind and driving sleet, to repeatedly tear the home defence apart. Tanners recorded their biggest win under Miller's tenure - 9-0, Lavers contributing four goals. The third round produced a battle royal with Hendon, who had earlier reached the third round of the FA Cup and taken Newcastle United to a replay. Games at Claremont Road and Fetcham Grove could not separate the two sides, both matches finishing 1-1. At the third time of asking Leatherhead got through 2-0 on the neutral slopes of Wycombe's Loakes Park. The quarter-final provided a local derby at Sutton and a 1-0 victory for the Tanners in a tense, scrappy match, Lavers tapping home the winning goal, after U's keeper, Stuart, had spilled a cross from Kelly. Ilford were the opponents for the semi-final to be played at the Den, home of Millwall. Leatherhead had high hopes of getting to Wembley having not lost in three previous meetings with Ilford that season. Alas it was not to be and a smallish crowd of 2,700 witnessed a poor game, Dave Guiver scoring the only goal for Ilford after 37 minutes. The Tanners failed to rise to the occasion and could not find a way back, Derek Casey coming closest with a shot against the underside of the bar. Miller was 'gutted' stating that, "*the tension just tied us up in knots*". Tanners played football with wingers and ball-players but did not always have the application or 'bottle' to grind out wins. To complete a miserable day for the supporters they had to endure extreme verbal and physical abuse from a hooligan element amongst the East Londoners.

Around this time, Leatherhead ran onto the pitch to Chelsea's 'Blue is the colour', professionally dubbed (Not!) with the words 'Chelsea' and 'blue' cunningly replaced by 'Leatherhead' and 'green'. For the Amateur Cup games at Hendon and Sutton the Tanners had worn a blue strip borrowed from Chelsea, perhaps in an attempt to make the words fit better.

Woking and Kingstonian were each defeated following replays in the Surrey Senior Cup but at the semi-final stage the Walton and Hersham side that had beaten Brian Clough's Brighton team 4-0 away in the FA Cup were again a stumbling block.

The miners' strike between December 1973 and February 1974 meant that floodlights could not be used, resulting in earlier kick-offs on Saturdays and no midweek games. Many clubs played on Sundays, but Leatherhead refused to on religious grounds. As a consequence of this and Leatherhead's cup involvements, a demanding three games a week schedule had to be undertaken during the last two months of the season. All things considered the run-in was fairly successfully completed and included an impressive 3-0 home success against Walton as the Tanners achieved fifth place in the final league table and received an award from Rothmans for being the League's second highest goal-scorers. £828 was earned from the Rothmans' sponsorship fund, high levels of sportsmanship (only three bookings were received) and having a settled side (only seventeen players were used), being significant factors. The local paper awarded Chris Kelly 'Player of the

Year', he having received nine Man of the Match nominations from their reporter, as against seven each for Reid and Cooper. Kelly was the leading individual marksman with 22 goals and both he and Peter Smith represented the England Amateur side, Smith playing at Wembley against West Germany, in the last international before the ending of amateur status.

1974/75

1974/ 75 saw the abolition of amateurism, or 'shamateurism' as it had become known in some quarters due to the proliferation of payments made to supposedly unpaid players. Long-serving Club Secretary Sid Ranger retired, a decision made largely due to the club's decision to go 'open'. Jack O'Malley replaced Ranger. It later transpired that the council lease banned semi-professional football at Fetcham Grove and for a while there were fears, fortunately unrealised, that Leatherhead would have to drop into the Surrey Senior League, the Isthmian League having decided that all members should be semi-professional. The reserve team had been scrapped for financial reasons and one method of fund raising at the time was newspaper collection. This was long before recycling became environmentally friendly.

It was also the season that the Surrey town was put firmly on the map. Leatherhead Football Club and Chris Kelly were to become household names. The campaign was to be dominated by cup football and details of the FA Cup run are given a separate section.

Five major new signings were made - goalkeeper John Swannell, holder of 61 England Amateur caps, from Hendon, winger John Doyle from Kingstonian, right-back Dave Sargent and midfielders Willie Smith and Colin Woffinden, all from the great Walton and Hersham side. Swannell was only signed on the eve of the season's opener, thus averting a potential goalkeeping crisis. Together with Barry Webb, John Cooper, Dave Reid, Derek Wells, Peter McGillicuddy, Peter Lavers and Kelly, who had been training with Fulham pre-season, an outstanding side was formed. Players leaving the club were Peter Smith for Hendon, Nobby Skinner, (after 346 games and 112 goals) and Ron Fruen for Kingstonian. Barry Friend made a temporary reappearance at the Grove with a Fulham XI.

The Tanners made a cracking start to the season proper and following the 4-0 victory over Slough Town in September went top of the Isthmian League for the first time. A nine match unbeaten run was ended by defeats at Ilford and Dulwich and the previous consistency of league form was never really regained once Leatherhead became heavily committed to cup competitions. Having said that, the Tanners remained unbeaten at home until February, when they lost 3-2 to Sutton. They gained their biggest Isthmian victory thus far, when winning 8-0 at Clapton and towards the end of the campaign a win at Enfield and a draw at Dagenham helped to decide the championship in Wycombe's favour.

With the Amateur Cup competition ended, the FA Trophy was entered for the first time. Southern League sides, Gravesend and Northfleet and Hastings United had been comfortably disposed of, 4 -1 and 5-1 respectively, the latter game subsequently being described by Kelly as the greatest team performance in his years at Leatherhead. The second round tie at Weymouth was the match after Leicester. The Tanners were still coming back to reality and a physical Weymouth side won the match 2-0. Leatherhead were to find that everyone tried that little bit harder to bring the FA Cup giant-killers down.

In both London and Surrey Senior Cups, hard fought semi-final replays were won away from home to give the Tanners two cup final appearances. Following the transfer of Chris Kelly to Millwall goal-scoring had became a problem and in neither final did the Tanners do themselves justice. The London Senior Cup Final with Wimbledon was billed as the battle of the giant-killers, Wimbledon having beaten Burnley and taken Leeds United to a replay in the FA Cup to at least match Leatherhead's exploits. It was also something of a Walton and Hersham old boy's reunion. The Dons, managed by Alan Batsford, had Dave Bassett, Dave Donaldson and Billy Edwards in their ranks. Tanners had Sargent, Smith and Woffinden. The game was staged at Dulwich Hamlet's

Champion Hill ground in front of a crowd in the region of 3,500. Two Ian Cooke goals in quick succession during the second half settled it in Wimbledon's favour.

The Surrey Senior Cup was even more disappointing, a lacklustre performance ending in another 2-0 defeat at the hands (and feet) of Dulwich, John Baker scoring Hamlet's second goal. So there was no silverware to show for such a magnificent season.

Support for the Tanners had obviously increased due to the cup run. Membership of the Supporters Club had reached record levels although this was partly due to abolishing the age limit of thirty. Average home gates were about 800. Leatherhead's version of the Kop, the Shack, at the far end of the ground near to the new clubroom, was usually full.

Dave Reid was the only player to appear in all 68 competitive matches this season, Peter Lavers was top scorer with 41 goals in all competitions and second highest scorer in the Isthmian League with 28. Doyle, Reid and Swannell were selected for the Middlesex Wanderers touring side. With no reserve side fringe players had limited chances to play. Among the youngsters making occasional appearances were Tony Mitchell, a full-back/midfielder still at school but later to play 77 first team games for Exeter City, and Peter Page a defender/midfielder from Crystal Palace. In a nod to the future, Fetcham Park United's under-10 side were sweeping all before them. Their side included Steve Lunn, Paul Otway and Barry Hempstead.

The 1974/75 season was when many became hooked as Leatherhead supporters. Some of the football being produced, by a part-time team mind you, was stunning. Every player had great qualities. You can have a team of wonderfully talented individuals, but unless they are orchestrated they can all be playing different tunes. It requires a good conductor to get them to play the same tune and Billy Miller obviously had a great ear for metaphorical music. The individual talents and the composite teamwork were never more apparent than during this season's FA Cup competition.

1974/75 FA CUP

The season was very much dominated by the FA Cup. It began quietly enough on a sunny Saturday in September, 300 spectators seeing a comfortable 2-0 win away to Croydon Amateurs in the 1st qualifying round. A diving header by Lavers and a low shot by Kelly provided the goals early in the second half. A convincing 5-0 victory over Hornchurch followed.

Next up Dagenham, who provided tough opposition. The Tanners were on top in a pulsating match at Fetcham Grove, but were constantly thwarted by Ian Huttley in the Dagger's goal and held 0-0. Dagenham were a formidable side, particularly at their Victoria Road home, but Doyle scored an early goal from a near impossible angle in the replay. Two dazzling second half strikes from Kelly ensured progress. Dagenham did score once in reply but Tanners performed impressively all-round, withstanding some heavy pressure to win the tie 3-1.

Walton and Hersham, who had won the Amateur Cup in 1973 and had thumped Brighton 4-0 away in the 73/74 FA Cup, were drawn at home to Leatherhead in the 4th and final qualifying round. However, the Swans fortunes had nose-dived. Only one of their Amateur Cup winning side remained and most of their stars were now at Wimbledon or, in the case of Woffinden, Smith and Sargent, Leatherhead. Woffinden and Sargent were among those on the mark as the Tanners ran riot, chalking up their biggest win of the season thus far - 7-1. The local newspaper dubbed Tanners, "*The Green Machine*" in honour of the calm and efficient manner that they went about steamrollering their opponents.

Leatherhead were through to the first round proper, already further than they had previously been, but there was much more to come. The 'big name' draw did not materialise, Amateur Cup holders and fellow Isthmians Bishop's Stortford, providing the next opposition. A hard fought 0-0 draw took place in Hertfordshire. Tanners had periods of dominance but could not ram home their advantage against a resilient Stortford defence. Supporters listened in secretly at school or work as the draw was made for the next round, at 12.30 p.m. on the Monday. By the time of the replay both sides knew that victory would set up a meeting with a Football League club. On a very muddy Fetcham Grove pitch a further half-hour of stalemate was eventually broken with a Lavers header from a Woffinden cross. Leatherhead went on to dominate the game. Webb had a penalty saved but victory was ensured when, following a brave run down the right by Cooper, Doyle's shot found the top corner of the net.

For Leatherhead's first competitive meeting with a League club, Colchester United, lying fourth in Division Three and FA Cup giant-killers themselves just four seasons earlier when they beat Leeds United on their way to the fifth round, were drawn to play at Fetcham Grove. Colchester were to gain promotion at the end of the season and their players included Ray Harford and Mike Walker. Both were to become better known for managerial roles and the Harford name was to become more closely linked with Leatherhead Football Club many years later. Jim Smith, the Essex club's manager was happy with the pitch at Leatherhead but not the floodlights so the match kicked-off at 2.15 p.m. The Greens attacked the Football League side from the off and were rewarded after twenty minutes when a Webb corner fell kindly for little winger John Doyle, still holding a sponge following treatment seconds earlier for a cut eye, to whack the ball home. Under current rules he would have been off the pitch being properly bandaged up. There was a frantic second half assault by Colchester, but Willie Smith drove the Tanners on, Lavers' aerial flick-on's helped relieve the pressure, Cooper covered every blade of grass and defenders Sargent, Webb and Reid remained solid, limiting Colchester to just a handful of scoring chances. The majority of the 3,500 spectators were in, "*a state of frenzied excitement*" as the Tanners had giant-killed the giant-killers 1-0. Billy Miller in true cliché form was, "*over the moon*" while even Jim Smith conceded that the better team had won. In his autobiography, Smith said that losing to Leatherhead was the worst moment in his managerial career. Having watched Tanners' replay with Bishop's Stortford, he thought that Leatherhead were a very poor side. However, in order to avoid complacency, he told his players that they were the best non-league team he had ever seen. Perhaps the Colchester players were overawed! Smith was also upset with Kelly. Offering his hand in congratulations at the end, Kelly in return offered a stream of derogatory remarks about the Football League side. Smith pursued Kelly but a melee of celebrating fans prevented further discussion on the matter. A post match party was held at Miller's house, where the players observed the 3rd round draw, made live on Match of the Day at 11 p.m. Leatherhead were paired with another Third Division club, Brighton and Hove Albion. Miller's reaction was, "*we would have preferred a First Division side but should make a lot of money at Brighton and at the same time take in a bit of sea air. We have an excellent chance of going through*". The Tanners certainly had a good psychological start because Sargent, Smith and Woffinden had all been in the Walton side that had trounced Brighton in the previous season's competition. Earlier in his career, Woffinden had actually made four appearances for the Seagulls at centre-forward. Kelly, who had not played against Stortford or Colchester, now returned to action only six weeks after a cartilage operation.

Twenty two coach loads of supporters, including parties from the Post Office, British Legion, Working Men's Club and several pubs, as well as official Football Club coaches and numerous private cars travelled to the Goldstone Ground, where the total attendance numbered 20,491. Leatherhead won the match with a wonder goal from Kelly. Cooper cleared the ball from defence to McGillicuddy, who swept the ball on to Kelly in the middle of the park. Kelly set off with calm assurance, running straight at the two Brighton defenders between him and the goal. A sway and a shimmy left the defenders floundering, allowing Kelly to cut in and shoot, the ball finding the net off the far post. It was a composed performance all-round by the Tanners. Reid blotted out Fred

Binney, the League's leading scorer for the previous two seasons, and Brighton were restricted to just two half chances all match. That said, fingers, arms, legs and anything else to hand, were crossed by Tanners supporters during the last few minutes when two risky back passes almost gave the advantage away. It was one of only three home defeats suffered by the Seagulls all season. Brighton boss Peter Taylor was gracious in defeat. Miller was ecstatic, "*Right now I could walk on top of the stands*". The unassuming Kelly commented, between mouthfuls of gin, "*If this performance had been at Old Trafford, they would have been proclaiming a new George Best*". Kelly, already known as 'Budgie' for his willingness to talk, now earned the nickname 'The Leatherhead Lip' as the national media picked up on the Surrey club's giant-killing exploits. He had to be pulled from a Brighton pub to be interviewed on 'Match of the Day' where, slightly inebriatedly, he declared, "*Leicester are rubbish. We'll stuff them in the next round*". Kelly was by now a bona fide celebrity and featured on 'Nationwide' and, oddly, 'Tomorrows World'. His name also appeard on the back of Fletch's copy of the Sun in 'Porridge' later that year. Kelly and Miller both appeared on 'The Big Match' and the Tanners' league game with Hitchin was filmed for 'Bob Wilson's Football Preview'. A bit of a betting scandal came to light. The team scooped £170 from a Worthing bookie, having gambled on themselves to win at Brighton. The Football Association investigated, but no action was taken.

The Tanners had got the First Division club they desperately wanted when they had been drawn at home to Leicester City, but due to safety reasons, the lack of terracing at Fetcham Grove and financial factors, it was decided to switch the match to Filbert Street. Budgie was quick to tell the press what he was going to do to Leicester, "*I beat Brighton with my magic shuffle. In the next round Leicester will get my double shuffle and that's something really special*". When asked what Leicester's view of him might be, he responded, "*They ought to thank me. I've probably sold a few more tickets for them. People will want to come and see if I can do it*". Mole Valley bookmakers had odds of 9-1 for a Leatherhead victory at Leicester, whereas a better price of 16-1 could be obtained in the East Midlands.

An estimated 8,000 Tanners supporters turned the M1 into a sea of green and white. Followers of other clubs were met at service stations or on the road and almost all waved and shouted support for the underdogs. A couple of hundred Nottingham Forest fans even came to the match at Filbert Street, after their own game had been called off. The eventual crowd of 32,090 was 11,000 above Leicester's average at the time and the largest ever attendance for a match involving the Tanners. Millions more tuned in to see the highlights featured on 'Match of the Day' later that night.

The home side included several ex-London club players such as Keith Weller, Alan Birchenall, Jon Sammels and the talented Frank Worthington. Kelly had an outstanding first half, setting up McGillicuddy for the first goal then scoring the second with a deft back-header from a Webb free-kick. Leatherhead 2-0 up at the interval, the Leicester supporters stood in stunned silence and Budgie's pre-match boasts were looking believable.

After the break, however, the game turned on two incidents. Early in the second half Kelly was clean through and rounded the keeper but was left with a very acute angle and Munro somehow got back to clear off the line. Every man continued to do his job for Tanners, who were still playing all out attacking football, even as Leicester came more into the game. A diving header by Jon Sammels pulled a goal back for Leicester. Then midway through the half the second turning point arrived. Swannell, who had played impeccably, failed to hold a Worthington free-kick and Steve Earle nipped in to score from the rebound. Leicester's supporters now found their voice and their team responded. Superior fitness began to show and they used the full width of the pitch to stretch Leatherhead's tiring defence. With just ten minutes left, Steve Whitworth's cross was headed on by Worthington, for Weller to volley the winner past the helpless Swannell. Derek Wells, who had been a regular in the earlier rounds, remained on the bench, which caused some criticism at the time, but in retrospect, Wells graciously conceded that it was the right decision.

The Tanners had lost 3-2 but, in the process, earned many plaudits for their performance. David Miller in the Daily Express wrote, "*Leatherhead did more for football on Saturday than some of our professionals have done in years".* Leicester manager, Jimmy Bloomfield, described his side's escape as, *"nothing short of a miracle"* and regarding Chris Kelly stated, *"he was almost as good as he said he was".* In the 'Complete Record of Match of the Day' this game was John Motson's choice as the Match of the 1974/75 season. One Leatherhead supporter with mixed feelings was Keith Oram, who could at least continue his wedding arrangements for cup final day knowing that Leatherhead Football Club would not get in the way.

The Tanners' ten match FA Cup run attracted a total attendance of over 60,000. A profit of £15,000 was made which helped clear the overdraft run up during the previous two years. In most seasons, Leatherhead's exploits would have been unparalleled in terms of non-league performances in the cup, but Wimbledon also had a fabulous run and shared the headlines. Nonetheless, Leatherhead was well and truly 'on the map'.

Chris Kelly's comments certainly boosted publicity. He even accused Johan Cruyff of copying one of his tricks. For his abilities on the field Kelly was rewarded with the Daily Mail Footballer of the Month award for January and decided to stay in the limelight by joining Second Division Football League club Millwall. He had been offered trials with Nottingham Forest, Ipswich and Leicester, but wanted to remain in the London area. Leatherhead had missed out on a transfer fee (possibly as much as £150,000) because he was not under contract. Kelly made his Millwall debut as substitute in a 2-0 defeat by Bolton and on his first full appearance played quite well in a 0-0 draw with Oldham. Overall he played eleven times, without scoring, but did manage a few assists. Chris soon became depressed with what he saw as an uncaring, motivated by money attitude from his fellow players. He saw football as a game to be taken seriously but played for fun. When Kelly's feelings became known, Millwall boss Gordon Jago suspended him and tried to sell him to Arsenal, who wanted to give him a go. Eventually Jago relented and allowed Kelly his wish to return to Leatherhead for the start of the 75/76 season.

1975/76

Leatherhead took the decision to turn fully professional following a directive from the Isthmian League. Fourteen players signed contracts, three students: John Cooper, Tony Mitchell and Chris Jolly, remained non-contract. There were not many changes in personnel during the close season. Coming to the club were forward John Adams from Walton and midfielder Steve Ibbotson from Horsham and, of course, Chris Kelly had returned from Millwall. Peter McGillicuddy moved to Enfield and soon after the season commenced, Barry Webb departed for Kingstonian. In twelve years at the club, Webb made 438 appearances, scoring 119 goals, 44 of which were penalties. The season started with an excellent exhibition of football when Leatherhead took on a Leicester City side, containing seven players with first team experience, in a friendly. The Tanners came from 3-1 and 4-3 behind to earn a 4-4 draw, Kelly scoring a hat-trick.

A 3-1 victory against Dagenham got the league programme off to a good start but a shock came in the next match, a 5-0 defeat at newly promoted Staines Town. A 2-1 win at Enfield suggested that this had only been a minor setback but league form continued to be erratic, particularly away from home. Miller lashed out at the, *"film stars"* in the team.

The best form of the season coincided with the FA Cup campaign. Following the previous year's success Leatherhead were exempted to the fourth qualifying round where they drew Ilford at home. In an excellent first half display newcomer Ibbotson controlled the midfield, but for all their superiority the Tanners could only score once through Doyle. Ilford came back into the match after the break but Leatherhead held on to their slender advantage, John Swannell making a magnificent save from Chester Brown in the final minute.

Fourth Division Cambridge United, the second youngest side in the league and with Ron Atkinson in his first Football League managerial role, were the Tanners opponents in the first round proper. Media interest was again high with Chris Kelly the prime target for newsworthy quotes, such as, "*I still believe the standards in the Football League are appallingly low. It's a good job for many of them that it is a team game, because they can be carried along*". A disappointing crowd of 2,450 watched the match, with the visitors displaying a solid no-nonsense approach in the early stages, but Leatherhead struck twice in the quarter of an hour before half-time. Firstly, Kelly's low cross following a fine run was turned into his own net by United defender, Brendon Batson. Then from another telling cross by Kelly, this time high to the far past, Cooper nodded the ball back for Doyle to head home. As 'Big Ron' walked round at the interval, he was asked what the score was. I am not sure if his response indicated the correct scoreline or was some other sort of gesture. Cambridge had more of the play in the second half but with great resilience and a little luck, the U's strike-force of Bobby Shinton and Geoff Horsfall were successfully repelled and the Tanners held out for a 2-0 success. Superstitions and habits are commonplace in football and Miller, for his part, always used to wear the same set of clothes for cup ties.

Some teams are ideally suited for knockout competitions. Not blessed with consistency or depth of squad to mount a serious league title challenge, they retain the ability to turn in breathtaking one-off performances. Certain West Ham and Chelsea teams have also displayed these same characteristics. In the second round Leatherhead faced fellow Isthmians, Tooting and Mitcham and although they had already performed a league double over the Sandy Lane outfit, found them much tougher opposition than Cambridge in the cup. At Fetcham Grove the dazzling skills of Doyle and Kelly created many chances during the opening half, but the finish was lacking. Tooting grew in confidence and had the better opportunities themselves after the break but they too failed to score and the match finished goalless. It did not take the Tanners too long to break the deadlock in the replay, John Cooper scoring with a 30-yard thunderbolt after thirteen minutes. Tooting gradually got more into the game and equalised with a penalty just before the interval. Ten minutes into the second half referee Alan Turvey decided that the ice on the pitch was becoming too dangerous and abandoned proceedings. A result was eventually achieved at the third time of asking. Again Leatherhead scored first, from a powerful free-kick by Dave Reid, but Tooting fought back well, equalised from a penalty converted by Juneman and scored the winner early in extra-time, through captain Ron Howell. The Green Machine's cup dream was over for another year.

There were still hopes of a good run in the FA Trophy. Southern League Wealdstone had been beaten in the opening tie after a replay. Staines Town provided the next opposition and proved a very tough nut to crack. 2-2 and 1-1 draws brought about a third match at Walton that the Tanners controlled. Sargent missed a penalty and Kelly hit the post in the first ninety minutes before Colin Woffinden's curling free-kick provided the winner during the additional half-hour. Fate did not seem to be on Leatherhead's side for the second round tie away to Bromsgrove Rovers. Peter Lavers had left the club for Hayes, after 296 appearances and 144 goals, Willie Smith was suspended and Kelly out with flu. The pitch was poor and it was bitterly cold. As it was, the Tanners dominated most of the match but badly lacked someone to score goals. With time running out Leatherhead pulled back and seemed to be settling for a draw. Bromsgrove had other ideas however, and in injury time scored the only goal from a free-kick which was practically their only shot of the game.

Lavers' departure had left a big hole in the Tanners attack. Attempts to fill it included an audacious approach to England World Cup winner Geoff Hurst. Hurst, having been released by West Bromwich Albion, was playing in Ireland at the time. The proposed deal fell through, however, because Tanners could not afford his wage demands.

Defeats by Dagenham and Woking had meant exits from the London and Surrey Senior Cups. This left just the Isthmian League and floodlit games to complete, Leatherhead having rejoined the Floodlight League this season. There was a fine home victory over champions Enfield but several lacklustre performances as the Tanners finished a season that had promised so much, rather disappointingly. Only £80 was won from the sponsorship pool, compared to over £1,600 in the two preceding years and in a 'General Assessment' by the League, based on such criteria as ground facilities, organisation and atmosphere, Leatherhead only finished 26th out of 44 clubs in the league's two divisions. The much improved matchday programme though was voted third best in the league, behind only Wycombe and Slough's offerings.

Billy Miller's managerial talents had been recognised when he was chosen to run the Isthmian League representative side. Swannell, Sargent and Kelly played. Reid was also in the squad, as were John Baker, Micky Preston, Larry Pritchard and Alan Devonshire, then at Southall before progressing to West Ham and England fame. Future England international Cyrille Regis was also in the Isthmian League around this time with Les Ferdinand soon to follow.
One new player coming into the team towards the end of the season was John Bailey, a midfielder signed from Crawley Town. Kelly's season ended with him representing the Rothmans National League XI in front of 30,000 spectators in Indonesia.

1976/77

In a bid to solve their striking problem the Tanners signed former Amateur international John Baker from Hendon. Also arriving were left-back Ray Eaton from Wycombe and 17-year-old, ex-Arsenal apprentice defender, Colin Brooks. Steve Ibbotson and John Adams left after only one season at the Grove while Alan Brazier was forced to retire as a player. Following two cartilage operations Brazier had found it difficult to come back at the age of 33, but he did join Johnny Phipps and Dave Wall on the coaching staff. He had made a record, at the time, 455 appearances, mostly as captain. Billy Miller believed it was his best ever squad and Kelly thought that if they could find the right level of consistency they were good enough to win the league. Friendlies included a match with a Chelsea XI that attracted over 1,500 paying customers. Tommy Langley and Clive Walker, who Kelly described as, "*a verbose goal-scoring machine*", were in the Blues' line-up.

John 'The Beast' Baker was straight on the goal trail as Leatherhead won their first seven league games to open up a gap at the top of the table, but after a draw with Tooting, the next six matches were lost in an inexplicable change of form. League results continued to be erratic although victory was achieved at Sutton, in Dario Gradi's first match in charge of the U's following his dismissal as first team coach at Chelsea.

It was hoped that the FA Cup could produce an upturn in fortunes. Mid-table Southern League Chelmsford City, whose side included ageing former Football League stars such as Jimmy Greaves and Bobby Kellard, were thrashed 4-0 on their own ground at the fourth qualifying round stage. On a pitch described as, "*resembling an elephant's bathroom*", Greaves went off with an injured back after just twenty minutes, as the Tanners dominated. John Bailey controlled the midfield and capped a fine performance with a goal, Baker (2) and Cooper netting the others.
Football League Division Three club, Northampton Town, managed by Pat Crerand and with John Gregory in their side, came to Fetcham Grove for the first round tie. The Tanners stuck to their superstition of never being photographed before a match. Watched by 3,550 spectators, Leatherhead were soon in command against a physically bigger Northampton side. Kelly with his corkscrew dribbles, Sargent with his overlapping runs, Doyle and Cooper all tormented the visitors defence which seemed to panic at every opportunity and Doyle was the ultimate executioner, poking home

Smith's headed cross after four minutes and heading in Baker's chip after half an hour. The League side began to have more of the play after the interval but the Tanners comfortably held on for another memorable victory. The men in green were exchanging confident winks and glances with spectators long before the end. Lance Masters in The Daily Telegraph wrote, "*Leatherhead emerged as a supremely fit, disciplined team capable of surprisingly fluent and sophisticated football*".

For the second round, the Green Machine received another home draw, this time against fellow non-league giant-killers Wimbledon. The match attracted Fetcham Grove's record attendance of 5,500 (some records vary and show the gate as anywhere between 3,500 and 4,500), including Jack Charlton, who's Middlesbrough side were to be the next opponents for the winners.

The Tanners had the better of the early exchanges, Woffinden missing a golden opportunity, but the class of Cooper and Doyle was countered by the organisation and stern professionalism of the Dons rearguard. The Leatherhead defence was undone, and the course of the game changed, after thirty minutes. As a Wimbledon corner came over, a whistle blew and everyone stood still. The ball dropped at the feet of Jeff Bryant who, almost as an afterthought, knocked the ball into the net. To everyone's astonishment the referee awarded a goal. The phantom whistler had struck. The culprit was never unmasked, but phantom whistles were heard at one or two subsequent games. When Marlowe hooked in a centre from Connell early in the second half to put the Dons 2-0 up Leatherhead might have crumbled. Instead they hit back with a clever goal from a free-kick. Using a trick that was often tried but only occasionally worked, Kelly ran over the ball, Smith stopped and Smith and Kelly looked at each other and exchanged expletives as though they had messed it up before Smith nonchalantly touched the ball for Reid, trundling forward unnoticed, to thunder in an unstoppable shot. Leatherhead pressed forward for an equaliser but Wimbledon always looked dangerous from breakaways. The Tanners had the class but not the physical strength. Three minutes from the end, Connell again set up Marlowe for their third goal. Prior to this match Leatherhead had gone more than 1,100 minutes (over twelve matches spanning 6 years), without conceding a goal at home in the FA Cup, and the previous team to score……Wimbledon! It was also to be the Tanners' only FA Cup defeat at Fetcham Grove throughout the 70s, a run encompassing 22 matches.

Dagenham prevented any progress in the FA Trophy and went on to reach the final, after their first round success over Leatherhead. Although they deserved a 3-0 victory in the replay at Victoria Road they had required an equaliser three minutes into injury time, when there had been no obvious stoppages, to gain that replay.

Shortly afterwards things at the club became a little unsettled. Sargent, Bailey and Page departed, to leave Leatherhead with a squad of just thirteen players including two goalkeepers. Manager Billy Miller resigned but, following a vote of confidence from the team, was back running the side in less than a week. Several newcomers were signed including midfielder Micky Cook from Kingstonian. The Tanners did reach the semi-final of the Surrey Senior Cup but after two evenly matched games, in which both sides missed numerous chances, Steve Grubb's goal in the second half of extra-time saw Tooting and Mitcham triumph.

The league campaign ended poorly with a run of five defeats and only one goal scored. Smith and Woffinden requested transfers and were dropped for the final match to end a disappointing season. There were, however, further representative honours for Leatherhead players. Billy Miller was one of three managers who selected an England squad for a semi-professional international with Italy and among the side were Chris Kelly and John Swannell. In June 1977, John Cooper captained the Rothmans England Select touring side for a tournament in the Canary Islands. Geoff Hurst, then at Telford, was one of the team. Also in June, Sutton United's prestigious annual six-a-side tournament was won by Epsom's Duke of Wellington Pub, the team consisting of Chris Jolly, Colin Brooks, Willie Smith, Micky Cook, John Doyle and Chris Kelly.

The brothers Dixon were involved in Fetcham Grove events in slightly different ways. Tom was appointed Membership Secretary while Mick 'streaked' across the pitch during the match with Ilford. Streaking was enjoying a wave of popularity at the time, but in January? Mick was duly arrested but only because one elderly lady spectator complained. Most of the players and crowd were merely amused. It is believed that the money he gained from the bet that dared him to do it outweighed the fine, however.

1977/78

Significant changes to playing personnel took place at the start of what was to be a marathon campaign, where a visit to Wembley would mean the stadium not the Vale Farm home of Wembley FC and, in all, three cup finals would be reached. Willie Smith left to try his luck with Football League newcomers Wimbledon. Smith appeared in the Dons' first ever league match, although a broken leg soon ruined his chance of proving himself at this level. Also departing were Colin Woffinden, to Tooting, and Derek Wells to Walthamstow. Prominent signings were midfielder Billy Salkeld from Staines and centre-back Dennis Malley from Slough. Malley had also played for Preston, Wimbledon and Guildford City, scoring the last ever goal at St. Joseph's Road. In his full-time job, he was a Customs Officer trying to stop smugglers. At Leatherhead, he was soon highly regarded for stopping opposing strikers and was appointed club captain. Returning to Fetcham Grove were John Bailey from Sutton and Barrie Davies from Wycombe. Publican and five years retired goalkeeper Micky Cuthbert was put on standby as cover for John Swannell, following Chris Jolly's departure. The newcomers joined Swannell, Micky Cook, John Cooper, Ray Eaton, Dave Reid, John Baker, John Doyle, Chris Kelly and Colin Brooks in a very strong squad. Many of the players had nicknames. John Baker was 'The Beast', John Doyle - 'The Ferret', Dennis Malley - 'Sam' or 'McCloud' for his resemblance to the television character, Dave Reid - 'The Shadow' for his ability to carry injuries and John Bailey - 'The Judge' because he made over 50 appearances from the bench in his time at the club.

Rothmans had ended their Isthmian involvement, leaving the league without a sponsor. During their period of sponsorship, which included financial rewards for fair play, Wycombe had only received five bookings. Leatherhead had a tally of twenty two bookings; while at the bottom of the table were Clapton, with sixty seven bookings and seven dismissals. The Isthmian News strongly fancied the Tanners to challenge Enfield, champions for the two previous years, for the title. An indifferent start was made, home victories against Hayes and Dagenham contrasting with a failure to win any of the first five away games, but the goals then started to flow with most games at Fetcham Grove being won comfortably and a fair amount of points collected on the road. The Tanners had moved up to third place in the table behind Wycombe and runaway leaders Enfield when their heavy cup commitments meant that only one league match was played in an eleven week spell between early January and late March 1978.

The FA Cup could always be relied upon to bring out the best in the Leatherhead players and Isthmian Division Two side Cheshunt found the Green Machine too hot to handle. 2-0 up inside ten minutes, Tanners cruised to a 4-1 victory and a place in the first round proper for the 4th year running.
A useful Swansea City side, lying fifth in Division Four and about to begin their surge up to the top division, were drawn to play at Fetcham Grove. Welsh internationals Robbie James, Alan Curtis and Jeremy Charles, nephew of former Leeds and Juventus legend John, were included in the Swansea team that showed more composure than previous Football League visitors and actually dominated at the start of the match. Cheered on by most of the 3,000 spectators Leatherhead got back into it and created the best openings. Kelly's amazing skills led to three chances but all were squandered and on other occasions, Swansea custodian Keith Barber produced fine saves to keep the Greens at bay, particularly late in the game when turning Cooper's shot round the post.
A large contingent of Leatherhead supporters made the trek to South Wales for the midweek replay and took their place in a crowd of 7,200 on a bitterly cold evening. Despite going 1-0 down to a

goal from Charles, the Tanners played some fine football as they tried to get back in the match. Swansea's ability to take their chances was the main difference between the two sides and Welsh international Curtis added a second goal soon after the interval. Baker pulled one back and Leatherhead battled gamely to the end, but their FA Cup run was over for another year.

Apart from the FA Trophy, more of which later, the Tanners progressed to the final of two other cup competitions but again could not produce their best form on the big day. Sutton United had been beaten eventually in the semi-final of the London Senior Cup, 2–1, after extra-time in a replay. Leatherhead totally dominated the first half of the final with Walthamstow Avenue, played at Dulwich, despite having Kelly reduced to the role of a passenger through a recurrence of a calf injury. They hit the woodwork twice and let countless other opportunities slip by and after the interval allowed Walthamstow back into the match, a 55th minute headed goal by Vince Cotter settling the issue.

Due to other cup commitments the Tanners did not play their Hitachi Isthmian League Cup 1st round tie with Molesey until near the end of March, at the ninth attempt. Molesey, Hendon, Wycombe and Boreham Wood were all defeated in quick succession and without conceding a goal as another final place was achieved. Champion Hill, Dulwich, was once again not a happy venue for Leatherhead, as cup finals continued to have a similar effect on the Tanners as kryptonite does on Superman. Micky Cuthbert replaced the injured Swannell in goal. The Tanners had almost all the play but Dagenham's Mal Harkins provided the only score of the match.

A home loss to Woking in the semi-final of the Surrey Senior Cup provided further disappointment. There was a large enough turnout for the game but the lack of noise left the programme editor wondering if the crowd were either spellbound or asleep. A Banstead side run by Tom Dixon, coached by Alan Brazier, and including Jimmy Rochester (son of Tommy) and future Tanner Peter Fitzgerald, had been defeated in an earlier round.

Cup commitments left Tanners with an almost impossible to fulfil Isthmian League programme, particularly having no reserve side. Rather than extend the date for the end of the season the league allowed Windsor and Eton on three occasions, and Banstead Athletic once, to masquerade as Leatherhead. Windsor gained the only point from these games, a 0-0 draw at Southall. Sutton United's supporters were most disgruntled when they found they were playing Banstead but it was just two days before the FA Trophy final. The week after Wembley was even crazier:

Monday 1st May	Home v Staines Town	Won 2-0
Tuesday 2nd May	(Windsor & Eton) Away v Hitchin Town	Lost 0-2
Wednesday 3rd May	Home v Tilbury	Won 2-1
Thursday 4th May	Home v Sutton United	Drew 2-2
Thursday 4th May	(Windsor & Eton) Away v Slough Town	Lost 1-3
Friday 5th May	Home v Walthamstow Avenue	Drew 0-0

Was the 4th May 1978 the only occasion that a team has fulfilled two fixtures in the same competition at the same time! Windsor's P. Duff scored at Slough, making him the only non-Leatherhead player (excluding own goals) to score for the club. Under the circumstances the final league placing of seventh was most reasonable.

A friendly with Dutch club AFC Amsterdam, was won 1–0 to complete a 78 match season. Baker and Kelly ended as top scorers with 27 and 26 goals respectively, while Dave Reid passed Alan Brazier's record appearance tally. Further representative honours came Leatherhead's way. Reid, Bailey, Eaton and Kelly played for a Surrey Select XI against Crystal Palace in a match to celebrate the centenary of the Surrey County FA and Doyle and Cooper appeared for the Isthmian League against champions Enfield. Tanners' boss Billy Miller managed both representative sides.

Leslie Ellis, having resigned from the committee, was made a Life Vice-President of the club to honour his involvement for most of their existence. Despite the lack of trophies, it had been a very successful season for the club. The celebrations were tinged with sadness, however, because of the sudden death of Chairman Chris Luff, in February 1978. His ambition had been to see his beloved Tanners play at Wembley Stadium but after watching the team train at Headley Court one Thursday evening he suddenly collapsed. Club physiotherapist John Deary and the Headley Court medical staff were called to the Guardroom, but regrettably to no avail.

1977/78 FA TROPHY

The Wembley trail began amongst the railway yards and warehouses of Banbury in January 1978. After an exciting end to end clash, Leatherhead made Banbury cross with a 2-1 victory. Cook's header from a Salkeld corner was soon equalised, but on the stroke of half-time Kelly struck after Reid's header had rebounded from the bar. A strong defensive showing through the second period saw the Tanners home. Sid Ranger and Keith Williams performed an impromptu cabaret during the post match celebrations, Keith singing while accompanying himself on a local newspaper!

The second round tie with Dartford produced some bizarre events. Doyle, Reid and Swannell were all injured as the game approached. On the day of the match torrential rain threatened a postponement, but the referee passed the pitch fit to play. The visitors, however, failed to arrive. They had apparently telephoned the ground and been told the game was off, but spectators, match officials and the Leatherhead team waited until 3.45 p.m. when it was actually called off due to the lack of opposition. In a recent interview, one Chris Kelly claims to have answered the call from Dartford and given them the dubious information. The Football Association accepted Dartford's explanation and ruled that the match should take place on the following Thursday, but the drama was not over. The Tanners, already missing Doyle and Reid, had to field a hobbling John Swannell in goal because stand-in Paul Whittaker was stuck in a traffic jam, as was John Cooper. Whittaker eventually arrived, having been stopped for speeding in his rush to get there and replaced Swannell just before half-time. Even without these circumstances, it turned out to be a magnificent performance by the Green Machine. The Southern League Darts who included experienced players such as Vic Akers, Arthur Horsfield and Pat Morrisey in their line-up, scored first after only eight minutes, but three minutes later Leatherhead were 2-1 in front through Kelly and Joe Palladino. Further goals from Salkeld, Kelly and Baker sealed a convincing 5-1 victory. Dartford may have wished that they had not turned up again and sacked manager Roy Dwight, cousin of Elton John, in the aftermath.

Northern Premier League championship contenders Wigan Athletic were next, again at Fetcham Grove. Wigan had only lost twice away from home that season, at Scarborough and in the FA Cup at Birmingham City and they had defeated Enfield 3-0 in the previous round of the Trophy. As anticipated the Lancastrians provided very tough opposition but Tanners produced another remarkable team performance, Kelly providing the finishing touches to two fine moves to settle it. For their part Wigan finished the season as Northern Premier League runners-up and gained election to the Football League for the following season.

Ugly scenes of hooliganism blighted the quarter-final at Bedford Town, with Northampton supporters out for revenge possibly to blame. Despite the Bedford 'followers' desire to tear their main stand down, and attack anyone in Leatherhead colours, the Green Machine did the business on the pitch. In a dour, hard fought struggle, Swannell and the defence were superb, although the rest of the team never really hit top form. Elwyn Roberts, with a shot against the bar for Southern League Bedford, then managed by Barry Fry, was closest to scoring in a 0-0 draw. The replay was similar to the Dartford tie, Leatherhead dominating the early exchanges but the visitors breaking away to take the lead with a deflected shot. Kelly then turned on the magic, setting up Salkeld and Doyle in quick succession. Doyle, again put through by Kelly, was this time brought down. Salkeld scored from the spot for the Tanners' third goal in just six minutes. Bedford pulled it back to 2-3 before the interval, but Leatherhead dominated the second half and added further goals through Cook and Doyle.

Only a two-legged semi-final with top Northern League club Spennymoor United stood between Leatherhead and their first Wembley appearance. After an initial 'cat and mouse' period, two goals in four minutes put the Tanners in command at the Grove. Kelly brilliantly beat four defenders in as many yards, got to the bye-line and pulled the ball back for Cooper to fire home. Soon after, a Cook corner was flicked on by Reid for Malley to thunder in a header, which had crossed the line before being cleared. With the second leg still to come caution possibly took over, Spennymoor defended stoutly and there was no further score. Five hundred fans travelled to Durham a week later, half of them on a British Rail special at a price of £8 a head. Double-decker buses then ferried them from Durham Station to the ground. However, the overall crowd of 4,500 consisted mainly of a fanatical north-eastern following. A lacklustre first half showing allowed Billy Ward and John Davies to provide the goals that pulled Spennymoor level on aggregate. As the Northerners continued to attack things looked grim for the Tanners. It took a gutsy, determined second half performance to pull through. Spennymoor's pressure was withheld and after 70 minutes, Salkeld took a corner, Reid headed on and Baker flew through a flurry of boots to squeeze in a diving header. Leatherhead went from strength to strength, controlled the remainder of the match and came close to an equaliser on the day. Baker's away goal, though not counting double, was priceless enough and secured a 3-2 aggregate victory.

The town was gripped by cup fever. Shop window displays, a 16 page special printed by the Surrey Advertiser and 'Wembley' suits sponsored by local firms all helped to mark the occasion. The club produced a souvenir brochure that paid tribute to long-serving officials such as John Hewlett and Sid Ranger and the management team of Billy Miller, John Phipps, Dave Wall and physiotherapist John Deary. Deary spent 32 years in the RAF and had been awarded the MBE in 1968. The only regret was that Chris Luff was not there to see the big day. The team set out early on the Friday morning prior to the final. They trained at Enfield FC, visited Wembley Stadium and stayed overnight in a local hotel before a light workout on the Saturday morning. Unfortunately, on the day the final was very much an anti-climax. Defensive errors in the first fifteen minutes saw the Tanners go 2-0 behind  against Northern Premier League Altrincham and effectively this ended the match as a contest. From this point on Leatherhead had more possession but could never find the right rhythm against resolute opponents. Kelly hit the bar with a snap shot but King's goal soon after half-time put Altrincham further ahead. A little pride was salvaged when Cook pulled one back near the end but overall it was a disappointing end to a marvellous run for the Leatherhead contingent in the 20,000 crowd. Altrincham boss Tony Sanders said, "We *proved today that northern guile and determination is too much for the ball players of the south*". The result was soon forgotten however, as the team was greeted by hundreds of singing and dancing supporters lining the streets as they paraded through the town in an open top bus. When they finally arrived back at the club Barrie Davies climbed on to the front of the bus to proudly display his lucky underpants decorated with fire engines which had, apparently, played a key part in the Tanners' run to Wembley. The players were reluctantly dragged off to a civic reception and banquet and Micky Cook later gifted me his Wembley tie. Leatherhead received the Isthmian Team of the Month award for May, to go with their runner's-up medals.

1978/79

The use of sponsorship in non-league football was becoming widespread as leagues and clubs battled to combat rising costs and dwindling attendances. Berger Paints became sponsors of the Isthmian League while Leatherhead, on the back of their Trophy run, signed a deal worth about £2,500 per year with Safety Equipment Centres. Matchday and match ball sponsorship was also introduced at Fetcham Grove. John Hewlett was now Chairman of Leatherhead Football Club following the death of Chris Luff, former club secretary Sid Ranger was Vice-Chairman and Tom Dixon returned, after a spell managing Banstead Athletic, as Executive Officer. Other club officials included the long-serving Club Secretary Jack O'Malley, Match Secretary Mike Crouch and Press and Publicity Secretary Nick Hunter-Henderson.

There were few changes on the playing side. Of the previous season's squad only John Bailey was missing, having taken over as player-manager at Three Bridges. 16-year-old schoolboy Graham Whitehead, who could play in defence or midfield, and former Fulham and Peterborough United striker Steve Camp, signed on for the Tanners, Camp scoring a hat-trick of headers on his first outing, a 4-1 victory over Kingstonian. League form was reasonable in the early months of the season with several convincing home successes including a 5-2 win against local rivals Sutton United. Six of the first seven league games at Fetcham Grove produced 3-goal win bonuses. Championship favourites, Enfield and Wycombe proved too strong for Leatherhead, however. The very professional Enfield side that had won the championship by a margin of 31 points the previous season managing the double. When the FA Cup campaign began the Tanners stood second in the league.

As FA Trophy finalists Leatherhead were exempt until the first round proper of the FA Cup where they were drawn at home to Southern League Merthyr Tydfil. A large crowd, including a good contingent from Wales, saw John Baker capitalise on a defensive error to put the Tanners in front. Camp's header made it 2-0 early in the second half as Leatherhead threatened to overrun their opponents but Merthyr came back strongly and after scoring once the Tanners defence, with Dennis Malley a tower of strength, needed to be at their best to hang on for a 2-1 win.
The second round paired Leatherhead with Colchester United, who they had beaten four seasons earlier. Both sides had a Micky Cook, the Essex side, mid-table in Division Three, also including Mike Walker, Steve Wignall and Bobby Gough. Colchester were determined not to be giant-killed again and took the lead through Gough after half an hour. It required a superb individual goal from Chris Kelly following a well worked free-kick to preserve the Tanners' unbeaten home record against Football League sides in the FA Cup and earn a second chance. In the replay Leatherhead held out until just before half-time when former Epsom and Ewell striker Trevor Lee gave Colchester a 1-0 advantage. Three goals in a ten minute spell after the break killed off the Tanners. The Essex club also hit the woodwork twice and ended up convincing 4-0 victors.

There were high hopes of another good run in the FA Trophy but right from the first round tie with Hillingdon Borough the Tanners found it tough going. Hillingdon took the lead at Fetcham Grove before Dave Reid and Billy Salkeld scored to earn a second round trip to Northern Premier League Lancaster City. Under the imposing shadow of the Cathedral, Lancaster forward Ian Innes hit the post twice and John Swannell made several fine saves. A fairly defensive minded Leatherhead side was happy to gain a 0-0 draw, although Reid hit the woodwork himself near the end.
The Green Machine controlled the first half of the replay and went ahead through Kelly, but an improved showing by Lancaster after the break produced an equaliser from Gary Benfold. A few shaky moments were withstood and the Tanners went on to dominate in extra-time, Salkeld and Baker (2) scoring to ensure a 4-1 victory. Renowned Southern League cup fighters Yeovil Town came to Leatherhead for the third round and Barry Lloyd's men from Somerset became the first visiting team to win an FA Trophy match at the Grove. Reid made his 500th appearance for Tanners but Davies and Doyle were out injured, Kelly was very tightly marked and not at his best and Camp missed two good chances with headers. Yeovil grew in strength the longer the match went on but thanks to the brilliance of Swannell did not clinch victory until the 73rd minute with a goal by

David Platt (not the David Platt!).

Form slumped badly after the Trophy defeat, exits from the Hitachi and London Senior Cups rapidly following, but Tanners capitalised on some weak forward play by Sutton United to achieve a 3-1 victory in the semi-final of the Surrey Senior Cup. The final against Isthmian Division Two members Camberley was played at Metropolitan Police's Imber Court ground, but it was not a very arresting performance by Leatherhead that day. John Doyle cancelled out an early Camberley goal but the side from Krooner Park showed more will to win and inspired by Richard Parkin scored three goals in the last eight minutes of extra-time to triumph 4-1. *"I was absolutely ashamed of them"* raged Miller, promising a clearout. The Tanners' cup final jinx had struck again, six finals in five years, all lost.

League form was also below par towards the end of the campaign and the Tanners had to settle for 10th place in the final analysis. Long-serving defender Dave Reid was rewarded with a testimonial match against Portsmouth. He had started out as a junior at Pompey and his famous father Dougie, who had made many appearances for Portsmouth and Scotland, had just retired as groundsman at Fratton Park. Dave's 523 appearances over ten years at Fetcham Grove set a club record which, at the time of writing, still stands. His 67 goals were a tremendous achievement for a centre-half and although most were scored with his head or from searing free-kicks his backside had been used to good effect when deflecting Chris Kelly's shot into the net at Slough earlier in this season. Portsmouth brought along their first team squad for the testimonial game and after Peter Denyer had given them the lead it was fittingly Reid himself who headed the equaliser just two minutes from time.

During an injury crisis earlier in the season Leatherhead had been forced to field 15-year-old Glyn Grammar schoolboy Kevin Gray and this may well have contributed to the decision to set up a reserve/youth side. Other events at the Grove included a Superstars competition for the players, which Chris Kelly won narrowly from Dennis Malley, and a Football Programme Fair, which was organised by programme shop manager, Aubrey Doran.

1979/80

1979 witnessed the 'winter of discontent' with hundreds of thousands of public sector workers going on strike whilst turmoil and change also engulfed Leatherhead Football Club. The loss of Dave Reid to Fareham, the stalwart centre-back finding the 120 mile round trip from his Portsmouth home three times a week too much after ten years, was a major factor. In addition, Ray Eaton left for Wycombe Wanderers, John Doyle suffered a knee injury that restricted him to just one appearance, Barrie Davies was put on the transfer list for a while after missing training and John Baker went on the list at his own request and almost moved to Hendon. The proposed transfer went to arbitration with the Isthmian League Appeals Committee deciding Baker's value at £4,000, at which point the player decided to stay put at Fetcham Grove and signed a new three year contract. Many of the new players coming into the side did not perform as well as had been hoped. Wycombe's former Welsh Amateur international centre-back Alan Phillips was signed to take Reid's place, Hillingdon's Steve Melledew, formerly with Aldershot and Reading came to bolster the midfield and Dagenham striker Mal Harkins was bought for a fee approaching £1,500 to score the goals. Former Brighton youth team defender/midfielder Russell Cox was also signed and Mark Quintyne became the first coloured player to appear for Leatherhead.

Home draws with Tilbury and Hendon and a defeat at Enfield opened the campaign. Successive victories against Oxford City, Hitchin and Slough suggested an improvement, but form dipped again and from mid-September successes were few and far between.

The FA Cup, for once, did not inspire the team to greater things. At home to Croydon in the 4th qualifying round, Steve Camp's header following a corner put the Tanners in front but the visitors equalised from the penalty spot within two minutes. On Monday 5th November, the only Leatherhead fireworks were in the annual display at Fetcham Grove and a poor performance at the Croydon Sports Arena resulted in a 3-0 defeat. Billy Salkeld, Phillips and Melledew were all promptly transfer listed and soon left the club, although Salkeld returned from Croydon within three months for the same £1,500 fee for which he had moved in the first place.

The Tanners scraped a 1-0 win at Wokingham in the 1st round of the FA Trophy but less than a week before the next round, Chairman John Hewlett asked Billy Miller to consider his position at the club. Miller quickly resigned, ending twenty three years association with the club, for the last fifteen of which he had been first team boss. He had been manager for 890 Tanners' first team games. To put this into perspective no-one else has even managed 200 games in charge! Miller soon found new employment at Woking. Dave Wall and Johnny Phipps were appointed dual caretaker-managers at Fetcham Grove, but it was not the best preparation for facing Alliance Premier League leaders Weymouth. Leatherhead performed reasonably well with John Swannell, Chris Kelly, Dennis Malley, Baker, Cox and Lee Harwood having good matches. Colin Brooks put through his own net to give the Terras the lead. Tanners tried hard to get back in the match but Weymouth's tough defence held out and with a young Graham Roberts (later to play for Tottenham, Rangers and England) battling in midfield, they snatched a second goal through Anniello Iannone near the end.

Youngster Harwood had been signed from Wimbledon to fill the problem centre-back position. After half a dozen appearances he returned to League football with Port Vale, where he played nineteen games for the first team, scoring one goal.

The re-introduction of the local derbies over Christmas and the New Year drew big crowds but no points and little cheer following a visit by Woking and a trip to Sutton United. Having already exited from the other cup competitions at an early stage there was little left to play for. The first away league win of the season, a 4-1 victory at Carshalton, followed the Weymouth game but only one of the final ten matches was won as the Tanners slid down the table to finish in 18th place. At the beginning of March, Martin Hinshelwood, the former Crystal Palace player, had moved from Selhurst Park, where he had been youth team coach, to take over the Fetcham Grove hot seat. He was given a three year contract and became Leatherhead's first player-manager and at the tender age of 26 he was the youngest manager in the Isthmian League at the time. Johnny Phipps left the club but Dave Wall decided to stay for the time being. New players drafted in included former Palace youth team members, Steve Dixson and Terry Page. Dixson had also featured in a Kevin Keegan soccer skills television programme, demonstrating the art of tackling on the permed superstar. At 41-years-old, John Swannell had decided to retire at the end of the season. His 'understudy' had been the semi-retired Micky Cuthbert, so the club signed former Crystal Palace and Crewe goalkeeper Peter Caswell (son of former Tanners stalwart Doug), from Alliance Premier League side Telford United then managed by Gordon Banks. Mal Harkins' brief period at the Grove ended with a move to Dartford, as the comings and goings continued.

The new reserve/youth side was sponsored by Hometune and managed by Keith Mills initially and then by Dominic McCarthy. A Leatherhead team including Wayne Falloon, Robert Dilger and Paul Otway, played for the first time in the FA Youth Cup.
Tom Dixon was now Vice-Chairman at the club while Jack O'Malley's sterling service as Honorary Secretary came to an end, Ian Gower-Williams taking over. Gates fell by over 10% but despite the poor playing performances generally there were still further representative honours gained by Malley, Salkeld, Cooper and Kelly who all appeared for the Middlesex Wanderers on a tour of Holland. Cooper, in his testimonial year, and Kelly were also in the Isthmian squad for the OCS Inter-League Cup but did not appear at Dulwich in a 2-0 defeat by the Southern League, for whom Kerry Dixon, then with Dunstable but later of Chelsea and England, scored one of the goals.

◤Poster advertising the big game at Bolton Wanderers.
▲Barrie Davies challenging for the ball at Burnden Park during the FA Amateur Cup semi-final defeat to Skelmersdale in 1971.

◀Ron Fruen scores the only goal of the Amateur Cup quarter-final replay at the Grove versus Hayes in 1974.
▼Goal-scoring hero John Doyle putting the Colchester United defence under more pressure as John Cooper and Peter McGillicuddy look on.

▲Pete Lavers challenges for a header at Brighton in front of a packed main stand at the Goldstone Ground whilst Colin Woffinden and John Cooper wait to pick up the loose ball.

▲Chris Kelly fires home a brilliant goal to win the game and is mobbed by his ecstatic team-mates as he wheels away to celebrate; in stark contrast to the crestfallen Brighton defenders▼.

▲The celebrations continue in the dressing room after the match and as far as the supporters are concerned carry on long into the night in the pubs and clubs of Leatherhead.

LEATHERED

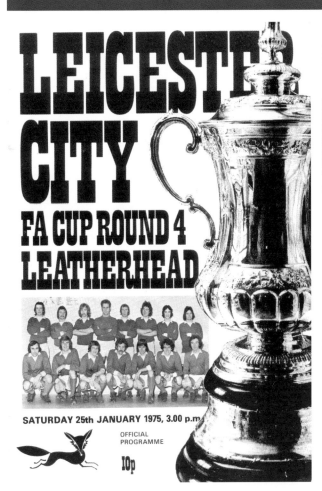

▲The Leicester City matchday programme.

▲The respective captains, Willie Smith and Jon Sammels, toss up at Filbert Street.

▲Tanners players rush to congratulate Peter McGillicuddy after he has put Leatherhead in front.

▲The turning point - Chris Kelly rounds Leicester keeper Mark Wallington and rolls the ball towards the empty net, only to watch in disbelief as Foxes defender Malcolm Munro seemingly appears from nowhere to scramble the ball to safety▼.

▲Brendan Batson heads the ball into his own net to put Leatherhead in front against Cambridge United in this FA Cup first round clash at the Grove in November 1975.

CALYPSO KELLY ROCKS BRIGHTON

Super Tanners topple giant-killer United

Brighton 0, Leatherhead 1

SIX weeks ago Chris Kelly was on the operating table, wondering whether his soccer career was to end at the age of twenty-five under the surgeon's scalpel.

This morning he is the Cup hero who put Leatherhead into a fourth round tie against Leicester with one of the best goals I have seen this season.

After a forty-yard run, in which he rounded past two defenders—"it was my Calypso shuffle that fooled them." said Kelly—and drew goalkeeper Peter Grummitt, he shot home with his left foot—the one on which he had been operated.

Kelly exploded : "That one is for you, doc, thank you very much !"

He is some player, which is why Millwall and Fulham are interested. But it will need a good offer to drag him

LEATHERHEAD 1   COLCHESTER UNITED 0

THE TANNERS players were submerged in a sea of frenzied excitement at the end of Saturday's shock FA Cup second round win at Fetcham Grove after they had killed off Colchester, the most famous of all giant-killers.

The men in green deserved this dramatic victory for they took a paltry Colchester outfit by the scruff of the neck and never allowed them to recover from a John Doyle goal after 20 minutes. Tanners played with confidence and ability. Colchester were half-hearted and their defence,

defenders, lashed a vicious right-foot shot as the ball dropped and it flew in at the far post.

The all-important goal came during a period of complete supremacy by Tanners. A minute earlier Doyle had put through Peter McGillicuddy whose shot was turned away for a corner by 'keeper Walker.

In the very first minute Tanners could have jumped into the lead. A Lavers back-header had Walker in trouble and he was forced to dive

Dominic and Harford, Colchester's two giants at the back, resorted to desperate, long kicks out

TANNERS GIVE COBBLERS THE BOOT:

Leatherhead 2 Northampton 0

MINUTIVE dribble wizard John Doyle took just half an hour to put Third Division Northampton Town inside out in Saturday's FA Cup first round proper tie at Fetcham Grove.

The little forward, so often the man to provide who continued his policy of scoring against every team he has played Leatherhead since the

Brighton on the rocks:

Sunk by Kelly shuffle

HERE WE GO AGAIN!

Leatherhead 2 Cambridge United 0

THE doubting Thomases who didn't believe Leatherhead could bring off yet another F.A. Cup sensation, and that includes me, should have known better. While the Tanners keep pulling performances like this out of the hat, it will take a far better team than Cambridge United to halt them—perhaps only a first or second division side.

Tanners give United a footballing lesson

Kelly's heroes blast City

Leicester 3   Leatherhead 2

THE NAME of Leatherhead resounded around a packed Filbert Street ground at the end of this pulsating, see-saw FA Cup battle as both sets of supporters joined in the chant for the brave Tanners.

They won't forget

Miller's merry men

But Weller lands knock-out punch

Tanners hail Doyle – mis-hit hero

Green Machine keeps on rolling

▲What the papers had to say about Tanners FA Cup giant-killing exploits of the seventies.

▲John Doyle *(on ground)* has just scored his, and Tanners, second goal as Leatherhead defeat Northampton Town in the FA Cup to claim their fourth Football League scalp in just three seasons.

▲Chris Kelly leaps high to keep Leatherhead on the road to Wembley with his second goal against Northern Premier League high-flyers Wigan Athletic in this FA Trophy clash.

▲The Leatherhead squad of 1977/78 *Back row:* Dave Wall (coach), John Deary (physio-therapist), John Bailey, Colin Brooks, John Swannell, Dave Reid, Paul Whittaker, John Baker, Billy Salkeld, John Cooper, Billy Miller (Manager) *Front row:* John Doyle, Micky Cook, Chris Kelly, Dennis Malley (captain), Ray Eaton, Barrie Davies and Kevin Mansell

▲How the local paper reported Tanners march to their first national final.

▼John Baker challenges Alty keeper Eales.

▲The Leatherhead players emerge from the tunnel at Wembley into the warm May sunshine to be greeted by their supporters amongst the 20,000 strong crowd.

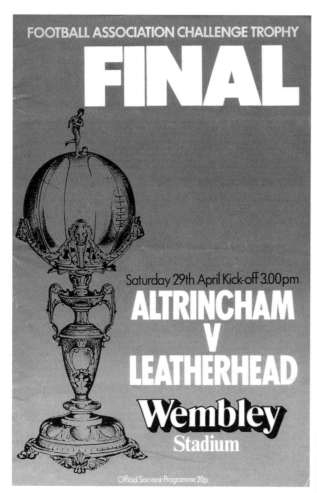

▲The Wembley matchday programme

▲Dave Reid outjumps the Altrincham defence but cannot direct his header on target.

▲The dejected Leatherhead players, led by Dennis Malley, coming down the Royal steps after collecting their medals.

▼Barrie Davies and the rest of the squad acknowledge the supporters, as they parade through the town streets in an open top bus.

◄Altrincham goalkeeper Eales grasps at thin air as Chris Kelly's volley beats him only for the ball to thud against the crossbar and rebound to safety.

CHAPTER THIRTEEN - DECLINE AND FALL

While many people tried 'to get rich quick' in Thatcher's Britain, Leatherhead saw the closure of the long established Goblin and Ronson factories. By way of compensation, the Swan Centre opened and the Reigate ~ Leatherhead ~ Wisley sections of the M25 were completed.

Football hooliganism and the dilapidated state of many grounds were highlighted by the Heysel, Bradford and Hillsborough disasters, leading to the Taylor report and enforced action on ground safety. Even minor leagues enhanced their ground grading criteria and many clubs, Leatherhead included, had to spend limited resources on improving their facilities, often just to stay at the same playing level.

1980/81

Dave Wall remained at Leatherhead as coach under Martin Hinshelwood's management, but several prominent players left in the first few months of the season. John Swannell was persuaded not retire and returned to his former club Hendon, who he helped to a 0-0 draw against the Tanners on the opening day. Swannell had made 333 appearances for Leatherhead, while John Cooper departed having played in 517 games, which left him just short of Dave Reid's record. After 236 games and 86 goals, John Baker also returned to Hendon, for a £1,500 fee (having been valued at £4,000 a year previously) and towards the end of 1980 Barrie Davies, having made 388 appearances in his two spells at Fetcham Grove, joined Cooper and former manager Miller at Woking.
Some of the departures were an effort to reduce the wage bill with the club's coffers none too healthy. The loss of major players was worsened by long term injuries to Billy Salkeld and Robin Kember. Salkeld missed the entire season and the unfortunate Kember, a midfielder signed from Carshalton Athletic and brother of the better known Steve, was stretchered off with a broken leg just five minutes into his home debut against Barking and was out for the rest of the campaign. Centre-back Dave Dyer was signed from Sutton United, following a loan spell the previous season, and John Doyle returned following his long lay off but was never as effective as he had been prior to his injury. Dave Bonner, Chris Wellman, Steve Brennan and Roy Botterill also appeared for the first team alongside Peter Caswell, Steve Dixson, Terry Page, Dennis Malley, Chris Kelly, Micky Cook, Colin Brooks and Russell Cox.

It was not surprisingly a season of struggle for the Tanners. Draws in the first three matches were followed by an embarrassing 5-0 defeat at Second Division Cheshunt in the Hitachi Cup and a 3-0 home reverse against Enfield.

By the time of the FA Cup 4th qualifying round tie with Bath City, Leatherhead had only won twice in twenty matches, scoring just eleven goals. Cup success was not anticipated but the team rose to the occasion producing a gritty display. Caswell and Dyer were outstanding and with Kelly having his best game for some time and scoring, the Tanners earned a 1-0 success.

Back in the 'bread and butter' business of the league, Kelly scored a hat-trick but could not prevent a 5-4 defeat in a thriller at Carshalton. Another loss followed at Slough and Leatherhead were bottom of the Isthmian League for the first time.

Third division Exeter City were the opposition in the FA Cup 1st round proper in front of a 4,607 crowd at St. James Park. Tony Mitchell was with Exeter at the time but missed the match against his former club through injury. Once again Tanners battled well, holding out for half an hour during which time Russell Cox went close from 20 yards. The Devon side then took command. Tony Kellow, the Football League's leading marksman, scored twice and Martin Hinshelwood netted a 'cracking' own goal and although Leatherhead continued to create chances, Hinshelwood hitting the bar at the right end as he tried to make amends, Exeter ran out easy 5-0 winners.

Around the turn of the year away victories at Hayes, Tooting and Woking produced a slight move up the league table but disappointment followed with successive cup defeats by Weymouth (FA Trophy), Barking (London Senior Cup) and lowly Merstham (Surrey Senior Cup).

The search for a new striker was paramount with Ricky Kidd and Alan Whittle among those being approached but budgetary constraints meant that in the end it was Andy Bushnell, who had been scoring well for the reserves, who answered the call. Bushnell scored in a friendly against a Southampton reserve side including Danny Wallace and netted again on his competitive debut against Bromley, the Tanners winning 3-0 to record their biggest victory for more than a year. Roy Elcombe also made the step up from the reserves as Leatherhead's form improved sufficiently for the relegation positions to be avoided. As it happened, there was no relegation due to Enfield and Dagenham gaining election to the Alliance Premier League. Leatherhead were the lowest scorers in the division with just 36 goals, but only the top three sides conceded less than the Tanners. Goalkeeper Peter Caswell, having kept 19 clean sheets, was not surprisingly voted Player of the Year.

Towards the end of the season John Hewlett's long association with the club was severed when, citing health reasons, he resigned from the post of Chairman. Since attending the club's first ever meeting in 1946 Hewlett had at some point in time held every official position except manager. Tom Dixon took over in 'the chair' while A. Lane replaced Ian Gower-Williams as Secretary. Bernard and Tim Edwards were both serving on the committee and Caroline Brouwer was physiotherapist with the reserves. Caroline had made history as the first ever female to be a registered referee with the men's FA and had also followed Leatherhead since the age of nine. She later joined the physiotherapy staff at Wimbledon and was seen leaping into the arms of Dennis Wise when the Dons pulled off their shock FA Cup final win over Liverpool.

Leatherhead concluded the season by winning their own six-a-side tournament. The end of year accounts showed an improvement, but a deficit of £10,800 was still unsatisfactory.

1981/82

This was another topsy-turvy season for the Tanners with more twists than the average Agatha Christie novel. Martin Hinshelwood gave up playing to concentrate on management although he did make a few appearances later on in the campaign. With the departure of Dave Wall, Chris Kelly was appointed player-coach. Wall was the victim of further financial cuts and was sad to be dismissed after twenty two years service. On the committee, Michael Rowell became Vice-Chairman, Steven Waldron - Treasurer and Tim Edwards - Press and Publicity Secretary.

Close season signings included former Dorking and Banstead striker Peter Fitzgerald, ex-Sutton, Woking, Kingstonian and England Amateur international centre-back Micky Preston and Crystal Palace midfielder Chris Sparks. Once the campaign started Terry Eames a midfielder/defender with Football League experience at Wimbledon, was signed from Dulwich. Lee Harwood returned from Port Vale and midfielder Robert Dilger made the step up from the reserves. Russell Cox, Terry Page, Dave Dyer and Roy Botterill were among those departing Fetcham Grove.

The unfortunate Robin Kember, having recovered from his original broken leg, suffered exactly the same fate in a pre-season friendly against a strong Queens Park Rangers side with Ian Gillard, Andy King and Ian Stewart in their line-up.

Despite beginning the season with only twelve contract players a reasonable start was made in the league, including an exciting 4-3 win at Bishop's Stortford, Andy Bushnell scoring a hat-trick. A victory at Croydon took Leatherhead to second place in the table after ten matches. At this stage form took a dramatic turn for the worse. Only one success was achieved in the next nineteen outings as the Tanners tumbled to 16th position in the league. This sequence also included early exits from the Hitachi and FA Cup's, Sutton and Dover respectively ending Leatherhead's interest in replays. The FA Cup 4th qualifying round tie at Dover produced a good performance. Chris Kelly gave the Tanners the lead with a typically skilful goal but Dover equalised and in a poor replay at Fetcham Grove, a below par showing by the men in green resulted in a 1-0 defeat.

The disappointing run caused Martin Hinshelwood to resign after less than two years in charge and return to Selhurst Park as youth team boss. Martin's next first team managerial role was not until 2002 at Brighton. Billy Miller, having parted company with Woking, and Chris Kelly were mentioned in connection with the Fetcham Grove vacancy but reserve team manager and former player Keith Mills took over, initially on a caretaker basis, assisted by Dominic McCarthy. Kelly refused to play against Addlestone but denied that it was because he did not get the manager's job. He was fined two weeks wages and placed on the transfer list but settled his differences with the new management team and agreed to stay. Chris Sparks, however, moved to Sutton.

There were quick exits from the remaining cup competitions and the financial problems caused player contracts to be cancelled when wage bills could not be met. At the end of the season only three players: Doyle, Caswell and Bushnell, were under contract and by the start of the following campaign there was only one. A collection was taken in an attempt to retain the gymnasium and medical facilities at Headley Court. The club, however, angrily denied rumours in the national press that they were on the verge of bankruptcy. The bank overdraft was nonetheless higher than anticipated, with poor results and a dearth of home fixtures compounding the problems.

Dennis Malley, after 252 appearances, and Steve Dixson departed but surprisingly things began to improve on the playing front. Youngsters such as Gerry Robinson and Paul Pritchard moved up from the reserves and Robert Dilger gained a regular place. Leatherhead in fact put together their best run since joining the Isthmian League, eleven matches unbeaten including a notable 3-1 victory at Wycombe. Keith Mills' position as full-time Leatherhead boss was confirmed and he gained the Isthmian Manager of the Month award for March. Against champions elect Leytonstone and Ilford the Tanners recorded a 2-1 home win and a 1-1 away draw and despite losing the final match 2-1 at home to Wycombe, a satisfactory league position of 9th was achieved. Micky Preston was voted Player of the Year and the financial position was a little healthier with the deficit for the year reduced to less than £700.

Former Leatherhead stars such as Sargent, Wells, Cooper, Smith, Woffinden, McGillicuddy, Reid and Lavers returned to Fetcham Grove for Chris Kelly's testimonial in which a Leatherhead Past and Present XI took on a London All-Stars XI which included Peter Osgood, Ron Harris, Ian Hutchinson and Stan Bowles. Keith Mills scored for the Leatherhead side in a 3-1 defeat.

The youth team had a highly successful season under Keith Oram's guidance. Keith's father, Bunny, was bar steward at the club and had been involved with Leatherhead for many years. Keith himself had supported the club since the age of eight and was destined to become first team manager. Paul Estall, Mark Dodman, Paul Otway, Peter Gee, Steve Lunn and Cliff West were in the side that lost to a last minute extra-time goal against Barking in the semi-final of the Isthmian Youth Cup. Paul Pritchard captained the squad that went to Raismes in France

CHRIS KELLY TESTIMONIAL
21st April 1982

LEATHERHEAD XI

v

LONDON ALL STARS XI

OFFICIAL PROGRAMME 50p

Champagne Raffle Draw No. . . 1 6

and won an International junior tournament. Teams from Senegal, Portugal, France and Switzerland were defeated before a final victory against Italian club Angelo Balardo. The young Tanners side included Wayne Falloon, John Hales and Gary MacDonald, as well as Pritchard who was voted Player of the Tournament.

Leatherhead (Sunday) FC included many of the Tanners semi-pro players. Peter Caswell played as a striker in the side that was managed by committee member Martin Collins, later to be in charge at Dorking.

1982/83

George Orwell painted a depressing picture of 1984. For Leatherhead doom and gloom came a year earlier. Three managers, seven goalkeepers and more than 50 players were involved as the Tanners suffered relegation for the first time in their history.

In the 1982 close season three players with over 1,000 appearances between them left the club. Chris Kelly who's 156 goals in 492 games had put him second in the all-time scorers list, John Doyle after 341 games and Colin Brooks after 223, all joined Kingstonian where Billy Miller was now manager. With finances tight the only real newcomer was full-back Peter Ranson from Tonbridge although several of the previous season's reserve and youth squad gained their first team chance, including goalkeeper Peter Trussell and Gary MacDonald, a forward and actor who went on to star in 'London's Burning' and 'Eastenders'. Prior to one match that was in doubt due to the weather, MacDonald gave a display of his thespian capabilities. As supporters rang up to check about the game, MacDonald adopted a different character to answer each call. The supporter who was told the game was off by the manager of a Chinese laundry must have been particularly confused.

A 1-0 victory against Carshalton opened the season and gave little sign of the disasters to come. After a couple of narrow defeats Staines were also beaten 1-0 but from this point on only two more league victories were achieved throughout the remainder of the campaign. Following the worst ever home defeat (8-0 by Tooting and Mitcham in September), the management team of Mills and McCarthy slammed their "*team of posers*" and resigned, only to be reinstated after receiving a vote of confidence at an emergency meeting. Form failed to improve and within another three weeks Mills and McCarthy were sacked. Former Tanners player Brian Caterer and Colin Lippiatt, previously in charge at Windsor and Woking, were appointed as the new manager and assistant manager respectively. Players came and went with alarming frequency as Caterer struggled to find the right blend. Micky Preston, Robert Dilger, Terry Eames, Andy Bushnell, Roy Elcombe and Gerry Robinson departed, the last three going to Dorking. The exodus was reaching biblical proportions.

Many of the newcomers only lasted one or two matches, such as goalkeeper Ian Bath, probably the least successful player in Leatherhead history, who signed on a Monday, played the following night then left. The match he played in was the nightmare 11-1 defeat at Sutton United, the Tanners' worst ever loss with Micky Joyce responsible for nine of the goals. John Rains got the other two and was even booed by some of his own supporters for having the temerity to interrupt Joyce's scoring blitz. Leatherhead's defence had so many leaks that they needed a plumber, not a manager. Mention of the team in match reports tended to be prefaced with the words hapless or hopeless.

Magic Micky hits Tanners —for nine!—

AMAZING scenes at Gander Green Lane on Tuesday night saw stupendous Sutton give poor Leatherhead an incredible 11-1 Servowarm Isthmian League Premier Division tanning — and the hero of the night was star striker Micky Joyce, who set a new club record by scoring nine of them.

Former Woking players Tommy Hewitt, Paul 'Noddy' Holder and Lance Cadogan, Dorking centre-back Andy Cullum and Wycombe midfielder Cliff Jones were among the other arrivals. Only once was the same side fielded in consecutive matches. After seven weeks in which a 2-1 result against Woking was the only victory, Caterer and Lippiatt were sacked and went to Maidenhead United along with Cadogan and several other players. Micky Cook was appointed player-manager, assisted by Joe Fascione the former Chelsea and Hampton player.

Tim Edwards reported that the club had reached the limit on their overdraft. They had lived beyond their means in the past and were now paying for it. The overdraft of £22,000 and outstanding creditors to the value of £8,000 led to further wage cuts. Bad publicity in the national press regarding the financial crisis and other problems caused the loss of a £6,000 sponsorship deal. It was a vicious circle of events. The league's £40 award for three goal wins had been scrapped but Leatherhead came up with a novel scheme to replace it. Supporters pledged £5, with £1 to be taken for every three goal win. This initiative was well supported but not called upon all season! Meanwhile back on the pitch a Waterlooville side including a returning Dave Reid, gained a comfortable 5-2 FA Trophy win at the Grove. A flying header from Gary MacDonald produced a fine victory against Wokingham and Woking were defeated again, this time in the Surrey Senior Cup, but the Tanners failed to win any of their last twenty matches, finishing rock bottom in the league with just seventeen points.

Peter Caswell, who had spent most of the season performing for Brentford's reserve side, returned to Fetcham Grove but for several matches was used as an emergency striker. In the final game against Hayes he came on as substitute to score Leatherhead's equaliser in a 1-1 draw, a result which ended Hayes championship hopes and gave the title to Wycombe.
Centre-back Phil Smith from Banstead, midfielder/defender Tony Coombe, formerly with Epsom, Carshalton and Malden Vale, and Keith Williams came into the side along with youth team players Johnny Hales, Peter Gee and Barry Hempstead. Lee Harwood and Peter Ranson were released.
The upheavals that affected club management and playing staff were also experienced in the boardroom. Brian Bird was Secretary for a while but resigned, Nick Hunter-Henderson regaining the role. Tom Dixon stood down as Chairman but was reinstated five weeks later following an Extraordinary General Meeting, with John Radford becoming Vice-Chairman. John Curran was among the newcomers to the committee.

The youth team had an excellent run in the FA Youth Cup, reaching the 2nd round proper before bowing out 2-0 to Chelsea. George Holland, founder member, Life Vice-President and involved with Leatherhead football for more than 60 years, celebrated his golden wedding anniversary. These were two bright spots in a dismal season.

1983/84

If Leatherhead thought life was going to be easier in Division One of the Isthmian League, now sponsored by Servowarm, they were in for a rude awakening in what was to be a season of two halves. Terry Eames returned from Walton and Hersham and forward Dave Worth was signed from Malden Vale while Holder (Woking), Fitzgerald (Bromley) and Otway (Dorking) left the club.

The opening fixture was in doubt due to cracks in the pitch, but remedial works allowed it to go ahead, Leatherhead losing 2-0 to Hertford Town. League games in the first few months of the season found goals very hard to come by and points were even more of a luxury, as sides such as Windsor and Eton and Farnborough comfortably outplayed the men in green. Miller and Kelly returned to the Grove with Kingstonian and triumphed 1-0. Football League referee Ray Lewis had to be summoned from his armchair in Great Bookham to take over in the middle during this game, when the original referee was injured, with no suitable replacement on hand. Goals did come in the cup matches. Hungerford Town were beaten 6-1 in the Hitachi Cup before defeat at Aveley in the next round.

The Tanners found themselves in the early qualifying stages of the FA Cup for the first time in nine years. Away wins at Littlehampton (2-0) and Egham (5-1, including a Dave Worth hat-trick) were produced before powerful Southern League side Fisher Athletic triumphed 4-0 at Fetcham Grove in the 3rd qualifying round.

Membership and attendances were at their lowest levels ever. After paying the match officials for one midweek game, the remaining £19 gate money did not even cover the cost of floodlighting. Tom Dixon pleaded with the people of the town to, *"help us or we could go out of business by Christmas"*. The club were threatened with closure by the council over unpaid rent and rates. They also demanded repairs to a list of defects, amounting to £30,000 worth of work. Things were so bad that one game was held up when the only ball was kicked out of the ground. Three players appeared in unnumbered shirts having lost the originals. A 'Save the Tanners' campaign was launched and in October, Beau Reynolds, having seen reports in the press about Leatherhead's plight, took over as Chairman. He had served Wimbledon in a similar capacity prior to their entry to the Football League and had also been involved with Epsom and Ewell. Tom Dixon assumed the mantle of Vice-Chairman and Fundraiser. A bank loan was taken out to pay off some of the arrears to the council and Tanners' officials even put themselves in debt to save the club.

Following defeat in the local derby with Kingstonian, the management team of Micky Cook and Joe Fascione resigned, Cook along with Terry Eames going to Kingston! Wayne Falloon's four years in the reserve side now made him the club's longest serving player and he was called up for his first team debut in the FA Trophy tie at Premier Division Staines Town. Against the odds the Tanners gained a battling 0-0 draw and Falloon kept his place in the side. The replay produced an even more surprising 4-1 extra-time victory, Johnny Hales scoring twice.

Micky Leach had now been appointed as the new manager. Leach had enjoyed a good playing career, mainly at Queen's Park Rangers and had been managing Chelsea's reserve side when Leatherhead signed him up. The Trophy victory against Staines flattered to deceive as league form continued in a poor vein including a 7-1 home thrashing by Oxford City in which former Wimbledon and Orient goalkeeper Ray Goddard played his only game for the club. Gradually Leach began to assemble a squad of players that might turn things round. Former Wimbledon midfielder Micky Belfield was signed from FC Ills in the Finnish First Division and Brian Perkins from Southern Amateur League Carshalton. Striker Peter Shodeinde from Hampton, Scottish centre-back Jimmy Richardson, formerly with Hendon, Fulham and in his youth Glasgow Rangers and left-back Dave Eden from Kingstonian also arrived. Youth team goalkeeper Les Cleevely made his first team debut in a 3-1 defeat away to a Chesham side including former England international Tony Currie, but later found things more successful with Carshalton Athletic. Richardson was sent-off on his debut and Perkins looked slow and ungainly at first but two more good performances in the FA Trophy suggested that the team could play a bit. Andover were beaten 2-0 and a useful Windsor side gained a narrow 3-2 victory in a fine match.

A 2-2 draw with Lewes began the New Year. At this point the Tanners were seven points adrift at the bottom of the table. The only way was up, and up they went with an astonishing transformation, as a more physical approach and the long ball game were adopted. A twelve match unbeaten run included victories by 4-2 at Kingstonian, 6-2 over Tilbury and home successes against the eventual top two in the league, Epsom and Ewell and Windsor and Eton. Micky Leach was duly awarded the Divisional Manager of the Month award for February.

The London Senior Cup produced convincing wins against Farnborough (3-0) and Premier Division Bromley (4-0) before an injury weakened side bowed out narrowly to Sutton United (1-0). The team was further strengthened with the arrival of striker Mark Annon from Croydon, former Aldershot midfielder Colin Fielder and centre-back Phil Caulfield from Molesey, although

Caulfield suffered a serious leg injury after just four appearances. Only Caswell, Phil Smith, Worth and Hempstead remained from the start of season line-up.

Despite the upsurge in form, relegation was still a threat as the other lowly clubs also picked up points. A number of convincing victories, including 6-0 thrashings for Feltham and Walton and Hersham, assured safety with two games to spare. An 8-1 win at Farnborough in the final match made most Leatherhead supporters believe that the season was ending too early. 11th place in the table was achieved and the following breakdown illustrates the mid-season turn about:

First 21 matches	Won 3	Drawn 4	Lost 14	Goals for 12	Goals Against 36	Points 13
Last 21 matches	Won 12	Drawn 6	Lost 3	Goals for 55	Goals against 20	Points 42

Top goal-scorers were Peter Shodeinde with 17, Dave Worth 16 and Brian Perkins 16. Shodeinde and Phil Smith were voted Joint Players of the Year by the supporters.

The Leatherhead youth side were defeated at the semi-final stage of the Isthmian Youth Cup for the second time in three years. Having led Farnborough 2-0 midway through the second half they eventually fell 3-2 after extra-time. The youngsters, who included Andy Fisher, also held Brentford, who had Les Cleevely in goal, to a 1-1 draw in the FA Youth Cup.
A certain Alex Inglethorpe was starring for Fetcham Park United and Bookham's junior sides.

The ambitious ground development plans of a few years previously had fallen by the wayside, due to the financial constraints. Nevertheless, a new enclosed players' tunnel was constructed at the far end of the ground and work carried out to try and cure the pitch drainage problem that had caused a number of postponements during the season.

1984/85

This season promised much but was to end in ultimate disappointment. On the playing front, Johnny Hales and Dave Eden were the only significant departures as in came defender Martin Clark from Dulwich, midfielder Marc Turkington from Farnborough and striker Paul Williams from Woking. Williams or 'Spider' had made two Football League appearances for Chelsea as a centre-back but became one of Tanners' most prolific scorers in his year and a half at Fetcham Grove.

Jeff Morrell was appointed General Manager and Secretary while Steve Waldron stepped down as Treasurer. The club's financial deficit had been substantially reduced despite over £2,000 being spent on ground improvements. Stationers Crisallen signed a £2,500 sponsorship deal and there was a pioneering scheme to admit under-12's free when accompanied by an adult.

A 7-1 win at Clapton began the campaign in style, although five Tanners were booked, in what was to be a poor disciplinary season - 45 bookings and 1 dismissal in all. Phil Smith was cautioned on nine occasions and even Peter Caswell had his name taken three times. There were narrow home defeats by Walton and Hersham and Boreham Wood, away draws at Kingstonian and Oxford City, each achieved with a late equaliser and cup exits to Southern League teams Hastings United and Basingstoke Town. Generally the goals continued to flow and league form was good, an eleven match unbeaten run between mid-September and New Year's Day keeping the Tanners in the promotion hunt. Andy Dear and Dave Rattue made the step up from youth and reserve football, Micky Belfield returned from Finland where his club FC Ills had taken on Juventus in the European Cup and former Wimbledon and Millwall midfielder Chris Dibble was signed and soon had everyone 'sorting their life out'. Brian Gayle, who later established himself in Wimbledon's First Division side, was drafted in to play one match at centre-back. Dave Worth left the club, Colin Fielder's appearances were limited through his involvement with Aldershot and Marc Turkington returned to Farnborough.

Into March and Leatherhead lost in the semi-final of the Surrey Senior Cup to Addlestone and Weybridge. Former Chelsea forward Steve Finnieston was kept quiet but England captain Gerry Francis' brother Martin scored the only goal two minutes from time. It was the only match of the season where the Tanners failed to find the net. For their part, Addlestone lost in the final and folded in the summer.

Paul 'Noddy' Holder returned to Leatherhead after spells with Woking and Carshalton, just in time for a vital spell of three games in five days. Maidenhead were comfortably beaten 5-0, and a further four points gleaned from top of the table clashes with Farnborough and Kingstonian. The Tanners came back from 1-0 down with ten men following Phil Smith's dismissal to draw with the former and beat Billy Miller's K's 2-0, in a highly charged atmosphere watched by a near 500 crowd. A spate of postponements produced a hectic end of season schedule. Jamie Nightingale was promoted from the reserves but with Belfield and Dibble returning to Finland the pressure was on. The promotion jitters began to show and at the Grove the players showed all the enthusiasm of a condemned man going to the gallows. Some supporters did not help, by being too quick to voice their displeasure and get on the players' backs. Tilbury and St Albans each recorded 5-2 victories over the Tanners, but sufficient points were gained to remain in the race. Aveley (7-0) and Bromley (3-0) were comfortably defeated and a last minute goal from Andy Dear rescued a draw against Lewes to leave Leatherhead knowing that a single point from their final match at Maidenhead United would clinch the second promotion spot behind champions Farnborough Town. The Tanners went a goal down when Lance Cadogan scored. Maidenhead were not going to make it easy, particularly as Leatherhead had stopped them going up a year previously. Chances of an equaliser came and went but with just a quarter of an hour to go substitute Peter Shodeinde lobbed the home keeper to make it 1-1. The celebrations began in the York Road clubhouse and continued long into the night back at Fetcham Grove.

Some days later came the cruel blow that the Isthmian League's Management Committee had fined Leatherhead £250 and, more crucially, deducted three league points for playing Micky Belfield without receiving the correct international clearance following his spell in Finland. The club appealed to the FA claiming that Wimbledon were believed to be handling his international clearance, as they also wanted him on a non-contract basis. The fine was reduced to £50 but the three point deduction remained. Kingstonian completed ground upgrading work in time so it was they and not Leatherhead  who were promoted. The Tanners were nevertheless top scorers in the league, Williams leading the way with 39 goals in all.

Beau Reynolds had stepped down as Chairman towards the end of the season due to unforeseen business and personal pressures, Gerald Darby taking over. Tim Edwards was now Programme Editor.

1985/86

Most of the previous season's side were retained with the exception of Brian Perkins who went to Farnborough Town but was back at Fetcham Grove by November. None of the new signings, midfielder David Price, striker Lance Pedlar and defender Martin Black were to make a major impact. Price had previously played for Crystal Palace, Orient and most particularly, Arsenal, where he made 116 appearances and gained an FA Cup winner's medal.

Tom Dixon was appointed Club President and Gerald Darby confirmed as Chairman with John

Radford Vice-Chairman. A financial loss of £19,000 on the previous year, mainly due to ground improvements and refurbishment of the clubrooms, was reported. The decision was also taken to disband the youth team. To help the financial situation sponsorship was received from the Swan Centre and a deal struck with Crystal Palace for their reserves to play 'home' games at Fetcham Grove, although this arrangement proved to be fairly short-lived. The Isthmian League also had new sponsors, car firm Vauxhall-Opel, which showed that they were on the right road.

Pre-season friendlies included a first experience of an artificial surface on the 'plastic' at Feltham Arena and a couple of practice matches at Wimbledon's training ground in Roehampton Vale.

Once the serious business started, the Tanners went straight to the top of the table with a six match unbeaten league run. Dave Worth, nicknamed 'Harry' for obvious reasons, returned after a year at Kingstonian, and there was a first team debut for striker Ian Huie, nicknamed 'Lucan' for his ability to disappear during games. Paul Williams was again knocking in the goals and was the only Division One player chosen in the League XI for a representative match with the FA. As well as Perkins and Worth, Andy Dear (Sweden) and Chris Dibble (Finland) returned from playing abroad, although there were great difficulties in obtaining clearance for Dibble.

All was not well, however. Although plenty of goals were being scored, too many were being conceded, a 6-2 hammering at St Albans being a prime example. Interest in the main FA competition had been ended at the first stage, the 2-0 FA Cup defeat by Redhill in the first qualifying round marking the Tanners' earliest exit for sixteen years.

Premier Division sides Boreham Wood and Kingstonian were defeated in the AC Delco (League) Cup and Leatherhead were second in the league going into December. However, following earlier rumours of a rift between manager Micky Leach and the committee, matters came to a head over disciplinary measures to be taken against Peter Shodeinde for refusing to play in a reserve match. Leach claimed it was, "*an unwarranted intrusion into his job*", promptly resigned and was soon coaching at Dulwich Hamlet, where Alan Batsford was manager. Within a few games Barry Hempstead, Jimmy Richardson, Andy Dear, Williams, Shodeinde and Paul Holder had also left. Roger Charland, formerly in charge of Hampton, came in as the new manager. Numerous newcomers were tried alongside the loyal few, such as Player of the Year Peter Caswell, Wayne Falloon, Dave Rattue, Worth and Perkins. Right-back Ray Metz, previously with Sutton United and Harrow Borough, David Hyner, Micky Brookman, Reg Gaston and Michael Rose all at least managed to reach double figures in appearances. Reserves' midfielder Andy Fisher stepped up for his first team bow. Leatherhead's defence was actually tighter than under Leach, but the goal-scoring dried up considerably. An attempt to re-sign the sorely missed 'Spider' Williams, who had scored 61 goals in just 76 games for the club, was unsuccessful. The Tanners plummeted down the league and finished in 14th place.

Some battling cup performances brought appearances in the semi-final of the Surrey Senior and quarter-final of the AC Delco competitions. Horrendous weather caused the Surrey Cup quarter-final with Walton to be postponed no fewer than nine times. Tanners eventually triumphed 1-0, but in the semi-final Chertsey were convincing 4-1 winners against a very inexperienced Leatherhead side. Even though the two games were very close together the anomalies of the qualification rules meant that one player who was able to play against Walton was ineligible for the Chertsey game! In the AC Delco Cup Hampton needed extra-time in a replay to get past the defiant team in green.

As the season ended Charland had announced his resignation as manager and more players left over non-payment of wages. For the suffering Leatherhead supporters - the young 'Molers' behind the goal, the middle aged 'Kop' in the Shack and the ageing 'Politburo' on the central seats, it was another blow.

Keith Oram, a 34-year-old local man, British Telecom engineer and a successful manager at youth level with Leatherhead and Surrey, was chosen as the new first team boss at Fetcham Grove. Keith's father, Bunny, had been a prominent Tanners supporter and fund-raiser in previous years. A number of important players were soon signed: centre-backs Paul Andrews from Molesey, Andy Cullum from Carshalton and Micky Payne from Colchester United, right-back John Cook from Molesey, left-back Andy Riley from Whyteleafe and midfielders Martin Gillings (Epsom & Ewell), Gavin Mayoss (Tooting and Mitcham) and Gary Richards (Crawley). The newcomers banded with Caswell, Falloon, Rattue, Perkins and Fisher in a very unfamiliar looking Tanners side. For the first time two substitutes were allowed, a move that would further test the squad's strength in depth. Peter Caswell, in addition to keeping goal, was a partner in the club's sponsors Lereda 1156 Ltd. A local decoration and design consultancy that took their name from the town's Anglo-Saxon origins.

On the opening day of the campaign the team coach got lost on the way to Stevenage Borough. The game eventually kicked off 40 minutes late and the home side were 2-0 winners. Things improved with only one more defeat in the next ten league games. In defence and midfield Leatherhead were a considerable force. With a bit more up front a pretty good side could have been a great one. Adrian Grant from Whyteleafe and Clive Youlton from Woking were signed in an attempt to boost the team's goal-scoring capabilities. Grant came on as a sub to score a last minute winner against Southern Premier Division side Shepshed Charterhouse in the FA Trophy. It was to be the only goal he managed for Leatherhead. Having already defeated Aveley and Dover the Tanners were in the competition proper for the first time in six years. Vauxhall-Opel Premier Division leaders Wycombe were the next opponents. An inspired battling performance produced a 0-0 draw at Loakes Park. Wanderers, who had only failed to score once that season, dominated the early stages of the Fetcham Grove replay but the woodwork twice and Peter Caswell once, with a stunning save, denied them. Leatherhead grew stronger as the game wore on and with twelve minutes of normal time remaining, Andy Fisher scored after Gillings' shot was only parried. Southern League Aylesbury United came to the Grove in round two. A crowd of 658 witnessed another tight game with chances at a premium. This time it was the visitors who took one, a superb strike from the prolific Cliff Hercules giving Aylesbury a 1-0 success.

Leatherhead gained revenge on Chertsey in the Surrey Senior Cup but suffered a 1-0 reverse to Kingstonian in the 2nd round. Having dominated the game but failing to score, Richard Parkin converted a late chance for a Kingston side run by Chris Kelly and Micky Cook. Incidentally, Billy Miller had by now been sacked as Walton and Hersham manager and been replaced by another ex-Tanner, Larry Pritchard.

There was a fine league victory against promotion seeking Leyton-Wingate despite having Caswell taken off with a bad facial injury in the days before substitute goalkeepers. Outfielder Richards performed heroics between the sticks. Youlton converted a penalty and the Tanners won 1-0. There was enough quality in the squad to give the impression of better results to come, but injuries and loss of form created problems in the last few months of the season. There were heavy defeats by Leytonstone-Ilford and Grays Athletic as the Tanners had to settle for a mid-table position. Only the top three sides conceded fewer goals than Leatherhead, but only the bottom three scored less. Reserve team members Brian Stannard and Mark Joyner had stepped up to the first eleven by the end of the campaign.

The final match of the season produced the best attendance, more than 1,000 watching the fund raising friendly with Bobby Charlton's International XI. Charlton, who had made an earlier visit to the Grove to assist with youth coaching, showed he had lost less of his shooting power than his speed or hair, and scored a hat-trick. Johnny Hollins, Bobby Moore, Dave Webb, Mike Summerbee and Chris Kelly were amongst the other celebrities appearing.

The season was concluded with a dinner dance and 40th anniversary celebration held at the Surrey Hills Hotel, Beare Green.

1987/88

With the exception of Andy Riley, who moved to Carshalton, Keith Oram retained most of the previous season's squad. Attacking options were improved with the arrival of Marc Smelt, a striker previously at Kings Lynn and Gravesend and Northfleet, and Carey Anderson from Corinthian Casuals. Midfielder Gary Carter was signed from Carshalton and there were reappearances at the Grove for Terry Eames and Peter Fitzgerald.

A fairly good start was made in the league with a draw at Stevenage, who were managed by former Tanner John Bailey, and a convincing 4-0 victory against Lewes. Smelt equalised with a great strike at Stevenage to open his account and had reached the eleven goal mark after the first ten games.

There were early exits from the main cup competitions. The magic of the FA Cup was not in evidence on a rain-soaked August day at Darenth Heathside, Leatherhead losing 2-1 to the Kent League outfit. Lewes were defeated in the Trophy, but Ashford Town from the Southern League Premier Division edged through in a 2nd qualifying round tie at Fetcham Grove. The visitors took the lead inside 90 seconds and although Tanners dominated for the remaining 88 minutes, they could not find a way back against a side with a midfield of, "*Brunoesque*" physique.

Fetcham Grove only suffered minor damage from the 'hurricane' of October 1987 but the next two away games had to be postponed through a lack of electricity at Basildon and the absence of a roof on the dressing rooms at Southwick.

Leatherhead had moved up to 5th place in the league, but soon began to slip. Bogey side Basildon United won 3-1 at the Grove as Smelt missed a penalty and Falloon scored at the wrong end with a misplaced back-pass from 20 yards. Smelt and Anderson played for an FA XI at the same time as Tanners' goalless draw with Woking, the Cardinals having refused to change the date of the match. In consecutive weeks during December the Tanners had captain Gary Richards and manager Keith Oram sent-off, Oram being dismissed from the touchline at Marlow. Youlton and Falloon left the club, whilst Kingstonian full-back Kevin Wedderburn was signed. For the return meeting with Stevenage, Borough were without their regular goalkeeper, who had been suspended for streaking at another match! A run of just one win in ten games between February and April saw the league position slide further, but only champions Marlow lowered the Tanners' colours in the last few outings and a respectable final placing of 10th was achieved.

In the County and League Cup competitions, Leatherhead produced battling but ultimately unsuccessful performances against Premier Division Carshalton Athletic.

Marc Smelt, who had to make a 200 mile round trip from Margate for every home game, finished top scorer with 32 goals and was voted Supporters' Player of the Year, but after the inconsistent Anderson left for Dulwich, lacked support up front. Wayne Falloon passed 200 appearances while Peter Caswell reached 350 and was awarded a much deserved testimonial match with Dorking. 'Cazzy' played the first half in goal and the second half as a striker, claiming that he scored the scrambled goal in 1-0 victory.

The lower clubroom at Fetcham Grove was converted for use as a disco/night club while Leatherhead were also honoured to stage the representative match between the Vauxhall Opel and Dan Air Leagues.

Several reserve players broke through into the first team, including strikers Robert Wadey, John Humphrey and Chris Vidal. The reserves went on to reach the final of the Suburban League Cup and took part in two hard fought encounters with Kingstonian's reserves at Tooting. The first game finished 2-2, K's equalising in the last minute of extra-time before going on to win the replay 3-2.

1988/89

Close season talks with potential sponsors had collapsed, showing the far-reaching ramifications of the violence involving England 'supporters' at the European Championship finals in Germany during the summer.

Newcomers to the club included Whyteleafe striker Trevor Smith, Tooting and Mitcham defender Danny Godwin, Feltham centre-back Martin Taylor and Redhill centre-back Tony Welch, while Chris Dibble returned to the Grove after spells at Dulwich and Carshalton. Of the previous season's side Marc Smelt, Andy Cullum, Martin Gillings, Paul Andrews and John Cook departed. Smelt came back to Leatherhead after a period at Thanet Utd, but never rediscovered his previous goal-scoring touch and was soon on his way again, to Hythe Town.

The Tanners had another mid-table season in the league, the biggest excitement being reserved for the final game at home to Chesham United. Having failed to win any of the previous twelve matches hopes were not high when Leatherhead trailed 1-4 with the half-time whistle due. Even when Godwin pulled one back in injury time before the break, not too much was expected, but after the interval and playing some fine attacking football, the men in green made an amazing recovery. Two goals in a minute midway through the half brought the scores level, then Trevor Smith and captain Gary Richards each struck in the last twelve minutes as Chesham went down 6-4.

The FA Cup tie at high-flying Conference side Barnet, managed by the ebullient Barry Fry, had also produced a fighting comeback. With an hour of the match gone, Barnet led 4-1, Dave Sansom (2), Frank Murphy and Gary Abbott the scorers to one by Trevor Smith. The Tanners continued to pile on the pressure as tragedy struck Barnet's goalkeeper who broke his leg in an awkward fall. With both substitutes on, Abbott had to fill in between the sticks. Dave Rattue struck twice in quick succession, and Leatherhead did everything but equalise as Barnet clung on for a 4-3 success.

FA Trophy interest ended in the 3rd qualifying round at Carshalton. Steve Tomlin, who had made one appearance for Leatherhead three seasons earlier, scored both the Robins' goals in a 2-1 success. In the previous round, at Thanet United, red and yellow cards were flashing like traffic lights. Ever so slightly strict referee Mr. Coffin, from the inappropriate location of Peacehaven, sent-off four Thanet players and booked four more as the Tanners coasted to a 3-0 victory. There was a rumour at the time that the Football Association had to employ a full-time administrator just to deal with Mr. Coffin's reports and player suspensions. A year later and five players went for an early bath during the Redhill v Folkestone FA Cup tie.

Tanners' record goal-scorer Fred Stenning, sadly passed away at the age of 73 and a minute's silence was observed prior to the game with Walton & Hersham.

In the Surrey Senior Cup, Cobham were defeated on the same day that local rivals Sutton United gained their famous FA Cup victory over Coventry City. Leatherhead then held rapidly rising Woking to a draw but crashed 4-1 in the replay at Kingfield, despite having scored first from the penalty spot and gone close to increasing this lead.

Former Woking midfielder John Cassidy was now a Leatherhead player and Steve Lammiman had progressed from the reserves to make a handful of first team appearances. The pace and finishing ability of striker John Humphrey was attracting Football League interest, Tottenham and Bristol Rovers each giving him trials. Vidal, Welch, Eames and Rattue all left the club before the end of the season. Vidal moved to Molesey for a £500 fee, but less than a year later was sold on to Hythe Town for £5,000. Coach Ronnie Wilson resigned in May due to pressure of work, after three years as assistant to Keith Oram.

The reserve team defeated Malden Vale's first team in a Southern Combination Cup tie and later reached the semi-final of the Surrey Premier Cup, going down 3-5 to Frinton Rovers after leading 3-1.

1989/90

Keith Oram resigned as manager and Adrian Hill, formerly in charge at Epsom & Ewell and Croydon, but out of the game for two years, was appointed in his place. The experienced Micky Stratford was signed from Grays as player-coach.

Most of the side that ended the previous season departed, including long-serving goalkeeper Peter Caswell, to Dorking, and captain Gary Richards, to Carshalton Athletic. Caswell had made 401 appearances for Leatherhead and later came out of retirement to play twice more in the 93/94 season. Only Kevin Wedderburn, who became Player of the Year, and some of the young squad members, Mayoss, Lammiman, Stannard and Humphrey (restricted to just six games though injury) remained. The new management team brought in winger Tony Boorman from Grays, midfielder Paul Rogers from Alma Swanley, striker Richard Smart, who had only played Old Boys football previously, and former Aldershot, Chelsea and Brentford forward Gary Johnson.

The new look line-up performed disappointingly on the whole with swift departures from the main cup competitions and a slide down the league. Leatherhead were second from bottom in the table in December when Ada Hill resigned. John Cassidy was re-signed from Worthing to take the role of player-manager while Keith Oram returned in an advisory capacity. As with most managerial changes, particularly at non-league level, a wholesale turn around of players swiftly ensued. Among those arriving were goalkeeper Paul Riley from Tooting and Mitcham, veteran striker Mark Davis and centre-back Paul Wooler from Woking, plus defender Tony Wright and striker Tommy Hewitt from Worthing. Midfielder Phil George was also signed from Worthing a little while later while centre-back Richard Strong remained from Hill's side.

From the end of September 1989 to the end of January 1990 Leatherhead had one of the worst runs in their history. Twenty one games without a victory, until Worthing were defeated 2-1 away, the additional motivation for manager and several players of performing well against their former club undoubtedly being a factor. Only a couple more league victories followed, however. Defeats included a 6-0 thrashing at Woking, and, with two games still to play, Leatherhead's relegation to Division II South was confirmed following seven years as members of Division I.

There was some minor consolation provided by the Southern Combination Cup. In the semi-final a Tanners side reduced to ten men came from behind to beat Dorking 2-1 and then in the final with Malden Vale played at Vale's Grand Drive ground, goals from Mark Davis and Steve Lammiman brought a 2-0 victory and Leatherhead's first trophy for 21 years.

The reserves, obviously influenced by first team events, had a poor season but the youth section was beginning to thrive again, the club running seven sides from under-10's to under-15's, most of them competing in the West Surrey Boys' League.

CHAPTER FOURTEEN - CLOSE TO THE EDGE

The growth in out of town superstores was having a negative effect on many of Britain's town centres including Leatherhead, although the prosperity of the area was improved with the arrival of several company headquarters, such as Esso (on the old Goblin site), Brown & Root and the National Grid. The population of the town was now around the 40,000 mark.

Hurricane force winds heralded the start of the decade and Fetcham Grove seemed to be flooded at least once each season. Was global warming taking effect?

Football was undergoing something of a resurgence in popularity, with big money sponsorship, The Premiership, Champions League, satellite TV coverage and Euro 96 all contributing factors. A number of clubs moved into smart new stadiums but at grass roots level, for teams like Leatherhead with their council owned ground and limited funds, things became even tougher, although they were now part of a recognised national pyramid.

1990/91

Manager John Cassidy had a new assistant, Bill Stoves (formerly at Dorking and Farnborough), for the Tanners' first season in Division II South of the Vauxhall (Isthmian) League. Newcomers on the playing staff included experienced former Fulham, Brentford and Aldershot defender Paul Shrubb, midfielder Andy Taylor from Bookham and striker/midfielder Noel Fletcher. Later in the season midfielder Tony Calvert from Cove and defender Roland Pierre from Southall arrived, while Carey Anderson and Clive Youlton were among the players returning for second spells at the Grove, following time at Sutton and Woking respectively.

WATCH OUT, WATCH OUT, THERE IS A HUMPHREY ABOUT

Rob Dilger also returned briefly and scored after just seventeen seconds of the opening day 2-0 win at Hampton. A cure for relegation blues perhaps? Defeat followed against the eventual champions Abingdon Town but early results were sufficiently good to keep Leatherhead in the promotion chasing pack. Some convincing victories were recorded; 5-0 at Cove, 5-1 at home to Petersfield, 5-0 at home to Chertsey and 7-0 in an away game with Camberley played at Epsom and Ewell. John Humphrey scored a pair of goals in each of the aforementioned matches, earning himself the nickname 'Noah' in the process. Humphrey was top scorer for all divisions of the Vauxhall League with 22 goals. Such striking prowess did not go unnoticed. After trials at Millwall and having also been watched by Ipswich Town, he eventually signed for Millwall earning Leatherhead an initial four figure sum. Humphrey actually made his Football League debut while on loan to Exeter City and his time at Millwall was spent in the reserves, until the injury jinx struck again leading to a long spell out of the game.

Two particularly good league performances by the Tanners were the 3-3 draw at Malden Vale (having been 3-1 down), a result which ended Vale's 100% record, and the 1-1 draw at champions elect Abingdon Town, a game in which Leatherhead held the lead until six minutes from time. After the loss of Humphrey in February the goals did not flow so freely and form suffered. Results included a 4-1 home defeat to Southall, for whom Justin Fashanu scored twice, and a 2-0 reverse at Banstead on Tanners' first league visit to Merland Rise for 40 years. Isthmian reorganisation meant that to ensure a place in Division II for the following season, a finishing place in the top half of the table was essential, those in the bottom half going down to Division III. The required position was only clinched in the last minute of the final game, short-sighted Ian Huie's dramatic goal earning a 1-1 draw with runners-up Maidenhead United.

Cup competitions saw Leatherhead's first FA Vase tie, a 2-1 defeat at Sussex County League

Pagham, and initial matches in the Loctite Trophy, a new competition for the lower divisions of the Isthmian League and, some would say, Walt Disney characters.

Paul Wooler who glided gracefully across the pitch and did sterling work at the back when over confidence did not get the better of him, still found time to score nine goals on his sorties upfield and was voted Supporters' Player of the Year.

Tim Edwards resigned after more than a decade of serving on the committee including stints as Press Secretary, Programme Editor, Club Photographer and matchday announcer. Team changes were always clearly read out though support had declined so much that it might have been easier to announce the crowd changes to the players.

In March, A. G. 'Bunny' Oram, who had spent 25 years of his life involved with Leatherhead Football Club, particularly as Commercial Manager, sadly passed away.

1991/92

Italian sports shoe manufacturer Diadora, whose UK Chairman was Sebastian Coe, took over sponsorship of the Isthmian League for the 1991/92 season. Serving officers at the club included A. J. Eldridge (President), Gerald Darby (Chairman), former player Ian McGuire (Vice-Chairman and Treasurer), Bill Cannon (Secretary), Bernard Edwards (Match Secretary), John Loveridge (Membership Secretary) and Keith Oram (General Manager).

Respected coach Micky Byrne, with previous experience at Southall, Hayes and Walthamstow, as well as abroad in the USA, New Zealand and Western Samoa, came to Leatherhead, originally as first team coach. However, just two days prior to the start of the season, manager John Cassidy was dismissed and Byrne appointed in his place. Officials felt that Cassidy was no longer up to it as a player and criticised his fitness level. A decade later and Cassidy was still turning out for Westfield in the Combined Counties League. Meanwhile, the new boss confidently predicted a top three finish and a good FA Vase run.

Byrne soon assembled his own squad, including battling midfielders John Lawler and Paul Steffe, both New Zealanders from the Papatoetoe Club that he formerly managed, goalkeeper Colin Caulfield from Woking, much travelled striker Steve Russell, Dorking forward Ray Arnett and winger Clevere Forde from Southall. Way back in 1978 Forde had fetched Hounslow Town's record transfer fee of £4,000 when he moved to Plymouth Argyle. Mark Joyner returned after a spell at Hampton and the long dreadlocks and fine dribbling skills of Andy McCollin also made a brief reappearance. Noel Fletcher, Paul Riley and Clive Youlton were among the players departing for pastures new. Once the season started Carey Anderson and Kevin Wedderburn both moved to Dorking.

A pre-season friendly with a Millwall XI including John Humphrey attracted, what proved to be, the biggest crowd of the season (400). The opening league game with Malden Vale was edged 1-0. The large rugged visitors were described as, "*a mining town side after the last pit had shut*".

More new arrivals soon followed, including another Kiwi - Paul Marshall, Hampton left-back Micky Dalton, Southall midfielder Jerry Alleyne, Yeading midfielder Earl Whiskey, goalkeeper Paul Martin from Wembley and strikers Lance Pedlar and Clifton Soares. The most interesting signing, however, was that of former 'Barnardos boy' and England Under-21 international striker Justin Fashanu. At club level he had made 163 appearances and scored 51 goals, including the 'Match of the Day' Goal of the Season in 79/80, for Norwich City. He then became the first black million pound footballer when signed by Brian Clough at Nottingham Forest and also played at Southampton and Notts County. On his return from Canada, where he had appeared for Toronto Blizzard, he chose a trial at Newcastle United instead of a place at Leatherhead, but after just eleven days and one substitute appearance with the Geordies, 'Fash' was released and came to Fetcham Grove, claiming he just wanted to play for fun and with no pressure. Rumours of alternative offers and his imminent departure surfaced daily but despite missing a penalty on his Tanners debut Fashanu remained for eight games, helping the club to the top of the table, as well as attracting a lot of press interest and increasing attendances. He was certainly influential as Ray Arnett became the first Leatherhead player to score four goals in a match for sixteen years, in a 4-2 victory at Saffron Walden. In the same game Micky Byrne became an emergency linesman for a ten minute spell up to half-time, following an injury to the original man with the flag. Fortunately there were no controversial incidents.

The Tanners made early exits from all the knockout competitions. Kevin Tilley became the first Leatherhead player to be sent-off in an FA competition, during the FA Cup tie with Corinthian Casuals (like buses, two more were to come the following season). Ex-Sutton United player and FA Cup goal-scoring hero Matt Hanlan scored both goals in Dorking's victory in the next round.

Promotion was certainly the number one priority, however. Following Fashanu's departure to Torquay United (for a fee of £2,000), form dipped a little but there were fine victories over champions elect Purfleet, by 3-1, and away to promotion rivals Billericay by 3-0, Billericay's main striker Steve Jones, later to play for West Ham and Charlton, missing several good chances. If Byrne's enthusiasm and confidence had been enough Leatherhead would have gone up. However, despite remaining undefeated in games with the three clubs that were subsequently promoted, too many silly points were dropped and 4th place was all that could be achieved in the end. The side bristled with skill and plenty of fine football was played but there was not always enough punch in the box, only Steve Russell scraped into double figures in the goal-scoring stakes, and problems were experienced against the more physical sides.

For the final match of the season against Worthing there was a 28 year age gap between the two substitutes. Joe Rayfield, only just 16-years-old, and manager Micky Byrne, aged 44. Both came on, Byrne's twenty minute appearance provoking intense excitement every time he got near the ball, which was surprisingly often. For the record, Leatherhead won the game 3-0.

Solid defender Roland Pierre was voted Supporters' Player of the Year, while Paul Steffe and Fijian international James Hoyte attracted League club interest from Millwall and West Ham respectively.

1992/93

Leatherhead had a new Treasurer (Richard Warren) and a new Secretary (Martyn Cole), following the death of the long-serving Bill Cannon. Founder member and Life Vice-President George Holland also passed away.

Carlton Mitchell, Tony Collins and Ian Bascombe were added to the previous season's squad, now often referred to as Micky Byrne's London All Stars. With the exception of Whiskey, Forde, Russell, Marshall and Lawler it looked likely that the rest would remain until the pre-season friendlies. Fine performances against Crawley Town, Windsor and Eton, Kingstonian and XI's from Wimbledon and Crystal Palace bode well for the forthcoming campaign. Once again there appeared to be light at the end of the tunnel, although this ignores the oncoming train about to arrive. The display at Crawley in a 3-2 victory was particularly good. Unfortunately, Crawley thought so too and promptly signed Paul Wooler, Colin Caulfield and Jerry Alleyne.

With little time left to rebuild it was not too surprising that a tough season ensued. Other factors did not help. In an effort to boost support midweek home matches were switched to Wednesdays, a day which clashed with a course that Ray Arnett had to attend. Goalkeeper Paul Martin failed to turn up for the game at Tilbury and for the home match with champions elect Worthing did turn up, but at Worthing not Fetcham Grove. As he had scored Leatherhead's goal from a penalty and punched an own goal into his net during the away game with Worthing earlier in the season he might have been expected to remember that he had already played there. Despite the above events, Arnett finished as top scorer, boasting four in a game for the second time, in a Surrey Cup tie at Merstham, and Paul Martin topped the appearance list, being ever present in all bar the two aforementioned matches. Martin also had to cope with the first season of goalkeepers not being able to handle back-passes.

Big names, Francis Joseph, the ex-Wimbledon and Brentford striker, and veteran Hayes defender Reg Leather arrived during the season but only stayed for a couple of games apiece. Full-back or winger Ramon Forrester and midfielder Neil Harlow, son of the Life Vice-President and former player Chris Harlow, were also signed and Paul Marshall returned after a period with Fareham.

The ever optimistic Micky Byrne reckoned that, "*we are playing the best football in the division*". The team's style won friends but, unfortunately, not enough matches. A final league placing of 14th was achieved but there was some drama in the cup competitions. The Tanners were drawn against Aldershot Town, the newly formed side arising from the ashes of the old Football League club, in the Isthmian League Cup. The 1-1 draw after extra-time at Fetcham Grove was witnessed by a crowd of 800 including a handful of troublemakers. Although only a handful in number they were more than a handful in deeds, fighting in the bar, stealing club mementos and striking Paul Wooler by the side of the pitch. 1,510 attended the replay a week later with the Shots winning 3-2.

First successes in the FA Vase were achieved with narrow victories over Alma Swanley and Ringmer but defeat followed in the Gloucestershire town of Nailsworth, 2-1 to Forest Green Rovers, Paul Steffe's penalty miss proving costly.

Two games later Steffe scored a superb hat-trick in a 5-0 league win against a Berkhamsted side that then underwent an amazing transformation which took them from a relegation threatening position to promotion. At one time Barnet and Chelsea were reported to be interested in Steffe but nothing came of it.

In the Surrey Senior Cup, Sutton Utd gave the Tanners a thrashing while the Associate Members Cup (formerly Loctite Trophy) produced the first penalty shoot-out involving Leatherhead, at the end of a pretty poor match with Camberley. Leatherhead won the shoot-out 4-3.

Towards the end of the season Lance Tooley and Tony Bates, nicknamed 'the Mitchell Brothers' by some and from a leisure industry background, took over as Joint-Chairmen with Gerald Darby becoming Club President. The lower bar was refurbished and reopened and further plans for ground improvements were made.

1993/94

Micky Byrne led Leatherhead into the season in new jade green shirts, declaring that the squad was capable of promotion and a good run in the Vase. Two ex-League players, Paul Canoville (Reading and Chelsea) and Frank Sheridan (Derby and Torquay), joined the ranks. Micky Payne, Dean Smith and briefly, Paul Wooler, returned to Fetcham Grove but there was the significant departure of defender Roland Pierre, who had undoubtedly been one of the most consistent players in his time at Leatherhead. Paul Steffe also left to try his luck with Stevenage Borough and then Welling United before returning to New Zealand.

The FA Cup campaign did not last long but produced plenty of goals. A Ray Arnett hat-trick and a brace from Micky Payne led the way to an 8-3 thrashing of Langney Sports from Sussex, although it had been 8-0 with about ten minutes left. In the next round Mario Russo exploited huge gaps in the home defence to score four for Metropolitan Police in a 5-3 success, Arnett's two injury time goals giving the final score an air of respectability.

The Tanners were desperately close to defeating First Division side Staines Town in the League Cup, but failed to take their chances and fell to two late goals in extra-time. More misfortune surrounded the FA Vase exit. Fetcham Grove became flooded after the River Mole burst its banks. A foot of water got into the recently renovated lower clubroom and further problems to the boiler room and electrics meant that the Vase tie with Whitehawk had to be played away. A narrow 1-0 defeat followed, Stannard's penalty miss proving costly in a game of few chances. Whitehawk went on to reach the quarter-finals. Micky Byrne decided it was time to resign, ending his increasingly fragile hold on the manager's job. Former player Trevor Smith, who had returned to Fetcham Grove as assistant manager in the close season, now took temporary charge but after eighteen days the job went to Terry Eames, another former player who had been at Molesey and, as youth team coach, at Carshalton. Terry Mills was appointed assistant manager with Keith Oram as General Manager.

The managerial changes provoked the almost inevitable turnaround of players. Canoville, Sheridan, Arnett, Paul Martin, Carlton Mitchell and Tony Collins all departed, most linking up with Byrne again at Egham Town. Newcomers included goalkeeper Steve Osgood from Wokingham, forwards Jamie Earp from Sutton Utd and Kevin Glavey from Carshalton Athletic and midfielder Paul Bentley from Feltham and Hounslow Borough. The upheavals did not assist league progress and the entire season was spent just off the bottom of the table. Tanners' supporters had to wait until mid-November to see the first home league goal, this solitary strike being enough to defeat Hampton. Heavy defeats were received from the three clubs running away at the top of the league - Chertsey (including ex-England internationals Kenny Sansom and Ricky Hill), Newbury and Aldershot. The Leatherhead players looked like, "rabbits caught in car headlights" as wave after wave of Aldershot attacks rained in on the Tanners' goal, final score - 0-5. Leatherhead's biggest ever home reverse was equalled when Thame Utd won 8-0 at the Grove. Visits to Ware continued to be marked by defeats and an inability for Tanners to complete the match with a full complement of players, Mark Dunn becoming the third Leatherhead player to be sent off in consecutive visits to Buryfield. Some consolation was provided by victory against 'Leatherhead Old Boys' - Micky Byrne's Egham side containing seven ex-Tanners, one of whom, Frank Sheridan, got himself sent-off. A healthy crowd approaching 1,000 attended for the visit of Aldershot and Kevin Glavey scored a hat-trick at Hampton to provide Leatherhead's first away win for seventeen matches. At the home game against Witham, Tanners supporter Dick Wilkinson was giving visiting defender Liam Cutbush 'a bit of stick' as he came off for half-time. Cutbush promptly removed his boots and leapt over the barrier to attack Dick. The referee saw the incident and immediately dismissed the offender. Perhaps Eric Cantona heard about it as well.

In April 1994 Tanners problems worsened. Joint-Chairmen Tooley and Bates resigned. They had organised the redecoration of the lower clubroom, changed the tea bar into an American style Diner and resurfaced the car park leaving it similar to Brighton Beach, but, in part due to the floods, the lower clubroom did not generate the required business. Manager Terry Eames was next to go.
A new consortium, ABA Leisure, comprising businessmen brothers Ben and Eamon Ashi and player and club captain Paul Bentley took over the running of the club. Bentley, Terry Mills and Robert Jackson, who had been running the reserves, were charged with joint running of the first team for the last two games. Relegation looked likely. With debts hanging over the club and players not being paid, credit is due to those that stayed to fight the struggle. Leatherhead lost their two remaining matches, 2-1 at Malden Vale and 6-3 at home to champions Newbury. On the final day Lewes had been leading Metropolitan Police 1-0 before having a player dismissed and going down 4-2. It was only this result that saved Tanners from the dreaded drop but it looked likely that it would be only a temporary reprieve unless there was a dramatic change of fortune..

It had been a hard season. A record 70 players appearing on first team duty, more than forty of whom made fewer than ten appearances. Mark Joyner was voted Player of the Year. He was one of only 5 players whose name appeared on the team sheet more than 30 times during the season - Glavey, Smith, Lammiman and Stannard being the others.

1994/95

Former player Paul Andrews moved from Feltham and Hounslow Borough to take over as first team manager, assisted by Terry 'Frenchie' Mills. Alan Salmon became the new Club Secretary.
On the playing side Roger Walcott, Chris Holding and Andy Jepson were among the new arrivals but Mark Joyner departed and Brian Stannard retired (although he later returned to help out in an injury crisis, and later still was enjoying a prolonged return at Dorking).

Double Olympic gold medallist Daley Thompson made his professional soccer debut for Reading in a pre-season friendly at Fetcham Grove, and scored the only goal of the game within two minutes of coming on as a substitute.

Leatherhead recorded their biggest competitive victory for 20 years when thrashing Letchworth Garden City 8-0 in the FA Cup with Mills describing six of the goals as, "*of World Cup quality*". Unfortunately, only 79 people were present to witness this goal-fest. In the next round Tanners held Diadora Premier Division leaders Hayes to a draw before crashing out 4-0 in a replay.

Early league form was poor, the Tanners perhaps taking time to get used to the kick-in, an alternative to throw-ins being tried out as part of a FIFA experiment. This idea had little merit and was dropped at the end of the season. The first success eventually came away to Micky Byrne's Egham and a good spell followed including an impressive 3-1 victory over league leaders and forthcoming FA Vase finalists Oxford City.

Leatherhead's Vase run appeared to be over before it had started when 3-0 down at Redhill after twenty five minutes but a battling performance produced a 4-3 success in extra-time. A narrow 2-1 victory followed, again after extra-time, at Thame United in the next round, Will Powell scoring two fine individual goals. Kevin Glavey unfortunately broke his ankle in this match and was out for the rest of the season. It was an injury weakened side that went down 4-0 at Sussex County League Stamco in the 2nd round. Stamco, including five players with Football League experience, went on to beat Tiverton in a later round before losing out at Canvey Island.

Hugh Mann, Tony Welch, Steve White and Nigel Webb all came into the first team squad and striker Ray Arnett returned from Egham and was soon on the goal trail. Results were generally mixed for the rest of the campaign but a comfortable mid-table position was secured. Attendances had sunk to an all-time low, only 48 spectators saw the game with Hemel Hempstead and the average home league gate was just 83. Leatherhead did, however, capture one trophy. A team of Nigel and Tony Webb, Bentley, Mann, Millard and Arnett defeated Kingstonian, Molesey, Cobham, Corinthian Casuals and Hampton to win the Ditton 5-a-side tournament.

In February 1995 the 20th anniversary of the 'Leicester match' was celebrated with a reunion organised by Derek Wells. All but one of the 1975 side, plus quite a few players from earlier years attended. Dave Sargent (Eastbourne Utd reserves) and Willie Smith (Old Boys football) were still regularly playing at the time.

As the season neared its conclusion a development fund was set up in order to try and raise £10,000, the sum required for ground improvements to take place and ensure Fetcham Grove met the new grading criteria.

1995/96

In the 1995 close season a new group took over key positions within the club to try and restore Leatherhead to their former glory. In came Keith Wenham, an ex-Football League referee, and David Zackheim, as Joint-Chairmen, Mike Thornton as Finance Director and twice capped former England international Mike Bailey as General Manager. At club level Bailey had made over 450 appearances for Wolves and Charlton and had served Portsmouth and Brighton in a managerial capacity. Bailey's duties now included washing the kit, something he probably did not have to do at Fratton Park or the Goldstone Ground. A three year sponsorship deal, worth £15,000, was signed with construction company Marchants. With an eye to the future the youth team was reformed. Sufficient ground improvements took place for Fetcham Grove to gain a satisfactory 'B' grading. The bar was also smartened up and an impressive wall of memorabilia formed, in general there was a far more optimistic air about the place.

Paul Andrews had been sacked before the season started with fellow co-manager Terry Mills taking sole charge of playing affairs. The team was fairly lightweight, however, usually being out muscled on the pitch. Fundamental defensive errors also proved costly. The playing surface was not conducive to passing football either with Mills describing the pitch after a 2-2 draw with Croydon in December as, "*like playing on the Norfolk Broads, especially when kicking towards the Boggy End*". Mills' position always seemed precarious and it was no surprise to most supporters when Mike Bailey took over team management in February 1996. Bailey was no stranger to non-league management having replaced Malcolm Allison at Fisher Athletic during the 1989/90 season. Under his guidance the south-east London side won their last four games to narrowly avoid relegation from the Conference. Newcomers on the pitch, where three outfield substitutes were now permitted, included Welsh defender Simon Jones, striker David D'Rosario and Dorking full-back Laurence Ennis. Brothers Tony and Nigel Webb, Paul Bentley, Steve Lammiman, Andy Jepson, Tony Leslie, Ray Arnett, Robin Welch and Hugh Mann all played prominent roles in the first team. Lammiman broke his sternum in a car crash, but soon returned to the side. Mann had been instrumental in Fisher's relegation escape mentioned above, scoring nine goals in the last five games of the season, including all four on the final day against Merthyr. Among later additions to the Tanners' squad were former Dorking striker and record goal-scorer Steve Lunn, Egham midfielder Paul Reed and Carshalton Athletic defenders Michael Brady and Steve Lawson.

As far as results were concerned it was a pretty unremarkable season with a league position below halfway and early exits in the major cup competitions. Five of the first six games under Bailey were won. A run of eight straight defeats followed, before a reasonable final sequence of one defeat in five. Rare highlights included a 5-2 win at Metropolitan Police, Nigel Webb contributing a hat-trick, and the games with eventual champions Canvey Island. A hard fought and well deserved 1-1 draw was gained in Essex and although the home match was lost 2-4, it was only after a fine match and a comeback from 0-2 down to level at 2-2 with ten minutes left, Tony Leslie scoring a cracker. On the downside was the sight of Leatherhead finishing the game at Bracknell in April with just eight players after Lammiman, Robin Welsh and Brady were all sent-off during a highly contentious match eventually won 3-1 by the home side.

In attack Leatherhead did appear to have the makings of a dangerous strike-force. Ray Arnett finished as top scorer despite missing one match of the season for his wedding and honeymoon, and was voted Supporters' Player of the Year.

Long-serving club stalwart and most recently Programme Editor Bernard Edwards sadly passed away, while supporter Michael Anderson became Chairman of Mole Valley District Council. Leatherhead's new limited company achieved turnover of £91,000 in their first year, nevertheless a loss of £8,000 resulted.

1996/97

Gani Ahmet, Chris Harris and Elliot Davidson were the major new signings as the Tanners entered their 50th anniversary season. Before the competitive action started, Leatherhead took on and defeated Football League outfit Brighton and Hove Albion 2-1 in Steve Lammiman's testimonial match, manager Jimmy Case, ex-Liverpool, among those playing for the Seagulls.

Early form was mixed, impressive league victories over Ware and Bracknell and a 9-3 FA Vase demolition of Broadbridge Heath being countered by exits from the FA Cup (1-0 at Tonbridge) and Guardian Insurance League Cup (5-1 at Aveley).

At this point Mike Bailey, who had experienced problems dealing with the players that he regarded as professionals, left the club and the more 'streetwise' Keith Wenham took over team management, as Director of Football. He made an inauspicious start with a 3-0 home reverse inflicted by Witham but this preceded an eleven match unbeaten run which took the Tanners to the top of the league. The goals were flying in with Steve Lunn, Ray Arnett, Nigel Webb and Paul Reed all moving quickly into double figures for the season. Hemel Hempstead were thrashed 9-0, Leatherhead's biggest league win for 28 years, since a 9-0 Athenian League success against …. Hemel Hempstead! Neil Hams, one of the subjects of a revealing Channel 4 documentary about apprentices under Graham Rix at Chelsea, and Alan Whiter signed on at Fetcham Grove while Michael Brady returned after a spell at Carshalton Athletic.

The Tanners came from 2-0 down to get a point at home to big spenders Collier Row and Romford and in front of a crowd of over 400 drew 1-1 in a top of the table clash with Horsham. An FA Vase defeat at Burgess Hill preceded a slightly shaky spell. Wenham branded the performance against Ware as, "a *pathetic display. There was more movement on the bench than on the pitch*". Good form soon returned however, and 19 of the last 23 league matches were won as the promotion charge gathered increasing momentum. Ross Edwards and Danny Bower had now joined to strengthen the Tanners' squad for the run-in and Steve Lunn rejected offers from Kingstonian and Dorking in order to stay at the Grove. Chairman Zackheim urged local people and businesses to get behind the club. The division's second best attendance of the season, 673, attended the Mole Valley derby with Dorking on Easter Monday, Tanners winning 3-0. Dorking chairman Jack Collins had floated the belief that the two clubs would in due course merge, as Mole Valley United perhaps. A few days later there was a vital match at the Sungate ground of Collier Row and Romford with posters around the ground billing it as 'Judgement Night'. The Tanners, already without Lunn and Steve Lawson, lost Reed through injury early in the game. Having gone behind to a penalty converted by ex-Arsenal player Martin Hayes, Nigel Webb levelled and a superb battling performance appeared likely to yield a point until Tony Welch snatched a late winner for the home side. Despite this setback promotion was still confirmed that night, with three matches still to play, due to results elsewhere. These last three matches were all won but 'the Romford' as they were about to become, pipped Leatherhead to the championship by just one point. Nevertheless, 95 points, well over 100 league goals and a first promotion for 33 years were pretty good compensation.

FINAL TABLE (TOP 3)

Team	Played	Won	Drawn	Lost	For	Against	Points
Collier Row & Romford	42	28	12	2	93	33	96
Leatherhead	**42**	**30**	**5**	**7**	**116**	**45**	**95**
Wembley	42	23	11	8	92	45	80

Had it not been for an injury to Steve Lawson, the Tanners would have uniquely fielded four sets of brothers for the final game, namely the Edwards, D'Rosarios, Lawsons and Webbs.

Steve Lunn finished top scorer for the whole of the league with 44 goals in Icis (Isthmian) competitions and was voted Player of the Year by both players and supporters. The team's league and cups goal tally of 158 for the season set a new club record.

The nearest thing to cup success was a run to the semi-final of the League's Associate Members Trophy, ended by Wealdstone in a replay.

The main men behind this excellent anniversary season were Gani Ahmet, Nigel Webb, Tony Webb, Chris Harris, Paul Reed, Elliott Davidson, Ray Arnett, Steve Lunn, Steve Lawson, Michael Brady, Alan Whiter, Ross Edwards, Steve Lammiman, Neil Hams, Danny Bower and Mark Byrne, while off the pitch David Zackheim, Keith Wenham, Terry Quick and Bob Davis all played important roles.

1997/98

Leatherhead, back in Division One of the Isthmian League after a seven year absence, gained backing from Cornhill Insurance and started a Clubcall telephone line for the first time. Icis were replaced by Ryman as League sponsors midway through the season.

More works were required to keep up with ground grading requirements. The club had to fund most of the improvements themselves. Mole Valley Council offered £2,000, a sum that Keith Wenham described as *"totally inadequate"*. A proposed public share issue never got off the ground due to a poor response.

Almost all of the previous season's side were retained, the squad further strengthened by the addition of Scott Tarr, the goalkeeper who had just helped Banstead to an FA Vase semi-final. Alex O'Brien, Danny Lavender, Simon Sobihy and Darren Anderson also joined the club. Berkhamsted were defeated 3-0 on the opening day, Ray Arnett scoring his 100th goal for the Tanners, thus becoming the first player to reach the century mark since Chris Kelly.

Tony Webb and Elliott Davidson both had brief spells away before returning. Leatherhead were removed from the League's Full Members Cup having reached the semi-final stage because Davidson played for the Tanners having appeared for Romford in an earlier round. Other cup progress was limited, although it took Vauxhall Conference side Woking to remove the men in green from the Surrey Senior Cup, in a match switched to Kingfield.

League form was fairly impressive until the turn of the year, when Leatherhead stood 2nd in the table, albeit from more matches than most of their closest rivals. There were particularly good wins against Chertsey, Romford, Uxbridge and Worthing. The games with Aldershot attracted excellent crowds. The Tanners lost narrowly 1-0 away in front of 1,888 and drew 0-0 at home in a fairly drab return, the attendance of 1,540 being the best at Fetcham Grove for some years and the largest ever confirmed home league gate at that time. Aldershot went on to win the championship in style.

Bob Davis stepped down after just nine months as Chief Executive of the club leaving Keith Wenham to take on more responsibility. The team turned in a series of 'Jekyll and Hyde' performances as the New Year was entered. Alex O'Brien was sent-off for fighting with an opponent at Berkhamsted. A frustrated Wenham relegated Ahmet, Lavender and Nigel Webb to the bench after defeat in this game, allowing Laurence Head and Ben Papa to make debuts. A last minute goal by lowly Thame inflicted Tanners' first home league defeat for almost a year, causing chairman Zackheim to read the riot act to the players. After a run of only one win in eleven league games, Wenham resigned as manager while retaining his role as Chief Executive and taking over the running of the reserve team. Former player Gary Richards, who had only returned to the club six months earlier, stepped up to take charge of the first team. Form improved under Richards and there was only one defeat in the last seven matches allowing a satisfactory top half of the table finish. Custodian Scott Tarr was voted Player of the Year.

The reserve side had a very successful season, finishing runners-up in the Southern Division of the Suburban League and winning the Suburban League Cup. In a very exciting final Chesham United were eventually defeated on penalties, after two hours of football had produced a 3-3 deadlock.

Leatherhead Ladies completed their first season in the Greater London League, having stepped up from the South East Counties League.

Chairman, David Zackheim reiterated his intentions to get Leatherhead up to a higher level stating, *"There's a train leaving for the Conference and you'd better get on board now"*. Whether the local council, and for that matter, the local population, would provide the necessary support for this quest remained to be seen.

1998/99

Tanners' colours reverted to green and white quartered shirts, as opposed to stripes, and the club also had the use of an impressive new training ground at Stoke D'Abernon (now the site of Chelsea's plush new multi-million pound training complex).

Gary Richards began the season as team manager, but after a mediocre start Keith Wenham surprisingly reassumed the role of first team boss, with Richards as his assistant. Experienced central defender Tommy Warrilow, left-sided midfielder Junior Harvey and full-back Wesley O'Connor arrived at the club. Steve Lammiman, after 249 first team appearances, Elliott Davidson, Alan Whiter and Danny Bower departed during the close season. Steve Lunn missed the first two months through work commitments while Chelsea's Football in the Community Officer, Chris Harris, only played a couple of times. As the season progressed some old friends returned to the club: Gani Ahmet from Carshalton Athletic, Paul Reed, following a brief spell at Hampton, and John Humphrey from Aldershot Town. Five players made their debuts in the opening day success against Worthing, victory owing much to the acrobatics of Tarr. A goal shy attack, lack of midfield creativity and lengthy injury list meant that it was often a struggle for league points, although the defence was fairly solid.

In September, Chairman David Zackheim once again bemoaned the lack of support from the local community, although interest increased a little during a fine FA Cup run to the final qualifying round. Whitehawk were comfortably despatched in Wenham's first game back in charge. In the next round a bad tempered match with Sheppey saw three players, including Tanners' David Ward, dismissed and Wenham sent from the dugout for abusing a linesman as his frustration at the team's ineptitude boiled over. Five days later Ward was again sent-off, in the league defeat at Berkhamsted, this time for headbutting his own centre-half Warrilow. Ward was promptly dismissed from the club. Having defeated

FA Cup, 4th qual round:
Heroes denied at the death

Leatherhead 1
Rushden & D 1

HEROIC Tanners came within an ace of smuggling the Diamonds out of the Cup.

the league table. Their manager Keith Wenham has often been their fiercest critic but he had

made a telling tackle o block at some time in : stirring second half.

Whitehawk, Sheppey and then Windsor and Eton, the Tanners were rewarded with a home tie against high-flying Conference side Rushden and Diamonds. With the financial clout of Doctor Martens footwear boss Max Griggs, Rushden had just splashed out £100,000 on experienced Northampton Town pair Carl Heggs and Ray Warburton. The eagerly awaited match was twice postponed after the River Mole flooded. When it did take place, Steve Lunn gave Leatherhead a shock lead on the stroke of half-time. This narrow advantage was defended admirably against a constant stream of crosses. Warrilow headed clear so often that he probably ended up with the ballmakers name imprinted on his forehead. Zackheim could not bear the tension and retreated to the boardroom for the last fifteen minutes. Agonisingly, just two minutes from time, Rushden equalised. At their superbly appointed ground Diamonds gained a comfortable 4-0 victory in the replay. They went on to defeat Third Division Shrewsbury Town and reach the 3rd round proper where they held Premiership side Leeds United to a draw and even took the lead in the Elland Road replay in front of a 40,000 crowd, before succumbing 3-1. Some consolation for Tanners was the ovation given by both sets of supporters and their share of gate receipts, 1,143 watched the game at the Grove and a further 1,855 saw the replay.

There was a flurry of goals towards the end of the year including wins by 6-4 (Leyton), 7-3 (Croydon) and, in the League Cup, 5-2 at Premier Division Hampton. The goal feast was followed by a famine, with a consequent marked downturn in results. A run of nine straight losses plunged the Tanners into the bottom three in the league. The home League Cup quarter-final with Aldershot was narrowly lost 1-0, in the midst of this sequence. The popular and long-serving Ray 'Razor' Arnett, after 259 appearances and 115 goals for the club, had now retired to concentrate on work and family commitments. A further blow was the loss of excellent goalkeeper Scott Tarr to Gravesend and Northfleet, amid reports of dressing room tensions. Some reasonable results, however, kept Leatherhead battling on against the threat of relegation. Victory in the final home game against Leyton Pennant was followed by a fine win at Worthing; Ross Edwards getting the vital goal in what was only Leatherhead's second away success of the season. Results elsewhere meant that safety was secured prior to the final day's 3-0 defeat at Bognor Regis. The Tanners finished in 17th spot but just one point above third bottom Molesey. Nigel Webb was top scorer with 19 goals and voted Supporters' Player of the Year.

> Saturday witnessed an appalling performance at Whyteleafe, where I don't recall us getting a shot or header on target in the whole ninety minutes, and that included a penalty! Had there been a prize for sticking the ball on the Leafe's Darren Anderson's head 400 times, we would have been laughing.
>
> DZ

A typically forthright assessment of Tanners performance in Chairman, David Zackheim's, programme notes.

It was still a struggle financially. A dispute with the council over rent arrears was eventually settled and the debt paid but a burglary caused extensive damage to the clubhouse, the playing budget was cut and it was decided to scrap the reserve side as a cost-cutting measure. Better relations with the council were cemented with the visit of Chairman John Butcher for the 4-1 victory against Whyteleafe. His son Peter, an experienced referee, got closer to the action than anticipated when one of the linesmen failed to arrive and he volunteered his services.

David 'Cigar Man' Zackheim, who had pumped £80,000 into the club over four years, urged the council to provide more financial help as other local councils, such as Woking, had for their own teams. Keith Wenham, who had given up his job with a liquidation company to become full-time Managing Director of Leatherhead FC, stood down as team manager (again) at the end of the season, to concentrate on building up the commercial side of the club.

1999/2000

Tommy Warrilow, despite having no managerial experience and not being first choice, took over as boss from Wenham, stating that he would only play when necessary. It was to become necessary on 34 occasions! Richards remained as number two, with former Leyton Orient and Watford player Alex Inglethorpe appointed as youth team coach, a particularly important role with the club having no reserve side. Ross Edwards (Gravesend & Northfleet), Steve Lunn (Whyteleafe), Gani Ahmet (Tooting & Mitcham), Stuart Lawson (Tooting & Mitcham) and John Humphrey left the club with Jimmy Bolton, Paul Malcolm, Michael Rootes, Tommy Williams and Richard Vercesi arriving. The release of the popular Lunn came as a particular shock to the fans.

The season started badly. It was not until the ninth game that victory was achieved. At least the matchday programme was much improved with Robert Wooldridge, formerly at Carshalton, as editor. After the initial success, against Uxbridge, results picked up for a while. Warrilow brought himself in as emergency striker and had soon become leading scorer. Both Webb's departed, Nigel later returning after five months with three different clubs - Yeading, Aveley and Whyteleafe. Paul Hart was signed from Molesey to take over in goal from Tony Webb. With some fine performances behind an often beleaguered Tanners defence, Hart went on to receive the Player of the Year award. Steve Lawson, Darrell Teasdale, Danny Lavender, Ben Papa and Ben Loney were the other mainstays of the side, along with captain Alex O'Brien, who had a brief spell at Walton and Hersham, following barracking from a section of the crowd, but soon returned.

Keith Wenham was replaced by Maurice Everest as General Manager and shortly after took over as manager at Aveley. Dean Worsfold, only just turned seventeen, stepped up to the first team and then gained a YTS place at Millwall.

Good performances came in the FA Trophy, with a 2-0 victory (the first win in the Trophy since 1988) over Beazer Premier Division side Kings Lynn who included ex-professionals Jeremy Goss and Gary Mills in their ranks, and in the Surrey Senior Cup, the Tanners only losing on penalties to Conference high-flyers Kingstonian following a 1-1 draw.

In the league, Leatherhead managed to hold the top four sides away from home but often stumbled against lesser opposition and Fetcham Grove form was generally not as good.
News that the future of the club was under threat first broke in December 1999, £60,000 in debt and losing £2,000 per week. Increased costs and wages since promotion to Division One, expenditure on the ground to comply with grading regulations and vandalism and flooding that could not be fully insured for, were all taking their toll. The club needed £3,000 a week to break even but were generating barely a third of that figure. Chairman David Zackheim, who had been paying player's wages out of his own pocket, threatened to pull out and warned that, *"one day soon, people are going to turn up at the gate and it will say 'Leatherhead FC - R.I.P.'"*. Players were not paid for a while and there were further rumours of a merger with Dorking. As if to prove that it never rains but it pours the River Mole flooded once again, causing extensive damage to the clubhouse and electrics, closure of the tea bar and the loss of much needed matchday revenue.

Lumps in the throat and tears as Tanners play the final game?

In December there was a fine 4-1 win against Braintree, but the home game with Thame United on the Saturday before Christmas only took place after the players agreed to turn out for nothing and some frantic activity behind the scenes by club stalwarts. Against the odds Tanners came from 2-0 down to draw with the then second in the table Oxfordshire side. There were emotional scenes at the end of what, at the time, was thought by many to be Leatherhead's last ever game. There was passionate support, lumps in the throat and a few tears at the entrance to the player's tunnel where a large group of supporters gathered to applaud the players off the pitch, however, fears that this could be the final match proved to be unfounded and the club managed to soldier on.

As the new millennium began a six man group from the senior side of the club and from those involved with the youth team agreed to sponsor running costs until the end of the season, but stressed the need for more people to become involved.

Four senior players: Bolton, Malcolm, Vercesi and Alan Cockram were released as a cost-cutting exercise and youth team players such as Matt Brewer and Darren Blight were given their chance. Five members of the youth side played against Worthing and the attendance of 252 was the best for two years. The enthusiasm was there, but a period of five months without a home win saw Tanners sink back into the relegation zone. This sequence was ended with a 2-0 victory, the first of the new millennium, over Bedford Town, in the penultimate game, but in the final outing Leatherhead crashed 5-2 to relegation rivals Harlow Town. Fortunately, they managed to finish ahead of Leyton Pennant and Chertsey, as 20th place was, by default, sufficient to stay up. Hemel Hempstead who had won the Division Two title were denied promotion through having failed to get the required ground grading by the appointed date. They provided a three and a half-hour presentation of their case at an FA appeal into the matter, but the appeal failed.

The under-18 side finished runners-up in the Southern Section of the Southern Youth League and might have won it but for the abandonment of a tempestuous match with Faygate Falcons, after four Leatherhead players had been sent-off.

Off the pitch, Warrilow resigned as manager, *"before he was pushed"*, claiming that, *"the reason I was having trouble with my back for the last month, was most probably to do with all the knives"*.

The 'consortium of six', with Tim Edwards as spokesman, vowed to put in £25,000 for each of the next two seasons provided that sponsors or other backers could be found to match that amount.   Ex-pros Alex Inglethorpe and Craig Maskell were being lined up as the new management team and there were rumours that film star and local resident Sir Michael Caine had put money in. Not a lot of people know that. After reports of the financial position appeared in the local press donations were received from far and wide, including £1 from a former resident now living in Australia.

Local companies failed the club however, and the financial backers pulled out. At a last ditch crisis meeting towards the end of May, Tim Edwards spoke passionately and eloquently about the club. He feared however, that they would have to drop down

No extra time for Tanners

THE axe is hanging over Leatherhead Football Club once again unless it can find £25,000 by the end of the month.
 Club secretary Gerald Darby this week warned that if a cash lifeline cannot be found then football will cease at Fetcham Grove.

to the Combined Counties League, or suspend operations for a year, in order to survive. The 70 or so diehard supporters that attended were vehemently opposed to either of these options. The swell of enthusiasm led to the formation of a Supporters Committee that would take over the running of Leatherhead FC as a members club. The Limited Company could then be wound up. Those present accepted that it would be a rough ride for a while. Colin Ward, author of 'Steaming In', 'All Quiet on the Hooligan Front' and other similar books had his own view of the situation, *"We have got into the lifeboats and we have been drifting without any oars. Now we have some and we are starting to row to the shore, but it's a long way off"*.

CHAPTER FIFTEEN - NEW MILLENNIUM, NEW HOPE

In the 21st century top level football is big business, with sponsorship, blanket television coverage and merchandising among the key issues. Attendances continue to rise, more clubs are relocating to new grounds and foreign players are to be found in ever increasing numbers. The gap between the haves and the have-nots is widening, however.

At grass roots level there are attempts to rationalise the non-league pyramid. It is still a struggle for many clubs. Leatherhead FC having almost folded at the start of the millennium, are gradually regaining stability and rekindling a spirit that has been lacking for a number of years.

Whilst managing to retain its rural setting the town itself is in a growth area with commerce and industry attracted by its convenient location close to the M25 and the London airports.

2000/01

Leatherhead Football Club had come desperately close to folding in the close season. Now, as a Members Club once again and with the slogan 'a club run by it's supporters for the benefit of its community', there was renewed hope. A new management board was elected, with Tim Edwards (Chairman), Graham Richards (Secretary), Laurence Herbert (Financial Director), Colin Ward (Commercial Director), John Loveridge, Dick Wilkinson, Matt Weller, Dave and Simon Blasczowski, Peter Botting, Derek Bywater, John Drake, Bob Elcombe, Roy Haines, Jim Smithers, Chris Woodward and Robert Wooldridge serving as the initial officers and committee members. Milner Carpets provided sponsorship, largely in the form of a new carpet for the main clubroom, once the leaky roof had been fixed. There were talks with Bookham about joining forces to become 'the biggest community club in the country' but these discussions ultimately fizzled out.

Earlier plans to have Leyton Orient player Alex Inglethorpe and former Southampton striker Craig Maskell as player-manager and player-coach were now out of reach. Inglethorpe went to Exeter City, Maskell to Hampton and Richmond Borough, where he was one of the top goal-scorers in the Ryman Premier Division. Steve Lunn was offered the manager's job but turned it down. Eventually Clive Howse, ex-Chertsey Town, Woking reserves and assistant manager at Kingstonian, was appointed team manager, with Chick Botley, formerly boss at Banstead, Hampton and Fleet, as his assistant. Howse said of his task, "*You don't need to be a rocket scientist to work out we will lose more than we will win. On the budget available we will use youngsters, with some experienced heads. There are no players left on contract, so we will trawl local parks looking for talent*". Players were only to be paid expenses, most of which was to be provided through supporters' pledges. Only Tommy Williams remained from the previous season's first team squad, so Howse and Botley did remarkably well to organise any sort of side. A programme note on Williams commented that he, "*likes to shoot from all distances, but refuses to go and find the ball afterwards*". New players included former professional Andy Sayer, who had made around 150 appearances with Wimbledon, Sheffield United, Leyton Orient, Cambridge United, Cardiff City and Fulham, goalkeeper Andy Hunt, Fleet defender Luke Jolly, Wealdstone midfielder Paul McKay, who had twelve Football League appearance's with Burnley to his name, defender Gareth Cope and midfielder Jamie Beer from Hampton. Also arriving were Julian Old, Iain Hendry, Matt Ottley, Croydon Athletic keeper Stewart Vaughan, Darrell Teasdale, returning after a brief spell at Redhill, Camberley Town striker Paul Harkness, Danny Oliver from Bookham plus Molesey and former Banstead Athletic forward Warren Burton, who did not play until February due to injury.

The pre-season friendlies were spiced up by the inaugural Advertiser Challenge Trophy and Maureen Wooldridge Memorial Trophy matches against Dorking and Banstead respectively, although both were lost. Referee for the Dorking game was Ray Lewis, a resident of Bookham and a match official who had graduated from the Isthmian League to the very top level of English and European football. He was referee at the Hillsborough disaster match, the Arsenal v Tottenham FA Cup semi-final at Wembley and Juventus v Napoli in the UEFA Cup, amongst other games. Back in the 70s Ray trained with the Leatherhead team at Headley Court and in more recent times could often be seen with his dog (No, not a guide dog) as a spectator at Fetcham Grove. His sportswear company was also a supplier of kit to the club.

Early league form was disappointing, only one point in the first ten games and that thanks to a dreadful last minute error by the Bromley goalkeeper, but many of the defeats were by narrow margins. Ben Papa had returned to the club and there were further new signings in the shape of Richard O'Connor, a classy midfielder from Kingstonian, Jeremy Jones from Yeading and defender Aaron Roberts on loan from Basingstoke Town. Clive Howse and Chick Botley reversed their managerial roles, before Howse left and former Fulham player Brian Cottington came in as coach. The first league success came in the eleventh game, at home to then 4th in the table Oxford City. The first away win followed shortly after, at Whyteleafe. From then to the end of February only two victories were recorded, a thumping 5-1 Boxing Day success against Walton and Hersham, Harkness scoring his second hat-trick for the club, and a 4-1 win over a Romford side playing their first game back after a spell of suspension from the league. The Tanners were deep into the relegation mire, although for a while it appeared that the Ryman League restructuring plans would save them once again. However, the FA ruled that the reorganisation could not take place until 2002-03. A mini revival took place in March. A 600 minute goal drought was ended with a 3-2 victory against Staines and further successes followed. Chick Botley (Division One Manager of the Month for March) and Stewart Vaughan (Safe Hands award), gaining recognition for their efforts. In the end, it was just too little too late. Leatherhead finished in the third relegation spot, five points behind Wealdstone, who the Tanners had defeated in both meetings.

One of the best cup performances of the season was the 3-1 victory at Premier Division Maidenhead United in the League Cup, Harkness scoring one stunning goal from a superbly delivered long pass by O'Connor.

Southern League Evesham United were run close in the FA Trophy and Tooting and Mitcham, including more than half a team of ex-Tanners, ended interest in the Surrey Senior Cup.

Sayer, Papa and Harkness were among those leaving during the season. Replacements included Egham full-back Stephen Garrood and Dean Worsfold, returning on loan from Millwall.

The dreaded floods struck again in what was a particularly wet season. Fetcham Grove was waist deep in water and featured on TV news reports. There were some bright spots. Notably, the club was still going and the dedication and enthusiasm shown by the Management Committee and others was an inspiration. A presentation evening in March highlighted the achievements thus far while stressing the continued efforts required for the future. An international branch of Leatherhead Supporters Club had been formed by Kjell Friestad, from near Stavanger in Norway. His father had lived in Leatherhead for more than twenty years.

Stewart Vaughan, who had performed admirably in goal and, for a time, outfield as an emergency striker, was voted Supporters' Player of the Year. The Players' Player award went to Iain Hendry. The Leatherhead Sunday side, run by Chris Woodward (Senior), did at least win some silverware in the Invicta Sunday League.

2001/02

A new sponsorship deal helped Tanners attract Alex Inglethorpe as a player and joint-manager.

Inglethorpe had gained Football League experience with Watford, Barnet, Leyton Orient and Exeter City and he opted to turn down job offers from clubs higher up the Pyramid and from abroad in favour of his local club. Chick Botley began the season as fellow joint-manager, but soon resigned to leave Alex in sole charge. Brian Cottington returned to assist Alex. Cottington had spent ten years at Fulham, making around 100 Football League appearances and earning the nickname 'The One-Goal Wonder' for his solitary contribution to the scoresheet during a League Cup tie with Bury. He also picked up fifteen Youth international caps for the Republic of Ireland and after persistent injuries forced him to leave the full-time game, an FA Trophy winner's medal with Enfield. His only previous managerial experience had been with Wimbledon Ladies and Ditton.

Officials Robert Wooldridge, Graham Richards and Bob Elcombe stepped down, the first two taking similar roles at Kingstonian, Elcombe to concentrate on Bookham FC with the planned links between Leatherhead and Bookham not being developed further. Maurice Everest and Paul Everett took over Colin Ward's commercial role. Gerald Darby and John Loveridge returned as Club Secretary and Matchday Secretary respectively. Sam Dubberley became the new Programme Editor and Jon Coombe assumed the mantle of webmaster, in charge of the Tanners internet site. The Norwegian branch set up their own website, P.I.L.S. (Peoples International Leatherhead Supporters). Chris Inglethorpe and John Syrett were added to the Management

Committee. Finances were still extremely tight with sponsors Milners and Toshiba, supporters' 'pledges and wedges' and the Pitstop Community Project providing vital assistance. Pitstop is a registered charity that provides a daytime drop-in centre for the homeless, unemployed and socially isolated in and around Leatherhead. To emphasise the disparity in football finance, a week of David Beckham's wages at the time (£100,000) would have covered the Tanners' playing budget for the next five years. A single day's earnings would have allowed a new clubhouse to be built. At least the pressure and competitiveness of Division 2 of the Ryman League was reduced, the league's restructuring plans meaning that there was to be no promotion or relegation at stake for this season.

Richard O'Connor (Hampton and Richmond Borough), Darrell Teasdale (Tooting and Mitcham) and Aaron Roberts left the club. A number of youngsters were signed, including Peter Maynard, Chris Hall, Chris Woodward and Dorking pair Craig Duffell and Gary Syrett. Striker Duffell had been for trials with Southampton and Syrett was Dorking's Young Player of the Year for 2000/01.

The pre-season build up went fairly well with victories in two minor cup competitions. Inglethorpe scored a hat-trick in a 4-2 win at Dorking to capture the Advertiser Trophy and Banstead were narrowly defeated in the Wooldridge Trophy match. The first two league matches were also won, forward Phil Ruggles, on loan from Woking, scoring five goals. A number of different front men appeared during the campaign, but most did not stay long enough. Ruggles' loan spell came to an end, Warren Burton went to Dulwich and Kezie Ibe (another loan player) and Stefan Ball each had brief successful spells before settling at Hampton and Tonbridge respectively. This left Inglethorpe to do the bulk of the scoring and when he was out injured the Tanners strike-force was very lightweight. Ibe scored four in an 8-0 demolition of Metropolitan Police and, in the very next league game, the Tanners trounced Wivenhoe 9-1 away, Inglethorpe contributing five. Alex finished the season as top scorer with 35 goals at a rate of about a goal a game. Other notable league performances saw a 4-1 victory against Leyton Pennant and a 0-0 draw with eventual champions

Lewes, as Leatherhead finished in a respectable 11th position.

In the FA Cup large financial incentives were available. £1,000 was gained by ousting Whitehawk in the preliminary round, but the Tanners missed out on £7,500 and the chance of further rewards by losing at Oxford City. The FA Vase produced a dismal 7-2 defeat at Combined Counties club Ash United, but Leatherhead gave a better account of themselves in the other cups, although still losing at the first stage. Holders, Crystal Palace, including a number of players with first team experience, came to Fetcham Grove in the Surrey Senior competition and won through 3-1 on their way to retaining the cup. The Tanners recovered a two goal deficit in the League Cup tie with Leyton Pennant, only to concede again in the final minute.

New players who appeared as the season progressed included Tommy Smith (Dorking), Tony Perfect and Richard Allicock (Hampton), Wesley Cain (Hemel Hempstead) and goalkeeper Justin Gray (Molesey). Gray replaced Stuart Vaughan who went to Corinthian Casuals, wanting to play as a striker! Smith and Stefan Ball cost Leatherhead a transfer fee - the £41 required to cover their League suspension fines!! Two former Tanners, Ben Papa and Danny Lavender, returned from Molesey and a number of youngsters from the London based Pro-Sports Youth Academy were given a chance.

There is little doubt that the most attractive wearer of the Leatherhead shirt this season was page three model Jo Hicks, the resultant photo appearing on the Tanners programme cover and in the Non-League Paper, on page three of course.

After a period of legal wrangling over minor points, Leatherhead managed to agree a new 25-year lease for Fetcham Grove with the council. The lease was in the name of the Limited Company, which the club had to retain in order to stay in the league and keep membership of the Football Association.

Paul McKay was voted Player of the Year by both players and supporters, Danny Oliver winning the Manager's award. Iain Hendry topped the appearance list for the second year running. Overall, it was a reasonable season with Alex finding local players committed to the club and building for the next campaign.

2002/03

Reorganisation of the Ryman League meant that Leatherhead were in the 24 team Division One South. A double financial boost from reduced travelling costs and increased matchday income was anticipated, with lots of local derbies, but it was a tougher league to play in. Big budget sides such as Carshalton Athletic and Bromley were among Tanners' opponents. Croydon and Croydon Athletic, who the previous season had competed three divisions apart, were now at the same level.

Alex Inglethorpe turned down lucrative coaching jobs at Premier Division clubs Kingstonian and Aylesbury, to stay at Leatherhead. Team spirit was good with the manager and players even helping with the usual pre-season makeover work on the pitch and ground maintenance. Links were formed with Surrey Intermediate League side Horsley (who were to serve as Leatherhead reserves) and Bookham Colts (to allow progression through to Tanners' under-18 youth side). Chris Hall, Dean Worsfold (Horsham) and Craig Duffell (Dorking) left the club and Ben Papa was forced to retire, but this was countered by the signings of young strikers Phil Ruggles and Ali Chabaan. Ruggles came from Woking, following his successful loan spell in 2001. Chabaan had been top scorer and Young Player of the Year for Dorking in 2001-02. Aldershot Town defender Jon Lloyd was also taken on.

Leatherhead were one of the first opponents for the new AFC Wimbledon, the breakaway club formed due to the decision of Football League Wimbledon to relocate to Milton Keynes. Former Tanners player and manager Terry Eames, was in charge of the new Dons who attracted a best of season crowd of about 1,200 to Fetcham Grove for the pre-season Maureen Wooldridge Memorial Trophy match. The bar takings were particularly good because, after Leatherhead had won the match 2-0, about 300 of the Dons' followers watched fellow supporter Darren Langley win a Commonwealth Games boxing silver medal, via the clubhouse TV. Later in the season Chessington United staged their Combined Counties League match with AFC Wimbledon at Fetcham Grove, pulling in around 900 spectators. The Tanners also retained the Advertiser Trophy, defeating Dorking 1-0. Commonwealth Games hammer gold medallist Mick Jones resisted the chance to throw the trophy and settled for presenting it to Leatherhead captain Danny Lavender at the end.

Early league performances were patchy, but the FA Cup provided some relief. Victories at Banstead Athletic and Abingdon Town set up a 2nd qualifying round tie with Bromley. Just four days before the cup match, Leatherhead met the same opponents in the league. Tanners' Chairman, Tim Edwards and Bromley manager, Stuart McIntyre were both senior management with Lloyds TSB. Tim and friends, in the guise of The Nobby Skinner Appreciation Society, sponsored the match and other Leatherhead officials arranged for former Tanners favourite Nobby Skinner to be a surprise guest at the game. Michael Webb came on as a late substitute to rescue a point in a 1-1 draw and then almost the same thing happened in the cup clash, again 1-1 with Webb appearing late in the day to snatch an equaliser. The replay at Bromley produced one of the best performances of the season, a 4-2 victory for the Tanners with Ruggles scoring a hat-trick. In the next round, a goal three minutes from time brought Ford United a 2-1 success and an end to Leatherhead's cup run, although they were £16,000 better off in terms of FA prize money. Part of the cash was used to purchase a tractor with attachments in order to assist with pitch maintenance. The tractor was later christened 'Bromley'.

As the turn of the year approached Leatherhead were perilously close to the foot of the table. There had been few successes in the league and early exits from the FA Trophy (6-0 at Berkhamsted) and Bryco League Cup (3-0 at Witham). Tall midfielder Paul Harford, ex-Arsenal youth, Blackburn Rovers (where dad Ray had been manager), Aldershot, Farnborough and Sutton, was signed from Bracknell. Following the departure of Brian Cottington, Harford was appointed to a player-coach role and form started to improve. It took a while for results to match performances as too often Tanners were made to pay for missed chances, the 1-1 draw with Epsom and Ewell, where both Chabaan and Inglethorpe failed from the penalty spot, being one example. However, wins over Walton (4-0) and Horsham (2-1 away) improved matters. High-flying Bognor Regis, second highest scorers in the division, were twice held 0-0, but then in a relegation 'six pointer' with Molesey, ex-Tanner Wes Cain scored the only goal, for the visitors. The Leatherhead faithful need not have worried, for the remaining games produced seven wins and a draw, including a highly impressive 3-1 success against promotion seeking Dulwich Hamlet and thrashings for the bottom two clubs, Chertsey (8-2, with four for Chabaan) and Met Police (6-2). A respectable 14th place was achieved in the end and Inglethorpe picked up a League Manager of the Month award.

Ruggles and Chabaan each finished with over 20 goals. Harford and ex-Molesey captain Dante Alighieri had added steel and poise to the midfield, Hendry, Lavender and Adam Gray were pretty solid at the back and goalkeeper Justin Gray (no relation) had made many stunning saves, resulting in the Supporters' Player of the Year award. Danny Oliver, Paul McKay, Jeremy Jones, Tommy Smith, Inglethorpe, Lloyd and Wes Harrison also played significant roles during the campaign.

Tanners' end of season resurgence was reflected in their best Surrey Senior Cup performance for seventeen years. After an easy win over Croydon, cup holders Crystal Palace provided quarter-final opposition. The Eagles had a mix of youth and reserve players but Latvian international Alex Kolinko was in goal. With an important league match two days away, Leatherhead rested several first choice players, but the stand-ins, including Chris Woodward and debutants Vitor Tavares at the back and tiny Jamzel Bonaparte up front, excelled. Following several fine stops during two hours of goalless football, Gray went on to save twice more in the penalty shoot-out as Tanners went through 5-4. Premier Division Kingstonian, including two England Semi-Professional internationals, came to Fetcham Grove for the semi-final, but Leatherhead stunned their opponents by taking a 2-0 lead after an hour. K's fought back to level and a penalty shoot-out was again required. This time Tanners did not get 'the rub of the green' and were edged out 7-6.

Justin Gray only missed one match during the season, for which Jamie Ribollo was loaned from Sutton to take his place. In the same game Julian Charles, the Aylesbury and former Brentford striker, also made his one loan appearance, but he was soon shown the red card for a passable Bruce Lee impression. Ali Chabaan's family sent videos of his performances to the manager of the Lebanese Olympic side, resulting in him being called up for international duty. Unfortunately, the proposed friendly with Syria twice had to be postponed because of a waterlogged pitch. Wes Harrison also found some fame when, along with Dante Alighieri, he appeared on the Channel 4 game show 'Your face or mine'.

The youth team reached the final of the Surrey County Cup and finished second in their section of the Southern Youth League, helped considerably by 45-goal Kevin Terry. 17-year-old James Mackie began the season in the Tanners' youth set up, proceeded to make 7 first team appearances for Leatherhead and ended it by gaining a YTS contract with Football League side Wimbledon.

Average first team attendances were around the 170 mark and overall it could be considered a reasonably satisfactory season.

2003/04

Due to the wonderful weather the AGM took place outdoors in the main stand at Fetcham Grove. Finances were fairly healthy. The club was actually in profit and in the unusual situation of chasing creditors. The existing officers and committee were all unanimously re-elected and the spirit and enthusiasm of all involved was most evident. The pitch was looking better than ever, a great credit to groundsman Dave Blaszkowski and the small army of volunteers that attended Saturday work parties during the summer months.

Paul Harford became co-manager with Inglethorpe and most of the previous season's playing squad remained, including five on contract. Ali Chabaan moved to Conference club Farnborough Town and Peter Maynard down the road to Dorking, where he went on to win their Player of the Year award as the Chicks gained promotion. The budget was still strictly limited with the club refusing to spend above their means and the only notable addition to the side was midfielder/striker Nko Ekoku, brother of former Nigerian international Efan.

A major reorganisation of the non-league pyramid was planned to take effect in 2004/05 and amid a great deal of confusion it seemed that Leatherhead would have to finish in the top six or seven to gain a place in a revised Isthmian Premier Division.

Pre-season games produced welcome crowd figures for the visits of AFC Wimbledon (around 800) and a Tottenham XI (approximately 550). The Advertiser Trophy was won for the third year running with a 2-0 success at Dorking.

The first half of the season produced some good league results, highlights including the 1-0 win at home to previously unbeaten Staines Town, a 6-0 thrashing of Banstead Athletic and a 2-1 victory at Hampton and Richmond Borough, the first home defeat for the Middlesex club. There were also some stirring comebacks. Against Walton and Hersham, Inglethorpe twice equalised in a 2-2 draw, the second leveller coming in the sixth minute of injury time after Lavender had been stretchered off and Harford red carded. At Marlow, Leatherhead trailed 2-3 with less than ten minutes to play but came through 4-3, Iain Hendry becoming the first Tanners defender to score a hat-trick. Ex-Everton and Wales international Neville Southall was present, in his capacity as Director of Football for Molesey, as the nine men of Leatherhead fought back to gain a point against the ten men of Molesey in a feisty match. By mid-January the boys in green had risen to 6th place in the league but inconsistency had already been noticeable; the only defeat in an eleven match run coming at lowly Corinthian Casuals.

Moneyfields and Deal Town were dispatched in the FA Cup before a disappointing loss at Leyton, while the FA Trophy and Isthmian League Cup produced immediate exits.

A few new players came into the squad, including Roger Joseph (ex-Brentford, Wimbledon, Millwall, West Brom and England 'B'), former England Semi-Professional international David Harlow (the son of Chris Harlow who had played for the Tanners in the 1960s) and experienced striker Damien Panter from Staines. Dean 'Chippy' Carpenter and Kevin Terry stepped up from the youth team, while Jeremy Jones left the club. Several long term injuries to key players had a debilitating effect on Leatherhead's fortunes. Captain Danny Lavender was out for a lengthy period early on. Goalkeeper Justin Gray suffered a serious leg injury away to Epsom and Ewell in October and only returned for the last few matches. Six other keepers were tried in the intervening period with Michael Johnston, like Gray signed from Camberley, proving the most consistent. Striker Marc Charles-Smith broke his ankle in February and Panter joined the casualty list towards the end of the campaign.

The Tanners management duo of Harford and Inglethorpe spent a few days with Everton Football Club, picking up coaching and management tips from the first team and the academy set up. Farnborough Town, struggling towards the foot of the Conference, were reported to be showing an interest in the Leatherhead pair. As it turned out Inglethorpe did depart, but to take charge of the Under-19 side at one of his former clubs, Leyton Orient. Paul Harford assumed sole charge of the Tanners first team and soon appointed David Harlow as his number two. Earlier in the season Paul's father Ray, had sadly passed away. Ray had been manager or coach at a number of clubs, including Luton Town when they won the Littlewoods (League) Cup and Blackburn Rovers, when they took the Premiership title in 1995. The last match he saw was Leatherhead's friendly with Sutton just a week before his death.

Inconsistency continued to be a hindrance to league progress. At Lewes towards the end of January, Tanners had to play in borrowed black and white striped shirts having turned up with a shortage of green kit. Lewes had won 11 and drawn the other of their 12 home league games with a 37-8 goal difference, but in a tremendous performance the boys in black and white (and green socks) led twice before being pegged back in a 2-2 draw. The erratic nature of Tanners' league games is best illustrated by the four home games in March. Leaders Windsor and Eton were defeated 1-0 (and it should have been more), a fortunate 3-3 draw was achieved against lowly Met Police, followed by a 2-1 reverse to bottom of the table Epsom and Ewell. Leatherhead then showed their good side in a thriller against champions elect Lewes. 4-1 ahead at one stage, they were pegged back to 4-4 before netting a last minute winner. The Brighton Argus was so shocked (or mathematically challenged) that they printed the headline "*Lewes on the wrong end of a seven goal thriller*". Narrow defeats by Staines and Slough put paid to any remaining hopes of promotion. Six of the last seven games were lost, although the final league position of 13th was still a one place improvement on the previous campaign.

The Surrey Senior Cup also provided some cheer. Having gone nearly twenty years without reaching the last four, a semi-final place was achieved for the second year running. Redhill, Horley

Town and Molesey were dispatched to set up a home clash with Woking. With a considerably under-strength front line Tanners fought hard in front of a 532 crowd, but the Conference visitors were too experienced and gained a comfortable 3-0 win.

Steve Sargent, son of 70s star Dave, had been signed from Bognor Regis and Dante Alighieri was back in the fold after a year travelling, perhaps trying to find out more about his namesake, the Italian renaissance author who wrote 'The Divine Comedy'. Nko Ekoku was sold to Worthing and predictably was Man of the Match in Tanners 2-0 defeat on the South Coast, scoring one goal and making the other. Phil Ruggles finished up as top scorer including several crackers in his 30 goal haul. Players' Player of the Year was Adam Gray with the Supporters' award going to Michael Webb who had developed considerably during his time at the club.

One former Tanner making a name for himself was 17-year-old James Mackie, with Wimbledon at their new Milton Keynes home. Early in the season he was a regular in the reserve side, scoring in a 2-1 win against Chelsea in front of a 3,000 crowd. He made his first team debut as substitute, in a 3-0 victory at Reading, having initially been mistaken for the club mascot. He made his first start in a 0-0 draw with West Bromwich Albion, twice coming close to scoring, and went on for an extended run in the first team of the struggling Division One side.

As the season came to a close Leatherhead supporters, along with followers of many other clubs, wondered what league they would be playing in and which new opponents they might face under the restructure. Chairman Tim Edwards' important April 1st announcement that the club were set to join the French Football Federation's pyramid structure suggested an alternative solution.

2004/05

The FA's re-structuring of non-league football was in full swing. With a new tier introduced, Conference North and South, Leatherhead were now at the 4th level of the pyramid. Several clubs were switched from the Southern League to the Isthmian in an attempt to reduce regional anomalies and create a more rational geographical structure.

Bar and gate income had been particularly good during the previous year and the club were operating at close to break-even, ignoring any money that may or may not have been 'behind Laurence's clock'. Pitstop who continued to rent the lower clubroom, had just received the Queen's Golden Jubilee award. David (Popeye) Pope was now Programme Editor and his wife Gail was Matchday Physio and Sports Therapist. The management duo of Harford and Harlow were joined by coaches Bobby Barnes and Steve Wood. Barnes had previously managed Epsom & Ewell, coached at Hampton and Sutton United and was also in charge of the Surrey under-18 side, while Wood had coached in the army.

Striker Phil Ruggles was the most prominent departure. Having scored 65 goals in 119 games Ruggles left to try his luck at Worthing, with the League tribunal setting his fee at £2,500. By the time his transfer fee was decided by tribunal he had already moved on to Kingstonian and he was to end the season with the relegation bound Kingsmeadow club. His replacement in the Tanners front-line was Dave Stevens, who had been in the Crystal Palace youth team alongside Clinton Morrison and Hayden Mullins and had played in Israel before dropping into non-league with Bromley and Dulwich. 49 goals in 54 games for the Hamlet persuaded Conference club Hayes to part with £35,000 for his services and another 12 goals in 18 games and a call-up to the England semi-professional squad further enhanced his reputation. Carshalton Athletic had been his most recent club and at the Grove he initially looked unfit and showed regular tendencies to stray offside and talk himself into referee's notebooks. Although the offside law and match officials continued to be bugbears the goals were soon flying in. Two other important signings were made prior to the start of the campaign. Former Sutton and Tooting goalkeeper Tommy Dunn was initially brought in as cover for Justin Gray, who still had to have the pins removed from his recovering leg and ex-Aldershot and Met. Police central defender Mark Harper came in to strengthen the back line. Most of the previous season's squad was retained with Steve Sargent having spent the summer playing for Minnesota Kicks in the USA.

Pre-season visitors included a Millwall XI containing seven players with first team experience, under the watchful eye of Ray Wilkins, Sutton, where match proceeds went to the Princess Alice Hospice to mark the memory of Paul Harford's father Ray and Dorking, who took the Advertiser Trophy back to Meadowbank for the first time in three years.

The opening five league games were negotiated without defeat before a 4-2 loss at Bashley. Victory against Met Police set the Tanners up for a visit to AFC Wimbledon. In front of a crowd of almost 2,400 Leatherhead trailed 2-0 and appeared to be down and out. A fighting spirit and never say die attitude was to be found in this Tanners side, however. Two goals by Stevens in the last three minutes ended the Dons 100% league record as the outnumbered but more vociferous away fans celebrated a very creditable point. Battling midfielder Tommy Moorhouse had signed from Walton & Hersham to further bolster Leatherhead's selection options. Fringe players Michael Webb and Kevin Terry departed, as did Justin Gray. Having recovered from injury he was unable to displace the reliable Dunn in goal.

Victories over Walton & Hersham, Cray Wanderers and Sandhurst Town brought the Tanners to an FA Cup 3rd qualifying round tie at home to Maidstone Utd. The crowd of over 500 saw Marc Charles-Smith give Leatherhead the early lead only for the Stones to equalise against the run of play. Stevens hit the bar prior to netting what proved to be the winner, although there was seven minutes of injury time to get through before the fat lady could sing. Stevens was unfortunately suspended for the next round at Southern Premier Bath City and the lack of firepower proved costly. In front of 938 spectators the Tanners were 1-0 down at the interval and could not find a way back despite a good second half, Sargent hitting the post among a number of chances that went begging. Bath went on to defeat Conference champions elect Barnet in the 1st round proper.

While involved in the FA Cup Tanners league form suffered with heavy defeats inflicted by Walton and Hersham and Horsham. Once out of the cup matters improved, notably at Burgess Hill where the 5th in the table home side were thrashed by a rampant Green Machine. There were two goals apiece for Stevens and Wes Harrison in a 4-0 victory that could easily have been doubled. In November, Paul Harford, "*wanting to progress in the game*" stepped down as manager and later spent time assisting with coaching at the youth academies of Fulham, Newcastle, Luton and Crystal Palace (he has recently been appointed as manager at Sutton United). Dave Harlow and Barry Barnes now stepped up as joint first team managers. Harford's predecessor in the Fetcham Grove hot seat, Alex Inglethorpe was now manager of Exeter City and soon pitting his wits against Sir Alex Ferguson and the mighty Manchester United in the 3rd round of the FA Cup. The Grecians earned a draw at Old Trafford and only went down narrowly in the replay. On Inglethorpe's appointment, Exeter's Director of Football, Steve Perryman stated that, "*he understands the compromise of achieving success while working within financial limitations*". Wonder where he learnt that?

League results continued in a reasonable vein, including a 5-1 thumping of Hastings Utd thanks to 4 goals in the last 8 minutes. Tanners began to climb the table and by January had fought their way into play-off contention. The Bryco (League) Cup provided a nice distraction for a while with two thrilling performances against Premier Division opposition. At Hendon a great comeback saw a 1-3 deficit turned into a 6-3 extra time victory. Stevens scored with a brilliant solo effort reminiscent of Archie Gemmill's goal for Scotland against Brazil to force extra-time and in the additional half-hour completed his second hat-trick in three games. The next round brought Yeading, including their renowned striker DJ Campbell (subsequently signed by Premiership Birmingham City from

Brentford for a £500,000 fee in January 2006), to the Grove. Yeading were on their way to the league title and just a few weeks earlier had given the Premiership stars of Newcastle a run for their money in the FA Cup. Stevens was rested and Sargent and Harper only started on the bench but Leatherhead held the visitors 3-3 after extra-time. Hero of the hour was undoubtedly Tommy Dunn. Having already saved two penalties in the match itself, he saved two more in the shoot-out. Not content with that he even scored one of Tanners' four successful spot kicks. In the quarter-final a severely weakened Leatherhead side, ravaged by injuries, suspension and unavailabilty were defeated (but not disgraced) in a blizzard by Chelmsford City.

Within two months of being appointed Harlow and Barnes were receiving the Ryman Division One Manager of the Month award. Through February and into early March every match seemed to be against promotion or play-off contenders but only Horsham managed to lower the Tanners colours in this fine run. The return meeting with champions elect AFC Wimbledon produced a hard fought 1-1 draw, the Dons needing a dubious penalty to get a point after a fine Sargent free-kick had put the greens in front. The attendance of 1,814 is probably an all-time record for a league match at Fetcham Grove and on the day was the second highest non-league crowd anywhere in the country. The only match against a lowly side during this period was at Fleet where a team including ex-England international Andy Sinton caused Leatherhead plenty of problems before Stevens came to the rescue again with a 93rd minute winner. Danny Lavender returned from a loan spell at Walton to get the winner in a 2-1 success at Tooting & Mitcham. There were only 2 defeats in the last 11 league matches but the losses to Ashford Town and Corinthian Casuals as well as points dropped to Banstead and Burgess Hill meant just missing out on a play-off place. A 3-0 victory over Croydon Athletic was achieved in the final game but Bromley and Met. Police obtained the points they required, leaving Tanners in 7th position on goal difference behind Cray Wanderers.

Despite this disappointment it had been a fine season and attendance figures had risen even discounting the AFC Wimbledon effect. There was even interest from the USA with a lady in Ohio following the Tanners fortunes via the Internet and two children in Houston attending school in Leatherhead replica shirts.

Tommy Dunn appeared with distinction in all 55 matches during the season and deservedly received Player of the Year awards from both players and supporters. Considering that seven different people

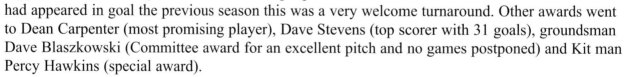

Season 2004/05 - Popeye's random memories

- Dunny the 'ever-present'
- Macca and the creep to 200 appearances
- Dave Stevens - on target and off side
- The Dante chant ("all we need is a team of Dantes)
- Goal of the seaon - Adam Graysie versus Met Police at the Grove in September
- Victory over Maidstone in the FA Cup with over 500 at the Grove
- The 4-0 demolition of Burgess Hill Town away in November (it could have been 10)
- Trip to Bath City in the FA Cup 4th Qualifying round- a great day out
- Sarge's 35 yarder during the 5-1 demolition of Hastings at the Grove in December
- Dave Stevens - two hatricks in just over a week (Bashley and Hendon)
- Beating Premier league leaders Yeading on penalties in the Bryco Cup 4th round - Dunny's night all around - saved 2 penalties during the game, saved more during the shoot out and then scored one!!
- Harps and Henders - solid as a rock
- The games against AFC W unbeaten —the last minute comeback in the away game, a packed Grove, the blocked toilets
- The strange snowy trip to Chelmsford as we got dumped out of the Bryco
- Beating Dorking
- Unsung hero - Ross 'super physio' Hanbury (pictured, right)
- Dave Harlow's skiing holiday
- Lavs winner away at Tooting & Mitcham - in the 8th minute of injury time
- The best non-league supporters in the country

had appeared in goal the previous season this was a very welcome turnaround. Other awards went to Dean Carpenter (most promising player), Dave Stevens (top scorer with 31 goals), groundsman Dave Blaszkowski (Committee award for an excellent pitch and no games postponed) and Kit man Percy Hawkins (special award).

2005/06

Following the previous season's near miss, hopes were high that Tanners could at least achieve a play-off place in their Diamond Jubilee season. For a long time this looked distinctly possible but a loss of form after Christmas and certain elements of bad luck conspired to dash these aims.

The pre-season programme offered grounds for optimism as Dorking were trounced 5-1 away in the Advertiser Trophy match and higher-league opposition in Sutton Utd and Hampton & Richmond Borough, were also defeated. Dave Blaszkowski and Dickie Wilkinson had now been elected as members of the Board with Michael Anderson and Ray Lewis as Associate Directors. The clubroom had new windows, ceiling and lighting and finances overall were in a pretty healthy state, largely thanks to increased gate and bar income.

The majority of the previous term's players remained alhough Danny Lavender (234 appearances) departed for Walton & Hersham, Paul McKay (200 appearances) retired and Damien Panter left for Kingstonian. Iain Hendry, Jamie Beer and Adam Gray were now the longest serving members of a good solid squad. Striker Julian Thompson returned to the Grove. Goalkeeper Tommy Dunn was considering a cricket coaching job in Australia but fortunately from a Tanners point of view decided to stay. At the end of the campaign he again topped the appearance chart having only missed one match in two years.

Nearly 500 fans attended the opening league match at home to Kingstonian. Leatherhead hit the bar, had a strong penalty appeal turned down and were held 0-0. Tanners legend Chris Kelly was now back at the club as Commercial Manager, and managed to survive the game despite death threats made by some K's 'supporters' who presumably held him accountable for their club's recent problems. There were as usual some comings and goings during the season. Newcomers that made an impact included striker Warren Waugh, defenders Lindval Duncan from Ashford Town and Paul Sears from Met Police and midfielders Scott Bennetts from Kingstonian and Richard O'Connor, returning to the Grove from Hampton. Ex-Kings Lynn player Phil Eagle was signed on but quickly released when he received a 58-week F.A. ban for sending off offences and unpaid fines stemming from his previous career. Dave Stevens and Tommy Moorhouse each had brief spells away, at Dulwich and Kingstonian respectively, but soon realised where the grass was greener. Stevens was again top goal-scorer despite his sabbatical.

Apart from the habitual early exit from the FA Trophy, there were decent runs in the other cup competitions. After exciting narrow victories over Ash Utd (3-2 in a replay) and Chatham (4-3) 'old boys' played a prominent part in the next two rounds of the FA Cup. At Hampton, Richard O'Connor equalised 11 minutes from time against his former club to earn Tanners a replay, this after Hampton had scored in two minutes, had a penalty saved by Dunn and missed a host of other chances. With home advantage Leatherhead dispatched the then Ryman Premier leaders thanks to two first half strikes from Stevens. A season's best home gate of 609 attended the 3rd qualifying round tie with Farnborough, managed by the only player to reach European Cup finals with two different English clubs, Frank Gray. Former Tanner, Paul Harkness scored the first of the Conference South club's two unanswered goals, Waugh going closest for 'the greens' with a header that went agonisingly wide of the far post.

The League cup included an excellent performance in defeating Met Police 4-1 and an exciting 5-3 extra time win over Cray Wanderers before Premier club Slough Town prevailed and two rounds of the Surrey Senior competition were negotiated only for Kingstonian to eliminate Tanners on penalties for the third time in seven years. Have they got a German coach?

League progress was generally good up to the turn of the year. The best unbeaten run for more than 20 years (12 matches) between September and the end of November took Leatherhead up to 5th place in the table. The highlight of this sequence was probably the 4-1 victory over Tonbridge Angels who were top of the table and undefeated at the time. Some of the worst weather conditions for a football match for many a year were experienced at Lymington & New Milton. The stand was no protection against the horizontal rain and gale force winds and Tim Edwards described the players as looking like extras from 'The Cruel Sea'. A wind-assisted howitzer of a free kick from Steve Sargent proved to be the only score. However, in some games, often against lowly opposition, Tanners threw away points by failing to hold onto a lead. Draws at Burgess Hill and Newport (Isle of Wight) are examples. Later on a three-goal lead at Cray ended 3-3 and two goals in the first three minutes at home to Horsham eventually resulted in a 4-2 defeat. There were also several contentious decisions that went against Tanners, often in critical games. Horsham's penalty winner at their ground and the 'goals' Leatherhead 'scored' in 1-0 defeats to Dulwich Hamlet and Dover spring to mind. The Kent club's video of the match indicates that the ball was several feet over the line but the goal was not given. This prompted an April Fools Day website spoof about the introduction of the Assistant Referees' Line Interpretation Processor (ARLIP) based on a sensor picking up the metal valve in the ball. There was concern over the effects that the pins holding Bennetts' injured leg would have on the system, however. Some poor results in February and March ended any realistic play-off hopes although Tonbridge, later to gain promotion through the play-offs, were again defeated 4-1. We will miss them! Form improved at the end, victories in the last three matches producing a final standing of 10th. Following an injury to the referee, Chris Kelly was changed and ready to step in to run the line at the last home game against Cray. The visitors objected, however, and an alternative substitute had to be found. Former Tanners' defender Dave Sargent commented that Chris could not work out offside as a player so what chance would he have as an official.

'Budgie' had more success in his commercial role at Fetcham Grove. A Sportsmen's Dinner was held in November, the guest speaker being Chelsea legend Peter Osgood, sadly to pass away a couple of months later. The Diamond Project was launched to help raise funding to terrace the grass banking at Fetcham Grove in line with ground grading and health and safety requirements. Chairman Tim Edwards made a substantial contribution and supporters were invited to buy £25 stakes and get a chance to name part of the new terracing. It was also proposed that the upper section of grass banking be retained in order to help preserve the rural character of the ground.

The season ended with the highly successful 60th anniversary dinner dance at the Preston Cross Hotel in Bookham. There was an excellent turnout of past players and officials with almost all of the glory year sides of 74-75 and 77-78 in attendance. Derek Wells was still playing regularly, for PLA Vets in the Essex Business Houses League. The role of officials such as Chris Luff and Billy Miller in the rise of the club and the tales of the players (many unprintable) were remembered. The current Board of Management and playing staff were well represented, auguring well for the spirit at the club. The enthusiasm and efforts of officials such as Gerald Darby and Tim Edwards in keeping the club going through the dark days must be mentioned. Manager Dave Harlow, having turned down a recent approach from Sutton United, stated that he wanted to remain at Leatherhead for the next few years. Mark Harper is now his number two following the departure of Barry Barnes and 'Harps' has pledged to delay his retirement from playing for another year. The loyalty and commitment of players such as Iain Hendry (280 appearances), Jamie Beer (200 appearances) and Adam Gray (192 appearances) should also be noted. Beer received the Player's Player of the Year Award while the never-say-die attitude of Marc Charles-Smith earned him the Supporter's vote.

▼Leatherhead Lip website editor Matt Le Ross with Tanners legend Billy Miller.

Leatherhead ➡
Football Club

Here's to the next 60 years. The future is bright. The future is green.

▲Goalkeeper Pete Caswell and full-back Colin Brooks. Between them clocked up well over 600 appearances for the club during the late 1970s and 1980s and, in Caswell's case, into the nineties as well.

▲Mick Leach, team manager from 1983 to 1985. In terms of the percentage of games won Micky is Leatherhead's most successful boss.

▲Mick Leach's squad that topped the table before breaking up in the wake of his resignation *Standing:* Paul 'Spider' Williams, Phil Smith, Peter Shodeinde, Peter Caswell, David Price, Lance Pedlar and Martin Black *Kneeling:* Barry Hempstead, Gary McDonald, Simon Cook, Paul 'Noddy' Holder and Dave Rattue

▲The Tanners players and management celebrate winning promotion after finisihing as Ryman Isthmian League Division Two runners-up in1996/97

▲Leatherhead skipper Alex O'Brien and Rushden and Diamonds captain Gary Butterworth line-up with the match officials prior to the FA Cup Fourth Qualifying round tie in November 1998.

▲Leatherhead secured their first silverware for more than a decade albeit in the shape of the Advertiser Challenge Trophy, after beating Mole Valley neighbours Dorking 4-2 in 2001.

Ace goal-scorers from the last fifteen seasons (*left to right*) -
▲Steve Lunn (100 goals in total), Ray Arnett (115) and Nigel Webb (103).
▼John Humphrey (41), Phil Ruggles (65), Marc Charles Smith (43 to date), and Alex Inglethorpe (56).

TANNERS BACK FROM THE BRINK

▲Leatherhead Secretary Gerald Darby and Chairman Tim Edwards present former player-manager Alex Inglethorpe (centre) with an engraved crystal set and a programme front cover, signed by the first team squad, following his move from the Grove to coach Leyton Orient's youth sides. Inglethorpe was Leatherhead's thirty fourth post-war manager in forty eight seasons.

▲Steve Sargent (*out of picture*) scores with a well struck free kick from the edge of the area to give the Tanners the lead against AFC Wimbledon in this top of the table clash in February 2005, played in front of over 1,800 spectators. However, the Dons equalised before half-time and the honours eventually finished even on the day.

▲The Levred massive behind the goal seem to be anticipating a goal, but this effort from Mark Harper is comfortably saved by the visitng Farnborough Town goalkeeper. The Conference South side went on to win this F A Cup third qualifying tie, played in October 2005, by 2-0.

▲The Tanners squad that narrowly missed out on the promotion play-offs in 2005. *Standing:* Ross Hanbury (Physio), Wes Harrison, Marc Charles-Smith, Dante Alighieri, Mark Harper, Iain Hendry, Tommy Moorhouse and Steve Wood (coach) *Kneeling:* Paul Wetherall, Paul McKay, Damien Panter, Jamie Beer, Dave Stevens, Dean Carpenter and Tommy Dunn

CHAPTER SIXTEEN - FOR THE RECORD (1946 - 2006)

Twenty memorable matches

There have been many highlights in the three thousand plus games played by the Tanners to date. The Amateur Cup produced fantastic memories from treks in the 1960s and 70s to the likes of Blyth Spartans, Enfield, Hendon, Middlewich Athletic, Stowmarket and Wealdstone, as well as exciting home ties with Carshalton Athletic, Dagenham, Hayes and Redhill amongst others. In the F A Cup Tanners have played out epics against Bishop Stortford, Dagenham, Guildford City, Ilford, Kingstonian, Swansea City and Wimbledon to name but a few. There have been Trophy thrillers involving Bedford Town, Dartford, Lancaster City, Wealdstone and a fantastic all round team performance to defeat northern giants Wigan Athletic as well as numerous enthralling blood and thunder local derbies with Walton & Hersham and league encounters with old adversaries such as Dagenham, Enfield, Hendon, Kingstonian, Slough Town, Sutton United, Tooting & Mitcham and Wycombe Wanderers. More recently there was an emotional promotion night at Collier Row and excellent cup wins over Crystal Palace and Hampton and Richmond Borough. None of the above, memorable as they were, made the final cut although it was a near impossible task to whittle down so many great afternoons and evenings to just twenty matches, but here is the final selection:

16th November 1946   Surrey Senior League
Leatherhead 13 v Leyland Motors 1
Motors dismantled

As the score suggests Leatherhead gained the easiest of victories (and one that still remains a Tanners record). One hopes that the Motormen were better at making cars than they were at playing football. From the outset Leatherhead attacked and after ten minutes Weller fastened onto a Collins centre to score. The brilliant scheming of Trout and Rochester time and again opened up the visitors defence and with the Tanners halves giving the forwards plenty of support Weller, Rochester and Collins (2) were able to add further goals before the half-time break.

On resumption, exchanges were more even for fifteen minutes before Collins and Rochester found the net. Motors pulled one back from the penalty spot but were soon made to pay. Leatherhead piled on the pressure to such an extent that goals came with great regularity. Trout worked through on his own and finished with a hard shot. This was followed by a lob and a header from Weller and a shot from Rochester. Temlett ran in from the left for number twelve and Trout completed the rout.

Team: *Syd Parker, Ernie Harvey, Rueben Leverington, G. Weatherill, Bryn Evans, Tommy Nunn, Jackie Collins, Tommy Rochester, Cecil Weller, Ernie Trout and Tommy Temlett*

15th November 1952   Delphian League
Dagenham 3 v Leatherhead 4
Daggers blunted

Three goals in arrears with less than twenty five minutes remaining Leatherhead fought back in sensational style to gain a deserved and rare victory at Victoria Road. Dagenham, the eventual runaway champions, went into the game on the back of seven wins in eight games and with a much vaunted defence that had conceded just three goals. Tanners' form in contrast had been indifferent and their chances weren't helped by being forced into three late team changes.

There was little to choose between the teams in the opening exchanges with both sides playing fast, attacking football. The game remained scoreless with chances going begging at either end until, with half-time approaching, Hill turned and shot past Lindsay to put the home side in front. Dagenham started the second half strongly and soon increased their lead when Lawson's shot hit the upright before dropping over the line. Shortly thereafter Lawson scored again to seemingly settle the issue. However, in the 68th minute Tanners got just reward for continuing to battle away when a through pass was collected by Collins who cut in from the wing to shoot past Skinner. This provided a real tonic to Tanners and four minutes later Collins centred for Drury to head home. Daggers started to panic and it wasn't long before Collins equalised with another well taken goal. Tanners were now rampant and ten minutes from time Don Smith went up the left wing, cut inside and beat Skinner with a low cross-shot to score Tanners' fourth goal in twelve amazing minutes. Dagenham made a last ditch effort to salvage the game and in a frantic finale were awarded a penalty. Cornish stepped up to take the kick but his shot hit the upright and was scrambled to safety. Almost immediately the final whistle sounded to give Leatherhead a great victory in which the whole side played an equal part although Tester at centre-half was exceptional.

Team: *Graham Lindsay, Ken Tester, B. Smith, Doug Caswell, Ronnie Read, Tommy Hall, Dave Benetton, Don Smith, Ernie Trout, Cyril Drury and Jackie Collins*

7th January 1956   Surrey Senior Cup Quarter-Final
Leatherhead 3 v Wimbledon 1
Dons downed

Leatherhead, lying mid-table in the Delphian League, upset Cup holders and Isthmian League pace setters Wimbledon in an exciting match to give Tanners a rare win over their bogey side.

The match started at a very fast pace with both sides creating and then squandering a number of good chances. The two goalkeepers, Lowder and Bragg, were kept busy but dealt with everything thrown at them in confident fashion to keep the scoreline blank going in at the interval.

The pace initially slackened in the second half though the good, clean football played by both sides delighted the large crowd of around 1,300. The deadlock was finally broken when Smith swung over a cross and Wallis deceived Lowder to put the Dons in front. The visitors lead did not last long though as Allbutt soon fired Tanners level. The tempo of the game picked up again as both teams strived for the decisive breakthrough. The Dons enjoyed more of the game with the home goal remaining intact despite several frantic goalmouth scrambles. Wimbledon were dealt a severe blow ten minutes from time when their centre-forward Joe Wallis was forced to leave the field through injury. Almost immediately Tanners took advantage of their extra man to take the lead. Ken Allbutt's viciously dipping free-kick deceiving Bragg. Bob Taylor wrapped up a memorable victory in the closing seconds, finishing off a sweeping Tanners' counter-attack as Dons desperately pressed forward in search of an equaliser.

Team: *Lou Lowder, Wally Pointer, George Mannings, Bill Godfrey, Peter Martin, Sid Gillett, Doug Caswell, Ken Allbutt, T. Stiles, Bob Taylor and Jackie Hughesdon*

17th November 1962   Corinthian League
Leatherhead 4 v Dorking 1
Chicks plucked

Victories over Mole Valley neighbours Dorking are always sweet and this one was particularly so as it put Tanners on top of the table, a position they did not relinquish for the rest of the season. Dorking were hampered by the loss of influential centre-forward Norman Dearlove who had broken his leg the previous weekend. Leatherhead were the better balanced side and took the lead in the 14th minute when Pell cracked a low free-kick from outside the penalty area in off the foot of the far post. Dorking equalised on the half-hour with Bell scoring from a Forrester pass from the right. Four minutes later Goodman restored Tanners' advantage. A strong run saw him evade a couple of challenges before unleashing a shot that young keeper Dunn seemed to have covered but the ball dipped past him into the net.

Chicks applied the pressure at the start of the second half but were caught on the break, Dobbs, Goodman and Pell combining superbly to set up Hickey for Tanners' third goal. Two minutes from time Dunn was beaten again, this time by a rasping shot from Harris after a fine interchange of passes with Brittin. There was little doubt that Tanners deserved their win as they continued their march towards the Corinthian League title.

Team: *Jack O'Malley, Johnny Lewis, Reg Oakes, Kenny Harris, Jock Wood, Johnny Phipps, Bill Hickey, Brian Pell, Kevin Brittin, Terry Dobbs and Neil Goodman*

8th April 1964   Athenian League Division One
Leatherhead 3 v Worthing 0
Rebels routed

Over 1,400 saw Leatherhead bring off one of their best achievements to date in this crucial floodlit game for promotion to the Premier Division of the Athenian League. On a rutted surface the light ball played some weird tricks but while the game never reached astronomical heights in artistry it was full of excitement and thrills. Hitting the ball hard and using their weight to advantage Tanners took the lead in the 14th minute when Brittin headed one of the finest goals anyone could wish to see from a lob by Bill Hickey.

Fellow promotion contenders Worthing had the greater share of the ball in the second half but they could make little impression on the commanding Tanners defence in which Jock Woods and Ken Bird tackled fearlessly and cleared with power and judgement. In the 55th minute Bill Hickey passed forward for Brian Pell to take in his stride, neatly side-step the keeper and shoot into the vacant goal. Worthing never gave up trying but in the last minute Terry Dobbs judiciously lobbed to the left of Best and just under the crossbar into the net for a fine third goal that sparked scenes of great celebration among the home fans as promotion was all but guaranteed.

Team: *Jack O'Malley, Johnny Lewis, Ken Bird, Ken Harris, Jock Wood, Johnny Phipps, Bill Hickey, Brian Pell, Neil Goodman, Kevin Brittin and Terry Dobbs*

28th January 1967   FA Amateur Cup 2nd Round
Tow Law Town 0 v Leatherhead 1
Lawyers dismissed

Northern League Tow Law, unbeaten in five months at their forbidding hilltop Ironworks ground, sported one of the most impressive records in the North and were strongly fancied to progress at Leatherhead's expense. Cup tie fervour filled the ground as Town attacked from the off. After ten minutes they were awarded a penalty but, much to the relief of the Tanners supporters in the 1,500 plus crowd who had set off from Fetcham Grove at 1a.m. for the 300 mile trip to County Durham, Brown fired the spot-kick wide. Buoyed by this let off Tanners went on the attack and were rewarded when Micky Goodall soared above the defenders at the far post to meet Alan Brazier's free-kick and nod the ball down for Brian Pell to poke home.

Defences were generally on top for the majority of the rest of the match and chances were few and far between. Leatherhead had to survive a severe second half grilling though. Bobby Adam, superb in blotting out England Amateur international George Brown, and full-backs Ray Francis and John Hilliard were outstanding in this rearguard action. All the hard work was nearly undone in the closing minutes when substitute Williams' shot hit the inside of the post before being hacked to safety. Billy Miller's after match comment summed it up, *"The whole team were magnificent"*.

Team: *Jack O'Malley, Ray Francis, John Hilliard, Brian Gibbs, Bobby Adam, Alan Brazier, Peter Keary, Brian Pell, Micky Goodall, Keith Mills and Ian Meekin Sub: Bill Scott*

25th February 1967   FA Amateur Cup Quarter-Final
Leatherhead 0 v Hendon 3
Penalty drama as Cup hopes are shattered

Leatherhead's Wembley hopes and dreams were shattered in the space of fifteen seconds against all-star Isthmian Leaguers Hendon. Before a huge crowd numbering over 4,000, including ten coach loads from North London, Hendon made the breakthrough in the 32nd minute in dramatic circum-stances. Leatherhead were awarded a penalty for a foul on Keith Mills but Ian Meekin's shot was deflected by John Swannell on to the under part of the crossbar. With spectators on the pitch celebrating what they thought was a goal, the rebound was quickly cleared upfield where Lakey found himself in acres of space to run through and pass for Swain to fire home.

Leatherhead had more than matched their illustrious opponents up to this point but Hendon grew in confidence and gradually took control thereafter. Shortly after half-time Sleap put over a centre that was headed on to Harding who netted from an awkward angle by the far upright. Late on Quail slipped a pass through for Harding to take in his stride and complete the scoring.

For a cup tie tempers were reasonably well controlled although the referee had to talk to Harding and Brian Gibbs after they were engaged in one or two tussles. In losing Leatherhead did not disgrace themselves but Hendon were indisputably the better side.

Team: *Jack O'Malley, Ray Francis, John Hilliard, Alan Brazier, Bobby Adam, Brian Gibbs, Brian Pell, Peter Keary, Ian Meekin, Keith Mills and Micky Goodall*

3rd May 1969   Surrey Senior Cup Final
Leatherhead 3 v Redhill 1
Third time lucky

At Sutton United's Gander Green Lane ground Leatherhead finally laid their Surrey Senior Cup Final jinx to rest. On this occasion there was never much doubt about the result. Leatherhead were too organised and too strong for a disappointing Redhill side. Fellow Athenian League outfit Redhill's rearguard had all sorts of trouble from the darting Skinner and the wily Mills, and they could never get a strong enough grip in midfield, where Davies' constant harrying never let them settle on the ball, to hope to build up their own attacks. Leatherhead began their drive for victory in the 10th minute, a poor clearance was forced out to Mills on the right and he unselfishly laid it back for Nobby Skinner to hammer the ball into the net. Tanners continued to hold the upper hand throughout the remainder of the half without being able to add to their slender advantage.

The Reds began the second half more purposefully but Tanners took a firm grip on the game in the first twenty minutes when they added two more goals. The first followed a throw from Alan Brazier, Mills hooked the ball over his head and Barry Webb caught Stewart off his line with a header that beat the goalkeeper's grasping fingers and dipped under the crossbar. Disconsolate Redhill soon fell further behind when Barrie Davies chipped over a square defence and Keith Mills fine, quick control enabled him to lift the ball past the onrushing Stewart. Tanners momentarily lost concentration after the goal and allowed Eddie Webb to reduce the arrears and complete the scoring. Alan Brazier was the man who proudly showed the trophy to the club's overjoyed fans as Leatherhead celebrated their first, and to date only, Surrey Senior Cup victory.

Team: *Micky Cuthbert, Bobby Taylor, Bobby Adam, Barrie Davies, Brian Caterer, Kevin Brittin, Barry Webb, Keith Mills, Nobby Skinner, Alan Brazier and Tony Slade*

20th March 1971   FA Amateur Cup Semi-Final
Skelmersdale United 2 v Leatherhead 0
Lack of strike power ends Cup run

The road to Wembley for the Amateur Cup, along which Leatherhead had marched in triumph for so long, involving a total of over fourteen hours playing time, came to an end at Bolton's Burnden Park. They were beaten by a Skelmersdale side that had reached the semi-finals for the third year running and who were to turn fully professional the following season. As the Leatherhead team trotted out onto the pitch they realised that their local opponents had by far the bigger numerical and vocal support among the official attendance of 7,085. With banners and streamers flying and the blue and green and white favours of the respective clubs prominent the scene was a most colourful one. With Nobby Skinner closely marked Leatherhead were seldom able to approach anything like the heights to which they ascended in earlier rounds. Skelmersdale pressed for most of the first half and Micky Cuthbert was one of the hardest worked players on the pitch but he managed to keep his goal intact until the interval. The game became scrappy in the second period with far too many glaring cases of shirt pulling by Skelmersdale being allowed to pass without punishment. Tanners had their chances but Dale took the lead in the 70th minute when a hard shot by Wolfe hit the bar and came straight down to the goal-line and Dickin rushed in and netted. The game was wrapped up in injury time when Barrie Davies slipped allowing Swift to run free before squaring to the unmarked Windsor to place into the net.

Team: *Micky Cuthbert, Jimmy Strong, Alan Brazier, Barrie Davies, Dave Reid, John Cooper, Freddie Slade, Keith Mills, Pete Lavers, Nobby Skinner and Barry Webb Sub: Ronnie Fruen*

14th December 1974   FA Challenge Cup 2nd Round Proper
Leatherhead 1 v Colchester United 0
Tanners hail miss-hit hero

Division Three promotion chasers and past giant-killers Colchester United crashed out of the Cup to an inspired Leatherhead side. On a pitch described as, *"yielding"* Tanners enjoyed the better of the early exchanges with the only goal arriving during this period of dominance. In the twentieth minute a corner from Webb was only partially cleared and John Doyle, still clutching a sponge to his head as a result of an earlier knock, volleyed the ball low into the net. Doyle admitted after the game it was a lucky goal as he had miss-hit the shot. Webb came close to doubling the lead with a 20-yard scorcher that shaved the bar whilst United could muster only a solitary effort on goal, comfortably saved by *"old warrior"* John Swannell, in the whole of the first half.

Suitably fired up by a half-time roasting from manager Jim Smith, United pressed forward in the second period. Inspirational skipper Willie Smith drove his men on in the face of U's frantic assault and with John Cooper covering every inch of the park and Dave Reid making the Division's leading scorer John Froggatt look slow and cumbersome Tanners weathered the storm with relatively few alarms. The supporter's most anxious moment occurred when Pete Lavers, back helping out his defenders, misdirected a header which was brilliantly turned round the post by John Swannell.

At the final whistle the Tanners players were submerged in a green sea of frenzied excitement. Billy Miller rated the team's first half performance as the best in the club's history whilst Jim Smith described his sides insipid performance as, *"diabolical"*.

Team: *John Swannell, Dave Sargent, Barry Webb, John Cooper, Dave Reid, Derek Wells, Colin Woffinden, Pete Lavers, Peter McGillicuddy, Willie Smith and John Doyle Sub: Chris Kelly*

4th January 1975   FA Challenge Cup 3rd Round Proper
Brighton and Hove Albion 0 v Leatherhead 1
Taylors outfit go for a Burton

The Tanners players looked nervous in the opening minutes of this cup tie at the Goldstone when the blood and thunder and the deafening noise of the massive 20,000 crowd seemed to unnerve them. However, they soon settled and once they realised that they were every bit as good as Brighton they began to look the more composed and threatening side. Kelly was at the centre of all Tanners' attacking ideas whilst the shock dropping of Wells to make way for his return did not upset the defence at all. Cooper and Reid performed heroically all afternoon as twin centre-backs and nullified the threat of the Seasiders prolific marksman Fred Binney. Twenty-five-year-old Kelly, who had had a cartilage operation only six weeks earlier, hit the most important goal in Tanners' history, and what a goal it was. With twenty five minutes remaining and Albion pressing forward Tanners broke swiftly out of defence. Cooper picked up the ball in his own area and quickly transferred it to the roaming McGillicuddy on the left. Mac in turn fed Budgie in the centre circle. Ignoring impassioned pleas from the Tanners bench, picked up by television microphones (not a pretty sound) to, *"****ing pass the **** ing ball"*, Kelly found himself confronted by two Albion defenders but first Winstanley and then Tiler were left on their backsides in his wake like whales floundering on a sandbank. Advancing into the penalty area Kelly looked up before coolly firing his shot beyond Grummitt and into the net via the far post. The Tanners supporters in the South Stand erupted and Kelly ran everywhere to celebrate. Albion's main threat came from tricky winger Towner but too often he failed to deliver a telling final ball and Swannell was largely untroubled, although Leatherhead hearts were made to beat faster as a couple of shots flew narrowly wide in the closing stages, but the Green Machine held firm.

Brighton boss Peter Taylor (ruing his, *"we will swat away those minnows" forecast*) acknowledged that Tanners were the better team commenting, *"No excuses we were outfought, outthought and outplayed"*. In the heady moments after this stunning victory the supremely self-confident Kelly drank gin and provided his own tonic for Tanners supporters announcing, *"I beat Brighton with my magic shuffle. In the next round Leicester will get my double shuffle and that's really something special!"*

Team: *John Swannell, Dave Sargent, Dave Reid, John Cooper, Barry Webb, John Doyle, Colin Woffinden, Willie Smith, Pete Lavers, Chris Kelly and Peter McGillicuddy Sub: Derek Wells*

25th January 1975   FA Challenge Cup 4th Round Proper

Leicester City 3 v Leatherhead 2

Miller's merry men so close to making history

The massed ranks of Leatherhead supporters were bolstered by several hundred Nottingham Forest and Derby County supporters whose own cup ties had fallen foul of the inclement weather and had instead turned up to cheer on the underdogs against their East Midlands rivals. Their presence helped to boost the crowd to a season's best of over 30,000. Leicester's pitch was protected by a large bubble and therefore there were no concerns about the match going ahead for the 8,000 travelling Tanners supporters as they made their way up the M1 in a huge convoy of green and white bedecked coaches and cars.

Despite the massive crowd the Tanners players displayed no trace of nerves. They started brightly and controlled the opening exchanges. The Leatherhead supporters, already in good voice, soon had reason to cheer even more loudly. McGillicuddy, who had passed a late fitness test after injuring his ankle falling off a ladder, was on hand in the twentieth minute to side-foot home after Lavers had bulldozed his way to the bye-line and cut the ball back across the area. Ten minutes later it was 2-0. McGillicuddy was chopped down by Whitworth on the touchline. Webb floated over the resultant free-kick and Kelly emerged ahead of Foxes keeper Wallington to glance the ball into the far corner with the deftest of headers. Play continued to switch fom end to end, a stranger coming into the ground would have assumed Tanners were in the First Division and Leicester the amateurs in that first half, so good were Tanners.

The half-time break seemed initially to have changed nothing as Tanners continued to look the more impressive side but, with the home fans contemplating invading the pitch as the only way of avoiding embarassment, the defining moment of the match arrived. Cross slipped as he tried to intercept a punt forward leaving Kelly one on one with Wallington. Time seemed to stand still as Kelly slowly dragged the ball around the diving keeper and rolled the ball goalwards. As the Tanners supports cleared their throats to celebrate, Munro made ground and with a desperate last ditch lunge diverted the ball behind for a corner. What was so nearly 3-0 became 2-1 within three minutes. The overlapping runs down the right flank by Whitworth were Leicester's major threat and it was from one of these marauding runs and crosses that Sammels arrived in front of Reid to send a diving header past Swannell. As Leatherhead began to run out of steam on the rain soaked pitch Leicester finally began to take control with Keith Weller and Frank Worthington (who would both feature in the full England side before the season was out) orchestrating the play. The scores were level in the 71st minute when the up to that moment immaculate handling of Swannell let him down. City were awarded a free-kick on the edge of the area. Swannell failed to hang on to Worthington's curling shot and Earle reacted the quickest to stab the rebound home. Just eleven minutes remained on the clock when a superb free-flowing move involving Whitworth, Birchenall and Worthington pulled Tanners' defence apart and left Weller unmarked in the box to thump home the winner.

At the final whistle the name of 'Leatherhead' resounded around the packed Filbert Street stadium at the end of what had been a pulsating cup tie. Both sets of supporters joined in the acclaim for the brave Tanners but it was little consolation to the players and supporters who knew they had come within inches of F A Cup immortality. Kelly later said "*I still dream about that moment. Where Munro came from to clear off the line I'll never know. I swear he just pops out of the ground*". Mick Lidbury, told off for chanting in the Press Box, started his colourful report in the Surrey Advertiser with the words, "*When the game was over a large slice of the population of Leatherhead weaved its weary way home. Mentally and physically shattered it was time to dream what might have been...*".

Once the fans got home they were able to catch the highlights of the game on 'Match of the Day' and relive once more those incredible moments of joy and anguish.

Team: *John Swannell, Dave Sargent, Barry Webb, John Cooper, Dave Reid, Peter McGillicuddy, Colin Woffinden, Pete Lavers, Chris Kelly, Willie Smith and John Doyle Sub: Derek Wells*

22nd November 1975   FA Challenge Cup 1st Round Proper
Leatherhead 2 v Cambridge United 0
Green Machine flatten United

Tanners set aside uninspiring league form to despatch another Football League side from the FA Cup. Although there were times, particularly in the second half, when Tanners were stretched, there was no denying that over the whole ninety minutes Cambridge were purely and simply outclassed. They say that cup ties can be won and lost in one moment of ill fate or good fortune and this game turned sharply in Tanners favour thanks to a large helping hand from Lady Luck. After a fairly even opening half-hour Kelly's twisting, turning run propelled him to the dead ball line from where he crossed into the penalty area. Batson, frantically chasing back, could not avoid deflecting the ball onto the post from where it rebounded back and hit him again before rolling almost apologetically over the line. There was certainly nothing fortunate about the knockout blow delivered shortly before half-time. Doyle, the scorer, started the move by dispossessing a United player near the halfway line. He made ground quickly before passing to Kelly on the left wing. The No. 9 spotted Cooper unmarked on the far post and delivered an inch perfect cross onto his forehead. Unselfishly Cooper nodded the ball back across goal for Doyle to head unchallenged into the net.

As expected Cambridge came at Tanners after the break but whether they attacked on the ground or in the air they got little reward out of Reid, Woffinden and Co. Cambridge knew it was not to be their day when Swannell miraculously turned the ball onto the crossbar as Horsfall bulleted the ball towards the goal from close range. A save, that post match, drew comparisons with Gordon Banks from United's flamboyant and rather disgruntled manager Ron Atkinson. Atkinson also probably bitterly regretted his decision, so confident had he been of his side winning, to invite two Fleet Street journalists to sit alongside him in the dugout. Lavers, Cooper and Doyle all came close to increasing Tanners' advantage but the last word belonged fittingly to the superb Swannell as he launched himself horizontally to turn Simmons far post header over the crossbar.

Team: *John Swannell, Dave Sargent, Steve Ibbitson, Colin Woffinden, Dave Reid, Derek Wells, John Cooper, Pete Lavers, Chris Kelly, John Doyle and Willie Smith Sub: Peter Page*

20th November 1976   FA Challenge Cup 1st Round Proper
Leatherhead 2 v Northampton Town 0
Tanners give Cobblers the boot!

For the third season running Leatherhead dumped Football League opposition out of the FA Cup. Even the BBC and the National Press were present, remembering Tanners ability to pull off the big upset in the Cup. Diminutive dribble wizard John Doyle took just half an hour to turn Third Division strugglers Northampton inside out. Doyle, who made a habit of scoring against the 'big boys', took just three minutes to open his account. John Baker, Chris Kelly and Willie Smith worked the opening and in the ensuing goalmouth scramble Doyle found an opening and calmly lobbed home. The Cobblers lacked imagination, a commodity Leatherhead enjoyed in excess and it was this vital factor that gave them another giant-killing victory. Chris Kelly was making Tanners tick and was at the heart of everything. On the half-hour mark he cheekily nutmegged Tucker before feeding Baker out on the right. John Baker's cross, from near the bye-line, was confidently nodded home at the far post by John Doyle. The closest the Cobblers came to scoring was when John Swannell lost a cross in the lights and was grateful to full-back Dave Sargent for heading George Reilly's header off the line. Tanners went into the break well pleased with their performance. Northampton improved after the interval but lacked the skill and technique possessed by Tanners to really trouble Swannell and his defenders. Tanners were able to see out the second half with relatively few alarms, roared home by the massed green ranks who cheered their heroes on evey step of the way until the final whistle blew. Once more the men in green had risen to the big occasion to claim another League scalp. Disappointed Town manager Paddy Crerand commented, *"I wish I could find an excuse but I can't. The best team won"*.

Team: *John Swannell, Dave Sargent, Ray Eaton, Colin Woffinden, Dave Reid, John Bailey, John Cooper, John Baker, Chris Kelly, Willie Smith and John Doyle Sub: Derek Wells*

8th April 1978   FA Trophy Semi-Final 2nd Leg

Spennymoor United 2 v Leatherhead 1 (aggregate 2 - 3)

True grit Tanners Wembley bound at last

On their sloping Brewery Field ground Spennymoor tore into Leatherhead like tigers from the outset and, roared on by a passionate crowd, launched a series of attacking forays that rocked Tanners back on their heels. It came as no surprise, therefore, when after sixteen minutes of almost continual pressure Ward leapt high above a packed defence to head past Swannell. The tension became almost unbearable for the travelling contingent in the 4,000 plus crowd as United continued to pour forward with unrelenting fury. Ten minutes before half-time the Moors were rewarded when Davies caught Tanners' defence square to ram home a second goal. Leatherhead were on the ropes and another goal at this juncture would probably have delivered the knockout blow but the greens managed to withstand further onslaughts to troop off at the break battered but unbowed.

After the interval Spennymoor's grip on the game became less pronounced and Tanners grew in stature and began to mount some attacks of their own. Then it happened. With sixty seven minutes on the clock Salkeld swung over a corner Reid headed on and Baker bravely dived in among the flying feet to connect with a header that sneaked under Porter's body to restore the aggregate lead. The remaining minutes were charged with high tension but amid the gripping intensity the Tanners players remained composed and Doyle could even have nicked an equaliser in the closing minutes. The final whistle blew and the fans that had travelled so far were justly rewarded. The player's ecstatic faces, the wives tears and the fans pitch invasion said it all - Wembley here we come. With the fans joyously singing and dancing it was a mystery how the drivers kept control of the wildly bouncing and swaying double-decker buses transporting them back to Durham Station to board the 'football special' for the long trek home to Surrey.

Team: *John Swannell, John Cooper, Ray Eaton, Barrie Davies, Dave Reid, Dennis Malley, Micky Cook, Billy Salkeld, Chris Kelly, John Baker and John Doyle Sub: John Bailey*

29th April 1978   FA Trophy Final

Altrincham 3 v Leatherhead 1

Off colour Greens Wembley wipe out

Leatherhead had finally made it to the hallowed turf of Wembley but there was to be no happy ending. They were caught cold by an Altrincham side that charged out of the blocks with all guns blazing. Within 180 seconds Johnson outstripped John Cooper down the left before centering for Rogers to power high into the net past John Swannell from close range. Ten minutes later it was two. Cooper, having a torrid time, was again left for dead, this time by Rogers who returned the favour for Johnson to slide the ball in at the near post. Tanners struggled to gain a foothold in the match but so nearly got it shortly before half-time when Chris Kelly's dipping volley from the edge of the box from John Baker's nod down crashed against the bar.

The match was effectively all over five minutes into the second period. John King heading home at the far post after the Tanners defence had failed to clear a corner. Kelly and Baker picked up bookings as their frustration boiled over. Both sides tired in the sweltering April sunshine but at least there was some consolation for the Tanners supporters, who had sung their hearts out all day, when Micky Cook stroked the ball into the bottom corner of the net five minutes from the end. A disconsolate Kelly, playing his first game in a month following injury, remained slumped in the centre circle with his head in his hands long after the final whistle had sounded. He would not have been amused by an attempt at humour by the northern side's supporters who displayed a large flag with the message, '*Alty have brains, not leather heads*'.

Even the rousing reception received from the supporters lining the High Street to greet the team as they paraded through the town in an open top bus later in the evening could do little to dispel the feeling of disappointment at their collective failure to perform to their true capabilities in the biggest game of their lives.

Team: *John Swannell, John Cooper, Ray Eaton, Barrie Davies, Dave Reid, Dennis Malley, Micky Cook, Billy Salkeld, Chris Kelly, John Baker and John Doyle Sub: John Bailey*

2nd May 1985   Servowarm Isthmian League Division One
Maidenhead United 1 v Leatherhead 1
Going Up ………
Having failed to secure the necessary points earlier in the week at home to Lewes, a jittery Leatherhead needed a single point from the final match to clinch promotion. In a nerve wracking finale Tanners started nervously and soon fell behind to a Lance Cadogan goal. Chances came and went and it began to look like Tanners had missed the boat, but with fifteen minutes remaining despair turned to joy as substitute Peter Shodeinde latched onto a Williams through ball and cleverly lobbed the home keeper to make it 1-1 to precipitate a mini pitch invasion by the delighted Tanners supporters. The drama wasn't over as the Magpies had an injury time goal disallowed for offside to further fray the travelling faithful's nerves but Tanners held on. The final whistle was the cue for another, more prolonged, pitch invasion by jubilant supporters and the popping of champagne corks as the Leatherhead players gave retiring chairman Beau Reynolds an emotional farewell. The celebrations continued long into the night in the Magpies clubhouse........ (the supporterrs blissfully unaware of the impending bad news).
Team: *Pete Caswell, Andy Dear, Barry Hempstead, Phil Smith, Jimmy Richardson, Dave Rattue, Wayne Falloon, Jamie Nightingale, Paul Williams, Brian Perkins and Micky Powell Sub: Peter Shodeinde*

23rd December 1986   FA Trophy 1st Round Replay
Leatherhead 1 v Wycombe Wanderers 0
Wanderers lose their way
Tanners secured one of their best ever wins in the Trophy with this superb victory over Isthmian League Premier Division leaders Wycombe Wanderers, despite being without the services of the influential Wayne Falloon, Micky Payne and captain Gary Richards.
In the opening quarter of an hour Wanderers threatened to overrun Leatherhead and only some desperate last ditch defending, the woodwork twice and one incredible 'Gordon Banks' type save from Caswell kept the scores level. Having weathered the storm Tanners grew in confidence and came more into the game. With Gittings orchestrating things in the middle of the park and the darting runs of Grant stretching the visitors defence it was Tanners who looked the more likely to score. It was therefore no great surprise when midway through the second half some fine approach play ended with Gittings' shot being only half cleared to Fisher who found time and space in the penalty area to control and fire home the decisive goal. Wycombe never recovered from this blow and only a fine save from the Wycombe keeper prevented Tanners from adding to their advantage.
Team: *Pete Caswell, John Cook, Andy Riley, Paul Andrews, Andy Cullum, Dave Rattue, Andy Fisher, Martin Gittings, Clive Youlton, Adrian Grant, Brian Stannard Sub: Micky Bennett*

9th November 1998   FA Cup 4th Qualifying Round
Leatherhead 1 v Rushden and Diamonds 1
Diamond choker
A heroic performance ended in heartbreak as the giants of the non-league game grabbed a late, late equaliser to finally breach Tanners' magnificent rearguard action. Rushden controlled much of the first half but only rarely threatened the home goal. In the closing minutes of the opening half a rare Tanners attack earned a corner. The ball was swung in from the left, glanced on by Ray Arnett and joyfully turned over the line at the back post by Steve Lunn to the huge delight of the home fans. After the break the expected siege of the Leatherhead goal duly materialised with Tanners rarely getting out of their own penalty area, let alone their own half. Diamonds resorted to playing four up front in a desperate bid to save the game. Tommy Warrilow and Steve Lawson dealt magnificently with a sustained aerial bombardment but with time running out and the home supporters looking forward to a home tie with Football League Shrewsbury Town in the first round proper, Diamonds £100,000 record signing Ray Warburton stole in to head home a debut goal from yet another cross to put a dampener on the home fans premature celebrations.
Manager Keith Wenham commented afterwards, "*Before the game I thought we were going to get*

stuffed but the team performance was outstanding and they did the club proud".
Team: *Scott Tarr, Ross Edwards, Stuart Lawson, Steve Lawson, Tommy Warrilow, Alex O'Brien, Darryl Teasdale, Paul Reed, Steve Lunn, Ray Arnett and Nigel Webb Subs: Danny Lavender and Gani Ahmet*

20th March 2004   Ryman Isthmian League Division One South
Leatherhead 5 v Lewes 4
Ruggles rocks Rooks

Lewes came to the Grove on a sunny March Saturday afternoon in second place in the league and destined for promotion. Facing a patched-up Tanners team missing several players through injury Lewes started the match brightly but were rocked when Leatherhead took the lead in their first attack. Centre-forward Phil Ruggles, whose pace and skill caused the visitors defence nightmares all afternoon, did well to elude a couple of challenges and although his shot was not cleanly struck it managed to squirm underneath Rooks keeper Jean-Zepherin and into the back of the net. Midway through the first half it was 2-0, Harford chipping home from 35 yards after the ball had fallen to him kindly off the body of the visiting keeper who had raced from his area to block the onrushing Panter's advance on goal. Within two minutes Lewes had pulled a goal back, leading scorer Haughton reducing the arrears with a spectacular overhead kick, however, ten minutes later the visitors found themselves trailing 4-1. Firstly Harford was allowed time and space in which to volley home a third and then another goalkeeping error allowed Ruggles to claim the fourth. With half-time fast approaching the Sussex side got themselves a lifeline when Haughton headed home. Fifteen minutes into the second half Haughton completed his hat-trick and within another ten the scores were level when Lovett headed home from a corner kick. Both sides pressed for a winner but it looked as though honours would finish even until, in time added on, Ruggles beat the last defender to a 50/50 ball and ran unchallenged to the edge of the six-yard box before smashing the ball high into the net to complete his hat-trick and send the home supporters into raptures.
Team: *Mike Johnston, Vitor Tavares, Mike Webb, Iain Hendry, Jon Lloyd, Steve Sargent, Dave Harlow, Paul Harford, Dean Carpenter, Phil Ruggles and Damien Panter Subs: Kevin Terry and Gary Syrett*

And one definitely to forget …

16th November 1982   Servowarm Isthmian League Premier Division
Sutton United 11 v Leatherhead 1
Mayhem as Joyce runs riot

With Leatherhead having lost twelve of their previous fourteen matches Tanners supporters hardly had high hopes of victory as they arrived at Gander Green Lane to see their side take on high-flying Sutton but they could not have anticipated what transpired.

Sutton gave poor Leatherhead an incredible tanning. Their hero of the night was striker Micky Joyce, who set a new club record by scoring nine of the goals. Joyce hit his first goal after just 97 seconds and completed his hat-trick in 13 momentous minutes and had reached five by the 20 minute mark. Fortunately that completed the first half scoring as United took a rest. Joyce soon added two more to his tally after the break. He then took a breather from his single- handed slaughter of the terrified Tanners to let skipper John Rains grab the next two while substitute John Reader interrupted the one-way traffic for a moment with Leatherhead's solitary goal, but Joyce was not finished yet. He netted again in the 75th and 77th minutes to complete the scoring then, thankfully for the sanity of the Tanners fans, missed several more chances as his team-mates made desperate attempts to put him into double figures. Yes, it was Joyce's night but spare a thought for goalkeeper Ian Bath, who was making his debut for Leatherhead, and recently appointed management duo Brian Caterer and Colin Lippiatt.
Team: *Ian Bath, Peter Ranson, Paul Estall, Micky Cook, Lee Harwood, Steve Hardwick, Mick Murphy, Kevin Davies, Andy Bushnell, Lance Cadogan and Tommy Hewitt Sub: John Reader*

Hall of Fame 1946 - 2006

Pete Caswell
1979 -1988, 1989 and 1994 (Goalkeeper) Appearances - 403 Goals - 1

Following a spell in the Football League with Crystal Palace (under Terry Venables) and Crewe Alexandra, Peter followed in his father's footsteps when manager Martin Hinshelwood signed him from Telford, in exchange for a fee of £1,000. He faced the unenviable task of replacing the great John Swannell but soon won over the sceptics in the crowd and was an ever present in 1980/81, keeping nineteen clean sheets and winning the Player of the Year award. His consistency was such that he was afforded the rare accolade of being awarded this trophy again, in 1986.

'Cass' briefly flirted with a return to the Football League when he turned out for Brentford Reserves, as well as for Tanners, during the 1982/83 campaign. One of many memorable performances came in an FA Trophy victory over Wycombe where he almost single handed defied the Wanderers forwards in the opening quarter of an hour. Aside from the playing front his Company were also Leatherhead's main sponsors for a couple of seasons. He joined neighbours Dorking in 1988, returning briefly in 1989, before retiring from the game. Such was his devotion to the club that after a couple of years of inactivity he was persuaded to come out of retirement in 1994 to help Tanners out of an injury crisis. 'Cass' always fancied himself as a goal-scoring centre-forward and he did make a couple of appearances as an outfield player when injury prevented him pulling on the gloves. He showed his ability too with a goal in a league match against Hayes.

John Cooper
1970 - 1980 (Defender / Midfield) Appearances - 517 Goals - 34

A mature student whose previous clubs included stints in the reserve sides of Brentford, West Ham United and Fulham. John arrived at the Grove in 1970 and was soon established as an integral part of the Green Machine. Tall with an elegant running stride and deceptively quick, 'Coops' was a very versatile player who filled every outfield position during his Leatherhead career. He spent the majority of his first four seasons patrolling the middle of the park before switching to a more defensive role of either full-back or centre-back. A strong runner he soon became noted for his powerful overlapping forays and accurate crosses.

He played for the FA XI as well as captaining the Rothmans England X1 on their tour to the Canary Islands. Woking paid a fee of £1,000 for his services and he subsequently had spells as a player at Walton and Hersham and Sutton United as well as a stint as manager at Athenian League Redhill.

Barrie Davies
1968 - 1973 and 1977 - 1981 (Midfield / Defender) Appearances - 388 Goals - 24

Barrie started his career in 1963 as a 16-year-old ball-winning midfielder with Southall in the Athenian League, before joining Leatherhead from Hendon five years later. He soon earned the respect of the fans with his tireless running, tigerish tackling and fierce competitiveness. Having made 243 appearances he left Tanners and subsequently had spells with Slough, Hayes, Hounslow and Wycombe before returning to Fetcham Grove in 1977. Small of stature Barrie was versatile, as well as volatile, and was equally at home at full-back, sweeper or in midfield and made a further 145 appearances before departing to team up with Billy Miller at Woking in exchange for a fee of £300. He was Leatherhead's first international and won 3 Welsh Amateur international caps in all.

John Doyle
1974 - 1982 (Winger) Appearances - 341 Goals - 59

Signed from Kingstonian, the skilful diminutive winger soon established himself as a firm favourite with the fans, especially as he had the happy knack of scoring goals against Football League opposition. League defenders seemed to neglect to mark John from crosses, perhaps fooled by his lack of inches. Honours bestowed on 'The Ferret', as he was nicknamed, included touring with Middlesex Wanderers and representing the Isthmian League. Injury curtailed his final couple of seasons at the Grove before he returned to Richmond Road in 1982 to team up with 'Budgie' and Billy Miller again.

Chris Kelly
1972 - 1982 (Forward) Appearances - 492 Goals - 156

The brash and highly talented Kelly started his career at Epsom and Ewell before moving on to Tooting and then Sutton United, from where he joined the Tanners in 1972. He was an ever present in that first season. Chris became a national figure during the course of the 1974/75 FA Cup run. He stated that he liked to be known as 'Kele' (as in Pele) but was more popularly known as 'Budgie' and was dubbed the 'Leatherhead Lip' by the national media. One national paper even described him as, "*a kind of Muhammed Ali with a cockney accent*". Love him or hate him the one thing you could not do was ignore him. His superb close control and mazy dribbling skills meant that he could usually back up his boasts on the football pitch. Chris was one of the few part-time footballers who could pull in the crowds. His style won games, his arrogance infuriated opposing players and fans but his sense of fun and obvious enjoyment of life and football usually converted his critics and at least brought a smile to those around him. He was never far from the referee's ear, a trait which earned him numerous bookings and an occasional early bath. 'Budgie' had a short but unhappy spell in the Football League with Millwall in 1975 before returning to the Grove inside six months, despite offers from other teams to stay in the professional game.

During his career he won just about every representative honour going: England Amateur, England Semi-Professional, FA X1, Isthmian League, Surrey and Middlesex Wanderers. This was just as well because as he so eloquently phrased it, "*We won sod all at Leatherhead*".

Chris had a short spell as player-coach but left at the end of the 1981/2 season, disappointed at not being offered the manager's job in succession to Martin Hinshelwood. He later had successful spells as manager, Commercial Manager and then Chief Executive of Surrey rivals Kingstonian. In 2005 Chris made a welcome return to Fetcham Grove in the capacity of Marketing Manager.

Billy Miller
1957 - 1980 (Defender / Manager) Appearances - 5 Games in charge - 890

Billy took over as first team manager, from Norman Douglas, in somewhat controversial circum-stances for the start of the 1965/66 season at a youthful 31-years of age. He had, by then, already spent eight years at the club initially playing and then, with some success, running the reserve side. Billy, a qualified FA coach, was considered a good administrator and motivator and a poor loser. As a player he had failed to break into the first team, making just five appearances during six years. As manager he carried on Douglas's good work and with the help of his able lieutenant Johnny Phipps, and subsequently Dave Wall, turned Tanners into one of the top amateur sides in the country. His tenure was not without its ups and downs though and on several occasions there were rumours of his imminent departure but he weathered these storms.

He was an excellent judge of players and helped engender a great team spirit amongst the squad, players wanted to play for Billy although he was not averse to issuing rollickings or turning the air blue with his tirades. He was described in the local press as, "*the unmistakable chubby figure, in trademark red jersey and sheepskin jacket, shrieking instructions from the touchline*".

Under his stewardship there were many memorable cup runs but perhaps the team lacked that extra consistency that was required to win league championships. His achievements included taking the side to two Amateur Cup semi-finals and three quarter-finals, an FA Trophy final, the FA Cup 4th round proper once, the 2nd round on three occasions and the 1st round once. Outside of national competitions he led the team to five Surrey Senior Cup, two London Senior Cup and an Isthmian League Cup final, as well as steering the club from the Athenian into the Isthmian League, although actual silverware remained hard to come by.

On a personal note and he was voted Isthmian League Manager of the Month on a couple of occasions. His abilities were highly respected by his peers and he managed various Isthmian League, FA and Surrey FA X1's, as well as being a selector for the first England Semi-Professional X1.

He resigned as Leatherhead boss in 1980 thus ending a 23 year association with the club. Following his resignation he managed Walton and Hersham, Woking and Kingstonian without ever quite replicating the tremendous success he had enjoyed at the Grove.

Brian Pell
1961 - 1968 (Inside-Left) Appearances - 281 Goals - 111
Brian made his debut in the opening game of the 1961/62 campaign following his arrival from Surrey rivals Banstead Athletic. A highly gifted ball player it remained a mystery to all Tanners supporters as to how he failed to gain recognition for England, although he did feature in an FA Amateur X1 and the Athenian League representative side. He was principally an inside left but liked to roam all over the pitch in search of space and the ball and provided the link between midfield and attack. His performances (not to mention goals) were instrumental in Tanners' rise through the Corinthian and Athenian League ranks as well as various Amateur Cup runs, most notably with his winning goal at Tow Law. He retired in 1968 after fighting a losing battle against injury.

Dave Reid
1969 - 1979 (Centre-half) Appearances - 523 Goals - 67
The son of famous Scottish international centre-half Doug Reid, Dave started as an apprentice with Portsmouth where he led the goal-scoring charts for their South East Counties side two years running before Pompey axed their youth team. 'Reidy' joined Tanners, from Andover. After a couple of games at centre-forward Billy Miller successfully converted him to an old fashioned centre-half. Dedicated, wholehearted, uncompromising but amiable he was soon being touted as one of the outstanding central defenders in non-league football. Following Alan Brazier's retirement he was appointed club captain, a position he held until his departure. Noted for his ability to hang in the air Dave or the 'Shadow' as he was nicknamed, never lost his eye for goal and was a regular contributor to the goals for column, twice reaching double figures in a season and was something of a specialist from dead ball situations possessing a, *"mule like free-kick"*. He finally tired of the regular commute from the South Coast and signed for Fareham. He subsequently had spells in charge of Hampshire sides Horndean, Waterlooville and Portsmouth Royal Navy. Dave appeared in the England Amateur squad on a number of occasions without ever making the starting eleven. He also won representative honours for the Isthmian and Athenian Leagues, Surrey, the FA and Middlesex Wanderers. Dave was awarded a well deserved testimonial against his home town team Portsmouth.

Dave 'Nobby' Skinner
1966 - 1974 (Outside-Left) Appearances - 346 Goals - 112
Nobby started his career with local side Leatherhead Casuals, before spending six months at West Ham under Ron Greenwood where he won a Football League Combination Cup winners medal. The Hammers failed to sign him and their loss was very much Leatherhead's gain.
Nobby earned rave reviews in making a goal-scoring debut for the Tanners in a Premier Midweek Floodlit League match against Hayes in 1967. He soon built on this initial success and quickly established himself as a favourite with the fans with his defence splitting runs and spectacular goals and was the natural ball playing successor to Brian Pell. Nobby was known as Leatherhead's George Best and led the Green's goal-scoring charts in both 1969 and 1970 as well as providing many assists for his colleagues with his mazy runs and accurate crosses. Among his many goals was a memorable one to win an Amateur Cup quarter- final tie against Boreham Wood in 1971. Among many representative honours Nobby's mercurial performances earned him selection for both the Great Britain Olympic and England Amateur squads. Ever the maverick he left the Tanners to join Kingstonian at the conclusion of the 1973/74 season. His memory is kept alive at the Grove through the workings of the mysterious group known as 'The Nobby Skinner Appreciation Society' who from time to time continue to sponsor Tanners home matches.

Willie Smith
1973 - 1977 (Midfield) Appearances - 177 Goals - 21

Willie was a former Chelsea trialist who had spells at Tooting and Mitcham and Sutton United before joining the great Walton and Hersham side of the early seventies. During his time at Stompond Lane he won an Amateur Cup winners medal and established himself as a regular in the England set up, gaining 14 caps. Impish and quixotic both on and off the pitch he was a natural leader although his efforts were perhaps more appreciated by his fellow players, for whom he provided the steel to allow their more expressive talents to flourish, than by the supporters. Willie was rated by none another than Chris Kelly as the most outstanding player he played with in semi-professional football. He was often to be seen hands on knees bellowing instructions at team-mates and urging them on. He left Tanners to play in the Football League with Wimbledon, but after appearing in their first two matches as a Football League club a serious leg injury prematurely ended his professional career.

Fred Stenning
1947 - 1952 (Centre-forward) Appearances - 139 Goals - 185

The mention of the name Fred Stenning still evokes much misty eyed nostalgia from all who witnessed his exploits. Fred of the thinning hair and wicked grin led Leatherhead to three of their four Surrey Senior League championship successes and was the most potent marksman in Surrey football either side of the war. His main strength was in the air but, as with most great goal-scorers, he had the happy knack of regularly being in the right place at the right time. Leatherhead has had many prolific scorers in their time but supporters still talk about Fred Stenning as the best of them all and more than 50 years since his retirement he still holds virtually all of Tanners' goal-scoring records. His senior football career started at the tender age of sixteen with Cobham but it was at Epsom Town that he first came to prominence. Whilst there he represented the London League and played in several trial matches for Crystal Palace. He was also approached by Spurs but any thoughts of a professional career were ended by the outbreak of war.

Upon demob he spent a season with Vickers before arriving at Fetcham Grove, via Walton and Hersham, in the autumn of 1947. He was soon breaking the hearts of many defences scoring freely for the remainder of the season, averaging a goal a game. His first full season, 1948/49, was memorable. Goals were again in plentiful supply, 61 in 39 games. Even that record was surpassed the following season. Fred was simply unstoppable netting an incredible 71 times in just 41 games. This tally included eleven occasions on which he scored three or more, and remains a club record. Fred also scored all six in a 6-1 win over McLaren Sports. His career was blighted by injury during the next two seasons. A serious leg injury resulted in him missing part of the 1950/51 season before he stunned the club and the supporters by following former manager Bill Whittaker to Malden in the New Year. He marked his return, against Cheshunt, in December 1951, by scoring one of his trademark glancing headers and missing a penalty (something he also did on a fairly regular basis). Fred's playing career was ended in February 1952 when he suffered a serious knee injury during a game against Rainham. In all Fred averaged nearly 1.5 goals a game, an incredible ratio at any level of senior football.

John Swannell
1974 - 1980 (Goalkeeper) Appearances - 333

Swannell was a goalkeeper extraordinaire whose athleticism and anticipation, at times, defied belief. In his day he was the most famous, as well as the best, keeper outside of the Football League. John started his distinguished career with Corinthian Casuals before joining the great Hendon team in 1964. He quickly established himself as a regular in the England Amateur set up, eventually gaining 61 caps, and the Great Britain Olympic team (8 caps). John appeared in three Amateur Cup finals as well as winning two Isthmian League championships with Hendon before he joined Leatherhead in 1974 at the age of 35, supposedly in the twilight of his career, although fellow players reckoned him to be Old Father Time and at least fifty. John was noted for his trait of always wearing white laces in his boots. Despite veteran status he turned in a series of near faultless performances in Tanners cup exploits of the mid-seventies and was still considered good enough to be selected for the first England Semi-Professional team that faced Italy in 1975. He left Tanners in 1980 to rejoin Hendon. Despite various ailments he was still playing well into his sixties, helping Corinthian Casuals to win the National Veterans over 50's Cup in the late 1990's.

Ernie Trout
1946 - 1954 (Right-Wing) Appearances - 255 Goals - 127
Ernie was a popular, nippy little winger, a great crosser of the ball, who provided the ammunition for the glamour boys - the centre-forwards - to score the goals, although he also chipped in with more than his fair share himself. Ernie was Fred Stenning's provider in chief and was instrumental in Tanners' early successes. The abiding memory of Ernie was his 'Tommy Lawton' centre parting which, even after ninety minutes play, always looked to be in place (good old Brylcreem)! On the subject of hair styles Fred Stenning never suffered from this problem for he was virtually bald. Perhaps he slapped the Brylcreem straight on his head which may explain why he scored so many glancing headers! Ernie, along with Fred Stenning and Cecil Weller were regular members of the Surrey Senior League Representative side.

Barry Webb
1965 - 1975 (Defender / Midfield) Appearances - 438 Goals - 119
Barry joined Tanners as a junior in 1964 and was promoted to the first team squad the following season. He had a brief spell at Bexley United before returning to the Grove and establishing a regular place in the starting eleven in the second half of the 67/68 season. The barrel-chested Webb was a midfield dictator in his early days and found the back of the net with great frequency and was deadly accurate from 12-yards. Barry was switched to left-back, a role he fulfilled with equal success making 170 consecutive league and cup appearances between 1971 and 1974. Barry moved to Kingstonian in September 1975. After retiring as a player in 1979 he had a successful five year spell as manager of Redhill before trying his hand, less successfully, with Croydon.

Derek Wells
1971 - 1977 (Centre-Half) Appearances - 336 Goals - 13
A taxi driver by profession, Derek arrived at Leatherhead at the tail-end of the 1970/71 season via Fulham and was one of Tanners' most consistent performers during his time at the Grove. A great 'team man' who was considered to be one of the best uncapped back four players in the country. Derek left for Walthamstow Avenue in 1977 and was immediately successful, helping the Avenue to a London Senior Cup success at Tanners expense.

Colin Woffinden
1974 - 1977 (Midfield / Defender) Appearances - 174 Goals - 20
Colin started out at Lewes before moving to Brighton and Hove Albion. He made his Football League debut against Gillingham in November 1970 and made three further appearances, scoring one goal, during the remainder of the season. He was released by the Seagulls and joined Sutton United before moving to Walton and Hersham the following summer. He won an Amateur Cup winners medal with the Swans and was a member of the England Amateur squad. Following the break up of the Walton team he joined Tanners, along with Willie Smith and Dave Sargent. Another versatile player, as so many of the squad seemed to be at the time, he was equally accomplished in either central midfield or central defence, good in the air and comfortable in possession. He was a player who always seemed to have time on the ball.
Colin moved to Tooting in 1977 and was still playing for his local side, Saltdean, in the Sussex County League in his mid-forties. Colin remains involved in youth soccer, he was responsible for setting up the Youth Development Scheme at Brighton, and was also co-author of the 'Guinness Book of Skilful Soccer'.

Selected seasons in full

1949/50 (Surrey Senior League)

Date	Opponents	H/A	Comp	Res	w/d/l	Scorers
20/08	Met Police	H	Fr	3-1	W	Cherigini 2 Trout
27/08	Camberley	A	Lge	4-2	W	Stenning 3 Hawksworth
03/09	Hounslow	H	FAC P	2-6	L	Stenning Hawksworth
10/09	Devas Institute	H	Lge	5-2	W	Stenning 4 Wheeler
14/09	Rest of League	H	Fr	2-2	D	Trout Own Goal
17/09	Guildford Pks	A	Lge	3-4	L	Stenning Hawksworth Honey
24/09	Chertsey Town	A	AC Pr	3-1	W	Stenning Tudor Weller
01/10	Hawkers Ath	A	Lge	3-0	W	Weller Caswell Tudor
08/10	Guildford Pks	A	AC 1Q	2-1	W	Stenning 2
15/10	McLaren Spts	H	Lge	6-1	W	Stenning 6
22/10	Banstead Ath	H	AC 2Q	4-3	W	Stenning 3 (1 pen) Bolton
29/10	Cobham	H	Lge	6-3	W	Caswell 3 Stenning Harvey Weller
05/11	Farnham	A	AC 3Q	4-3	W	Stenning 3 Hawksworth
12/11	Worcester Pk	A	Lge	4-4	D	Stenning 3 (1 pen) Graffham
03/12	Hayes	H	AC 1	1-3	L	Hawksworth
10/12	Chertsey	A	Lge	3-1	W	Stenning 3
17/12	McLaren Spts	A	Lge	1-1	D	Stenning
24/12	Surbiton Town	H	Lge	4-1	W	Stenning 2 Trout Caswell
26/12	Dorking	A	Lge	2-0	W	Hawksworth 2
31/12	Woking	A	SSC 1	2-3	L	Stenning Caswell
07/01	Worcester Pk	A	Lge	1-0	W	Caswell
14/01	McLaren Spts	A	SLC 1	7-3	W	Caswell 3 Trout 2 Hawksworth 2
21/01	Byfleet	H	Lge	6-1	W	Stenning 3 Trout 3
28/01	Chertsey Town	H	Lge	3-1	W	Stenning 2 Trout
04/02	Banstead	A	Lge	1-1	D	Temlett
11/02	Byfleet	A	Lge	2-1	W	Stenning 2
18/02	Camberley	H	Lge	7-2	W	Stenning 2 Trout Temlett Weller Caswell OG
25/02	Farnham	H	Lge	3-2	W	Trout 2 Temlett
04/03	Hawkers Ath	H	Lge	2-2	D	Trout Temlett
11/03	Worcester Pk	H	SLC 2	5-0	W	Stenning 3 Temlett 2
18/03	Cobham	A	Lge	2-1	W	Stenning 2
25/03	Chertsey Town	H	CC 1	6-1	W	Stenning 4 Trout Own Goal
01/04	Farnham	A	Lge	1-0	W	Stenning
08/04	Catford Wndrs	H	Fr	3-1	W	Stenning Hawksworth Temlett
10/04	Dorking	H	Lge	2-3	L	Stenning Weller
15/04	Worcester Pk	H	CC 2	6-2	W	Hawksworth 2 Stenning Trout Temlett Caswell
19/04	Farnham	H	SLC s/f	5-0	W	Hawksworth 2 Stenning Trout Smith
22/04	Devas Institute	A	Lge	5-2	W	Stenning 3 (1 pen) Temlett 2
24/04	Banstead Ath	H	Lge	1-0	W	Temlett
29/04	Banstead Ath	H	CC s/f	2-1	W	Stenning Trout
01/05	Surbiton Town	A	Lge	0-0	D	----------
03/05	Guildford Pks	H	Lge	8-0	W	Stenning 4 Trout 4
10/05	Banstead Ath	H	SLC F	5-2	W	Trout 2 Stenning Hawksworth Wheeler
17/05	Hawkers Ath	H	CC F	7-0	W	Stenning 5 Hawksworth Trout

Season's record: Played - 44 Won - 33 Drawn - 6 Lost - 5 Goals For - 154 Goals Against - 68

1962 / 63 (Corinthian League)

Date	Opponents	H/A	Comp	Res	w/d/l	Scorers
18/08	Slough Town	A	Lge	5-0	W	Brittin 2 Harris Dobbs Hickey
23/08	Dagenham	H	Lge	5-1	W	Brittin Pell Phipps Hickey Mollatt
25/08	Slough Town	H	Lge	3-3	D	Brittin Hickey Wood (pen)
30/08	Horsham	A	Lge	3-1	W	Brittin Dobbs Mollatt
01/09	Maidenhead Ud	H	Lge	7-1	W	Brittin Pell Mollatt Hickey Phipps Wood (pen) Dobbs
08/09	Wimbledon	H	FAC 1Q	1-4	L	Mollatt
15/09	Horsham	A	CMS 1	3-2	W	Pell 2 Mollatt
22/09	Letchworth Tn	A	Lge	1-3	L	Hickey
29/09	Hermes	H	AC Pr	3-1	W	Brittin Pell Goodman
06/10	Wokingham	A	Lge	2-1	W	Pell 2
13/10	Epsom & Ewell	H	AC IQ	3-2	W	Brittin 2 Goodman
20/10	Erith & Blvdre	H	Lge	4-1	W	Pell 2 Hickey Wood (pen)
27/10	Molesey	H	AC 2Q	6-3	W	Brittin 2 Hickey 2 Pell Goodman
03/11	Uxbridge	H	Lge	2-3	L	Brittin 2
10/11	Malden Town	A	AC 3Q	3-2	W	Pell 2 Own Goal
17/11	Dorking	H	Lge	4-1	W	Pell Goodman Harris Hickey
01/12	Carshalton Ath	A	AC 4Q	4-1	W	Goodman 2 Pell Brittin
08/12	Dagenham	A	Lge	3-0	W	Goodman Pell Oakes
15/12	Erith & Blvdre	A	Lge	0-0	D	----------
26/12	Epsom & Ewell	H	Lge	2-0	W	Pell Hickey
19/01	Pinehurst	H	AC 1	3-0	W	Goodman 2 Pell
26/01	Farncombe	H	SSC 1	7-0	W	Goodman 3 Brittin 3 Hickey
02/03	Hitchin Town	H	AC 2	1-4	L	Hickey
09/03	Wokingham	H	Lge	4-0	W	Goodman Pell Oakes Wood (pen)
15/03	Corinthian Cas	A	SSC 2	3-1	W	Brittin Pell Wood (pen)
22/03	Horsham	H	Lge	5-0	W	Goodman 2 Brittin Pell Hickey
29/03	Edgware	H	Lge	3-0	W	Goodman Brittin Own Goal
02/04	Maidenhead Ud	A	Lge	2-1	W	Goodman Brittin
06/04	Edgware	A	CMS 2	0-0*	D	----------
13/04	Eastbourne	A	Lge	2-1	W	Goodman 2
15/04	Letchworth Tn	H	Lge	5-2	W	Brittin 2 Pell 2 Goodman
17/04	Eastbourne	H	Lge	3-2	W	Brittin 2 Goodman (pen)
20/04	Epsom & Ewell	A	Lge	5-2	W	Brittin 2 Goodman Hickey Dobbs
27/04	Sutton Utd	H	SSC s/f	0-4	L	----------
30/04	Edgware	H	CMS 2r	0-1*	L	----------
02/05	Worthing	H	Lge	2-1	W	Goodman 2 (1 pen)
04/05	Wembley	H	Lge	1-0	W	Mollatt
07/05	Edgware	A	Lge	1-3	L	Hickey
09/05	Worthing	A	Lge	3-3	D	Goodman Hickey Brittin
11/05	Wembley	A	Lge	3-2	W	Brittin 3
15/05	Dorking	A	Lge	2-2	D	Hickey Goodman (pen)
21/05	Chesham Utd	A	Lge	1-1	D	Brittin
25/05	Chesham Utd	H	Lge	3-0	W	Brittin Goodman Mollatt

Season's record: Played - 44 Won - 31 Drawn - 6 Lost - 7 Goals For - 125 Goals Against - 61

1974/75 (Rothmans Isthmian League)

Date	Opponents	H/A	Comp	Res	w/d/l	Scorers
03/08	Arundel	A	Fr	8-0	W	McGillicuddy 3 Lavers 2 Fruen 2 Kelly
06/08	Lewes	H	Fr	5-1	W	Lavers Cooper Kelly Wells Skinner
08/08	Redhill	H	Fr	3-0	W	Lavers 2 McGillicuddy
10/08	Fulham XI	H	Fr	3-0	W	Reid 2 Doyle
17/08	Oxford City	A	Lge	4-1	W	Lavers Kelly Cooper Webb (pen)
20/08	Hayes	H	Lge	1-0	W	Cooper
24/08	Dulwich Hmlt	H	Lge	3-1	W	Lavers Reid Own Goal
27/08	Walton & Hshm	A	Lge	5-0	W	Doyle 2 Kelly Woffinden Own Goal
31/08	Hendon	A	Lge	2-2	D	Lavers Dade
03/09	Woking	H	Lge	3-3	D	Lavers Reid Webb (pen)
07/09	Kingstonian	A	Lge	2-0	W	Kelly Woffinden
10/09	Slough Town	H	Lge	4-0	W	Lavers 3 Smith
14/09	Croydon Amtrs	A	FAC 1Q	2-0	W	Lavers Kelly
17/09	Wycombe Wdrs	H	Lge	2-1	W	Lavers Kelly
21/09	Ilford	A	Lge	1-3	L	Lavers
24/09	Dulwich Hmlt	A	Lge	1-2	L	Lavers
28/09	Kingsbury Tn	A	LSC 1	2-0	W	Reid Smith
01/10	Walton & Hshm	H	Lge	3-0	W	Lavers Webb Cooper
05/10	Hornchurch	H	FAC 2Q	5-0	W	Lavers 2 Cooper Doyle Webb (pen)
12/10	Ilford	H	Lge	2-1	W	Lavers 2
15/10	Wycombe Wdrs	A	Lge	0-1	L	----------
19/10	Dagenham	H	FAC 3Q	0-0	D	----------
22/10	Dagenham	A	FAC 3Qr	3-1	W	Kelly 2 Doyle
26/10	Hounslow Tn	H	LSC 2	2-2	D	Doyle Reid
29/10	Hounslow Tn	A	LSC 2r	5-1	W	Doyle 3 Lavers Kelly
02/11	Walton & Hshm	A	FAC 4Q	7-1	W	Sargent 2 McGillicuddy 2 Lavers Doyle Woffinden
09/11	Bishops Stortfrd	H	Lge	2-0	W	Wells Sargent
11/11	Woking	A	Lge	1-1	D	Woffinden
16/11	Barking	H	Lge	5-1	W	Lavers 2 Webb Wells McGillicuddy
23/11	Bishops Stortfrd	A	FAC 1	0-0	D	----------
26/11	Bishops Stortfrd	H	FAC 1r	2-0	W	Lavers Doyle
30/11	Gravesnd & Nft	H	FAT 3Q	4-1	W	Lavers Doyle McGillicuddy Webb (pen)
04/12	Tooting & Mtm	H	Lge	1-1	D	Cooper
07/12	Hendon	H	LSC 3	2-1	W	Lavers Cooper
14/12	Colchester Utd	H	FAC 2	1-0	W	Doyle
21/12	Oxford City	H	Lge	2-1	W	Lavers Smith
28/12	Hayes	A	Lge	1-2	L	Webb (pen)
04/01	Brighton & Hv	A	FAC 3	1-0	W	Kelly
07/01	Sutton Utd	A	Lge	2-1	W	Lavers Woffinden
11/01	Hastings Utd	H	FAT 1	5-1	W	Reid 2 Lavers Kelly Webb (pen)
14/01	Redhill	A	SSC1	5-1	W	Lavers 2 Kelly Cooper Woffinden
18/01	Hitchin Town	A	LSC4	3-2	W	Lavers Kelly Reid
25/01	Leicester City	A	FAC 4	2-3	L	Kelly McGillicuddy
01/02	Weymouth	A	FAT 2	0-2	L	----------
08/02	Walthamstow A	A	Lge	2-1	W	Lavers Reid
10/02	Slough Town	A	Lge	1-2	L	Lavers

Date	Opponents	H/A	Comp	Res	w/d/l	Scorers
15/02	Enfield	H	Lge	1-0	W	Webb (pen)
18/02	Sutton Utd	H	Lge	2-3	L	Doyle Webb (pen)
22/02	Walton & Hshm	A	SSC 2	1-0	W	Doyle
25/02	Kingstonian	H	Lge	2-2	D	Cooper 2
01/03	Bishops Stortfrd	A	Lge	1-0	W	Doyle
04/03	Bromley	H	Lge	3-0	W	Lavers 2 Woffinden
08/03	Barking	A	Lge	1-2	L	Reid
18/03	Leytonstone	A	Lge	0-2	L	----------
22/03	Enfield	H	LSC s/f	0-0	D	----------
25/03	Enfield	A	LSC s/f r	1-0	W	Doyle
29/03	Tooting & Mtm	H	SSC s/f	0-0	D	----------
31/03	Leytonstone	H	Lge	2-0	W	Reid Wells
02/04	Tooting & Mtm	A	SSC s/f r	3-0	W	Lavers Reid Webb (pen)
05/04	Clapton	A	Lge	8-0	W	Lavers 4 McGillicuddy 2 Woffinden Reid
08/04	Hendon	H	Lge	1-1	D	Doyle
12/04	Wimbledon	N	LSC F	0-2	L	----------
14/04	Tooting & Mtm	A	Lge	0-0	D	----------
19/04	Enfield	A	Lge	1-0	W	Webb (pen)
23/04	Clapton	H	Lge	3-0	W	Doyle Page Sargent (pen)
25/04	Dagenham	A	Lge	1-1	D	McGillicuddy
29/04	Walthamstow A	H	Lge	2-1	W	Lavers McGillicuddy
02/05	Dulwich Hmlt	N	SSC F	0-2	L	----------
06/05	Dagenham	H	Lge	1-2	L	Smith
08/05	Bromley	A	Lge	1-1	D	Lavers
10/05	Hitchin Town	A	Lge	1-1	D	Lavers
17/05	Hitchin Town	H	Lge	2-1	W	Lavers Wells

Season's record: Played - 72 Won - 44 Drawn - 15 Lost - 13 Goals For - 158 Goals Against - 63

1977/78 (Isthmian League Premier Division)

Date	Opponents	H/A	Comp	Res	w/d/l	Scorers
06/08	Waterlooville	A	Fr	1-1	D	Baker (pen)
11/08	Farnborough Tn	A	Fr	2-0	W	Reid Purvis
13/08	Arundel	A	Fr	5-1	W	Kelly 2 Doyle Salkeld Own Goal
20/08	Hayes	H	Lge	1-0	W	Reid
23/08	Leytonstone	A	Lge	0-0	D	----------
27/08	Wycombe Wndrs	A	Lge	1-1	D	Kelly
30/08	Dagenham	H	Lge	3-0	W	Kelly Baker Cook
03/09	Hendon	A	Lge	1-1	D	Cook
07/09	Carshalton Ath	A	Lge	1-2	L	Baker
10/09	Staines Town	A	Lge	0-1	L	----------
13/09	Woking	H	Lge	4-1	W	Kelly Baker Malley Salkeld (pen)
17/09	Kingstonian	H	Lge	3-1	W	Baker Doyle Cook
24/09	Croydon	A	Lge	2-1	W	Baker Salkeld (pen)
01/10	Hendon	H	Lge	4-1	W	Baker 2 Malley Salkeld (pen)
04/10	Leytonstone	H	Lge	4-1	W	Kelly 2 Doyle Own Goal
08/10	Hitchin Town	H	Lge	1-1	D	Salkeld (pen)
10/10	Dagenham	A	Lge	1-3	L	Kelly

Date	Opponents	H/A	Comp	Res	w/d/l	Scorers
15/10	Tooting & Mtm	A	Lge	2-1	W	Kelly Doyle
18/10	Carshalton Ath	H	Lge	3-0	W	Doyle 2 Baker
22/10	Southall & Ealing	H	Lge	5-1	W	Kelly 2 Baker 2 Malley
25/10	Woking	A	Lge	3-0	W	Baker 2 Doyle
29/10	Boreham Wood	A	Lge	0-0	D	----------
05/11	Cheshunt	H	FAC 4Q	4-1	W	Salkeld 2 (1 pen) Kelly Baker
08/11	Enfield	H	Lge	1-2	L	Kelly
12/11	Bishops Stortford	A	Lge	0-0	D	----------
15/11	Windsor & Eton	H	PMFL	3-1	W	Kelly Reid Palladino
19/11	Kingstonian	A	Lge	3-2	W	Kelly 2 Cook
26/11	Swansea City	H	FAC 1	0-0	D	----------
29/11	Swansea City	A	FAC 1r	1-2	L	Baker
03/12	Tilbury	A	Lge	0-2	L	----------
10/12	Letchworth GC	H	LSC 1	3-1	W	Kelly Baker Salkeld
13/12	Bracknell Town	H	PMFL	6-1	W	Kelly 3 Salkeld Cook Palladino
17/12	Wycombe Wndrs	H	Lge	1-0	W	Cooper
31/12	Banstead Ath	H	SSC 1	2-1	W	Baker Doyle
02/01	Slough Town	H	Lge	1-1	D	Salkeld
07/01	Boreham Wood	H	Lge	1-0	W	Kelly
10/01	Windsor & Eton	A	PMFL	2-0	W	Salkeld Palladino
14/01	Banbury Utd	A	FAT 1	2-1	W	Kelly Cook
21/01	Harrow Borough	A	LSC 2	0-0	D	----------
24/01	Harrow Borough	H	LSC 2r	3-1	W	Baker 2 Cook
28/01	Walton & Hrshm	H	SSC 2	1-1	D	Kelly
31/01	Walton & Hrshm	A	SSC 2r	2-0	W	Baker Cook
09/02	Dartford	H	FAT 2	5-1	W	Kelly 2 Baker Salkeld Palladino
11/02	Croydon	H	Lge	2-3	L	Baker Cook
21/02	Boreham Wood	A	LSC 3	1-1	D	Baker
25/02	Wigan Ath	H	FAT 3	2-0	W	Kelly 2
28/02	Boreham Wood	H	LSC 3r	1-0	W	Bailey
04/03	Woking	H	SSC s/f	1-2	L	Salkeld
11/03	Bedford Town	A	FAT 4	0-0	D	----------
14/03	Bedford Town	H	FAT 4r	5-2	W	Doyle 2 Salkeld 2 (1 pen) Cook
18/03	Sutton Utd	A	LSC s/f	0-0	D	----------
21/03	Sutton Utd	H	LSC s/f r	2-1*	W	Malley Salkeld (pen)
23/03	Molesey	H	ILC 1	2-0	W	Cooper Salkeld (pen)
25/03	Barking	A	Lge	1-4	L	Malley
27/03	Hayes	A	Lge	0-2	L	----------
01/04	Spennymoor Utd	H	FAT s/f1	2-0	W	Malley Cooper
08/04	Spennymoor Utd	A	FAT s/f2	1-2	L	Baker
11/04	Barking	H	Lge	1-1	D	Baker
13/04	Hendon	H	ILC 2	1-0	W	Doyle
15/04	Walthamstow Ave	N	LSC F	0-1	L	----------
17/04	Tooting & Mtm	H	Lge	0-1	L	----------
18/04	Bishops Stortford	H	Lge	1-0	W	Salkeld
20/04	Wycombe Wndrs	H	ILC 3	1-0	W	Bailey
22/04	Enfield	A	Lge	0-2	L	----------

Date	Opponents	H/A	Comp	Res	w/d/l	Scorers
27/04	Sutton Utd	A	Lge	0-3#	L	----------
29/04	Altrincham	N	FAT F	1-3	L	Cook
01/05	Staines Town	H	Lge	2-0	W	Baker Reid
02/05	Hitchin Town	A	Lge	0-2#	L	----------
03/05	Tilbury	H	Lge	2-1	W	Baker Own Goal
04/05	Slough Town	A	Lge	1-3#	L	(Duff)
04/05	Sutton Utd	H	Lge	2-2	D	Baker Kelly
05/05	Walthamstow Ave	H	Lge	0-0	D	----------
08/05	Southall & Ealing	A	Lge	0-0#	D	----------
09/05	Boreham Wood	A	ILC s/f	1-0	W	Doyle
11/05	Walthamstow Ave	A	Lge	4-1	W	Cooper Doyle Cook Bailey
13/05	Dagenham	N	ILC F	0-1	L	----------
15/05	AFC Amsterdam	H	Fr	1-0	W	Salkeld

Season's record: Played - 77 Won - 40 Drawn - 18 Lost -19 Goals For -126 Goals Against -74

1996/97 (Icis Isthmian League Division Two)

Date	Opponents	H/A	Comp	Res	w/d/l	Scorers
27/07	Whitehawk	H	Fr	4-2	W	Lunn 2 Arnett 2
31/07	Charlton Ath XI	H	Fr	2-0	W	Lunn Webb
02/08	Brighton & Hv XI	H	Fr	2-1	W	Lunn 2
08/08	Erith & Belvedere	A	Fr	1-2	L	Own Goal
10/08	Carshalton Ath	H	Fr	1-6	L	Lunn
17/08	Ware	H	Lge	2-1	W	Lunn Arnett
20/08	Bracknell Town	A	Lge	4-2	W	Webb 2 Lunn Arnett
24/08	Leighton Town	A	Lge	2-2	D	Lunn Arnett
26/08	Harlow Town	H	ILC Pr	2-2*	D	Lunn Arnett
31/08	Tonbridge Angels	A	FAC Pr	0-1	L	----------
04/09	Harlow Town	A	ILC Pr r	3-2*	W	Reed 2 Webb
07/09	Broadbridge Heath	A	FAV 1Q	9-3	W	Webb 4 Reed 3 Davidson Arnett
10/09	Aveley	A	ILC 1	1-5	L	Lammiman
14/09	Witham Town	H	Lge	0-3	L	----------
17/09	Tilbury	A	Lge	1-0	W	Arnett
21/09	Edgware Town	A	Lge	3-2	W	Lunn 2 Arnett
24/09	Collier Row	H	Lge	2-2	D	Arnett Lammiman
28/09	Hemel Hempstead	H	Lge	9-0	W	Lunn 4 Webb 2 Reed 2 Glavey
01/10	Cheshunt	A	Lge	5-2	W	Reed 2 Lunn Webb Brady
05/10	Worthing Utd	A	FAV 2Q	6-1	W	Webb 2 Reed Davidson Whiter Lunn (p)
12/10	Met Police	H	Lge	3-0	W	Lunn Reed Ahmet
19/10	Hemel Hempstead	A	Lge	3-0	W	Webb Whiter Lunn (pen)
22/10	Egham Town	H	Lge	4-0	W	Lunn 3 Whiter
26/10	Horsham	H	Lge	1-1	D	Lunn
29/10	Godalming & Glfd	A	SSC 1	4-1	W	Arnett 2 Reed Lammiman
02/11	Burgess Hill	A	FAV 1	0-1	L	----------
05/11	Hungerford Town	H	Lge	2-0	W	Whiter Harris
09/11	Barking	H	Lge	0-1	L	----------
12/11	Bedford Town	A	Lge	0-3	L	----------
16/11	Wivenhoe Town	A	Lge	1-1	D	Reed

Date	Opponents	H/A	Comp	Res	w/d/l	Scorers
30/11	Chalfont St Peter	A	Lge	3-0	W	Lunn 3 (1 pen)
07/12	Wembley	H	Lge	1-1	D	Own Goal
09/12	Sutton Utd	A	SSC 2	0-4	L	----------
17/12	Northwood	H	AMT 1	5-3	W	Reed 3 Lunn Arnett
21/12	Windsor & Eton	H	Lge	4-2	W	Lunn 2 (1 pen) Webb Arnett
18/01	Egham Town	A	Lge	4-1	W	Arnett 2 Lunn 2 (1 pen)
25/01	Leighton Town	H	Lge	2-0	W	Lunn 2 (1 pen)
28/01	Croydon Ath	H	SCC 1	1-2	L	Arnett
01/02	Witham Town	A	Lge	4-1	W	Webb 2 Lunn Arnett
04/02	Banstead Ath	H	AMT 2	3-1*	W	Lunn Harris Edwards
08/02	Tilbury	H	Lge	5-2	W	Lunn 3 (1 pen) Reed Lawson
15/02	Ware	A	Lge	2-3	L	Webb 2
27/02	Wembley	H	AMT 3	1-0	W	Edwards
01/03	Met Police	A	Lge	4-2	W	Lunn Arnett Edwards Own Goal
08/03	Cheshunt	H	Lge	3-1	W	Lunn Arnett Reed
11/03	Bracknell Town	H	Lge	4-1	W	Reed 2 Lawson Edwards
15/03	Hungerford Town	A	Lge	4-0	W	Lunn 2 Webb Edwards
18/03	Barking	A	Lge	1-2	L	Lunn (pen)
20/03	Hungerford Town	H	AMT 4	6-2	W	Webb 3 Arnett Reed Ahmet
22/03	Bedford Town	H	Lge	0-2	L	----------
25/03	Edgware Town	H	Lge	5-1	W	Arnett 2 Reed 2 Lunn (pen)
29/03	Horsham	A	Lge	2-1	W	Lunn Davidson
31/03	Dorking	H	Lge	3-0	W	Lunn 2 Brady
03/04	Banstead Ath	H	Lge	3-1	W	Reed Webb Edwards
05/04	Windsor & Eton	A	Lge	4-1	W	Lunn 2 Arnett 2
10/04	Dorking	A	Lge	3-0	W	Webb 2 Lunn
12/04	Wivenhoe Town	H	Lge	1-0	W	Webb
15/04	Collier Row	A	Lge	1-2	L	Webb
17/04	Wealdstone	H	AMT s/f	0-0	D	----------
19/04	Banstead Ath	A	Lge	2-1	W	Webb Ahmet
22/04	Wealdstone	A	AMT s/fr	1-3	L	Edwards
26/04	Chalfont St Peter	H	Lge	7-0	W	Webb 4 (1p) Arnett Lawson Harris (p)
03/05	Wembley	A	Lge	2-0	W	Webb Edwards

Season's record: Played - 63 Won - 41 Drawn - 7 Lost - 15 Goals For -168 Goals Against - 87

KEY	Competition	KEY	Competition
AC	FA Amateur Cup	Lge	League
AMT	Associate Members Trophy	LSC	London Senior Cup
CC	Surrey Senior League Charity Cup	PMFL	Premier Midweek Floodlit League
CMS	Corinthian League Memorial Shield	r	Replay
FAC	FA Challenge Cup	s/f	Semi-final
FAT	FA Trophy	SCC	Southern Combination Cup
FAV	FA Vase	SLC	Surrey Senior League Cup
Fr	Friendly	SSC	Surrey Senior Cup
F	Final	*	After extra-time
ILC	Isthmian League Cup	#	Played by Banstead or Windsor & Eton

HONOURS BOARD - 1946 - 2006

First Team

Advertiser Challenge Trophy: *Winners - 2001/02, 2002/03, 2003/04 and 2005/06*
Athenian League Division One: *Champions - 1963/64*
Corinthian League: *Champions - 1962/63*
Ditton five-a-side Tournament: *Winners - 1994/95*
East Surrey Charities Cup: *Winners - 1958/59, 1963/64 and 1968/69 (joint) Finalists - 1969/70*
Epsom Challenge Cup: *Winners - 1950/51*
FA Amateur Cup: *Semi-finalists - 1970/71 and 1973/74 Quarter-finalists - 1965/66 and 1966/67*
FA Challenge Cup: *Fourth Round Proper - 1974/75 Second Round Proper - 1975/76, 1976/77 and 1978/79 First Round Proper - 1977/78 and 1980/81*
FA Challenge Trophy: *Finalists - 1977/78*
Isthmian League Cup: *Finalists - 1977/78*
Isthmian League Division Two: *Runners-Up - 1996/97*
Jack Davis Cup: *Winners - 1991/92*
John Grun International Tournament (Luxembourg): *Winners - 1965/66*
Leatherhead Hospital Shield: *Winners - 1946/47 Finalists - 1947/48*
Leatherhead six-a-side Tournament: *Winners - 1950/51 and 1980/81*
London Senior Cup: *Finalists - 1974/75 and 1977/78*
Maureen Wooldridge Trophy: *Winners - 2001/02, 2002/03 and 2003/04 (joint)*
Michael's Plaice Cup: *Winners - 1984/85 (joint)*
Premier Midweek Floodlit League: *Overall League Runners-Up - 1969/70 Section Winners - 1969/70 and 1970/71*
Sir Cyril Black Visitors Trophy (Jersey): *Winners - 1972/73*
Southern Combination Cup: *Winners - 1989/90*
Surrey Invitation Cup: *Finalists - 1964/65*
Surrey Senior Cup: *Winners - 1968/69* Finalists - 1964/65, 1966/67, 1974/75 and 1978/79*
Surrey Senior League: *Champions - 1946/7, 1947/48, 1948/49 and 1949/50*
Surrey Senior League Charity Cup: *Winners - 1946/47 and 1949/50*
Surrey Senior League Cup: *Winners - 1949/50*
Surrey Senior Shield: *Winners - 1968/69* Finalists - 1967/68*
Sutton Hospital Cup: *Finalists - 1947/48*
Sutton United six-a-side Tournament: *Winners - 1965/66*
Victory Cup (Guernsey): *Winners - 1972/73*
Wells Challenge Cup: *Winners - 1952/53, 1957/58 and 1964/65*

Isthmian League Manager of the Month Awards: *Billy Miller (1978), Keith Mills (1982), Micky Leach (1984), Micky Byrne (1991), Chic Botley (2001), Alex Inglethorpe (2003) and Dave Harlow / Barry Barnes (2005)*
League Clubs Defeated in the F A Challenge Cup: *Brighton and Hove Albion, Cambridge United, Colchester United and Northampton Town*

Players Progressing into the Football League: *Brian Caterer (Brentford), Barry Friend (Fulham), Lee Harwood (Port Vale), John Humphrey (Millwall and Exeter City), Chris Kelly (Millwall), Jamie Mackie (Wimbledon), Tony Mitchell (Exeter City), Willie Smith (Wimbledon) and Bob Taylor (Gillingham and Millwall)*

Amateur International Honours:
Great Britain: *Derek Gamblin (2 caps). Nobby Skinner featured in the squad for the Olympic Games qualifying tournament in 1971 but did not make an appearance in the team.*

England: *Barry Friend (6 caps), Derek Gamblin (4 caps), Chris Kelly (1 cap) and Peter Smith (1 cap). Nobby Skinner and Dave Reid were selected for squads but did not make an appearance.*
Wales: *Barry Davies (3 caps)*

Representative Honours:
Athenian League: *Alan Brazier, Kevin Brittin, Colin Brumpton, Brian Caterer, Tony Chappell, Jim Cooley, Barry Davies, Chris Harlow, Dave Juneman, Ian Meekin, Keith Mills, Brian Pell, John Phipps, Jack O'Malley, John O'Shea, Dave Reid, Nobby Skinner, Jimmy Strong, Bob Taylor, Barry Webb and Jock Wood*
Corinthian League: *John Phipps*
Delphian League: *Peter Rogers and Ken Tester*
Isthmian League: *Pete Caswell, John Cooper, John Doyle, Chris Kelly, Billy Miller (Manager), Dave Reid, Dave Sargent and John Swannell*
Surrey Senior League: *Bryn Evans, Ruben Leverington, Tommy Nunn, Tommy Rochester, Charlie Stenning, Fred Stenning, Ernie Trout and Cecil Weller*
British Army: *Alan Goucher*
England Semi Professional XI: *Chris Kelly and John Swannell*
Football Association Amateur X1: *Kenny Harris, Dave Reid and Brian Pell*
Football Association X1: *Bobby Adam, Carey Anderson, Alan Brazier, Pete Caswell, John Cooper, Barry Davies, Steve Dixon, Barry Friend, Derek Gamblin, Ada Hill, Chris Kelly, Dave Reid, Nobby Skinner, Marc Smelt, Peter Smith and Derek Wells*
Middlesex Wanderers: *John Cooper, John Doyle, Chris Kelly, Dennis Malley, Dave Reid, Billy Salkeld, Peter Smith, John Swannell and Derek Wells*
Rothmans England X1: *John Cooper*
Rothmans National X1: *Chris Kelly*
Surrey FA: *John Bailey, Kevin Brittin, Ray Eaton, Micky Goodall, Chris Kelly, Johnny Lewis, Peter Keary, Billy Miller (Manager), Brian Pell, Dave Reid, Mick Simmonds, Barry Webb and Jock Wood*

Reserves

Athenian League Premier Division (Reserve Section): *Champions - 1969/70*
Cobham Hospital Cup: *Winners - 1947/48*
Corinthian League (Reserve Section) Neale Trophy: *Finalists - 1963/64*
Delphian League (Reserve Section) Challenge Cup: *Winners - 1956/57 and 1957/58*
Suburban League: *Champions - 1971/72*
Suburban League Challenge Cup: *Winners - 1971/72 and 1997/98 Finalists - 1972/73 and 1987/88*
Suburban League South: *Runners-Up - 1997/98*
Surrey Intermediate Charity Cup: *Winners - 1951/52 (joint) and 1961/62 Finalists - 1956/57 and 1959/60*
Surrey Intermediate Cup: *Winners - 1968/69**
Surrey Senior League (Reserve Section): *Champions - 1947/48 and 1948/49*
Surrey Senior League (Reserve Section) League Cup: *Finalists - 1948/49*

* A special commemorative Plaque was presented to the club by the Surrey County Football Association to acknowledge the club's feat of winning all the County Senior and Intermediate Challenge Cups in one season.

Leatherhead clear the board !

▲The Tanners team that completed the treble in1949/50 pictured after adding the
Surrey Senior League Cup to the Surrey Senior League title, shortly to be
followed by victory in the Surrey Senior League Charity Cup final.
Standing: Mr. Lush (Trainer), J. Townsend, J. Bolton, Eric Bristow, Fred Stenning,
Bob Bishop, Ernie Hawksworth and Bill Whittaker (Manager) *Seated:* Ernie
Trout, Charlie Stenning, Ernie Francis, Tommy Wheeler and Tommy Temlett

▲The first team, reserves and committee celebrate the club's unique achievement of winning the
Surrey Senior Cup, Surrey Senior Shield and Surrey Intermediate Cup in the same season.

▲John Grun International Tournament winners 1966
Standing: Billy Miller (Manager), Alan Brazier, Dave Wall, Bobby Adam, Jack O'Malley, Ray Francis, Bill Hickey and Dave Farley *Kneeling:* Barry Webb, Keith Mills, Kevin Brittin, Brian Pell, Micky Goodall and Brian Cook (guest)

▲The Tanners squad take a break from training on the Tuesday night before they took on First Division Leicester City in the F A Cup Fourth round at Filbert Street.

▲In the F A Cup Tanners remain unbeaten against Football League opposition at the Grove. The list of opponents - Cambridge United, Colchester United (twice), Northampton Town and Swansea City.

▲Neil Goodman - most goals (30) in an Athenian League season, achieved in 1963/64.

▲Kilby Edward soars high to score the first goal in a 3-0 Amateur Cup win over Ulysses in October 1959.▼Jack O'Malley, who did not concede a goal in the Corinthian League between 17th November 1962 and 13th April 1963, a period of nearly five months.

▲Peter Smith - 20 clean sheets in the Isthmian League in 1972/73.▼Nobby Skinner (challenging keeper) and Keith Mills.

▲Dave Reid - club record holder with 523 appearances, spanning nine years.

▼The joy of an Amateur Cup goal is evident as Barry Webb, Barrie Davies and Ronnie Fruen celebrate another Tanners success.

▲Barry Webb - most consecutive appearances (170), and most successful penalties (44).

▲Pete Lavers - most goals in the FA Cup (14).
▼John Cooper - 517 appearances.

▼John Swannell - a club record of over 600 minutes without conceding a goal in 1975.
Willie Smith◢ - captain of the great 1974 team.

▲John Doyle - scorer of four FA Cup
goals against Football League opposition.

▶Dave Stevens
- 7 goals in the
2005/06 FA
Cup campaign.

▲The inimitable Chris Kelly, 350 appearances for
the Tanners in the Isthmian League, and ▼Kevin
Brittin scorer of 94 goals in 187 games.

▲Fred Stenning - the holder of almost all
of Tanners main goal-scoring records.

CLUB RECORDS - 1946 - 2006

Biggest Victories:	
League: Home	**13 - 1** v Leyland Motors, Surrey Senior League (1946/47)
League: Away	**9 - 0** v Leyland Motors, Surrey Senior League (1946/47)
Cup: Home	**8 - 0** v Addlestone and Surbiton Town, FA Amateur Cup (both 1959/60) and Letchworth Garden City, F A Cup (1994/95)
Cup: Away	**9 - 0** v Middlewich Athletic, FA Amateur Cup (1973/74)
Heaviest Defeats:	
League: Home	**0 - 8** v Thame Utd, Isthmian League Division Two (1993/94), Tooting and Mitcham Utd, Isthmian League Premier Division (1982/83)
League: Away	**1 - 11** v Sutton Utd, Isthmian League Premier Division (1982/83)
Cup: Home	**0 - 6** v Sutton Utd, Surrey Senior Cup (1992/93)
Cup: Away	**1 - 8** v Kingstonian, Wells Challenge Cup (1958/59)
Highest Aggregate:	**14 - 13 -1** v Leyland Motors, Surrey Senior League (1946/47)
Season's Records - League:	
Without defeat	**18** - Surrey Senior League (1948/49 and 1949/50)
Without victory	**19** - Isthmian League Premier Division (1982/83)
Successive wins	**12** - Corinthian League (1962/63)
Successive defeats	**8** - Isthmian League Premier Division (1982/83)
Most draws	**14** - Isthmian League Premier Division (1980/81)
Most clean sheets	**20** - Isthmian League (1972/73) 42 games
Fewest goals scored	**34** - Isthmian League Division One (1989/90) - 42 games
Most goals scored	**127** - Surrey Senior League (1946/47) 24 games **116 -** Isthmian League Division Two (1996/97) - 42 games
Fewest goals conceded	**28** - Surrey Senior League (1946/47) 24 games **32** - Isthmian League (1972/73) 42 games
Most goals conceded	**121** - Isthmian League Premier Division (1982/83) - 42 games **93** - Corinthian League (1960/61) 30 games
Most Wins	**27** - Isthmian League Division Two (1996/97) - 42 games **22** - Corinthian League (1962/63) - 30 games
Most Defeats	**33** - Isthmian League Premier Division (1982/83) - 42 games
All Games:	
Without defeat	**15** - 19/10/1974 to 21/12/1974
Without victory	**21** - 07/10/1989 to 10/02/1990
Successive wins	**11** - 15/01/1948 to 26/03/1948
Successive defeats	**9** - 26/09/1953 to 21/11/1953 and 02/01/1999 to 17/02/1999
Successive clean sheets	**6** - **John Swannell** 22/03/1975 to 05/04/1975
Points in a Season:	
Most: 2 pts for a win	**47** - Surrey Senior League (1948/49) - 26 games
Most: 3 pts for a win	**95** - Isthmian League Division Two (1996/97) - 42 games
Least: 2 pts for a win	**11** - Delphian League (1953/54) - 28 games
Least: 3 pts for a win	**17** - Isthmian League Premier Division (1982/83) - 42 games
Record Attendances:	
Highest: League	**1,814** v AFC Wimbledon, Isthmian League Division One (05/02/2005)
FA Cup	**5,500** v Wimbledon (14/12/1976)
FA Amateur Cup	**4,100** v Hendon (25/02/1967)
FA Trophy	**2,060** v Yeovil Town (24/02/1979)
Surrey Senior Cup	**1,913** v Sutton United (27/04/1963)

FA Vase	**95** v Burnham (05/10/1991)
Lowest: League	**48** v Hemel Hempstead, Cheshunt, Isthmian League Div Two (1994/95)
Individual Goal -scoring records:	
Career: All games	**185 - Fred Stenning** (1947 - 52)
League	**127 - Fred Stenning** (1947 - 52)
All Cups	**58 - Fred Stenning** (1947 - 52)
Hat-Tricks	**25 - Fred Stenning** (1947 -52)
In a Season: League	**45 - Fred Stenning**, Surrey Senior League (1948/49)
All games	**71 - Fred Stenning**, Surrey Senior League (1949/50)
In one game: League	**6 - Fred Stenning** v McLarens Sports, Surrey Senior League (1949/50) and **Gordon Cairns** v Berkhamsted Town, Delphian League (1957/58)
In one game: Cup	**6 - Cecil Weller** v Farnham, Surrey Senior League Charity Cup (1947/48)
Goals in consecutive League games	**16 - Fred Stenning** - Surrey Senior League (1948/49)
Appearances:	
Career	**523 - Dave Reid** (1969 - 79)
League games	**350 - Chris Kelly** (1972 - 82)
Cup matches	**197 - Alan Brazier** (1965 - 76)
Consecutive	**170 - Barry Webb** (30/10/1971 to 02/11/1974)
In a Season	**68 - Dave Reid** (1974/75)
As Manager	**890 - Billy Miller** (1965 - 80)
Competition Records:	
Most Goals in total:	
Isthmian League	**100 - Chris Kelly** (1972 - 82)
FA Amateur Cup	**24 - Fred Stenning** (1947 - 52)
FA Cup	**14 - Pete Lavers** (1970 - 76)
FA Trophy	**10 - Chris Kelly** (1974 - 82)
FA Vase	**6 - Nigel Webb** (1995 - 97)
Surrey Senior Cup	**13 - Ray Arnett** (1991 - 98)
In a Season:	
Isthmian League	**41 - Steve Lunn** (1996/97)
Athenian League	**30 - Neil Goodman** (1963/64)
Corinthian League	**28 - Kilby Edwards** (1960/61)
Delphian League	**27 - Gordon Cairns** (1957/58)
Biggest Victories:	
Isthmian League	**9 - 0** v Hemel Hempstead (1996/97)
FA Amateur Cup	**9 - 0** v Middlewich Athletic (26/01/1974)
FA Cup	**8 - 0** v Letchworth Garden City (27/08/1994)
FA Trophy	**5 - 1** v Hastings United (11/01/1975) and Dartford (09/02/1978)
FA Vase	**9 - 3** v Broadbridge Heath (07/09/1996)
Surrey Senior Cup	**8 - 0** v Croydon Amateurs (03/09/1955)
Heaviest Defeats:	
Isthmian League	**1 - 11** v Sutton United (16/11/1982)
FA Amateur Cup	**1 - 5** v Redhill (24/11/1956) and Carshalton Athletic (25/10/1958)
FA Cup	**0 - 6** v Sutton United (19/09/1959)
FA Trophy	**0 - 6** v Berkhamsted Town (05/10/2002)
FA Vase	**2 - 7** v Ash United (25/10/2001)
Surrey Senior Cup	**0 - 7** v Dulwich Hamlet (13/12/1958)

Leatherhead's complete playing record in League and Cup Competitions 1946 - 2006

LEAGUE	Seasons	Played	Won	Lost	Drawn	For	Against	% Wins	Best
Surrey Senior	4	102	79	10	13	396	134	77	1st
Metropolitan	1	31	13	3	15	64	67	42	9th
Delphian	7	194	74	32	88	384	446	38	4th
Corinthian	5	146	66	23	57	333	298	45	1st
Athenian Division 1	1	26	18	3	5	86	45	69	1st
Athenian Premier	8	240	120	48	72	400	295	50	3rd
Isthmian Premier	11	462	184	105	173	662	594	40	3rd
Isthmian Division 1	13	546	195	132	219	776	793	36	4th
Isthmian Div 1 South	2	92	35	22	35	154	154	38	13th
Isthmian Division 2	7	292	115	62	115	510	452	39	2nd
Isthmian Div 2 South	1	42	17	9	16	182	55	40	10th
ALL LEAGUES	**60**	**2,173**	**916**	**449**	**808**	**3,847**	**3,333**	**42**	

CUP	Played	Won	Drawn	Lost	For	Against	% Wins	Best
Athenian League	16	7	2	7	32	31	44	Winners
Corinthian League	11	5	1	5	17	23	45	Semi-final
East Surrey Charities	9	5	1	3	20	13	56	Winners
FA Amateur	107	59	21	27	244	146	55	Semi-final
FA Challenge	132	58	23	51	236	193	44	4th Round
FA Trophy	60	23	12	25	85	87	38	Runners-Up
FA Vase	14	6	0	8	29	31	43	2nd Round
Isthmian League	90	42	9	39	149	150	47	Runners-Up
London Senior	35	17	7	11	51	34	49	Runners-Up
Premier Midweek	125	58	24	43	222	183	47	Runners-Up
Southern Combination	22	11	1	10	42	38	50	Winners
Surrey Senior League	7	6	0	1	32	9	86	Winners
Surrey Senior Charity	11	10	0	1	48	16	91	Winners
Surrey Senior Shield	14	6	0	8	22	24	43	Winners
Surrey Senior	146	67	20	59	256	245	46	Winners
Others	62	29	10	23	114	116	47	Winners
ALL CUPS	**861**	**409**	**131**	**321**	**1,599**	**1,339**	**48**	

COMPETITION	Played	Won	Drawn	Lost	For	Against	% wins
Leagues	2,173	916	449	808	3,847	3,333	42
Cups	861	409	131	321	1,599	1,339	48
All Matches	**3034**	**1,325**	**580**	**1,129**	**5,446**	**4,672**	**44**

Tanners all time leading goal-scorers

Pos	Player	Seasons	Goals	Appearances	15 + goals in a season	Highest Total
1	Fred Stenning	1947 - 52	185	139	3	71
2	Chris Kelly	1972 - 82	156	492	5	26
3	Pete Lavers	1970 - 76	144	296	5	41
4	Ernie Trout	1946 - 54	127	255	5	24
5	Barry Webb	1965 - 75	119	438	5	21
6	Ray Arnett	1991 - 98	115	259	4	24
7	Nobby Skinner	1967 - 74	112	346	3	28
8	Brian Pell	1961 - 68	111	281	4	25
9	Neil Goodman	1961 - 65	108	133	3	46
10	Nigel Webb	1994 - 2000	103	256	4	33
11	Steve Lunn	1996 - 99	100	155	3	45
12	Kevin Brittin	1962 - 69	94	187	4	34
13	Keith Mills	1965 - 72	91	266	3	28
14	Kilby Edwards	1959 - 61	88	83	3	38
15	John Baker	1976 - 81	86	236	4	27
16=	Cecil Weller	1946 - 51	67	111	1	47
16=	Dave Reid	1970 - 79	67	523	0	12
18	Phil Ruggles	2001 & 2002 - 04	65	119	2	30
19	Paul Williams	1984 - 86	61	76	2	39
20	John Doyle	1974 - 82	59	341	1	18
21	Ronnie Fruen	1970 - 74	57	143	2	26
22	Alex Inglethorpe	2001 - 04	56	103	1	35
23	Dave Stevens	2004 - 06*	53	82	2	31
24	Brian Perkins	1983 - 87	50	124	2	19
25	Paul Reed	1996 - 99	49	109	1	24
26	Gordon Cairns	1957 - 58	48	48	1	36
27	Ian Meekin	1966 - 70	47	124	1	17
28=	Peter Shodeinde	1983 - 86	43	97	2	20
28=	Marc Charles Smith	2002 - 06*	43	162	1	19
30	John Humphrey	1987 - 91 & 1999	41	104	1	26

Leatherhead's longest serving Managers

Pos	Manager	Period in charge	Number of games	Wins	Draws	Losses	% of wins
1	Billy Miller	1965 - 80	890	429	180	281	48
2	Norman Douglas	1961 - 65	183	94	29	60	51
3	George Hollings	1954 - 59	168	70	24	74	42
4	Keith Oram	1986 - 89	160	61	39	60	38
5	Keith Wenham	1996 - 99	144	72	22	50	50
6	Alex Inglethorpe	2001 - 04	138	56	26	56	41
7	Micky Byrne	1991 - 93	119	51	21	47	43
8	Chris Luff	1958 - 61	113	44	14	55	39
9	Bill Berry	1951 - 54	109	42	18	49	39
10	Mick Leach	1983 - 85	105	57	24	34	54

Tanners all time leading appearance makers

Rank	Player	Position	Seasons	Appearances
1	Dave Reid	Centre-half	1970 - 79**	523
2	John Cooper	Right-back / Midfield	1970 - 81**	517
3	Chris Kelly	Outside-Right	1972 - 82**	492
4	Alan Brazier	Left-Back / Midfield	1965 - 76	453
5	Barry Webb	Left-Back / Midfield	1965 - 75	438
6	Pete Caswell	Goalkeeper	1979 - 88,1989 & 1994**	403
7	Barrie Davies	Midfield / Defender	1968 - 73 &1977 - 81	388
8	Nobby Skinner	Outside-Left	1967 - 74	346
9	John Doyle	Left-Wing	1974 - 82	341
10	Derek Wells	Centre-half	1971 - 77	336
11	John Swannell	Goalkeeper	1974 - 80	333
12	Micky Cook	Midfield	1977 - 83	317
13	Pete Lavers	Centre-forward	1970 - 76	296
14	Bobby Adam	Centre-half	1965 - 71	288
15	Brian Pell	Inside-Left	1961 - 68	281
16	Iain Hendry	Centre-half	2000 - 06*	280
17	Keith Mills	Centre-forward	1965 - 72	266
18	Jack O'Malley	Goalkeeper	1962 - 69	260
19	Ray Arnett	Centre-forward	1991 - 98	259
20	Nigel Webb	Right-Wing	1994 - 2000	256
21	Ernie Trout	Right-Wing	1946 - 54	255
22	Dennis Malley	Centre-half	1977 - 82	252
23	Steve Lammiman	Defender	1988 - 98**	249
24	John Baker	Centre-forward	1976 - 81	236
25	Brian Stannard	Defender	1986 - 95	235
26	Danny Lavender	Centre-half	1997 - 2000 & 2002 - 05	234
27	Micky Cuthbert	Goalkeeper	1967 - 73 & 1978 - 80	228
28	Colin Brooks	Right-back	1976 - 82	223
29	Phil Dade	Midfield	1968 - 75	220
30	Wayne Falloon	Midfield	1983 - 88 & 1990	215
31	Doug Caswell	Midfield	1949 - 59	210
32	Dave Rattue	Midfield	1984 - 89	205
33	Jamie Beer	Right back / Midfield	2000 - 06*	200
34	Paul Mckay	Midfield	2000 - 05	200
35=	Kenny Harris	Centre-half	1961 - 66	196
35=	Mark Joyner	Right-back	1986 - 94	196
37	Adam Gray	Left-back	2002 - 06*	192
38	Kevin Brittin	Centre-forward	1962 - 66 & 1968 - 69	187
39	Tony Webb	Goalkeeper	1994 - 97 & 1998 - 99	178
40	Willie Smith	Midfield	1974 -77	177
41=	Colin Woffinden	Centre-half / Midfield	1974 - 77	174
41=	Johnny Phipps	Midfield	1961 - 66	174
43=	Ray Francis	Right-back	1964 - 69	163
43=	Wes Harrison	Midfield	2002 - 06	163
45	Marc Charles-Smith	Centre-forward	2002 - 06*	162
46	Steve Lawson	Centre-half	1995 - 2000 & 2003	161
47	Dave Sargent	Right-back	1974 - 77	159

* Current Player   **Awarded Testimonials

CHAPTER SEVENTEEN - CUP RESULTS AND LEAGUE TABLES

Leatherhead's complete playing record in national competitions

FA AMATEUR CUP

Season	Round	Opponents	H/A	Result	W/D/L	Attendance
1947/48	1Q	Dorking	A	4-0	W	
	2Q	Post Office Telecomms	H	4-2*	W	
	3Q	Carshalton Athletic	H	1-0	W	2,000
	4Q	Erith & Belvedere	A	2-3*	L	
1948/49	Pr	RASC Farnborough	H	7-1	W	
	1Q	Epsom Town	H	4-1	W	
	2Q	Dorking	A	3-1	W	
	3Q	Redhill	H	2-2*	D	
	3Q(r)	Redhill	A	0-3	L	
1949/50	Pr	Chertsey Town	A	3-1	W	
	1Q	Guildford Pinks	A	2-1	W	
	2Q	Banstead Athletic	H	4-3	W	1,500
	3Q	Farnham	A	4-3	W	
	4Q	Hayes	H	1-3	L	2,500
1950/51	Pr	Hawker Athletic	H	3-0	W	
	1Q	Devas Institute	A	4-5	L	
1951/52	Pr	Cobham	H	4-3	W	
	1Q	Haywards Heath	A	4-3	W	
	2Q	Skyways	H	2-2	D	
	2Q(r)	Skyways	H	2-0	W	
	3Q	Banstead Athletic	A	0-0	D	
	3Q(r)	Banstead Athletic	H	3-2*	W	
	4Q	Sutton United	A	2-4*	L	
1952/53	Pr	Haywards Heath	A	2-0	W	
	1Q	Newhaven	A	5-1	W	
	2Q	East Grinstead	H	2-3	L	
1953/54	Pr	Eastbourne	H	1-0	W	
	1Q	Bexhill Town	A	1-2	L	
1954/55	Pr	Horsham	H	1-0	W	
	1Q	Eastbourne	H	2-2	D	
	1Q(r)	Eastbourne	A	0-2	L	3,100
1955/56	Ex Pr	Newhaven	A	0-1	L	
1956/57	Pr	Metropolitan Police	H	4-1	W	
	1Q	Croydon Amateurs	A	1-0	W	
	2Q	Bexhill Town	H	4-1	W	
	3Q	Banstead Athletic	H	2-1	W	1,100
	4Q	Redhill	H	1-5	L	1,300
1957/58	Ex Pr	Cobham	H	4-1	W	
	Pr	Chertsey Town	A	4-2	W	
	1Q	Farnham Town	H	0-1	L	1,000
1958/59	Pr	Whitehawk	H	3-0	W	
	1Q	Royal Ordnance Factory	H	3-1	W	
	2Q	Carshalton Athletic	A	1-5	L	2,000

Season	Round	Opponents	H/A	Result	W/D/L	Attendance
1959/60	Pr	Ulysses	H	1-1	D	
	Pr(r)	Ulysses	H	3-0	W	
	1Q	Surbiton Town	H	8-0	W	
	2Q	Chertsey Town	H	2-2	D	
	2Q(r)	Chertsey Town	A	2-1	W	
	3Q	Addlestone	H	8-0	W	
	4Q	Sheppey United	H	2-0	W	
	1	Redhill	A	1-1	D	3,158
	1(r)	Redhill	H	0-1	L	
1960/61	1Q	Vickers	A	3-4	L	
1961/62	Pr	Royal Ordnance Factory	H	7-0	W	
	1Q	Addlestone	A	1-1	D	
	1Q(r)	Addlestone	H	1-3	L	
1962/63	Pr	Hermes	H	3-1	W	
	1Q	Epsom & Ewell	H	3-2	W	
	2Q	Molesey	H	6-3	W	
	3Q	Malden Town	A	3-2	W	
	4Q	Carshalton Athletic	A	4-1	W	
	1	Pinehurst	H	3-0	W	500
	2	Hitchin Town	H	1-4	L	1,424
1963/64	4Q	Redhill	H	2-0	W	1,400
	1	Harwich & Parkeston	A	2-4	L	800
1964/65	4Q	BAC (Weybridge)	A	4-1	W	
	1	Eastbourne	A	1-2	L	854
1965/66	4Q	Wembley	A	5-1	W	
	1	Oxford City	A	3-2	W	1,268
	2	Maidenhead United	A	2-0	W	
	3	Hayes	H	2-2	D	1,600
	3(r)	Hayes	A	1-0	W	2,200
	QF	Wealdstone	A	1-2	L	5,000
1966/67	1	Bishop Stortford	H	1-1	D	800
	1(r)	Bishop Stortford	A	2-1	W	1,400
	2	Tow Law Town	A	1-0	W	1,536
	3	Clapton	A	3-2	W	850
	QF	Hendon	H	0-3	L	4,100
1967/68	1	Dagenham	H	1-2	L	1,500
1968/69	1	Enfield	A	0-0	D	
	1(r)	Enfield	H	1-1	D	1,266
at Dulwich	1(r)	Enfield	N	0-1	L	
1969/70	1	Sutton United	A	0-2	L	1,700
1970/71	1	Stowmarket Town	A	2-2	D	680
	1(r)	Stowmarket Town	H	2-2*	D	550
at Enfield	1(r)	Stowmarket Town	N	3-2	W	278
	2	Dulwich Hamlet	H	0-0	D	600
	2(r)	Dulwich Hamlet	A	1-0	W	500
	3	Boreham Wood	A	1-1	D	
	3(r)	Boreham Wood	H	2-1*	W	1,300
	QF	Hayes	A	1-1	D	2,611
	QF(r)	Hayes	H	1-0	W	1,514

Season	Round	Opponents	H/A	Result	W/D/L	Attendance
at Bolton	SF	Skelmersdale	N	0-2	L	7,085
1971/72	1	Dagenham	H	2-1	W	1,500
	2	Oxford City	A	3-0	W	
	3	Leytonstone	A	2-2	D	1,050
	3(r)	Leytonstone	H	3-0	W	1,304
	QF	Blyth Spartans	A	1-1	D	4,000
	QF(r)	Blyth Spartans	H	0-1	L	2,500
1972/73	1	Harwich & Parkeston	A	1-3	L	
1973/74	1	Enfield	H	4-0	W	550
	2	Middlewich Athletic	A	9-0	W	1,312
	3	Hendon	A	1-1	D	1,320
	3(r)	Hendon	H	1-1	D	1,991
at Wycombe	3(r)	Hendon	N	2-0	W	1,900
	QF	Sutton United	A	1-0	W	1,964
at Millwall	SF	Ilford	N	0-1	L	2,716

FA CUP

Season	Round	Opponents	H/A	Result	WD/L	Attendance
1947/48	1Q	Woking	A	0-2	L	
1948/49	Ex Pr	Vickers	A	4-1	W	
	Pr	Cobham	H	2-0	W	
	1Q	Sutton United	H	0-2	L	2,597
1949/50	1Q	Hounslow	H	2-6	L	
1950/51	1Q	Walton & Hersham	H	1-3	L	
1959/60	1Q	Sutton United	A	0-6	L	
1960/61	1Q	Dorking	H	1-2	L	
1961/62	1Q	Kingstonian	H	2-2	D	
	1Q(r)	Kingstonian	A	2-4*	L	
1962/63	1Q	Wimbledon	H	1-4	L	1,500
1963/64	1Q	Kingstonian	H	3-2	W	1,300
	2Q	Guildford City	A	1-5	L	3,074
1964/65	1Q	Petters Sports	A	5-0	W	
	2Q	Kingstonian	A	1-1	D	1,300
	2Q(r)	Kingstonian	H	1-0	W	2,325
	3Q	Guildford City	H	1-2	L	2,038
1965/66	1Q	Chertsey Town	H	3-3	D	
	1Q(r)	Chertsey Town	A	5-2*	W	
	2Q	Guildford City	H	2-2	D	1,400
	2Q(r)	Guildford City	A	0-3	L	3,020
1966/67	1Q	Barking	H	1-0	W	
	2Q	Maidenhead United	A	2-0	W	730
	3Q	Corinthian Casuals	H	2-1	W	
	4Q	Chesham United	H	1-2	L	1,060
1967/68	1Q	Clapton	A	1-2	L	410
1968/69	1Q	Molesey	H	5-0	W	
	2Q	Walton & Hersham	A	1-4	L	1,974
1969/70	1Q	Walton & Hersham	H	0-1	L	2,400
1970/71	1Q	Barking	H	3-1	W	

Season	Round	Opponents	H/A	Result	W/D/L	Attendance
	2Q	Tooting & Mitcham United	A	2-1	W	
	3Q	Grays Athletic	H	3-0	W	
	4Q	Wimbledon	H	1-2	L	1,350
1971/72	1Q	Erith & Belvedere	A	2-2	D	
	1Q(r)	Erith & Belvedere	H	3-0	W	
	2Q	Bexley United	A	2-3	L	850
1972/73	1Q	Worthing	H	3-0	W	
	2Q	Bognor Regis Town	A	0-2	L	
1973/74	1Q	Erith & Belvedere	A	6-1	W	
	2Q	Ilford	A	1-1	D	
	2Q(r)	Ilford	H	2-0	W	
	3Q	Leytonstone	H	0-0	D	
	3Q(r)	Leytonstone	A	0-1	L	
1974/75	1Q	Croydon Amateurs	A	2-0	W	300
	2Q	Hornchurch	H	5-0	W	
	3Q	Dagenham	H	0-0	D	
	3Q(r)	Dagenham	A	3-1	W	
	4Q	Walton & Hersham	A	7-1	W	
	1	Bishop Stortford	A	0-0	D	750
	1(r)	Bishop Stortford	H	2-0	W	1,750
	2	Colchester United	H	1-0	W	3,500
	3	Brighton & Hove Albion	A	1-0	W	20,491
	4	Leicester City	A	2-3	L	32,090
1975/76	4Q	Ilford	H	1-0	W	
	1	Cambridge United	H	2-0	W	2,450
	2	Tooting & Mitcham United	H	0-0	D	2,500
	2(r)	Tooting & Mitcham United	A	1-2*	L	2,500
1976/77	4Q	Chelmsford City	A	4-0	W	2,292
	1	Northampton Town	H	2-0	W	3,550
	2	Wimbledon	H	1-3	L	5,500
1977/78	4Q	Cheshunt	H	4-1	W	
	1	Swansea City	H	0-0	D	3,000
	1(r)	Swansea City	A	1-2	L	7,235
1978/79	1	Merthyr Tydfil	H	2-1	W	2,100
	2	Colchester United	H	1-1	D	2,550
	2(r)	Colchester United	A	0-4	L	3,920
1979/80	4Q	Croydon	H	1-1	D	
	4Q(r)	Croydon	A	0-3	L	
1980/81	4Q	Bath City	H	1-0	W	631
	1	Exeter City	A	0-5	L	4,607
1981/82	4Q	Dover Athletic	A	1-1	D	1,032
	4Q(r)	Dover Athletic	H	0-1	L	723
1982/83	4Q	Wokingham	A	0-1	L	693
1983/84	1Q	Littlehampton Town	A	2-0	W	215
	2Q	Egham Town	A	5-1	W	160
	3Q	Fisher Athletic	H	0-4	L	205
1984/85	1Q	Pagham	A	5-0	W	109
	2Q	Dover Athletic	A	4-1	W	322
	3Q	Hastings United	H	1-2	L	423

Season	Round	Opponents	H/A	Result	W/D/L	Attendance
1985/86	1Q	Redhill	H	0-2	L	241
1986/87	Pr	Eastbourne Town	H	1-1	D	200
	Pr(r)	Eastbourne Town	A	1-3	L	183
1987/88	Pr	Darenth Heathside	A	1-2	L	121
1988/89	Pr	Hounslow Town	H	1-1	D	159
	Pr(r)	Hounslow Town	A	2-1	W	180
	1Q	Stowmarket Town	H	1-0	W	154
	2Q	Barnet	A	3-4	L	857
1989/90	1Q	Folkestone	A	1-2	L	319
1990/91	Pr	Ashford Town	A	1-3	L	345
1991/92	Pr	Corinthian Casuals	H	3-1	W	130
	1Q	Dorking	H	1-2	L	370
1992/93	Pr	Lewes	A	0-1	L	132
1993/94	1Q	Langney Sports	A	8-3	W	168
	2Q	Metropolitan Police	H	3-5	L	140
1994/95	Pr	Letchworth Garden City	H	8-0	W	79
	1Q	Hayes	H	1-1	D	260
	1Q(r)	Hayes	A	0-4	L	252
1995/96	Pr	Milton Keynes Borough	A	4-0	W	50
	1Q	Harrow Borough	A	1-2	L	198
1996/97	Pr	Tonbridge Angels	A	0-1	L	443
1997/98	Pr	Wealdstone	H	2-0	W	337
	1Q	Langney Sports	A	1-2	L	270
1998/99	1Q	Whitehawk	H	5-0	W	150
	2Q	Sheppey United	A	0-0	D	127
	2Q(r)	Sheppey United	H	3-1*	W	174
	3Q	Windsor & Eton	H	2-0	W	283
	4Q	Rushden & Diamonds	H	1-1	D	1,143
	4Q(r)	Rushden & Diamonds	A	0-4	L	1,855
1999/2000	Pr	Cowes Sports	H	0-1	L	168
2000/01	Pr	Metropolitan Police	A	1-2	L	155
2001/02	Pr	Whitehawk	A	2-2	D	85
	Pr(r)	Whitehawk	H	2-0	W	118
	1Q	Oxford City	A	0-2	L	185
2002/03	Pr	Banstead Athletic	A	4-1	W	133
	1Q	Abingdon United	A	3-2	W	178
	2Q	Bromley	H	1-1	D	325
	2Q(r)	Bromley	A	4-2	W	515
	3Q	Ford United	H	1-2	L	333
2003/04	Pr	Moneyfield Sports	H	3-1	W	113
	1Q	Deal Town	A	2-1	W	170
	2Q	Leyton	A	0-1	L	140
2004/05	Pr	Walton & Hersham	A	2-1	W	156
	1Q	Cray Wanderers	H	1-0	W	121
	2Q	Sandhurst Town	A	2-0	W	210
	3Q	Maidstone United	H	2-1	W	528
	4Q	Bath City	A	0-1	L	938
2005/06	Pr	Ash United	A	1-1	D	111
	Pr(r)	Ash United	H	3-2	W	235

Season	Round	Opponents	H/A	Result	W/D/L	Attendance
2005/06	1Q	Chatham Town	A	4-3	W	251
	2Q	Hampton & Richmond Boro	A	1-1	D	357
	2Q(r)	Hampton & Richmond Boro	H	2-1	W	273
	3Q	Farnborough Town	H	0-2	L	609

FA TROPHY

Season	Round	Opponents	H/A	Result	W/D/L	Attendance
1974/75	3Q	Gravesend & Northfleet	H	4-1	W	
	1	Hastings United	H	5-1	W	
	2	Weymouth	A	0-2	L	1,873
1975/76	3Q	Wealdstone	A	2-2	D	1,521
	3Q(r)	Wealdstone	H	1-0	W	
	1	Staines Town	H	2-2	D	
	1(r)	Staines Town	A	1-1*	D	1,300
at Walton	1(r)	Staines Town	N	1-0*	W	
	2	Bromsgrove Rovers	A	0-1	L	
1976/77	1	Dagenham	H	1-1	D	
	1(r)	Dagenham	A	0-3	L	
1977/78	1	Banbury United	A	2-1	W	1,077
	2	Dartford	H	5-1	W	
	3	Wigan Athletic	H	2-0	W	
	QF	Bedford	A	0-0	D	1,201
	QF(r)	Bedford	H	5-2	W	1,091
	SF1	Spennymoor United	H	2-0	W	1,697
	SF2	Spennymoor United	A	1-2	L	4,500
at Wembley	F	Altrincham	N	1-3	L	20,000
1978/79	1	Hillingdon Borough	H	2-1	W	
	2	Lancaster City	A	0-0	D	1,041
	2(r)	Lancaster City	H	4-1	W	
	3	Yeovil Town	H	0-1	L	2,060
1979/80	1	Wokingham Town	A	1-0	W	410
	2	Weymouth	H	0-2	L	1,044
1980/81	1	Weymouth	H	1-3	L	588
1981/82	3Q	Addlestone & Weybridge	H	2-2	D	293
	3Q(r)	Addlestone & Weybridge	A	1-0	W	206
	1	Dartford	A	1-2	L	566
1982/83	3Q	Waterlooville	H	2-5	L	163
1983/84	1Q	Staines Town	A	0-0	D	145
	1Q(r)	Staines Town	H	4-1*	W	174
	2Q	Andover	H	2-0	W	162
	3Q	Windsor & Eton	H	2-3	L	284
1984/85	1Q	Basingstoke Town	A	1-3	L	310
1985/86	1Q	Hastings United	H	w/o	W	-
	2Q	Farnborough Town	A	1-4	L	462
1986/87	1Q	Aveley	A	0-0	D	49
	1Q(r)	Aveley	H	4-2	W	123
	2Q	Dover Athletic	A	2-1	W	308
	3Q	Shepshed Charterhouse	H	1-0	W	257

Season	Round	Opponents	H/A	Result	W/D/L	Attendance
	1	Wycombe Wanderers	A	0-0	D	834
	1(r)	Wycombe Wanderers	H	1-0	W	385
	2	Aylesbury United	H	0-1	L	658
1987/88	1Q	Lewes	H	4-2	W	129
	2Q	Ashford Town	H	0-1	L	182
1988/89	1Q	Kingsbury Town	H	2-1	W	138
	2Q	Thanet United	A	3-0	W	260
	3Q	Carshalton Athletic	A	1-2	L	228
1989/90	1Q	Marlow	H	1-1	D	128
	1Q(r)	Marlow	A	0-2	L	261
1997/98	1Q	Basingstoke Town	A	0-2	L	402
1998/99	1	Crawley Town	H	1-2	L	335
1999/2000	1	Kings Lynn	H	2-0	W	177
	2	Bedford Town	H	0-0	D	258
	2(r)	Bedford Town	A	0-2	L	369
2000/01	1	Evesham United	H	1-2	L	145
2002/03	1	Berkhamsted Town	A	0-6	L	137
2003/04	Pr	Wealdstone	H	1-3	L	232
2004/05	Pr	Dartford	A	2-5	L	201
2005/06	1	East Thurrock Utd	H	0-1	L	141

FA VASE

Season	Round	Opponents	H/A	Result	W/D/L	Attendance
1990/91	Pr	Pagham	A	1-2	L	116
1991/92	Pr	Burnham	H	0-1	L	95
1992/93	Pr	Alma Swanley	H	2-0	W	79
	1	Ringmer	H	1-0	W	76
	2	Forest Green Rovers	A	1-2	L	123
1993/94	Pr	Whitehawk	A	0-1	L	160
1994/95	Pr	Redhill	A	4-3*	W	150
	1	Thame United	A	2-1*	W	83
	2	Stamco	A	0-4	L	306
1995/96	2Q	Slade Green	A	1-5	L	68
1996/97	1Q	Broadbridge Heath	A	9-3	W	121
	2Q	Worthing United	A	6-1	W	126
	1	Burgess Hill	A	0-1	L	315
2001/02	Pr	Ash United	A	2-7	L	119

Main Cup Final Appearances 1946 - 2006

Season	Opponents	Cup	Result	W/D/L	Scorers	Att
1946/47	Dorking	SLCC	2-1	W	Own Goals 2	3,000
1949/50	Banstead	SLC	5-2	W	Trout 2 Stenning Wheeler Hawksworth	
1949/50	Hawkers Athletic	SLCC	7-0	W	Stenning 5 Hawksworth Trout	
1964/65	Guildford City	SIC	1-2	L	Brittin	1,200
1964/65	Sutton United	SSC	2-3	L	Pritchard 2	2,000
1966/67	Kingstonian	SSC	1-2	L	Meekin	1,600
1967/68	Woking	SSS	2-3	L	Webb Mills	
1968/69	Redhill	SSS	1-0	W	Webb (pen)	
1968/69	Redhill	SSC	3-1	W	Skinner Webb Mills	1,151
1974/75	Dulwich Hamlet	SSC	0-2	L	----------	
1974/75	Wimbledon	LSC	0-2	L	----------	3,281
1977/78	Altrincham	FAT	1-3	L	Cook	20,000
1977/78	Walthamstow Ave	LSC	0-1	L	----------	
1977/78	Dagenham	ILC	0-1	L	----------	
1978/79	Camberley Town	SSC	1-4*	L	Doyle	1,400
1989/90	Malden Vale	SCC	2-0	W	Davis Lammiman	

KEY		KEY	
*	After extra-time	(r)	Replay
Ex Pr	Extra Preliminary Round	SCC	Southern Combination Cup
FAT	FA Trophy	SF	Semi-final
F	Final	SIC	Surrey Invitation Cup
ILC	Isthmian League Cup	SLC	Surrey Senior League Cup
LSC	London Senior Cup	SLCC	Surrey Senior League Charity Cup
Pr	Preliminary Round	SSC	Surrey Senior Cup
Q	Qualifying round	SSS	Surrey Senior Shield
QF	Quarter-Final	w/o	Walkover

Supporters' Player of the Year 1978 - 2006

Season	Player	Position	Season	Player	Position
1978/79	Dave Reid	Centre-half	1992/93	Ray Arnett	Centre-forward
1979/80	John Baker	Centre-forward	1993/94	Mark Joyner	Right-back
1980/81	Peter Caswell	Goalkeeper	1994/95	Robin Welch	Midfield
1981/82	Micky Preston	Centre-half	1995/96	Ray Arnett	Centre-forward
1982/83	Phil Holder	Midfield	1996/97	Steve Lunn	Centre-forward
1983/84	Phil Smith / Peter Shodeinde (Joint)	Centre-half / Centre-forward	1997/98	Scott Tarr	Goalkeeper
1984/85	Paul Williams	Centre-forward	1998/99	Nigel Webb	Forward
1985/86	Peter Caswell	Goalkeeper	1999/00	Paul Hart	Goalkeeper
1986/87	Martin Gillings	Midfield	2000/01	Stewart Vaughan	Goalkeeper
1987/88	Marc Smelt	Centre-forward	2001/02	Paul McKay	Midfield
1988/89	Gary Richards	Midfield	2002/03	Justin Gray	Goalkeeper
1989/90	Kevin Wedderburn	Right-back	2003/04	Michael Webb	Defence/Midfield
1990/91	Paul Wooler	Centre-half	2004/05	Tommy Dunn	Goalkeeper
1991/92	Roland Pierre	Centre-half	2005/06	Marc Charles-Smith	Forward

LEAGUE TABLES 1946 - 2006

Surrey Senior League 1946/47

	Pl	W	D	L	F	A	Pts
Leatherhead	**24**	**17**	**3**	**4**	**127**	**28**	**37**
Camberley	24	16	3	5	72	47	35
Vickers Armstrong	24	14	2	8	77	53	30
Dorking	24	14	2	8	60	56	30
Chertsey Town	24	12	2	10	76	65	26
Walton & Hershm	23	11	3	9	52	64	25
Worcester Park	24	10	4	10	67	51	24
Brookwood Hosp	24	10	4	10	67	70	24
Guildford (Pinks)	24	6	6	12	51	74	18
Cobham	24	8	1	15	46	83	17
Devas Institute	24	6	4	14	48	65	16
Leyland Motors	23	6	4	13	40	71	16
Lagonda Sports	24	5	2	17	39	86	12

* Walton & Hersham v Leyland Motors not played

Surrey Senior League 1947/48

	Pl	W	D	L	F	A	Pts
Leatherhead	**26**	**20**	**1**	**5**	**88**	**41**	**41**
Carshalton Ath	26	14	5	7	60	42	33
Chertsey Town	26	12	7	7	73	57	31
McLaren Sports	26	10	10	6	58	51	30
Devas Institute	26	11	7	8	55	53	29
Walton & Hersham	26	12	4	10	58	54	28
Worcester Park	26	12	3	11	64	55	27
Farnham Town	26	11	4	11	77	72	26
Met Police	26	9	6	11	58	70	24
Cobham	26	8	5	13	41	61	21
Dorking	26	8	4	14	49	62	20
Camberley	26	8	3	15	63	71	19
Brookwood Hosp	26	6	6	14	55	80	18
Guildford (Pinks)	26	7	3	16	44	74	17

Surrey Senior League 1948/49

	Pl	W	D	L	F	A	Pts
Leatherhead	**26**	**23**	**1**	**2**	**95**	**29**	**47**
Carshalton Ath	26	17	3	6	78	45	37
Dorking	26	15	3	8	82	51	33
Cobham	26	12	6	8	57	56	30
Byfleet	26	11	7	8	52	41	29
Devas Institute	26	12	4	10	50	46	28
Camberley	26	11	4	11	47	61	26
Guildford (Pinks)	26	11	2	13	76	63	24
Farnham Town	26	10	3	13	45	53	23
Chertsey Town	26	8	5	13	56	71	21
Met Police	26	7	3	16	56	77	17
Worcester Park	26	7	3	16	45	82	17
Brookwood Hosp	26	7	2	17	46	72	16
McLaren Sports	26	7	2	17	41	79	16

Surrey Senior League 1949/50

	Pl	W	D	L	F	A	Pts
Leatherhead	**26**	**19**	**5**	**2**	**85**	**35**	**43**
Banstead Athletic	26	18	5	3	95	35	41
Farnham Town	26	16	5	5	74	53	37
Dorking	26	17	2	7	73	39	36
Surbiton Town	26	12	2	12	70	53	26
Cobham	26	10	6	10	69	58	26
Worcester Park	26	10	3	13	60	70	23
Hawker Athletic	26	9	4	13	51	53	22
McLaren Sports	26	10	2	14	48	60	22
Devas Institute	26	9	2	15	57	75	20
Chertsey Town	26	9	1	16	60	88	19
Byfleet	26	8	3	15	41	75	19
Camberley	26	6	3	17	45	82	15
Guildford (Pinks)	26	7	1	18	52	104	15

Joined Metropolitan League

Metropolitan League 1950/51

	Pl	W	D	L	F	A	Pts
Dagenham	30	24	3	3	95	28	51
Vickers Armstrong	30	22	3	5	98	50	47
Croydon Rovers	30	22	1	7	67	37	45
St. Neots & Dist	30	18	4	8	87	47	40
Luton Town 'A'	30	17	3	10	95	47	37
Windsor & Eton	30	16	4	10	70	61	36
Headington Utd	30	14	4	12	68	62	32
Brighton & Hove A	30	10	10	10	56	53	30
Leatherhead	**30**	**12**	**3**	**15**	**59**	**68**	**27**
Dunstable Town	30	11	2	17	62	83	24
Callenders Ath	30	10	2	18	55	76	22
Twickenham	30	8	6	16	49	75	22
Chingford Town	30	8	5	17	51	71	21
Hastings Utd res.	30	6	5	19	38	72	17
Dickinsons	30	5	5	20	60	136	15
Hove United	30	5	4	21	36	80	14

*Chipperfield withdrew

Joined Delphian League

Delphian League 1951/52

	Pl	W	D	L	F	A	Pts
Brentwood & Wrly	26	16	4	6	65	37	36
Dagenham	26	16	3	7	68	35	35
Yiewsley	26	14	5	7	70	48	33
Leatherhead	**26**	**14**	**4**	**8**	**51**	**43**	**32**
Woodford Town	26	12	7	7	59	44	31
Aylesbury United	26	12	6	8	67	40	30
Rainham Town	26	13	3	10	41	43	29
Slough Centre	26	10	6	10	58	61	26
Willesden	26	10	3	13	48	50	23
Bishop's Stortford	26	10	3	13	55	80	23
Berkhamsted Town	26	9	3	14	47	58	21
Stevenage Town	26	6	7	13	50	75	19
Cheshunt	26	5	6	15	46	69	16
Wembley	26	2	6	18	30	72	10

Delphian League 1952/53

	Pl	W	D	L	F	A	Pts
Dagenham	30	22	3	5	78	34	47
Aylesbury United	30	18	3	9	70	43	39
Yiewsley	30	14	11	5	62	48	39
Slough Centre	30	16	4	10	60	35	36
Stevenage Town	30	17	2	11	63	51	36
Brentwood & Wrly	30	15	5	10	60	50	35
Woodford Town	30	14	6	10	66	52	34
Rainham Town	30	14	3	13	47	41	31
Leatherhead	**30**	**12**	**7**	**11**	**53**	**59**	**31**
Hornchurch & Up	30	12	5	13	48	48	29
Berkhamsted Town	30	11	6	13	57	71	28
Wembley	30	8	7	15	52	58	23
Cheshunt	30	9	4	17	48	66	22
Hemel Hempstead	30	7	3	20	46	77	17
Bishop's Stortford	30	6	5	19	47	94	17
Willesden	30	4	8	18	29	59	16

Delphian League 1953/54

	Pl	W	D	L	F	A	Pts
Aylesbury United	28	18	5	5	97	45	41
Dagenham	28	18	4	6	64	35	40
Rainham Town	28	17	6	5	64	40	40
Wembley	28	14	4	10	52	49	32
Slough Centre	28	13	5	10	58	52	31
Bishop's Stortford	28	12	4	12	64	56	28
Stevenage Town	28	12	4	12	65	61	28
Woodford Town	28	11	5	12	41	59	27
Yiewsley	28	11	4	13	51	45	26
Brentwood & Wrly	28	8	9	11	55	62	25
Berkhamsted Town	28	9	7	12	54	61	25
Cheshunt	28	10	5	13	50	59	25
Hemel Hempstead	28	9	5	14	48	66	23
Hornchurch & Up	28	6	6	16	46	72	18
Leatherhead	**28**	**4**	**3**	**21**	**45**	**92**	**11**

Delphian League 1954/55

	Pl	W	D	L	F	A	Pts
Bishop's Stortford	28	22	3	3	98	29	47
Dagenham	28	19	3	6	82	29	41
Aylesbury United	28	18	1	9	77	43	37
Rainham Town	28	16	4	8	66	47	36
Slough Centre	28	15	5	8	62	46	35
Hemel Hempstead	28	14	1	13	56	53	29
Woodford Town	28	11	6	11	55	58	28
Wembley	28	11	4	13	48	40	26
Stevenage Town	28	10	6	12	53	72	26
Tufnell Park	28	9	6	13	41	61	24
Leatherhead	**28**	**8**	**5**	**15**	**48**	**65**	**21**
Hornchurch & Up	28	9	3	16	49	68	21
Berkhamsted Town	28	9	3	16	42	70	21
Cheshunt	28	6	3	19	37	76	13*
Brentwood & Wrly	28	4	5	19	36	83	13

* 2 points deducted

Delphian League 1955/56

	Pl	W	D	L	F	A	Pts
Dagenham	28	20	3	5	83	28	43
Wembley	28	18	6	4	72	32	42
Rainham Town	28	18	3	7	71	45	39
Bishop's Stortford	28	16	5	7	84	43	37
Aylesbury United	28	14	4	10	57	63	32
Hornchurch & Up	28	13	5	10	60	59	31
Hemel Hempstead	28	11	8	9	61	56	30
Leatherhead	**28**	**11**	**5**	**12**	**53**	**63**	**27**
Tufnell Park	28	9	7	12	51	59	25
Ware	28	8	9	11	63	73	25
Berkhamsted Town	28	10	3	15	53	72	23
Woodford Town	28	8	7	13	52	74	23
Slough Centre	28	6	6	16	50	68	18
Brentwood & Wrly	28	5	3	20	42	80	13
Stevenage Town	28	2	8	18	35	72	12

Delphian League 1956/57

	Pl	W	D	L	F	A	Pts
Dagenham	26	18	5	3	66	29	41
Rainham Town	26	15	4	7	68	45	34
Brentwood & Wrly	26	14	6	6	68	46	34
Aylesbury United	26	11	7	8	55	41	29
Bishop's Stortford	26	13	3	10	70	56	29
Ware	26	13	2	11	78	65	28
Letchworth Town	26	12	3	11	57	47	27
Hornchurch & Up	26	12	3	11	47	44	27
Leatherhead	**26**	**11**	**4**	**11**	**57**	**67**	**26**
Hemel Hempstead	26	8	6	12	50	56	22
Stevenage Town	26	6	7	13	39	70	19
Tufnell Park	26	5	8	13	40	59	18
Berkhamsted Town	26	6	5	15	35	64	17
Woodford Town	26	5	3	18	43	84	13

Delphian League 1957/58

	Pl	W	D	L	F	A	Pts
Letchworth Town	28	22	4	2	96	27	48
Aveley	28	18	4	6	77	46	40
Rainham Town	28	17	5	6	67	45	39
Brentwood & Wrly	28	15	5	8	78	47	35
Aylesbury United	28	14	6	8	69	49	34
Leatherhead	**28**	**14**	**4**	**10**	**77**	**56**	**32**
Hornchurch & Up	28	13	5	10	50	38	31
Bishop's Stortford	28	12	6	10	62	54	30
Tufnell Park	28	11	6	11	44	53	28
Woodford Town	28	8	6	14	44	66	22
Ware	28	8	5	15	41	60	21
Wokingham Town	28	8	5	15	44	69	21
Hemel Hempstead	28	6	5	17	30	72	17
Stevenage Town	28	5	3	20	40	79	13
Berkhamsted Town	28	4	1	23	24	82	9

Joined Corinthian League

Corinthian League 1958/59

	Pl	W	D	L	F	A	Pts
Dagenham	26	19	2	5	70	36	40
Maidenhead Utd	26	14	7	5	63	38	35
Slough Town	26	14	5	7	75	41	33
Wembley	26	13	4	9	61	44	30
Leatherhead	**26**	**13**	**4**	**9**	**58**	**54**	**30**
Dorking	26	9	8	9	45	40	26
Uxbridge	26	11	3	12	58	63	25
Edgware	26	11	3	12	49	67	25
Horsham	26	9	5	12	66	68	23
Erith & Belvedere	26	8	7	11	43	53	23
Chesham Utd	26	8	6	12	45	57	22
Epsom Town	26	8	6	12	44	57	22
Eastbourne	26	5	7	14	28	50	17
Worthing	26	5	3	18	45	82	13

Corinthian League 1959/60

	Pl	W	D	L	F	A	Pts
Uxbridge	30	20	4	6	72	40	44
Maidenhead Utd	30	16	6	8	70	40	38
Dorking	30	17	3	10	69	47	37
Epsom Town	30	17	2	11	70	55	36
Letchworth Town	30	14	6	10	68	62	34
Dagenham	30	13	7	10	50	40	33
Slough Town	30	14	4	12	54	53	32
Horsham	30	13	5	12	68	64	31
Wokingham Town	30	11	7	12	62	51	29
Worthing	30	11	7	12	70	74	29
Erith & Belvedere	30	10	9	11	62	66	29
Leatherhead	**30**	**12**	**3**	**15**	**56**	**63**	**27**
Chesham Utd	30	11	4	15	45	60	26
Wembley	30	11	3	16	56	77	25
Eastbourne	30	8	4	18	41	67	20
Edgware	30	4	2	24	37	91	10

Corinthian League 1960/61

	Pl	W	D	L	F	A	Pts
Maidenhead Utd	30	19	5	6	65	39	43
Chesham Utd	30	19	2	9	73	38	40
Edgware Town	30	17	6	7	70	40	40
Dagenham	30	18	3	9	82	55	39
Horsham	30	17	3	10	85	77	37
Uxbridge	30	15	5	10	50	40	35
Worthing	30	14	5	11	85	67	33
Letchworth Town	30	15	3	12	64	66	33
Dorking	30	12	6	12	64	61	30
Erith & Belvedere	30	10	7	13	59	57	27
Eastbourne	30	10	6	14	50	59	26
Epsom & Ewell	30	11	3	16	46	77	25
Leatherhead	**30**	**9**	**4**	**17**	**68**	**93**	**22**
Wokingham Town	30	8	5	17	44	60	21
Wembley	30	6	6	18	51	80	18
Slough Town	30	4	3	23	48	95	11

Corinthian League 1961/62

	Pl	W	D	L	F	A	Pts
Maidenhead Utd	30	23	3	4	77	31	49
Chesham Utd	30	19	4	7	64	34	42
Horsham	30	18	3	9	88	57	39
Edgware Town	30	15	7	8	47	40	37
Dagenham	30	16	3	11	65	49	35
Uxbridge	30	14	5	11	47	41	33
Erith & Belvedere	30	14	5	11	56	57	33
Slough Town	30	13	4	13	47	49	30
Wokingham Town	30	11	6	13	50	49	28
Leatherhead	**30**	**10**	**7**	**13**	**63**	**52**	**27**
Letchworth Town	30	8	9	13	55	65	25
Worthing	30	10	5	15	52	67	25
Eastbourne	30	8	6	16	39	57	22
Dorking	30	8	6	16	55	90	22
Epsom & Ewell	30	8	2	20	47	81	18
Wembley	30	7	2	21	40	73	16

Corinthian League 1962/63

	Pl	W	D	L	F	A	Pts
Leatherhead	**30**	**22**	**5**	**3**	**88**	**36**	**49**
Erith & Belvedere	30	18	6	6	61	32	42
Wokingham Town	30	18	5	7	53	41	41
Dagenham	30	15	8	7	64	47	38
Uxbridge	30	15	7	8	73	51	37
Letchworth Town	30	16	3	11	75	50	35
Maidenhead Utd	30	12	9	9	61	46	33
Slough Town	30	12	9	9	62	54	33
Chesham Utd	30	11	6	13	66	59	28
Worthing	30	12	4	14	63	78	28
Dorking	30	9	6	15	56	70	24
Horsham	30	10	3	17	50	74	23
Edgware Town	30	9	5	16	43	66	23
Eastbourne	30	7	5	18	43	76	19
Epsom & Ewell	30	5	5	20	31	82	15
Wembley	30	4	4	22	46	73	12

Corinthian, Athenian and Delphian Leagues merged

Athenian League Division One 1963/64

	Pl	W	D	L	F	A	Pts
Leatherhead	**26**	**18**	**3**	**5**	**86**	**45**	**39**
Worthing	26	18	2	6	76	40	38
Edgware Town	26	17	4	5	72	40	38
Erith & Belvedere	26	12	8	6	46	30	32
Slough Town	26	15	2	9	54	37	32
Letchworth Town	26	12	6	8	80	52	30
Chesham Utd	26	14	2	10	75	57	30
Uxbridge	26	11	5	10	45	42	27
Wokingham Town	26	11	3	12	42	54	25
Wembley	26	8	4	14	48	67	20
Eastbourne	26	7	3	16	44	75	17
Dorking	26	7	2	17	44	74	16
Horsham	26	4	3	19	27	67	11
Epsom & Ewell	26	4	1	21	45	104	9

Promoted to Athenian League Premier Division

Athenian League Premier Division 1964/65

	Pl	W	D	L	F	A	Pts
Barnet	30	23	4	3	107	29	50
Leyton	30	19	3	8	67	41	41
Finchley	30	19	1	10	67	45	39
Worthing	30	15	8	7	70	65	38
Walton & Hersham	30	16	3	11	69	55	35
Hayes	30	14	5	11	71	56	33
Hounslow Town	30	14	5	11	69	61	33
Carshalton Ath	30	13	4	13	62	54	30
Maidenhead Utd	30	12	6	12	60	53	30
Leatherhead	**30**	**13**	**3**	**14**	**51**	**54**	**29**
Hornchurch	30	11	6	13	61	67	28
Dagenham	30	8	8	14	40	57	24
Edgware Town	30	8	5	17	33	78	21
Grays Athletic	30	8	4	18	48	75	20
Southall	30	7	5	18	37	67	19
Redhill	30	4	2	24	32	87	10

Athenian League Premier Division 1965/66

	Pl	W	D	L	F	A	Pts
Leyton	30	21	6	3	76	28	48
Finchley	30	22	4	4	83	39	48
Maidenhead Utd	30	21	3	6	63	29	45
Leatherhead	**30**	**14**	**9**	**7**	**41**	**34**	**37**
Hounslow Town	30	15	4	11	66	60	34
Dagenham	30	14	4	12	61	49	32
Southall	30	13	4	13	38	57	30
Slough Town	30	12	5	13	69	50	29
Hemel Hempstead	30	11	6	13	57	51	28
Grays Athletic	30	8	10	12	41	54	26
Walton & Hersham	30	9	6	15	56	66	24
Worthing	30	10	4	16	51	66	24
Hayes	30	9	5	16	50	55	23
Edgware Town	30	8	7	15	37	62	23
Carshalton Ath	30	7	2	21	48	93	16
Hornchurch	30	3	7	20	34	78	13

Athenian League Premier Division 1966/67

	Pl	W	D	L	F	A	Pts
Leyton	30	18	7	5	73	32	43
Bishop's Stortford	30	19	5	6	56	33	43
Finchley	30	16	6	8	72	38	38
Leatherhead	**30**	**17**	**3**	**10**	**53**	**42**	**37**
Harwich & Parkstn	30	15	5	10	64	42	35
Hounslow Town	30	14	6	10	62	49	34
Slough Town	30	14	5	11	52	38	33
Dagenham	30	13	7	10	48	40	33
Hayes	30	13	6	11	51	45	32
Grays Athletic	30	11	7	12	45	50	29
Hemel Hempstead	30	8	11	11	39	42	27
Southall	30	8	9	13	43	47	25
Walton & Hersham	30	10	5	15	46	58	25
Maidenhead Utd	30	7	10	13	49	65	24
Worthing	30	5	4	21	32	85	14
Edgware Town	30	2	4	24	19	98	8

Athenian League Premier Division 1967/68

	Pl	W	D	L	F	A	Pts
Slough Town	30	23	5	2	93	23	51
Dagenham	30	20	4	6	73	34	44
Bishop's Stortford	30	18	3	9	75	38	39
Hayes	30	15	5	10	57	40	35
Leatherhead	**30**	**15**	**4**	**11**	**55**	**44**	**34**
Maidenhead Utd	30	15	4	11	50	48	34
Hounslow Town	30	13	6	11	50	50	32
Walton & Hersham	30	13	5	12	61	39	31
Hornchurch	30	10	9	11	42	46	29
Redhill	30	11	7	12	43	48	29
Grays Athletic	30	11	6	13	45	54	28
Southall	30	9	8	13	34	65	26
Finchley	30	6	9	15	42	53	21
Harwich & Parkstn	30	7	5	18	36	60	19
Leyton	30	5	6	19	22	63	16
Hemel Hempstead	30	4	4	22	23	86	12

Athenian League Premier Division 1968/69

	Pl	W	D	L	F	A	Pts
Walton & Hersham	30	24	4	2	79	22	52
Slough Town	30	21	6	3	65	30	48
Southall	30	18	3	9	55	31	39
Leatherhead	**30**	**16**	**6**	**8**	**48**	**32**	**38**
Dagenham	30	15	7	8	51	34	37
Bishop's Stortford	30	14	6	10	57	44	34
Maidenhead Utd	30	10	11	9	42	35	31
Cheshunt	30	10	9	11	33	39	29
Wembley	30	11	7	12	35	45	29
Harwich & Parkstn	30	9	7	14	33	47	25
Redhill	30	10	5	15	31	51	25
Hayes	30	7	10	13	31	45	24
Grays Athletic	30	7	7	16	34	48	21
Finchley	30	5	10	15	19	39	20
Hornchurch	30	3	10	17	23	53	16
Hounslow Town	30	5	2	23	26	67	12

Athenian League Premier Division 1969/70

	Pl	W	D	L	F	A	Pts
Bishop's Stortford	30	20	5	5	72	33	45
Walton & Hersham	30	16	8	6	56	32	40
Dagenham	30	15	9	6	62	22	39
Slough Town	30	15	9	6	52	21	39
Leatherhead	**30**	**15**	**9**	**6**	**51**	**29**	**39**
Redhill	30	17	5	8	48	36	39
Hayes	30	11	9	10	47	45	31
Tilbury	30	10	9	11	48	43	29
Cheshunt	30	9	9	12	33	30	27
Harwich & Parkstn	30	7	12	11	44	43	26
Southall	30	10	6	14	33	48	26
Grays Athletic	30	9	8	13	26	40	26
Wembley	30	9	7	14	34	46	25
Maidenhead Utd	30	6	9	15	29	54	21
Finchley	30	7	5	18	30	73	19
Eastbourne Utd	30	3	3	24	27	97	9

Athenian League Premier Division 1970/71

	Pl	W	D	L	F	A	Pts
Dagenham	30	23	5	2	54	19	51
Walton & Hersham	30	20	7	3	56	21	47
Slough Town	30	17	7	6	48	21	41
Cheshunt	30	18	3	9	48	34	39
Maidenhead Utd	30	14	8	8	53	29	36
Leatherhead	**30**	**14**	**6**	**10**	**45**	**31**	**34**
Tilbury	30	13	4	13	48	44	30
Hayes	30	11	7	12	43	41	29
Lewes	30	11	6	13	42	42	28
Boreham Wood	30	9	9	12	39	41	27
Redhill	30	10	7	13	36	48	27
Bishop's Stortford	30	11	4	15	45	61	26
Harwich & Parkstn	30	8	6	16	43	62	22
Wembley	30	4	8	18	33	62	16
Grays Athletic	30	7	2	21	27	68	16
Southall	30	4	3	21	17	53	11

Athenian League Premier Division 1971/72

	Pl	W	D	L	F	A	Pts
Slough Town	30	22	4	4	60	17	48
Dagenham	30	19	5	6	61	27	43
Leatherhead	**30**	**16**	**8**	**6**	**56**	**29**	**40**
Tilbury	30	15	9	6	62	46	39
Harwich & Parkstn	30	14	9	7	47	40	37
Maidenhead Utd	30	13	8	9	38	31	34
Redhill	30	11	10	9	51	35	32
Cheshunt	30	10	11	9	43	37	31
Aveley	30	12	6	12	46	37	30
Hornchurch	30	10	8	12	39	38	28
Boreham Wood	30	11	6	13	40	45	28
Lewes	30	10	8	12	48	52	28
Erith & Belvedere	30	9	8	13	39	54	26
Southall	30	5	9	16	25	49	19
Wembley	30	3	5	22	26	58	11
Grays Athletic	30	1	4	25	25	111	6

Joined Isthmian League

Isthmian League 1972/73

	Pl	W	D	L	F	A	Pts
Hendon	42	34	6	2	88	18	74
Walton & Hersham	42	25	11	6	60	25	61
Leatherhead	**42**	**23**	**10**	**9**	**76**	**32**	**56**
Wycombe Wndrs	42	25	6	11	66	32	56
Walthamstow Ave	42	20	12	10	66	48	52
Tooting & Mtcham	42	20	11	11	73	39	51
Sutton United	42	21	9	12	69	48	51
Kingstonian	42	20	10	12	60	49	50
Enfield	42	20	8	14	90	54	48
Bishop's Stortford	42	18	12	12	58	51	48
Hayes	42	19	8	15	69	42	46
Dulwich Hamlet	42	18	9	15	59	52	45
Ilford	42	18	9	15	61	59	45
Leytonstone	42	17	11	14	55	54	45
Woking	42	18	8	16	61	56	44
Hitchin Town	42	15	9	18	52	64	39

Rothmans Isthmian League 1972/73 (continued)

	Pl	W	D	L	F	A	Pts
Barking	42	8	7	27	45	88	23
St. Albans City	42	5	12	25	34	76	22
Oxford City	42	6	7	29	30	101	19
Bromley	42	4	10	28	31	70	18
Clapton	42	3	11	28	31	100	17
Corinthian Casuals	42	3	8	31	30	106	14

Rothmans Isthmian League 1973/74

	Pl	W	D	L	F	A	Pts
Wycombe Wndrs	42	27	9	6	96	34	90
Hendon	42	25	13	4	63	20	88
Bishop's Stortford	42	26	9	7	78	26	87
Dulwich Hamlet	42	22	11	9	71	38	77
Leatherhead	**42**	**23**	**6**	**13**	**81**	**44**	**75**
Walton & Hersham	42	20	12	10	68	50	72
Woking	42	22	6	14	63	55	72
Leytonstone	42	20	9	13	63	44	69
Ilford	42	20	8	14	60	44	68
Hayes	42	17	14	11	65	43	65
Oxford City	42	15	16	11	45	47	61
Sutton United	42	13	16	13	51	52	55
Hitchin Town	42	15	10	17	68	73	55
Barking	42	14	12	16	57	58	54
Kingstonian	42	12	15	15	47	46	51
Tooting & Mtchm	42	14	9	19	57	62	51
Enfield	42	13	11	18	50	57	50
Walthamstow Ave	42	11	13	18	46	62	46
Bromley	42	7	9	26	37	81	30
Clapton	42	8	3	31	36	128	27
St. Albans City	42	4	7	31	30	92	19
Corinthian Casuals	42	3	4	35	31	107	13

#3 points for a win introduced

Rothmans Isthmian League 1974/75

	Pl	W	D	L	F	A	Pts
Wycombe Wndrs	42	28	11	3	93	30	95
Enfield	42	29	8	5	78	26	95
Dagenham	42	28	5	9	95	44	89
Tooting & Mtchm	42	25	9	8	78	46	84
Dulwich Hamlet	42	24	10	8	75	38	82
Leatherhead	**42**	**23**	**10**	**9**	**83**	**42**	**79**
Ilford	42	23	10	9	98	51	79
Oxford City	42	17	9	16	63	56	60
Slough Town	42	17	6	19	68	52	57
Sutton United	42	17	6	19	68	63	57
Bishop's Stortford	42	17	6	19	56	64	57
Hitchin Town	42	15	10	17	57	71	55
Hendon	42	15	7	20	59	74	52
Walthamstow Ave	42	13	9	20	56	62	48
Woking	42	12	10	20	53	73	46
Hayes	42	10	14	18	52	66	44
Barking	42	12	8	22	57	81	44
Leytonstone	42	12	7	23	42	61	43
Kingstonian	42	13	4	25	48	73	43
Clapton	42	12	4	26	46	96	40
Walton & Hersham	42	9	4	29	37	108	31
Bromley	42	6	3	33	25	110	21

Rothmans Isthmian League 1975/76

	Pl	W	D	L	F	A	Pts
Enfield	42	25	9	8	83	37	87
Wycombe Wndrs	42	24	10	8	71	41	82
Dagenham	42	25	6	11	89	55	81
Ilford	42	22	10	10	58	39	76
Dulwich Hamlet	42	22	5	15	67	41	71
Hendon	42	20	11	11	60	41	71
Tooting & Mtchm	42	19	11	12	73	49	68
Leatherhead	**42**	**19**	**10**	**13**	**63**	**53**	**67**
Staines Town	42	19	9	14	46	37	66
Slough Town	42	17	12	13	58	45	63
Sutton United	42	17	11	14	71	60	62
Bishop's Stortford	42	15	12	15	51	47	57
Walthamstow Ave	42	14	11	17	47	60	53
Woking	42	14	9	19	58	62	51
Barking	42	15	6	21	57	70	51
Hitchin Town	42	13	11	18	45	57	50
Hayes	42	10	19	13	44	48	49
Kingstonian	42	13	8	21	53	87	47
Southall & Ealing	42	11	9	22	56	69	42
Leytonstone	42	10	10	22	41	63	40
Oxford City	42	9	8	25	29	65	35
Clapton	42	3	3	36	19	112	12

Rothmans Isthmian League 1976/77

	Pl	W	D	L	F	A	Pts
Enfield	42	24	12	6	63	34	84
Wycombe Wndrs	42	25	8	9	71	34	83
Dagenham	42	23	10	9	80	39	79
Hendon	42	19	10	13	60	48	67
Tilbury	42	18	13	11	57	49	67
Tooting & Mtcham	42	18	10	14	85	72	64
Walthamstow Ave	42	19	7	16	61	55	64
Slough Town	42	18	9	15	51	46	63
Hitchin Town	42	19	6	17	60	66	63
Leatherhead	**42**	**18**	**7**	**17**	**61**	**47**	**61**
Staines Town	42	16	13	13	52	48	61
Leytonstone	42	16	11	15	59	57	59
Barking	42	16	9	17	63	61	57
Southall & Ealing	42	15	8	19	52	64	53
Croydon	42	13	10	19	38	52	49
Sutton United	42	14	7	21	40	55	49
Kingstonian	42	13	7	22	45	60	46
Hayes	42	12	10	20	49	69	46
Woking	42	11	12	19	47	61	45
Bishop's Stortford	42	11	11	20	51	71	44
Dulwich Hamlet	42	11	8	23	52	68	41
Ilford	42	10	8	24	32	73	38

Rothmans Isthmian League Premier Division 1977/78

	Pl	W	D	L	F	A	Pts
Enfield	42	35	5	2	96	27	110
Dagenham	42	24	7	11	78	55	79
Wycombe Wndrs	42	22	9	11	66	41	75
Tooting & Mtchm	42	22	8	12	64	49	74
Hitchin Town	42	20	9	13	69	53	69
Sutton United	42	18	12	12	66	57	66
Leatherhead	**42**	**18**	**11**	**13**	**62**	**48**	**65**
Croydon	42	18	10	14	61	52	64
Walthamstow Ave	42	17	12	13	64	61	63
Barking	42	17	7	18	76	66	58
Carshalton Ath	42	15	11	16	61	63	56
Hayes	42	15	11	16	46	53	56
Hendon	42	16	7	19	57	55	55
Woking	42	14	11	17	62	62	53
Boreham Wood	42	15	8	19	48	65	53
Slough Town	42	14	8	20	52	69	50
Staines Town	42	12	13	17	46	60	49
Tilbury	42	11	12	19	57	68	45
Kingstonian	42	8	13	21	43	65	37
Leytonstone	42	7	15	20	44	71	36
Southall & Ealing	42	6	15	21	43	74	33
Bishop's Stortford	42	7	8	27	36	83	29

Berger Isthmian League Premier Division 1978/79

	Pl	W	D	L	F	A	Pts
Barking	42	28	9	5	92	50	93
Dagenham	42	25	6	11	83	63	81
Enfield	42	22	11	9	69	39	77
Dulwich Hamlet	42	21	13	8	69	39	76
Slough Town	42	20	12	10	61	44	72
Wycombe Wndrs	42	20	9	13	59	44	69
Woking	42	18	14	10	79	59	68
Croydon	42	19	9	14	61	51	66
Hendon	42	16	14	12	55	48	62
Leatherhead	**42**	**17**	**9**	**16**	**57**	**45**	**60**
Sutton United	42	17	9	16	62	51	60
Tooting & Mtchm	42	15	14	13	52	52	59
Walthamstow Ave	42	15	6	21	61	69	51
Tilbury	42	13	11	18	60	76	50
Boreham Wood	42	13	10	19	50	67	49
Hitchin Town	42	12	11	19	59	71	47
Carshalton Ath	42	10	16	16	49	69	46
Hayes	42	9	18	15	45	58	45
Oxford City	42	12	7	23	50	80	43
Staines Town	42	6	16	20	40	64	34
Leytonstone	42	8	7	27	36	75	31
Kingstonian	42	3	15	24	35	72	24

Non-League Pyramid formed

Berger Isthmian League
Premier Division 1979/80

	Pl	W	D	L	F	A	Pts
Enfield	42	25	9	8	74	32	84
Walthamstow Ave	42	24	9	9	87	48	81
Dulwich Hamlet	42	21	16	5	66	37	79
Sutton United	42	20	13	9	67	40	73
Dagenham	42	20	13	9	82	56	73
Tooting & Mtchm	42	21	6	15	62	59	69
Barking	42	19	10	13	72	51	67
Harrow Borough	42	17	15	10	64	51	66
Woking	42	17	13	12	78	59	64
Wycombe Wndrs	42	17	13	12	72	53	64
Harlow Town	42	14	12	16	54	60	54
Hitchin Town	42	13	15	14	54	68	54
Hendon	42	12	13	17	50	57	49
Slough Town	42	13	10	19	54	71	49
Boreham Wood	42	13	10	19	50	69	49
Staines Town	42	14	6	22	46	67	48
Hayes	42	12	9	21	48	68	45
Leatherhead	**42**	**11**	**11**	**20**	**51**	**60**	**44**
Carshalton Ath	42	12	7	23	48	78	43
Croydon	42	12	7	23	48	78	43
Oxford City	42	10	9	23	49	87	39
Tilbury	42	7	11	24	41	90	30

Berger Isthmian League
Premier Division 1981/82

	Pl	W	D	L	F	A	Pts
Leytonstone & Ilfd	42	26	5	11	91	52	83
Sutton United	42	22	9	11	72	49	75
Wycombe Wndrs	42	21	10	11	63	48	73
Staines Town	42	21	9	12	59	46	72
Walthamstow Ave	42	21	7	14	81	62	70
Harrow Borough	42	18	13	11	77	55	67
Tooting & Mtchm	42	19	10	13	58	47	67
Slough Town	42	17	13	12	64	54	64
Leatherhead	**42**	**16**	**12**	**14**	**57**	**52**	**60**
Hayes	42	16	10	16	58	52	58
Croydon	42	16	9	17	59	57	57
Barking	42	14	14	14	53	51	56
Hendon	42	13	13	16	56	65	52
Dulwich Hamlet	42	14	10	18	47	59	52
Bishop's Stortford	42	15	5	22	50	70	50
Carshalton Ath	42	14	8	20	58	86	50
Billericay Town	42	11	16	15	41	50	49
Hitchin Town	42	12	11	19	56	77	47
Bromley	42	13	7	22	63	79	46
Woking	42	11	13	18	57	75	46
Harlow Town	42	10	11	21	50	73	41
Boreham Wood	42	8	13	21	47	58	37

Berger Isthmian League
Premier Division 1980/81

	Pl	W	D	L	F	A	Pts
Slough Town	42	23	13	6	73	34	82
Enfield	42	23	11	8	81	43	80
Wycombe Wndrs	42	22	9	11	76	49	75
Leytonstone & Ilfd	42	19	12	11	78	57	69
Sutton United	42	19	12	11	82	65	69
Hendon	42	18	10	14	66	58	64
Hayes	42	18	8	16	45	50	62
Dagenham	42	17	11	14	79	66	62
Harrow Borough	42	16	11	15	57	52	59
Bromley	42	16	9	17	63	69	57
Staines Town	42	15	9	18	60	61	54
Tooting & Mtchm	42	15	8	19	49	53	53
Hitchin Town	42	14	10	18	64	62	52
Croydon	42	12	15	15	51	51	51
Dulwich Hamlet	42	13	12	17	62	67	51
Leatherhead	**42**	**12**	**14**	**16**	**36**	**50**	**50**
Carshalton Ath	42	14	8	20	57	82	50
Barking	42	13	12	17	58	72	49*
Harlow Town	42	11	15	16	53	66	48
Walthamstow Ave	42	13	7	22	50	81	46
Boreham Wood	42	10	13	19	46	69	43
Woking	42	11	7	24	40	69	37#

* 2 points deducted   # 3 points deducted

Servowarm Isthmian League
Premier Division 1982/83

	Pl	W	D	L	F	A	Pts
Wycombe Wndrs	42	26	7	9	79	47	85
Leytonstone & Ilfd	42	24	9	9	71	39	81
Harrow Borough	42	24	7	11	91	58	79
Hayes	42	23	9	10	63	41	78
Sutton United	42	20	8	14	96	71	68
Dulwich Hamlet	42	18	14	10	59	52	68
Slough Town	42	18	13	11	73	36	67
Bognor Regis Tn	42	19	8	15	53	48	65
Tooting & Mtchm	42	18	9	15	58	56	63
Billericay Town	42	17	10	15	54	51	61
Croydon	42	17	9	16	68	58	60
Hendon	42	18	6	18	68	61	60
Bishop's Stortford	42	17	9	16	61	58	60
Barking	42	14	14	14	47	55	56
Bromley	42	14	12	16	51	50	54
Carshalton Ath	42	15	9	18	58	60	54
Wokingham Town	42	13	9	20	37	51	48
Walthamstow Ave	42	12	11	19	48	64	47
Staines Town	42	12	11	19	62	79	47
Hitchin Town	42	11	9	22	49	77	42
Woking	42	6	6	30	30	79	24
Leatherhead	**42**	**4**	**5**	**33**	**36**	**121**	**17**

**Relegated to Servowarm Isthmian
League Division One**

Servowarm Isthmian League
Division One 1983/84

	Pl	W	D	L	F	A	Pts
Windsor & Eton	42	26	7	9	89	44	85
Epsom & Ewell	42	23	9	10	73	51	78
Wembley	42	21	11	10	65	32	74
Maidenhead Utd	42	22	8	12	65	42	74
Boreham Wood	42	22	7	13	70	47	73
Farnborough Town	42	18	12	12	78	60	66
Hampton	42	18	12	12	65	49	66
Met Police	42	20	5	17	79	64	65
Chesham Utd	42	18	8	16	54	57	63
Tilbury	42	17	10	15	54	64	61
Leatherhead	**42**	**15**	**10**	**17**	**67**	**56**	**55**
Aveley	42	15	10	17	49	55	55
Woking	42	16	7	19	66	73	55
Hertford Town	42	15	9	18	55	75	54
Oxford City	42	14	9	19	57	56	51
Lewes	42	13	12	17	49	65	51
Walton & Hersham	42	13	10	19	52	70	49
Hornchurch	42	13	10	19	43	63	49
Kingstonian	42	13	9	20	47	67	48
Clapton	42	12	11	19	49	67	47
Cheshunt	42	12	8	22	47	64	44
Feltham	42	7	4	31	31	106	25

Vauxhall-Opel Isthmian League
Division One 1985/86

	Pl	W	D	L	F	A	Pts
St. Albans City	42	23	11	8	92	61	80
Bromley	42	24	8	10	68	41	80
Wembley	42	22	12	8	59	30	78
Oxford City	42	22	11	9	75	51	77
Hampton	42	21	11	10	63	45	74
Leyton-Wingate	42	21	10	11	77	56	73
Uxbridge	42	20	8	14	64	49	68
Staines Town	42	18	10	14	69	66	64
Boreham Wood	42	15	16	11	62	54	61
Walton & Hersham	42	16	10	16	68	71	58
Lewes	42	16	8	18	61	75	56
Leytonstone & Ilfd	42	13	15	14	57	67	54
Finchley	42	12	17	13	61	59	53
Grays Athletic	42	13	11	18	69	75	50
Leatherhead	**42**	**14**	**8**	**20**	**62**	**68**	**50**
Tilbury	42	13	11	18	60	66	50
Maidenhead Utd	42	13	7	22	61	67	46
Basildon Utd	42	12	9	21	52	72	45
Hornchurch	42	11	11	20	44	59	44
Chesham Utd	42	12	6	24	51	87	42
Harlow Town	42	8	14	20	53	70	38
Aveley	42	8	6	28	59	98	30

Servowarm Isthmian League
Division One 1984/85

	Pl	W	D	L	F	A	Pts
Farnborough Town	42	26	8	8	101	45	86
Kingstonian	42	23	10	9	67	39	79
Leatherhead	**42**	**23**	**10**	**9**	**109**	**61**	**76#**
Chesham Utd	42	22	8	12	78	46	74
Wembley	42	20	10	12	59	40	70
St. Albans City	42	19	10	13	79	59	67
Tilbury	42	18	13	11	86	68	67
Bromley	42	18	9	15	71	65	63
Hampton	42	17	11	14	75	62	62
Staines Town	42	16	11	15	59	53	59
Maidenhead Utd	42	17	8	17	65	64	59
Walton & Hersham	42	16	8	18	60	69	55+
Aveley	42	16	7	19	62	78	55
Oxford City	42	14	12	16	62	53	54
Lewes	42	15	9	18	70	72	54
Basildon Utd	42	15	8	19	55	61	53
Hornchurch	42	15	7	20	72	83	52
Boreham Wood	42	15	6	21	55	74	51
Woking	42	15	6	21	60	91	51
Met Police	42	10	12	20	65	92	42
Clapton	42	5	11	26	50	124	26
Hertford Town	42	5	10	27	36	97	25

Vauxhall-Opel Isthmian League
Division One 1986/87

	Pl	W	D	L	F	A	Pts
Leytonstone & Ilfd	42	30	5	7	78	29	95
Leyton-Wingate	42	23	13	6	68	31	82
Bracknell Town	42	24	9	9	92	48	81
Southwick	42	23	7	12	80	66	76
Wembley	42	21	9	12	61	47	72
Grays Athletic	42	19	10	13	76	64	67
Kingsbury Town	42	20	7	15	69	67	67
Boreham Wood	42	20	6	16	59	52	66
Uxbridge	42	18	9	15	60	59	63
Leatherhead	**42**	**17**	**11**	**14**	**45**	**48**	**62**
Hampton	42	18	5	19	57	55	59
Basildon Utd	42	16	10	16	58	60	58
Billericay Town	42	14	12	16	57	52	54
Staines Town	42	13	13	16	40	51	52
Lewes	42	15	6	21	55	65	51
Stevenage Borough	42	12	11	19	61	67	47
Oxford City	42	11	10	21	64	72	43
Walton & Hersham	42	11	10	21	53	74	43
Tilbury	42	12	7	23	46	70	43
Epsom & Ewell	42	12	7	23	44	68	43
Maidenhead Utd	42	11	4	27	44	76	37
Finchley	42	6	11	25	44	90	29

+ 1 point deducted   # 3 points deducted

Vauxhall-Opel Isthmian League
Division One 1987/88

	Pl	W	D	L	F	A	Pts
Marlow	42	32	5	5	100	44	101
Grays Athletic	42	30	10	2	74	25	100
Woking	42	25	7	10	91	52	82
Boreham Wood	42	21	9	12	65	45	72
Staines Town	42	19	11	12	71	48	68
Wembley	42	18	11	13	54	46	65
Basildon Utd	42	18	9	15	65	58	63
Walton & Hersham	42	15	16	11	53	44	61
Hampton	42	17	10	15	59	54	61
Leatherhead	**42**	**16**	**11**	**15**	**64**	**53**	**59**
Southwick	42	13	12	17	59	63	51
Oxford City	42	13	12	17	70	77	51
Worthing	42	14	8	20	67	73	50
Kingsbury Town	42	11	17	14	62	69	50
Walthamstow Ave	42	13	11	18	53	63	50
Lewes	42	12	13	17	83	77	49
Uxbridge	42	11	16	15	41	47	49
Chesham Utd	42	12	10	20	69	77	46
Bracknell Town	42	12	9	21	54	80	45
Billericay Town	42	11	11	20	58	88	44
Stevenage Borough	42	11	9	22	36	64	42
Wolverton Town	42	3	3	36	23	124	12

Vauxhall Isthmian League
Division One 1988/89

	Pl	W	D	L	F	A	Pts
Staines Town	40	26	9	5	79	29	87
Basingstoke Town	40	25	8	7	85	30	83
Woking	40	24	10	6	72	36	82
Hitchin Town	40	21	11	8	60	32	74
Wivenhoe Town	40	22	6	12	62	44	72
Lewes	40	21	8	11	72	54	71
Walton & Hersham	40	21	7	12	56	36	70
Kingsbury Town	40	20	7	13	65	41	67
Uxbridge	40	19	7	14	60	54	64
Wembley	40	18	6	16	45	58	60
Boreham Wood	40	16	9	15	57	52	57
Leatherhead	**40**	**14**	**8**	**18**	**56**	**58**	**50**
Met Police	40	13	9	18	52	68	48
Chesham Utd	40	12	9	19	54	67	45
Southwick	40	9	15	16	44	58	42
Chalfont St Peter	40	11	9	20	56	82	42
Hampton	40	7	14	19	37	62	35
Worthing	40	8	10	22	49	80	32*
Collier Row	40	8	7	25	37	82	31
Bracknell Town	40	8	6	26	38	70	30
Basildon United	40	6	7	27	34	77	25

2 points deducted

Vauxhall Isthmian League
Division One 1989/90

	Pl	W	D	L	F	A	Pts
Wivenhoe Town	42	31	7	4	94	36	100
Woking	42	30	8	4	102	29	98
Southwick	42	23	15	4	68	30	84
Hitchin Town	42	22	13	7	60	30	79
Walton & Hersham	42	20	10	12	68	50	70
Dorking	42	19	12	11	66	41	69
Boreham Wood	42	17	13	12	60	59	64
Harlow Town	42	16	13	13	60	53	61
Met Police	42	16	11	15	54	59	59
Chesham Utd	42	15	12	15	46	49	57
Chalfont St Peter	42	14	13	15	50	59	55
Tooting & Mtchm	42	14	13	15	42	51	55
Worthing	42	15	8	19	56	63	53
Whyteleafe	42	11	16	15	50	65	49
Lewes	42	12	11	19	55	65	47
Wembley	42	11	10	21	57	68	43
Croydon	42	9	16	17	43	57	43
Uxbridge	42	11	10	21	52	75	43
Hampton	42	8	13	21	28	51	37
Leatherhead	**42**	**7**	**10**	**25**	**34**	**77**	**31**
Purfleet	42	7	8	27	33	78	29
Kingsbury Town	42	8	10	24	45	78	25^

^ 9 points deducted

> **Relegated to Vauxhall Isthmian League Division Two South**

Vauxhall Isthmian League
Division Two South 1990/91

	Pl	W	D	L	F	A	Pts
Abingdon Town	42	29	7	6	95	28	94
Maidenhead Utd	42	28	8	6	85	33	92
Egham Town	42	27	6	9	100	46	87
Malden Vale	42	26	5	11	72	44	83
Ruislip Manor	42	25	5	12	93	44	80
Southall	42	23	10	9	84	43	79
Harefield Utd	42	23	10	9	81	56	79
Newbury Town	42	23	8	11	71	45	77
Hungerford Town	42	16	13	13	84	69	61
Leatherhead	**42**	**17**	**9**	**16**	**82**	**55**	**60**
Banstead Athletic	42	15	13	14	58	62	58
Hampton	42	14	15	13	62	43	57
Epsom & Ewell	42	15	12	15	49	50	57
Chertsey Town	42	15	9	18	76	72	54
Horsham	42	14	7	21	58	67	49
Flackwell Heath	42	11	11	20	56	78	44
Bracknell Town	42	11	7	24	60	97	40
Feltham	42	10	8	24	45	80	38
Cove	42	10	7	25	51	94	37
Eastbourne Utd	42	10	7	25	53	109	37
Petersfield Utd	42	6	3	33	25	119	21
Camberley Town	42	1	6	35	27	143	9

> **Isthmian League reorganisation**

Diadora Isthmian League
Division Two 1991/92

	Pl	W	D	L	F	A	Pts
Purfleet	42	27	8	7	97	48	89
Lewes	42	23	14	5	74	36	83
Billericay Town	42	24	8	10	75	44	80
Leatherhead	**42**	**23**	**6**	**13**	**68**	**40**	**75**
Ruislip Manor	42	20	9	13	74	51	69
Egham Town	42	19	12	11	81	62	69
Met Police	42	20	9	13	76	58	68
Saffron Walden	42	19	11	12	86	67	68
Hemel Hempstead	42	18	10	14	63	50	64
Hungerford Town	42	18	7	17	53	58	61
Barton Rovers	42	17	8	17	61	64	59
Worthing	42	17	8	17	67	72	59
Witham Town	42	16	11	15	56	61	59
Banstead Ath	42	16	10	16	69	58	58
Malden Vale	42	15	12	15	63	48	57
Rainham Town	42	14	13	15	53	48	55
Ware	42	14	9	19	58	62	51
Berkhamsted Town	42	13	11	18	56	57	50
Harefield Utd	42	11	7	24	47	66	40
Southall	42	8	7	27	39	93	31
Southwick	42	6	2	34	29	115	20
Newbury Town	42	4	8	30	30	117	20

Diadora Isthmian League
Division Two 1993/94

	Pl	W	D	L	F	A	Pts
Newbury Town	42	32	7	3	115	36	103
Chertsey Town	42	33	3	6	121	48	102
Aldershot Town	42	30	7	5	78	27	97
Barton Rovers	42	25	8	9	68	37	83
Witham Town	42	21	10	11	68	51	73
Malden Vale	42	20	10	12	70	49	70
Thame United	42	19	12	11	87	51	69
Met Police	42	20	9	13	75	54	69
Banstead Athletic	42	19	9	14	56	53	66
Aveley	42	19	5	18	60	66	62
Edgware Town	42	16	10	16	88	76	58
Saffron Walden	42	17	7	18	61	62	58
Hemel Hempstead	42	14	11	17	47	43	53
Egham Town	42	14	8	20	48	65	50
Ware	42	14	7	21	48	76	49
Hungerford Town	42	13	7	22	56	66	46
Tilbury	42	13	3	26	59	81	42
Hampton	42	12	5	25	42	70	41
Leatherhead	**42**	**10**	**6**	**26**	**46**	**92**	**36**
Lewes	42	8	10	24	38	85	34
Collier Row	42	7	8	27	37	88	29
Rainham Town	42	4	2	36	24	116	14

Diadora Isthmian League
Division Two 1992/93

	Pl	W	D	L	F	A	Pts
Worthing	42	28	7	7	105	50	91
Ruislip Manor	42	25	12	5	78	33	87
Berkhamsted Town	42	24	8	10	77	55	80
Hemel Hempstead	42	22	12	8	84	52	78
Met Police	42	22	6	14	84	51	72
Malden Vale	42	20	9	13	78	54	69
Chertsey Town	42	20	7	15	84	60	67
Saffron Walden	42	19	10	13	63	49	67
Newbury Town	42	14	18	10	53	51	60
Hampton	42	16	11	15	59	59	59
Edgware Town	42	16	10	16	84	75	58
Egham Town	42	16	9	17	60	71	57
Banstead Athletic	42	14	13	15	67	52	55
Leatherhead	**42**	**14**	**11**	**17**	**66**	**61**	**53**
Ware	42	12	11	19	68	76	47
Witham Town	42	10	16	16	54	65	46
Tilbury	42	12	8	22	55	101	44
Barton Rovers	42	9	14	19	40	66	41
Hungerford Town	42	11	8	23	37	93	41
Rainham Town	42	9	10	23	56	80	37
Harefield Utd	42	10	7	25	37	72	37
Southall	42	7	7	28	43	106	28

Diadora Isthmian League
Division Two 1994/95

	Pl	W	D	L	F	A	Pts
Thame United	42	30	3	9	97	49	93
Barton Rovers	42	25	7	10	93	51	82
Oxford City	42	24	8	10	86	47	80
Bracknell Town	42	23	9	10	86	47	78
Met Police	42	19	12	11	81	65	69
Hampton	42	20	9	13	79	74	69
Croydon	42	20	5	17	85	65	65
Banstead Athletic	42	18	10	14	73	59	64
Saffron Walden	42	17	13	12	64	59	64
Chalfont St Peter	42	17	12	13	67	54	63
Witham Town	42	18	9	15	75	64	63
Leatherhead	**42**	**16**	**12**	**14**	**71**	**75**	**60**
Edgware Town	42	16	10	16	70	66	58
Tilbury	42	15	9	18	62	82	54
Cheshunt	42	13	13	16	66	81	52
Ware	42	14	7	21	61	81	49
Egham Town	42	11	14	17	60	65	47
Hemel Hempstead	42	10	11	21	45	76	41
Hungerford Town	42	11	7	24	55	81	40
Windsor & Eton	42	10	8	24	58	84	38
Aveley	42	9	5	28	48	95	32
Malden Vale	42	5	9	28	46	108	24

Icis Isthmian League
Division Two 1995/96

	Pl	W	D	L	F	A	Pts
Canvey Island	40	25	12	3	91	36	87
Croydon	40	25	6	9	78	42	81
Hampton	40	23	10	7	74	44	79
Banstead Athletic	40	21	11	8	72	36	74
Collier Row	40	21	11	8	73	41	74
Wivenhoe Town	40	21	8	11	82	57	71
Met Police	40	18	10	12	57	45	64
Bedford Town	40	18	10	12	67	59	64
Bracknell Town	40	18	8	14	69	50	62
Edgware Town	40	16	9	15	72	67	57
Tilbury	40	12	11	17	52	62	47
Ware	40	13	8	19	55	80	47
Chalfont St Peter	40	11	13	16	58	63	46
Leatherhead	**40**	**12**	**10**	**18**	**71**	**77**	**46**
Saffron Walden	40	11	12	17	56	58	45
Cheshunt	40	10	12	18	56	90	42
Hemel Hempstead	40	10	10	20	46	62	40
Egham Town	40	12	3	25	42	74	39
Witham Town	40	8	10	22	35	68	34
Hungerford Town	40	9	7	24	44	79	34
Dorking	40	8	5	27	44	104	29

Newbury Town expelled

Icis Isthmian League
Division Two 1996/97

	Pl	W	D	L	F	A	Pts
Collier Row	42	28	12	2	93	33	96
Leatherhead	**42**	**30**	**5**	**7**	**116**	**45**	**95**
Wembley	42	23	11	8	92	45	80
Barking	42	22	13	7	69	40	79
Horsham	42	22	11	9	78	48	77
Edgware Town	42	20	14	8	74	50	74
Bedford Town	42	21	8	13	77	43	71
Banstead Athletic	42	21	5	16	75	52	68
Windsor & Eton	42	17	13	12	65	62	64
Leighton Town	42	17	12	13	64	52	63
Bracknell Town	42	17	9	16	78	71	60
Wivenhoe Town	42	17	9	16	69	62	60
Chalfont St Peter	42	14	13	15	53	61	55
Hungerford Town	42	14	13	15	68	77	55
Met Police	42	14	7	21	72	75	49
Tilbury	42	14	7	21	68	77	49
Witham Town	42	11	10	21	39	67	43
Egham Town	42	10	9	23	47	86	39
Cheshunt	42	9	3	31	36	101	30
Ware	42	7	8	27	44	80	29
Dorking	42	7	6	29	40	100	27
Hemel Hempstead	42	5	6	31	34	125	21

Promoted to Ryman Isthmian League Division One

www.isthmian.co.uk

Ryman Isthmian League
Division One 1997/98

	Pl	W	D	L	F	A	Pts
Aldershot Town	42	28	8	6	89	36	92
Billericay Town	42	25	6	11	78	44	81
Hampton	42	22	15	5	75	47	81
Maidenhead Utd	42	25	5	12	76	37	80
Uxbridge	42	23	6	13	66	59	75
Grays Athletic	42	21	10	11	79	49	73
Romford	42	21	8	13	92	59	71
Bognor Regis Tn	42	20	9	13	77	45	69
Leatherhead	**42**	**18**	**11**	**13**	**70**	**51**	**65**
Leyton-Pennant	42	17	11	14	66	58	62
Chertsey Town	42	16	13	13	83	70	61
Worthing	42	17	6	19	64	71	57
Berkhamsted Town	42	15	8	19	59	69	53
Staines Town	42	13	10	19	54	71	49
Croydon	42	13	10	19	47	64	49
Barton Rovers	42	11	13	18	53	72	46
Wembley	42	10	15	17	38	61	45
Molesey	42	10	11	21	47	65	41
Whyteleafe	42	10	10	22	48	83	40
Wokingham Town	42	7	10	25	41	74	31
Abingdon Utd	42	9	4	29	47	101	31
Thame United	42	7	9	26	33	96	30

Ryman Isthmian League
Division One 1998/99

	Pl	W	D	L	F	A	Pts
Canvey Island	42	28	6	8	76	41	90
Hitchin Town	42	25	10	7	75	38	85
Wealdstone	42	26	6	10	75	48	84
Braintree Town	42	20	10	12	74	48	70
Bognor Regis Tn	42	20	8	14	63	44	68
Grays Athletic	42	19	11	12	56	42	68
Oxford City	42	16	14	12	58	51	62
Croydon	42	16	13	13	53	53	61
Chertsey Town	42	14	16	12	57	57	58
Romford	42	14	15	13	58	63	57
Maidenhead Utd	42	13	15	14	50	46	54
Worthing	42	13	13	16	47	61	52
Leyton-Pennant	42	13	12	17	62	70	51
Uxbridge	42	13	11	18	54	51	50
Barton Rovers	42	11	15	16	43	49	48
Yeading	42	12	10	20	51	55	46
Leatherhead	**42**	**12**	**9**	**21**	**48**	**59**	**45**
Whyteleafe	42	13	6	23	51	72	45
Staines Town	42	10	15	17	33	56	45
Molesey	42	8	20	14	35	52	44
Wembley	42	10	10	22	36	71	40
Berkhamsted Town	42	10	7	25	53	81	37

Ryman Isthmian League
Division One 1999/2000

	Pl	W	D	L	F	A	Pts
Croydon	42	25	9	8	85	47	84
Grays Athletic	42	21	12	9	80	44	75
Maidenhead Utd	42	20	15	7	72	45	75
Thame United	42	20	13	9	61	38	73
Worthing	42	19	12	11	80	60	69
Staines Town	42	19	12	11	63	52	69
Whyteleafe	42	20	9	13	60	49	69
Bedford Town	42	17	12	13	59	52	63
Bromley	42	17	9	16	62	65	60
Uxbridge	42	15	13	14	60	44	58
Bishop's Stortford	42	16	10	16	57	62	58
Barton Rovers	42	16	8	18	64	83	56
Oxford City	42	17	4	21	57	55	55
Braintree Town	42	15	10	17	65	74	55
Yeading	42	12	18	12	53	54	54
Wealdstone	42	13	12	17	51	58	51
Bognor Regis Tn	42	12	13	17	47	53	49
Harlow Town	42	11	13	18	62	76	46
Romford	42	12	9	21	51	70	45
Leatherhead*	42	9	13	20	47	70	40
Chertsey Town	42	9	5	28	50	84	32
Leyton-Pennant	42	7	9	26	34	85	30

*Saved from relegation as Hemel Hempsteads
ground did not meet ground grading criteria

Ryman Isthmian League
Division One 2000/01

	Pl	W	D	L	F	A	Pts
Boreham Wood	42	26	7	9	82	49	85
Bedford Town	42	22	16	4	81	40	82
Braintree Town	42	25	6	11	112	60	81
Bishop's Stortford	42	24	6	12	103	76	78
Thame United	42	22	8	12	86	54	74
Ford United	42	19	12	11	70	58	69
Uxbridge	42	21	5	16	73	55	68
Northwood	42	20	8	14	89	81	68
Whyteleafe	42	20	6	16	62	69	66
Oxford City	42	16	13	13	64	49	61
Harlow Town	42	15	16	11	70	66	61
Worthing	42	16	9	17	69	69	57
Staines Town	42	16	8	18	60	66	56
Aylesbury Utd	42	17	4	21	65	55	55
Yeading	42	15	9	18	72	74	54
Bognor Regis Tn	42	13	11	18	71	71	50
Walton & Hersham	42	14	8	20	59	80	50
Bromley	42	14	6	22	63	86	48
Wealdstone	42	12	9	21	54	73	45
Leatherhead	42	12	4	26	37	87	40
Romford	42	9	4	29	53	113	31
Barton Rovers	42	2	9	31	30	94	15

**Relegated to Ryman Isthmian League
Division Two**

Ryman Isthmian League
Division Two 2001/02

	Pl	W	D	L	F	A	Pts
Lewes	42	29	9	4	108	31	96
Horsham	42	27	9	6	104	44	90
Berkhamsted Town	42	23	10	9	82	51	79
Arlesey Town	42	23	6	13	89	55	75
Banstead Athletic	42	22	8	12	83	54	74
Leyton Pennant	42	22	8	12	84	60	74
Great Wakering	42	21	8	13	64	37	71
East Thurrock	42	21	8	13	67	59	71
Marlow	42	18	13	11	73	63	67
Hemel Hempstead	42	18	10	14	82	66	64
Leatherhead	42	17	6	19	72	62	57
Ashford Town	42	15	11	16	58	71	56
Met Police	42	16	7	19	84	84	55
Barton Rovers	42	15	9	18	54	60	54
Hungerford Town	42	14	9	19	56	75	51
Tilbury	42	15	6	21	55	74	51
Chertsey Town	42	10	14	18	79	112	44
Wembley	42	9	10	23	51	82	37
Molesey	42	10	6	26	40	93	36
Cheshunt	42	7	13	22	51	84	34
Wivenhoe Town	42	8	9	25	55	111	33
Romford	42	4	7	31	42	105	19

Isthmian League reorganisation

Ryman Isthmian League
Division One South 2002/03

	Pl	W	D	L	F	A	Pts
Carshalton Ath	46	28	8	10	73	44	92
Bognor Regis Tn	46	26	10	10	92	34	88
Lewes	46	24	16	6	106	50	88
Dulwich Hamlet	46	23	12	11	73	49	81
Whyteleafe	46	21	13	12	74	51	76
Bromley	46	21	13	12	70	53	76
Walton & Hersham	46	20	13	13	87	63	73
Horsham	46	21	9	16	80	58	72
Epsom & Ewell	46	19	12	15	67	66	69
Egham Town	46	19	10	17	62	71	67
Tooting & Mtchm	46	18	9	19	83	78	63
Worthing	46	17	12	17	78	75	63
Windsor & Eton	46	18	9	19	66	65	63
Leatherhead	46	16	13	17	71	66	61
Staines Town	46	14	16	16	57	63	58
Banstead Athletic	46	14	15	17	58	59	57
Ashford Town	46	14	11	21	47	70	53
Croydon	46	15	8	23	56	87	53
Croydon Athletic	46	13	13	20	52	66	52
Bracknell Town	46	12	16	18	57	74	52
Corinthian Casuals	46	12	14	20	50	68	50
Molesey	46	13	9	24	52	79	48
Met Police	46	12	10	24	50	76	46
Chertsey Town	46	3	7	36	43	139	16

Ryman Isthmian League
Division One South 2003/04

	Pl	W	D	L	F	A	Pts
Lewes	46	29	7	10	113	61	94
Worthing	46	26	14	6	87	46	92
Windsor & Eton	46	26	13	7	75	39	91
Slough Town	46	28	6	12	103	63	90
Hampton & Rchmd	46	26	11	9	82	45	89
Staines Town	46	26	9	11	85	52	87
Dulwich Hamlet	46	23	15	8	77	57	84
Bromley	46	22	10	14	80	58	76
Walton & Hersham	46	20	14	12	76	55	74
Croydon Athletic	46	20	10	16	70	54	70
Tooting & Mtchm	46	20	9	17	82	68	69
Ashford Tn (Mx)	46	18	13	15	69	62	67
Leatherhead	**46**	**19**	**9**	**18**	**83**	**88**	**66**
Bracknell Town	46	19	6	21	81	87	63
Horsham	46	16	11	19	71	69	59
Marlow	46	16	11	19	50	64	59
Whyteleafe	46	17	4	24	66	91	55
Banstead Athletic	46	15	8	23	56	73	53
Molesey	46	12	6	28	45	84	42
Met Police	46	9	14	23	58	84	41
Croydon	46	10	10	26	57	88	40
Egham Town	46	8	8	30	55	92	32
Corinthian Casuals	46	6	6	34	48	110	24
Epsom & Ewell	46	5	8	33	40	117	23

Non-League Pyramid restructured

Ryman Isthmian League
Division One 2004/05

	Pl	W	D	L	F	A	Pts
AFC Wimbledon	42	29	10	3	91	33	97
Walton & Hersham	42	28	4	10	69	34	88
Horsham	42	24	6	12	90	61	78
Bromley	42	22	9	11	69	44	75
Cray Wanderers	42	22	8	12	72	51	74
Met Police	42	19	16	7	95	54	73
Leatherhead	**42**	**20**	**13**	**9**	**73**	**55**	**73**
Tooting & Mtchm	42	18	15	9	92	60	69
Whyteleafe	42	20	6	16	60	59	66
Burgess Hill Town	42	19	6	17	73	62	63
Hastings Utd	42	15	11	16	55	57	56
Croydon Athletic	42	13	16	13	66	65	55
Corinthian Casuals	42	15	9	18	56	64	54
Bashley	42	13	13	16	68	74	52
Dulwich Hamlet	42	10	14	18	61	64	44
Molesey	42	12	8	22	46	70	44
Banstead Athletic	42	10	10	22	50	64	40
Newport IOW	42	10	10	22	50	88	40
Fleet Town	42	11	5	26	47	86	38
Ashford Town	42	8	12	22	47	85	36
Dorking	42	8	11	23	43	89	35
Croydon	42	5	10	27	37	91	25

League Statistics		1946 - 76	1976 - 06
League Seasons / Championships		*30 / 5*	*30 / 0*
Promotions / Relegations		*1 / 0*	*1 / 2*
Finishes in the top / bottom half		*20 / 10*	*16 / 14*

Ryman Isthmian League
Division One 2005/06

	Pl	W	D	L	F	A	Pts
Ramsgate	44	24	14	6	84	38	86
Horsham	44	25	11	8	95	55	86
Tonbridge Angels	44	24	8	12	71	48	80
Met Police	44	24	7	13	72	46	79
Dover Ath	44	21	14	9	69	46	77
Tooting & Mtchm	44	22	9	13	93	62	75
Kingstonian	44	20	14	10	82	56	74
Croydon Athletic	44	20	13	11	56	41	73
Bashley	44	20	10	14	63	61	70
Leatherhead	**44**	**18**	**14**	**12**	**64**	**50**	**68**
Cray Wanderers	44	20	8	16	80	74	68
Hastings Utd	44	19	10	15	65	58	67
Dulwich Hamlet	44	19	8	17	55	43	65
Fleet Town	44	13	19	12	50	56	58
Walton Casuals	44	16	10	18	68	75	58
Lymington & NM	44	12	11	21	61	80	47
Molesey	44	12	10	22	56	79	46
Whyteleafe	44	10	14	20	50	66	44
Burgess Hill Town	44	10	10	24	57	83	40
Banstead Athletic	44	8	13	23	43	71	37
Ashford Town	44	8	11	25	41	81	35
Newport IOW	44	6	11	27	38	97	29
Corinthian Casuals	44	6	9	29	39	85	27

Leatherhead Football Club
A club run by its supporters for the benefit of its community

Average League Attendances

Season	Average	Season	Average
1949/50	600*	1990/91	111
1952/53	500*	1991/92	122
1954/55	400*	1992/93	101
1955/56	400*	1993/94	141
1956/57	300*	1994/95	83
1957/58	400*	1995/96	121
1961/62	350*	1996/97	242
1962/63	400*	1997/98	265
1963/64	550*	1998/99	165
1964/65	600*	1999/2000	151
1965/66	600*	2000/01	151
1972/73	800*	2001/02	120
1973/74	850*	2002/03	155
1974/75	800*	2003/04	180
1975/76	600*	2004/05	272
1988/89	132	2005/06	225
1989/90	140	*Approx	

Season by Season Records (League and Cup)

Season	Lge Pos	Leading Goal-scorer	Most Appearances	Highest Attendance
1946/47	1st	47 - Cecil Weller	33*-Vic Harvey / Ernie Trout / Tommy Temlett	1,500 v Dorking (SSL)
1947/48	1st	37 - Fred Stenning	38* - Bryn Evans	2,000 v Carshalton Ath (AC)
1948/49	1st	61 - Fred Stenning	39* - Eric Bristow/ Fred/Charlie Stenning	2,597 v Sutton Utd (FAC)
1949/50	1st	71 - Fred Stenning	41* - Fred Stenning	2,500 v Hayes (AC)
1950/51	9th	18 - Ernie Trout	38* - Doug Caswell	Not known
1951/52	4th	17 - Ernie Trout / Don Smith	40 - Graham Lindsay / Len Barnes / Don Smith	Not known
1952/53	9th	14 - Cyril Drury	37* - Ernie Trout	Not known
1953/54	15th	8 - Jack Bastable	30 - Eric Bristow / Arthur Massey	Not known
1954/55	11th	13 - Bert Willox	33 - George Mannings	Not known
1955/56	8th	11 - Roy Springett	35 - George Mannings	1,300 v Wimbledon (SSC)
1956/57	9th	13 - Jackie Hughesdon	38 - Ken Allbutt	1,300 v Redhill (AC
1957/58	6th	36 - Gordon Cairns	34 - Tommy Johnson	1,000 v Farnham (AC)
1958/59	5th	16 - Kilby Edwards	38* - Ken Allbutt / Roy Reader	600 v Kingstonian (WCC)
1959/60	13th	34 - Kilby Edwards	46 - Arnold Bates	1,100 v Dorking (CLMS)
1960/61	13th	38 - Kilby Edwards	36 - Ray Dowse	Not known
1961/62	10th	13 - Dave Mollatt	40* - Arthur Hammond	Not known
1962/63	1st	34 - Kevin Brittin	44* - Jock Wood	1,913 v Sutton Utd (SSC)
1963/64	1st	46 - Neil Goodman	39* - Jock Wood / Ken Harris	3,000 v Fulham (FO)
1964/65	10th	25 - Neil Goodman	49 - Jack O'Malley	2,325 v Kingstonian (FAC)
1965/66	4th	25 - Brian Pell	61 - Ray Francis / Bobby Adam	1,600 v Hayes (AC)
1966/67	5th	18 - Micky Goodall	59 - Jack O'Malley / Alan Brazier	4,100 v Hendon (AC)
1967/68	4th	16 - Keith Mills	50 - Dave Juneman	1,500 v Dagenham (AC)
1968/69	4th	28 - Nobby Skinner	58 - Bobby Taylor	1,266 v Enfield (AC)
1969/70	5th	21 - Barry Webb	54* - Micky Cuthbert	2,400 v Walton & Hersham (FAC)
1970/71	6th	28 - Keith Mills	67 - Barry Davies	1,514 v Hayes (AC)
1971/72	3rd	26 - Pete Lavers / Ronnie Fruen	55 - Dave Reid / BarryWebb	2,500 v Blyth Spartans (AC)
1972/73	3rd	27 - Pete Lavers	53* - Derek Wells / Barry Webb / Chris Kelly	1,050 v Walton & Hersham (ILP)
1973/74	5th	22 - Chris Kelly	60* - Barry Webb / Derek Wells	1,991 v Hendon (AC)
1974/75	6th	41 - Pete Lavers	68* - Dave Reid	3,500 v Colchester Utd (FAC)
1975/76	8th	15 - Chris Kelly	61 - Derek Wells	2,450 v Cambridge Utd (FAC)
1976/77	10th	19 - John Baker / Chris Kelly	57 - Willie Smith / John Doyle	5,500 v Wimbledon (FAC)
1977/78	7th	27 - John Baker	65 - Micky Cook	3,000 v Swansea City (FAC)

Season	Lge Pos	Leading Goal-scorer	Most Appearances	Highest Attendance
1978/79	10th	22 - John Baker	60* - John Swannell	2,550 v Colchester Utd (FAC)
1979/80	18th	16 - John Baker	51* - Dennis Malley	1,044 v Weymouth (FAT)
1980/81	16th	13 - Chris Kelly	49* - Pete Caswell / Steve Dixon	631 v Bath City (FAC)
1981/82	9th	19 - Andy Bushnell	53 - Micky Preston	723 v Dover Ath (FAC)
1982/83	22nd	6 - Micky Cook	44 - Micky Cook	Not known
1983/84	11th	17 - Peter Shodeinde	51 - Phil Smith	284 v Windsor & Eton (FAT)
1984/85	4th	39 - Paul Williams	52* - Pete Caswell	500 v Kingstonian (IL1)
1985/86	15th	22 - Paul Williams	49 - Pete Caswell	241 v Redhill (FAC)
1986/87	10th	12 - Gary Richards	56 - Dave Rattue	1,020 v Bobby Charlton XI (Fr)
1987/88	10th	32 - Marc Smelt	44 - Gary Richards	375 v Woking (IL1)
1988/89	12th	18 - Gary Richards	51 - Kevin Wedderburn	404 v Woking (IL1)
1989/90	20th	10 - Richard Smart	49 - Kevin Wedderburn	385 v Woking (IL1)
1990/91	10th	26 - John Humphrey	51* - Paul Riley	166 v Epsom & Ewell (1L2S)
1991/92	4th	10 - Steve Russell	53* - Mark Joyner / Paul Wooler	410 v Millwall (Fr)
1992/93	14th	21 - Ray Arnett	53 - Paul Martin	780 v Aldershot Town (ILC)
1993/94	19th	11 - Mark Joyner / Kevin Glavey	44 - Mark Joyner	970 v Aldershot Town (IL2)
1994/95	12th	15 - Ray Arnett	47 - Robin Welch	400 v Reading (Fr)
1995/96	14th	23 - Ray Arnett	53 - Tony Webb	165 v Bedford Town (IL2)
1996/97	2nd	45 - Steve Lunn	58* - Gani Ahmet	673 v Dorking (IL2)
1997/98	9th	26 - Steve Lunn	49 - Gani Ahmet	1,540 v Aldershot Town (1L1)
1998/99	17th	9 - Nigel Webb	55 - Nigel Webb	1,143 v Rushden & Diamonds (FAC)
1999/00	20th	12 - Ben Papa / Tommy Warrilow	50 - Michael Rootes	410 v Kingstonian (SSC)
2000/01	20th	11 - Paul Harkness / Richard O'Connor	46 - Paul McKay / Tommy Williams	257 v Bedford Town (IL1)
2001/02	11th	35 - Alex Inglethorpe	49 - Iain Hendry	200 v Crystal Palace (SSC)
2002/03	14th	28 - Phil Ruggles	57 - Justin Gray	1,165 v AFC Wimbledon (MWT)
2003/04	13th	30 - Phil Ruggles	57* - Phil Ruggles	800 v AFC Wimbledon (MWT)
2004/05	7th	31 - Dave Stevens	55* - Tommy Dunn	1,814 v AFC Wimbledon (IL1)
2005/06	10th	22 - Dave Stevens	58 - Tommy Dunn	609 v Farnborough Tn (FAC)

KEY		KEY	
AC	Amateur Cup	ILP	Isthmian League Premier Division
CLMS	Corinthian League Memorial Shield	IL2S	Isthmian League Division 2 South
FAC	FA Cup	Lge Pos	League Position
FAT	FA Trophy	MWT	Maureen Wooldridge Memorial Trophy
FO	Floodlight Opener	SSC	Surrey Senior Cup
Fr	Friendly	SSL	Surrey Senior League
ILC	Isthmian League Cup	WCC	Wells Challenge Cup
IL1	Isthmian League Division 1	*	Ever present

Leatherhead success story

EXTRA~TIME
CHAPTER EIGHTEEN - TANNERS TRIVIA

Odds and Sods

Net minding - Keeper John Swannell remained unbeaten for 600 minutes during March and April 1975, whilst the Tanners forwards failed to find the net for the same length of time throughout February 2001. On the subject of struggling to score, full-back Johnny Lewis made 152 appearances without locating the back of the opponents net. The meanest defence was that fielded in the 1972/3 season which recorded 23 clean sheets and conceded just 43 goals in 51 outings. In the FA Cup, Tanners kept eleven successive clean sheets at Fetcham Grove between November 1970 and December 1976.

All change - 53 players appeared for Tanners during the 1960/1 campaign in only 38 games and no fewer than 70 different men donned the green shirt during the 1993/94 season. This compares to the 1978/79 season when just 16 players were used in 60 league and cup matches.

Spot On - Barry Webb converted 44 of 48 penalties during his Tanners career (rather more accurate than Danny 'Corner Flag' Lavender, Wes 'River' Harrison or Tommy 'Back Garden' Moorhouse then) whilst record goal-scorer Fred Stenning's habit of employing brute force over subtlety saw him convert less than two thirds of his 30 or so spot-kicks.

Bad Boys - Leatherhead negotiated the forties, fifties and sixties with the solitary sending-off of George Allen the only blemish. However, rugged centre-half Bobby Adam soon put paid to Leatherhead's image as a soft touch by receiving his marching orders three times in the late sixties for various misdemeanours involving the use of fists and boots. His total has only been surpassed by Steve Lammiman and Tommy 'Madhouse' Moorhouse, both incurred the wrath of the ref four times in the space of two seasons. Collectively the team reached a high (or should that be low) of close to a century of bookings and boasted one of the worst disciplinary records in the Pyramid leagues during the 2000/1 campaign. Opponents Thanet saw four men depart during their 1988/89 FA Trophy clash with Tanners whilst the Green's best effort saw them finish with just eight men in an Isthmian League game at Larges Lane, Bracknell in 1996. Strangely no Tanners' keeper has featured in the total, to date, of ninety four dismissals, although plenty of opposing keepers have been rather less successful at staying on the pitch for the whole of the ninety minutes.

A record twenty one players went for an early bath in games involving Leatherhead during the course of the 2005/6 season - thirteen opponents and eight Tanners.

Loyal Supporters - Tanners' supporters can certainly not be accused of following the club for the sight of silverware. Leatherhead's record in the more senior cup competitions is a little lacking in an end product. Defeats have come at the semi-final stages of the Surrey Senior Cup on eleven occasions and the FA Amateur and Isthmian League Cups twice. Tanners have been no more successful once they reach a final. Defeat has been suffered in the finals of the Surrey Senior Cup on four occasions, London Senior Cup twice, FA Trophy once and Isthmian League Cup once, the solitary success coming in the 1969 Surrey Senior Cup final. In addition, since 1975, Tanners long suffering supporters have seen their heroes finish in the top six of their division on just six occasions.

Record breaking seasons - 1982/3 and 1996/7 were record breaking seasons for vastly different reasons. The disastrous 1982/3 league season produced the highest number of goals conceded (116), the most losses (33), the fewest wins (4), the heaviest home and away league defeats, most successive defeats (8) and the longest run without a victory (19). By contrast the rather more successful 1996/7 campaign produced the most wins (30), fewest defeats in a 42 game programme (7), the highest number of goals scored in all games (158) and the highest aggregate total of goals (234).

Green is the colour - Leatherhead were the first team to wear green shirts on 'Match of the Day'.

Happy Anniversary - The club's 1000th game, in November 1969, ended in a 1-0 win over Wembley at the Grove with the only goal coming from a Barry Webb penalty. Coincidentally the 2000th game, in March 1987, against Basildon United also ended 1-0 with this time Gary Richards converting a penalty for the only score. The 3000th, in November 2005, resulted in a 2-1 win over

Tanners Dream Team

Attempting to select an all-star team from the players that have represented Tanners over the last sixty years made me realise just how many fine and talented players had turned out for Leatherhead down the years. In order to narrow the list down I have made my selection only from those players who have made in excess of 100 appearances in a green shirt. Nevertheless, this still meant leaving out many players who would have walked into any team in their day. You may well have your own favourites that I have omitted from my line-up, but here are my selections to kick-off the debate.

Tanners have had their fair share of excellent net minders with Jack O'Malley and Micky Cuthbert pressing for a place but in the end the sheer class and calmness under pressure of John Swannell earns him selection just ahead of another fine keeper, Pete Caswell. There were a whole host of defenders who could very easily have been in the final X1. Dennis Malley, Johnny Lewis, Kenny Harris, Bobby Adam, Jock Wood, Ray Eaton, Bobby Taylor, Derek Wells, Colin Brooks and Brian Stannard to name but a few, but the defence picked looks solid and dependable with all those chosen displaying an eye for a goal given half a chance.

The centre-forward berth was the hardest decision of all, with the likes of Neil Goodman, Keith Mills, Brian Pell, Pete Lavers, Ray Arnett, John Baker, Micky Goodall, Kevin Brittin, Steve Lunn and Pete Lavers to choose from. Fred Stenning earns the role though. He was a proven and prolific goal-scorer and would almost certainly have scored goals at any level had he had the chance. For players to excite and entertain the crowd and create the chances I was spoilt for choice. Who would mind forking out the entrance fee if Kelly, Skinner, Doyle, Trout and Pell could all be integrated into the same team? There certainly would not have been many goalless draws around!

With so many ball players in the side the team would need a midfield enforcer or two. Willie Smith gets the nod, along with the all action terrier-like Barrie Davies, for his all-round ability and leadership qualities. Smith was not always a crowd favourite but his talents were certainly appreciated by his fellow players, as he broke up opposition attacks and quietly and efficiently distributed the ball to enable the more flamboyant players to do their business. Mr. Dependable, John Cooper would provide the running power alongside Smith with his ability to break forward whilst still having the stamina and energy to chase back and make crucial interceptions. Other midfield players worthy of consideration included Johnny Phipps, Billy Salkeld, Phil Dade, Peter Keary, the versatile Barry Webb and Micky Cook.

Billy Miller's motivational abilities and tactical awareness make him the only realistic choice as manager although Mick Leach and Norman Douglas also enjoyed successful spells in charge at the Grove. So here is the final choice of starting eleven, together with the substitutes:

Leatherhead All Star X1

John Swannell

Dave Sargent   Colin Woffinden   Dave Reid   Alan Brazier

John Cooper   Willie Smith   Barrie Davies

Chris Kelly   Fred Stenning   Nobby Skinner

Substitutes - Pete Caswell, Derek Wells, Brian Pell, John Doyle and John Baker

Manager - Billy Miller

▲Well the boss did say get stripped off and show them a thing or two! Colin Woffinden enjoys the moment as streaker Mick Dixon celebrates the Tanners opening goal at Fetcham Grove in a 4-0 win over Ilford in 1976, whilst the referee notes down his particulars.

▲An early Tanners training session comes to a juddering halt when Bob asks the coach what the round thing under his foot is for.

SCOT F.A. CUP
First Round

Leatherhead	1	E Stirling	0
(Half-time: 1-0)			
Forrest M	P	Berwick	P
Stirling Alb	3	Cowdnbeath	0
(Half-time: 2-0)			
Larn	2	Alloa	2
(Half-time: 2-0)			
Albion R	2	Arbroath	1
(Half-time: 1-0)			
Ayr Utd	3	Annan Ath	1
(Half-time: 1-0)			

'HEAD LINES
Off colour Greens get the Blues
Jolly Greens Giant reprieve
Leather lose their Heads
TIP TOP TANNERS TROUNCE TOOTING
Tanners cast a spell over 'Wich
Happiness is a victory over Hamlet
Kelly shuffles the Cards and comes up trumps

▲It is a little known fact that Leatherhead entered the Scottish FA Cup. In 1986 (at least according to this regional newspaper) the Tanners progressed into the latter stages of the competition after brushing aside the challenge of Scottish League side East Stirling.

▲Going quackers at the Grove. This was a quacking good game with the opposition proving to be far from washed up or the lame ducks that had been anticipated. They were clearly more suited to the playing conditions and although they ruffled some feathers with their blatant diving, they never ducked out of any challenges.

▲The ball juggling girls who enlivened the matchday programmes of the seventies.

▲The 'Untouchables', pictured on the long return journey from Spennymoor on the Leatherhead Football Special, passing the time by supping a few bevvies to celebrate Tanners finally reaching Wembley.

▲The players and management drown their sorrows at a civic reception and banquet in their honour at Tyrells Wood Golf Club following the team's Wembley FA Trophy final defeat.

▲Tanners had been working hard in training on their revolutionary 'gurning' method of defence. Alas, despite the combined efforts of Dante Aligheri, Tommy Dunn and Adam Gray it failed to have the desired effect on Farnborough Town's's Pauk Harkness and he calmly headed home this corner in the FA Cup meeting between Leatherhead and their Hampshire opponents in October 2005.

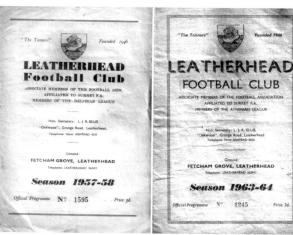

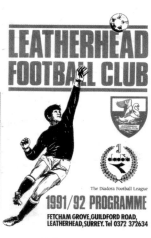

FINAL WHISTLE

THE LAST WORD - by CHRIS KELLY

Having been asked to write a small contribution to this book it soon became evident that it would be difficult to say anything about the club, its memories and the part it has played in my life, without descending into a nostalgic trip that would have many of those who shared those times with me saying, "*O God here he goes again*".

When I joined, Leatherhead Football Club was beginning a journey that reached a crescendo when they appeared in a Wembley final, at a time when the FA Trophy was still regarded as something special and the highlight of any non-league player's career. Amongst my first memories was the camaraderie of the players and officials, which was so different from my previous club, Sutton United. I hated training but enjoyed the social life that was part of the club. The manager Bill Miller was a fantastic man, what he lacked in technical ability he made up for in man management. He knew what he wanted (good players) and he had an eye for players who had skill, attitude and the same hatred of losing as he did. Bill taught me how to be a bad loser, if you accepted defeat then you would inevitably end up losing more than you ever won. Alongside him he had Dave Wall and Johnny Phipps, both contributed greatly to the success we achieved during our six years together.

Coupled with a great management team we also had possibly the best Physio and one of the finest men I ever met in John Deary. If he told you that you could walk on water you would try. In those days the club had a committee which had as many characters as the playing staff. Tom Dixon, Ian Taylor, Eric Wickens, Bernard Edwards and the Chairman, Chris Luff. Chris was a one off, totally committed to the club, I could tell a hundred stories that would illustrate this but one stands out. In my second season with the club we had reached the semi-final of the Amateur Cup only to lose to Ilford at Millwall's ground. It was a heartbreaking experience for everyone. Bill Miller knew at that stage he had taken this side as far as it could possibly go, so in the summer he decided, along with Chris Luff, that we needed to recruit some new players. How he persuaded them to join I don't know but he brought in Willie Smith, possibly the best player ever to play for Leatherhead (in my opinion), Dave Sargent, Colin Woffinden, and John Doyle (the most skilful player you could wish to see). In addition he acquired John Swannell, then the current England Amateur No.1 goalkeeper. All those players who remained from the previous season realised that with these new recruits they had a squad really capable of achieving something special. Sadly as a result of the new players coming in many of the old guard had to make way. These included Nobby Skinner, a legend at the club, Derek Casey, Ronnie Fruen, Phil Dade and Paul Proctor who all, funnily enough, made their way to Kingstonian. The pre-season saw us play a variety of teams and we seemed to be gelling well. The first game of the season saw us drawn away at Hendon. On the evening prior to the game Bill phoned all the players and told them to meet at the ground at 11am for an emergency meeting. No one knew until they arrived what it entailed. On arrival we learned that with the addition of all the new players the playing budget had gone through the roof and that the club would not be able to meet its commitments to the players. In the midst of the discussion that followed, with everyone totally confused and being told by Bill that if they did not wish to play at Hendon that afternoon he would understand, there was a roar of screeching tyres in the car park and in strode Chris Luff. He told the players that whatever happened they would be paid the wages they had agreed to accept and to get on the coach and play for his club. The rest, as they say, is history as that proved to be the club's finest season up till that point in time. Many may argue that 1978 was the greatest year in the club's history but it's difficult to differentiate between them because, in their way, they were both equally memorable.

I make no excuses for saying that the team of 1975 contained the best players in the club's history. We had five Amateur internationals in the team as well as players like John Cooper and Peter

My own personal high came at Spennymoor when, despite losing the second leg of the FA Trophy semi-final, I realised that we were going to play at Wembley. Losing the final was a bitter disappointment, and at the time it felt like the end of the world, but with hindsight I would rather have got there and lost than never have got there at all. There are a thousand other memories which would need a book of their own to recount. For those with long memories it is impossible to forget our first ever win over a league side when we defeated Colchester United at the Grove. For the players there was the night before the Leicester game when they played a practical joke at my expense involving a bogus TV interview or indeed the night coming back from Lancaster when John Doyle invaded a hotel kitchen and was chased out by the chef wielding a very large knife. I'm sure we caused Bill Miller no end of nightmares. I know that as a result of the goal I scored at Brighton I was elevated far above my station but there appeared to be no resentment from the other players, indeed they were often my scriptwriters whenever I was asked to say anything to the media

The Leicester defence won't know what to do,
When I start to shuffle they won't have a clue,
I drop my shoulder and swivel my hip,
Some will fall over, others slip.
I've got a new trick I want to test,
They'll think that we have resurrected George Best.
This shuffle's so quick Leicester won't realise,
What's going on in front of their eyes,
They will think it's magic they ain't seen before,
And while they're working it out we will go on to score.

I met so many great people and made so many friends during my time at the Grove as a player and, now that I am back in an administrative capacity, it's brilliant to see so many of them still involved or associated with the club. The difficulties the club found itself in a few years ago have been well documented, the fact that it is now well back on its way to re-establishing itself as a strong non-league side again is to the credit of the new committee. Gerald Darby and Tim Edwards deserve to be mentioned in the same breath as the likes of Chris Luff for their unswerving efforts to resurrect the club from those dark days, along with their committee they have ensured that Leatherhead Football Club still has history to make.

Leatherhead Football Club is, and will always be, special to me, as it will be to all those who participated in creating its history. I hope this book has given you the opportunity to remember those great moments from the past and appreciate what it was that made what the club achieved so special. I hope that in the future the club can capture more great memories and continue to be the special club that we all believe it to be.

Chris pictured in 1978, ▲ shortly before the FA Trophy final at Wembley and ▲scoring Tanners second goal against First Division Leicester City in the FA Cup in 1974 as Leatherhead added their name to the list of minnows to have scared the living daylights out of top flight Football League aristocrats.

THE CHAIRMAN'S CHATTERINGS ....
LOOKING TO THE FUTURE

I write these notes on the eve of Leatherhead Football club's Diamond Jubilee Year - an opportune moment to reflect on the history of our famous club in a wonderful book exploring the history of football in Leatherhead.

It has been suggested to me that we should now date the Leatherhead Football Club history from the summer of 2000, when the supporters of the club stepped in to keep the Tanners going after it seemed we would go out of existence. I disagree with that, my firm belief is that without the past success of the club and the emotional attachment that those previous great days generated, we would not have found enough enthusiasm to rebuild our club from what seemed to be a hopeless position. Therefore, in addition to giving us so much enjoyment over many years, the past players of the Tanners can take some credit for the continued existence of the team they played for!

When the club's new Board of Management was formed in 2000 there were a number of us 'of a certain age'. By that I mean supporters like me who had been on the terraces for our FA Cup and FA Trophy successes. Those of my generation could also remember the clean sweep of Surrey FA Trophies in 1969. We have a great heritage - we were not prepared to let that go if there was a chance of saving Leatherhead Football Club. The reaction to our call for a supporters' meeting was amazing and the resounding answer from everyone present was to keep the club going. Now there is much talk of the big 'fans' clubs' like AFC Wimbledon, but we were well ahead of them all and we still stay true to our guiding principle that we are a 'club run by its' supporters for the benefit of its' community'.

We inherited a clubroom where the water came in through the roof and additionally the boiler was so worn out we frequently had no hot water. Generally the club was in a state of disrepair and we had no players! The Football Association and the Ryman League had to be satisfied that we were in a fit financial and legal state to continue. Looking back I wonder how we managed it all but we did, and the Tanners have come back from the dead!

Certainly the response of the Tanners fans played the most important part, not only with their cash but their incredibly hard work, particularly from the hard core of fans who joined the Board of Management. So did the help of the previous management of the club - our continuing stalwart Gerald Darby and out going Chairman David Zackheim - because they honoured the substantial financial guarantees they had previously given and enabled us to take the club over without any acrimony. Later the granting of a new lease by Mole Valley District Council was an important step forward for us.

Since then we have managed to balance our finances by growing our revenue in line with our expenditure. The facilities have been repaired and improved. On the pitch we have a team that is doing well. Our business model is that the club has to be able to operate using its' own sustainable resources as we are not prepared to rely again on one major benefactor to bankroll the Tanners. That does not mean that we are a club without ambition, far from it! Every season we try to progress both on the pitch, and off it, and so far we have succeeded. I am very proud of how well the current Leatherhead team plays and how many more people come to support the Tanners - our gates have doubled in five years. We are now able to take strength from our past, although for a long time I felt it was a millstone around our necks. Now I take great pleasure from having Chris Kelly involved at Fetcham Grove again and seeing Dave Sargent watching his son play for us.

My friends in the 'Nobby Skinner Appreciation Society' remind me of my youth watching the

Tanners. I hope we get to meet many of those previous players during our Diamond Jubilee year.

▲Tim (*at the head of the table*) and the rest of his colleagues on the Management Committee who worked so tirelessly to rescue the Tanners in the summer of 2000.

We have a great history that we can look back on and we will cherish those memories during 2006 and the years to come. I sincerely hope that everyone who has built Leatherhead Football Club since 1946 would approve of what we've achieved in recent years. When I remember the many people that I've known at Fetcham Grove who were involved in those earlier times but are no longer with us, I am sure that they would give us the 'thumbs up' and would be enjoying the football that the Tanners are playing these days,

My one wish now is that we can give our current players, our younger supporters and the new people who have joined our Board of Management some similar memories to take forward when we celebrate our 70th, 80th, 90th and 100th anniversaries.

In 2006 we will need to raise substantial funds to make improvements to Fetcham Grove that are needed not only to retain our current status but also to achieve our objective of moving up the football pyramid. So in our Diamond Jubilee Year we will be looking to celebrate the past and secure our future!

COME ON YOU TANNERS!

Tim Edwards
Chairman, Leatherhead Football Club
31st December 2005

tanners club officials...

TEAM OFFICIALS

TEAM MANAGER.........................David Harlow
ASSISTANT MANAGER................Mark Harper
COACH...Steve Wood

TEAM THERAPIST......................Ross Hanbury
SPORTS THERAPIST........................Gail Pope

MANAGEMENT OFFICIALS

CHAIRMAN...Tim Edwards
SECRETARY.......................................Gerald Darby
MATCHDAY SECRETARY...............John Loveridge
TREASURER..................................Laurence Herbert
MARKETING MANAGER.........................Chris Kelly
BAR/MEMBERSHIP MANAGER.........Dick Wilkinson
SAFETY OFFICER...............................John Loveridge
HEAD GROUNDSMAN.................Dave Blaszkowski
PR/PRESS OFFICER...............................Steve Dennis
PROGRAMME EDITOR.........................David Pope
WEBSITES...Matt 'Le' Ross
BOARDROOM HOSPITALITY.......Barbara Edwards
CLUB SHOP MANAGER..........................Tony Neilson
KIT MAN/CARETAKER....................Percy Hawkins

MANAGEMENT COMMITTEE

Dave Blaszkowski   Gerald Darby   Steve Dennis
Tim Edwards   Chris Kelly   Roy Haines
Laurence Herbert   Chris Inglethorpe
John Loveridge   John Syrett   Dick Wilkinson
David Pope   Matt Le Ross   Les Ranger

(Clockwise) **The promotion winning squad of 1963/64. Ian Meekin. Leatherhead v Colchester United in 1974. Tanners v Brighton & Hove Albion, FA Cup 3rd Round January 1975. The Greens in Amateur Cup action. Chris Kelly. Surrey Senior Cup winners 1969. Tony Slade.**

THE tanners

Super Tanners notch seven on way to clinching promotion

The magnificent Tanners bandwagon continued rolling on Saturday. The 7-0 victory over their outclassed Kent opponents was enough to clinch promotion with a month of the season still remaining. Goals for the deadly striking duo of Dave 'Hitman' Stevens and Marc 'The Marksman' Charles-Smith took their collective total past the century mark whilst the team as a whole have now topped two hundred goals. The defence was as rock solid as ever, keeping a 25th clean sheet.

With promotion now sealed Tanners and their ever growing band of supporters can turn their minds to the little matter of the FA Cup final, and their clash at Wembley Stadium with Premiership champions Chelsea.

(Well we can dream)

Clockwise from left to right: **Dave Stevens** in typical goal - scoring action. **Iain Hendry** and **Steve Sargent**. **Phil Ruggles.** The supporters applauding the team off the pitch at the conclusion of the 2004/5 season. **Marc Charles-Smith.**